T0382202

Between God and Hitler

During World War II, approximately 1,000 Christian chaplains accompanied Wehrmacht forces wherever they went, from Poland to France, Greece, North Africa, and the Soviet Union. Chaplains were witnesses to atrocity and by their presence helped normalize extreme violence and legitimate its perpetrators. Military chaplains played a key role in propagating a narrative of righteousness that erased Germany's victims and transformed the aggressors into noble figures who suffered but triumphed over their foes. *Between God and Hitler* is the first book to examine Protestant and Catholic military chaplains in Germany from Hitler's rise to power, to defeat, collapse, and Allied occupation. Drawing on a wide array of sources – chaplains' letters and memoirs, military reports, Jewish testimonies, photographs, and popular culture – this book offers insight into how Christian clergy served the cause of genocide, sometimes eagerly, sometimes reluctantly, even unknowingly, but always loyally.

DORIS L. BERGEN is the Chancellor Rose and Ray Wolfe Professor of Holocaust Studies at the University of Toronto. Her research focuses on issues of religion, gender, and ethnicity in the Holocaust and World War II and comparatively in other cases of extreme violence. Her publications include *War and Genocide: A Concise History of the Holocaust*, now going into its fourth edition, with translations into Polish and Ukrainian. She is a Fellow of the Royal Society of Canada, and has taught in Canada, the USA, Germany, Poland, Bosnia, and Kosovo.

Between God and Hitler

Military Chaplains in Nazi Germany

Doris L. Bergen

University of Toronto

CAMBRIDGE
UNIVERSITY PRESS

Shaftesbury Road, Cambridge CB2 8EA, United Kingdom

One Liberty Plaza, 20th Floor, New York, NY 10006, USA

477 Williamstown Road, Port Melbourne, VIC 3207, Australia

314–321, 3rd Floor, Plot 3, Splendor Forum, Jasola District Centre,
New Delhi – 110025, India

103 Penang Road, #05-06/07, Visioncrest Commercial, Singapore 238467

Cambridge University Press is part of Cambridge University Press & Assessment,
a department of the University of Cambridge.

We share the University's mission to contribute to society through the pursuit of
education, learning and research at the highest international levels of excellence.

www.cambridge.org
Information on this title: www.cambridge.org/9781108487702

DOI: 10.1017/9781108767712

First published 2023

A catalogue record for this publication is available from the British Library.

Library of Congress Cataloging-in-Publication Data
Names: Bergen, Doris L., author.
Title: Between God and Hitler : military chaplains in Nazi Germany / Doris L. Bergen,
    University of Toronto.
Other titles: Military chaplains in Nazi Germany
Description: Cambridge, United Kingdom ; New York, NY : Cambridge University
    Press, 2023. | Includes bibliographical references and index.
Identifiers: LCCN 2023001139 (print) | LCCN 2023001140 (ebook) |
    ISBN 9781108487702 (hardback) | ISBN 9781108720823 (paperback) |
    ISBN 9781108767712 (epub)
Subjects: LCSH: World War, 1939-1945–Chaplains–Germany. | Germany.
    Wehrmacht–Chaplains. | Germany–Armed Forces–Chaplains. | Military
    chaplains–Germany–History–20th century. | Church and state–Germany–
    History–20th century. | World War, 1939–1945–Moral and ethical aspects. |
    World War, 1939–1945–Religious aspects–Christianity. | Holocaust, Jewish
    (1939–1945)–Religious aspects–Christianity. | Nazi propaganda.
Classification: LCC D810.C36 G33 2023 (print) | LCC D810.C36 (ebook) |
    DDC 940.54/78–dc23/eng/20230208
LC record available at https://lccn.loc.gov/2023001139
LC ebook record available at https://lccn.loc.gov/2023001140

ISBN 978-1-108-48770-2 Hardback

Contents

Figures

Maps

Table

Preface

It took me a long time to write this book.

Initially, I thought it would be easy. I first encountered the Wehrmacht chaplains in the late 1980s, when I was working on my dissertation on the German Christian Movement, a pro-Nazi Protestant group. In a church archive, I came across a letter from a Lutheran pastor who begged Reich Bishop Ludwig Müller to get him a job in the military chaplaincy. It was the first I had heard of Christian chaplains in the army of National Socialist Germany, and some checking revealed that there was almost no scholarship on the subject, beyond a pair of articles published twenty years earlier by a German military historian.[1] Here was a gap I could fill.

In 1990, a friend who was completing a dissertation on the *Volkssturm* – Nazi Germany's last-ditch effort to mobilize its civilian fighting power against the advancing Allies – asked me to join a panel at the annual meeting of the American Military Institute.[2] The location that year was Duke University, convenient for us as graduate students at the University of North Carolina in Chapel Hill, and I agreed. Some intensive research at the German Military Archive in Freiburg turned up a wealth of sources, and I gave a paper titled "'Germany Is Our Mission, Christ Is Our Strength!' The Wehrmacht Chaplaincy and the 'German Christian' Movement."[3] The audience responded positively, and a publisher suggested the subject would make a good book. Excited, I quickly came up with a plan to address this neglected topic. I would write a short, straightforward history built around three questions: Who were the Wehrmacht chaplains? What did they do? What was their relationship to Nazi crimes? I expected to be done within a year, two at the most.

Of course it was the third question, about Nazi crimes and specifically the crimes of the Wehrmacht, that sparked the most interest, including from me. In the meantime, I had a new position at the University of Vermont, where my responsibilities included teaching undergraduate and master's classes on the Holocaust. Thinking harder about the Nazi German murder of Jews complicated my approach to the Wehrmacht chaplains. So did a crucial piece of advice from Gerhard Weinberg: "Do not separate the Holocaust and the war."[4]

Instead of a simple narrative, I began to see my task as analyzing the failure of Christianity in the midst of massive violence. Where were the chaplains at Iaşi and Kamianets-Podilskyi, at Ponary, Babyn Yar, Lidice, Oradour-sur-Glane, and hundreds of other sites of mass murder?

Early in my archival research I discovered the incident I describe in the Introduction, about German chaplains and the killing of Jewish children at Bila Tserkva (Belaya Tserkov) in the summer of 1941.[5] Subsequently I learned I was not the first to have noticed it: Ernst Klee, Willi Dressen, and Volker Riess had included some of the key documents in a remarkable collection, published in English as *"The Good Old Days": The Holocaust as Seen by Its Perpetrators and Bystanders.*[6] And there were other glimpses of chaplains in the midst of atrocities. An article on the Wehrmacht in Greece quoted a Protestant chaplain who described the "heavy burden" that killing civilians and burning down their villages placed on the men of his unit.[7] A collection of reminiscences from the war years by Catholic priests and seminarians included a few poignant, if brief, allusions to witnessing murder of Jews in German-occupied territory.[8]

Now I decided my story was a moral tale, about the chaplains' failure, their weakness, and their efforts to uphold Christianity that ended up serving the cause of genocide. This version of my book would be centered in 1941 on Germany's eastern front, and it would basically expand on a presentation I gave at the United States Holocaust Memorial Museum in 1997, at a conference on Religion and Genocide organized by Omer Bartov and Phyllis Mack and subsequently published in the volume *In God's Name.*[9]

The revised project was more demanding emotionally, but I still expected it would be straightforward to write. I had gathered a lot of material and knew what I wanted to say: the Wehrmacht chaplains were witnesses to the murder of Jews, they were complicit in the Holocaust, and their history was a warning to Christians and people of faith everywhere about the high cost of partnership with a brutal state – perhaps with any state.

But somehow the idea felt flat. For one thing, much of the material I had found seemed oddly bland. Although chaplains operated in the thick of war and genocide, the records they produced rarely acknowledged German violence or its victims, and when they did so, it was briefly and obliquely, as if they were viewing events from a vast distance. Was I stretching the evidence? Would anyone be convinced? Or would I need to spend years chasing down every lead in search of a smoking gun, preferably in the hands of a Wehrmacht chaplain?

Another problem involved tone. Although I was convinced chaplains had come down on the side of the perpetrators and it distressed me when readers interpreted my analytical approach as sympathetic, it seemed shallow and sanctimonious to hammer away at the German chaplains, page after page.

Was I even saying anything new? So many social and professional groups had been studied and found to have been eager partners in the Nazi system: the middle class, "Aryan" women, physicians, lawyers, teachers, pastors, nurses, university professors, and more. Why would anyone expect anything different from military chaplains?

Meanwhile, other projects and commitments demanded my attention, and I put the chaplains aside. When I left the University of Notre Dame for Toronto, a friend predicted that I would never finish the book. Once you are no longer inside a Christian institution, he intimated, military chaplains will seem irrelevant. It took the events of September 11, 2001, the multivalent aftermath, and another invitation to jolt me to return to the chaplains and to recognize the importance of chronology. That insight changed my book again.

In 2010, a colleague at the University of Toronto asked me to co-organize a workshop on the last year of World War II.[10] Thinking it would be a good opportunity to revisit the Wehrmacht chaplains, I agreed. As I dug through boxes, files, and half-written chapters, seeking material on the period from early 1944 to May 1945, I was struck by how much the chaplains' situation changed over the course of the war. Thinking chronologically also made it clear that I had been so fixated on the chaplains as flawed individuals I had failed to notice the power of chaplaincy as an *institution*. Suddenly the chaplains' defensive posture, the collective eager-to-please dynamic I call "compensatory compliance," their "subtle duel" with Nazi authorities,[11] and the reciprocal processes of legitimation snapped into focus. No doubt my own experience, by this time of many years, working in institutions, from the provincial government of Alberta to a series of universities, most influentially the University of Notre Dame, played a role too. I came to appreciate the ways that institutions, offices, and systems shape, limit, and sometimes enable and magnify individual efforts.

Now I had a structure for my study of the Wehrmacht chaplains, and I knew the book needed to extend chronologically in both directions from 1941. This revamped approach was going to be difficult practically – there were holes in my research that I would need to address, particularly for the prewar and early war years – and in the meantime, exciting new scholarship by others – notably Martin Röw, Dagmar Pöpping, Lauren Faulkner Rossi, and David Harrisville – meant there was now a historiography to engage.[12] But the book seemed possible and also potentially important to counter a tendency in the historical scholarship, and in North American society as a whole, to reduce Nazism to the work of bad or weak individuals.

I returned to the manuscript even though I never felt like I had enough time. As a professor at a large research university, I always seemed to be reading other people's work: student papers, dissertations, article and book manuscripts, fellowship applications, and so on. Increasingly I was dissatisfied by methodologies that left people out of historical analyses and reproduced silences in the archives.[13] But for a long time I failed to notice that my work on the military chaplains did the same thing. Feminist and postcolonial approaches, scholarship on enslaved people, and Indigenous histories helped prompt my rethinking,[14] and although I had put it to the back of my mind, I slowly came to understand the advice I had received years earlier from a friend, the medievalist Kathleen Biddick,[15] when she read my draft of an article on the military chaplains: try not to replicate the perpetrators' gaze, she had told me.

For a few years I had been urging PhD students and anyone else who would listen to look for counter-voices and let some actual people interrupt the smooth surface of your analysis. These admonitions applied to me, too. Teaching a class on the Holocaust in Literature with Anna Shternshis deepened this insight.[16] The practice of integrated history, so powerfully implemented in works by Dalia Ofer, Saul Friedländer, Marion Kaplan, Alexandra Garbarini, Laura Jockusch, Zoë Waxman, and others,[17] also turns out to have been the original methodology of study of the Holocaust, as evidenced in the 1940s by Emanuel Ringelblum, Cecilia Slepak, Rachel Auerbach, Philip Friedman, the Black Book project of Ilya Ehrenburg and Vasily Grossman, David Boder, and many other contemporaries.[18]

Commitment to an integrated history generated new challenges. For one thing, the amount of potentially relevant material was boundless, yet chaplains themselves were elusive. How could I know where to even begin looking for glimpses of them in the tens of thousands of interviews of Jewish survivors in the USC Shoah Foundation Visual History Archive alone? Hiring research assistants from our University of Toronto undergraduate and graduate students, many of whom know languages other than English, has made it possible to carry out a number of targeted searches.[19] You will read some of the results in the pages that follow. The Jews, Poles, French, Ukrainians, Russians, Italians, and others whose words, voices, and experiences are recorded in personal accounts and various collections of survivor testimonies do not necessarily talk about military chaplains – in fact, only a minuscule number of them do so explicitly – but they make it possible to see chaplains and the issues they embody from the outside.

Working on this book in the summer of 2020 – as protests insisting that Black Lives Matter swept through the United States, Canada, and the world, and as the president of the United States had peaceful demonstrators driven away with tear gas and pepper balls so he could pose in front of a church, brandishing a Bible – added a particular urgency to the need to open up Holocaust Studies, acknowledge racism, and recognize its targets and victims. The urgency of seeing from the outside hit me with the murder of George Floyd and the subsequent reckoning with systemic anti-Black racism, and in

Canada with systemic anti-Indigenous racism. I came to see the Wehrmacht chaplains as important not only as members of an institution but as people embedded in systems and structures that fed on destruction even while they denied it and erased its victims – in other words, as part of what I call "genocidal culture."

Switching the perspective and approaching the Wehrmacht chaplains in multiple ways reframes and illuminates familiar questions: What is the place of religion in war and conflict? How do structures and systems shape people's behavior and with what repercussions? What narratives frame possibilities for finding meaning in violent encounters in the past, present, and future? What and whom do dominant narratives silence?

This book is as far as I got. So much more could be done to realize the potential of integrated history. And there is another layer of integration I have only begun to explore. It involves examining the Wehrmacht chaplains in connection with religion and violence in other settings. Consider the roles of clergy, including chaplains, in the genocides in Rwanda, Guatemala, and Indonesia in the 1990s, 1980s, and 1960s, or the Buddhist chaplains in the Japanese military in World War II, or Christians who preached murder and justified the destruction of Indigenous peoples in North America over the course of centuries.[20] I am not saying all situations of violence are the same, because of course they are not, and each is distinct. So is the Holocaust and the particular role of Christian chaplains who were part of a system intent on eradicating Jews and Judaism. But in our shared human history, different cases of religion and violence are both separate and linked, and although I have finally stopped writing this book and handed it over to you, the reader, I am still thinking about these connections.

Acknowledgments

The best part of completing this book after so many years is having the opportunity publicly to thank the many wonderful professionals, colleagues, and friends who helped me get to this point. Let me start with Liz Friend-Smith, whose insight, patience, and good judgment I have relied on since our first conversation about this project. Earlier, her colleague Michael Watson had encouraged me to return to the Wehrmacht chaplains, and even earlier, my friend Lewis Bateman convinced me that when I was ready, Cambridge University Press would be too. Thank you all!

I will be forever grateful to members of the workshop group that convened in March 2020 in Toronto to discuss a draft of this book. We had no idea what COVID-19 would bring. Now, after two years of isolation and disruptions, our time together seems even more precious. Martina Cucchiara, Michaela Hoenicke-Moore, Hartmut Lehmann, Silke Lehmann, Michael Moore, Julia Torrie, James Retallack, and Anna Shternshis, your brilliant, generous, creative engagement with my uneven and incomplete manuscript made all the difference. Also invaluable to the workshop were the contributions of Jessica Bush, Stephanie Corazza, Masha Koyama, Natasha Richichi-Fried, Mayar Shahin, and Galina Vaisman.

For funding the workshop in 2020, I am grateful to the Anne Tanenbaum Centre for Jewish Studies, the Wolfe Chair of Holocaust Studies, and the Centre for European, Russian, and Eurasian Studies, all at the University of Toronto, and to the Peter and Melanie Munk Foundation. Over the years, many organizations have supported my research: the Alexander von Humboldt Foundation, the Max Planck Institute for History, the Institute for Scholarship in the Liberal Arts at the University of Notre Dame, and the Social Sciences and Humanities Research Council of Canada. Librarians, archivists, and photo archivists in Germany, the USA, Israel, and Austria have helped at every step. I want to mention in particular Michael Noth at the Bundesarchiv-Militärchiv in Freiburg/Br., whose skilled assistance has been vital.

I started thinking about Christian chaplains in the Wehrmacht when I was still a graduate student. Gerhard Weinberg immediately recognized the significance of the topic and has shown a keen interest in my findings ever since. Peter Kracht, then at Westview Press, first suggested I write a book, and Carol Rittner RSM, John Roth, and Saul Friedländer all enthusiastically backed the idea. Sadly, some of the people whose early (and later) support inspired me are no longer alive to be thanked in person: Helen Bergen, Sam Bergen, John Conway, Lee Ann Fujii, Sara Ginaite, Ronald Hamowy, Michael Marrus, Livia Prince, Gerhart Riegner, Beate Ruhm von Oppen, Annelise Thimme, and Rabbi Max B. Wall. I will never forget you.

I owe a debt of gratitude to Marc-André Dufour, Peter Fritzsche, Konstantin Fuks, Manfred Gailus, Steven Maddox, Eliot Nidam, Na'ama Shik, Kevin Spicer, Fabien Théofilakis, and Gavin Wiens for pointing me toward specific sources. At the Universities of Toronto and Notre Dame, I received outstanding assistance from Hadas Binyamini, Imani Browne, Camila Collins Araiza, Josiah Cohen, James Raully Donahue, Anna Heffernan, Eli Jany, Mark Jantzen, Sam Meyerson, Sharon Minos, Michał Młynarz, Glen Ryland, Steven Schroeder, Elizabeth Strauss, and other students past and present, many of whom are named in the notes. Ryan Masters provided indispensable editorial assistance, and Michael J. Fisher, as always, did a superb job with the maps.

A wonderful array of people and institutions invited me to speak to them about my work on the Wehrmacht chaplains. I am profoundly grateful for discussions at events organized by Hilary Earl in North Bay, Rafal Witkowski in Poznań, Gerhard Besier in Heidelberg, Jochen-Christoph Kaiser in Marburg, Bella Gutterman and Dan Michman in Jerusalem, Krista Hegburg at the United States Holocaust Memorial Museum in Washington, DC, Gerald Ziedenberg and Nancy Machtinger in Toronto, Belinda Davis and Johanna Schoen at Rutgers University, Gaëlle Fisher and Caroline Mezger at the Zentrum für Holocaust-Studien in Munich, Ulinka Rublack and Paul Moore in London, and Tatjana Lichtenstein at the University of Texas at Austin.

Conversations, formal and informal, at conferences and on panels dealing with chaplains and related issues have been vitally important for me. I appreciate all of the following for their insights and questions: Natalia Aleksiun, Joyce Apsel, Victoria J. Barnett, David Bachrach, Omer Bartov, Rebecca Carter-Chand, Rev. David A. R. Clark, Natalie Zemon Davis, Jonathan Ebel, Robert Ericksen, Lauren Faulkner Rossi, David Frey, Geoffrey Giles, Sol Goldberg, Randall Hansen, Patricia Heberer-Rice, Susannah Heschel, Patrick Houlihan, Konrad Jarausch, Irene Kacandes, Thomas Kühne, Wendy Lower, Lindsay Macumber, Jürgen Matthäus, Jeanine Ntihirageza, Ute Planert, Dagmar Pöpping, Mark Ruff, Naomi Seidman, Caroline Sharples, Michael Snape, Nicholas Stargardt, Jacqueline Whitt, and many others.

Some amazing colleagues and friends read parts or all of my manuscript at various stages. Special thanks to Deborah Barton, Kathleen Biddick, Sandra Chaney, Mita Choudhury, Norman Goda, Howard D. Grier, Gary Hamburg, Jochen Hellbeck, Joanna Krongold, Catherine Schlegel, Edward Westermann, and David Yelton. Your responses, suggestions, and corrections have been a lifeline! I also deeply appreciate the University of Toronto History Department writing group, which devoted two meetings to discussing parts of my work-in-progress. Warm thanks to my brilliant and openhearted friends Nhung Tuyet Tran and Yvon Wang for all they have done to create a dynamic intellectual community, and to Christopher Lawson, Julie MacArthur, Natalie Rothman, Alison Smith, Luis van Isschot, Anna Veprinska, and Tamara Walker for their perceptive feedback. I also want to express my gratitude to the two anonymous and outstanding reviewers from Cambridge University Press. Of course, all mistakes and shortcomings in this book are my own.

Close friends and family provided intellectual and personal encouragement, ideas, companionship, perspective, and much-needed laughs. In addition to those already named, I want to thank Sylvia Bergen, Karen Epp, Marla Epp, Arlo Harink, Clement Ho, Mary Rose D'Angelo, Nancy Cardwell, Daphna Heller, Malavika Kasturi, Nina Lübbren, Daniel Mattern, Nakanyike Musisi, Melanie Newton, Linda Pardo, Dianne Sawatzky, and Joni Seager. I am so fortunate to have all of you in my life. To you and everyone I have named here, and to the many whom I have no doubt failed to mention but who have been part of this process, I want to say thank you. Even if you do not care that much about military chaplains in Nazi Germany, your wisdom and kindness are present in this book.

Note on the Text

A lot has changed since I began working on this project. Entire countries in which I conducted research no longer exist. Some archives have moved, and others have new names. I first consulted the files of the Reich Ministry for Church Affairs in the late 1980s, in the Central State Archive (*Zentrales Staatsarchiv*) of the German Democratic Republic in Potsdam. Two years later, I returned to those files in the same location, but it was now the Federal Archive (*Bundesarchiv*) Potsdam in the newly unified Germany. That archive has since disappeared, and readers who wish to consult those files can find them in the Federal Archive in Berlin-Lichterfelde. In the 1990s, I conducted research in the Political Archive of the German Foreign Office (*Politisches Archiv des Auswärtigen Amts*) and the Archive of the Catholic Military Bishop (*Archiv des Katholischen Militärbischofs*) in Bonn. Both have since moved to Berlin. In Warsaw, I benefited from research in the Archive of the Main Commission for the Investigation of Crimes against the Polish Nation. That entity has been replaced by the Institute of National Remembrance. In this book, I have retained the names of archives at the time I used them and provided as much information as possible in the notes in the hope that fellow researchers will be able to find the materials in their new locations.

Spelling of place names in Holocaust Studies is always a challenge. In the text and on the maps, I have tried to balance familiarity, consistency, and sensitivity to political considerations. When there is a widely used Anglicized version of a name, I use that. Rather than the German names, I prefer the Polish (or Czech, Yiddish, Lithuanian, Belarusian, and other) place names. I reject those names invented by Nazi Germany, for example Litzmannstadt, but do use German variants when those are most likely to be recognized by English-language readers. Thus, in the text and on the maps in this book, you will see Munich, Prague, and Krakow, rather than München, Praha, and Kraków; Wrocław and Poznań, not Breslau and Posen, but Sobibor and Auschwitz, rather than Sobibór and Oświęcim.

As I was preparing my manuscript for publication, the present crashed into this past in an unexpected way. The Russian attack on Ukraine that began in February 2022 raised countless questions, including practical ones about the spelling of place names: Kiev or Kyiv? Zhitomir or Zhytomyr, Odessa or Odesa, Zaporozhye or Zaporizhzhia? These choices, in the midst of a war that has already displaced and devastated millions of people, seem at the same time petty and of urgent significance. I have opted for Ukrainian place names (or more accurately, the common transliterations of those names) even in cases where a different name is more familiar in English-language Holocaust discourse. Accordingly, I use Kharkiv rather than Kharkov, and Bila Tserkva and Babyn Yar instead of Belaya Tserkov and Babi Yar. No doubt, looking back, some of my choices will seem inappropriate and even wrong, a reflection of the current upheavals.

Abbreviations

AA	Politisches Archiv des Auswärtigen Amts
AELKZ	*Allgemeine Evangelisch-lutherische Kirchenzeitung*
AKM	Archiv des Katholischen Militärbischofsamts
AOK	Armee-Oberkommando
AP	Archiwum Pansytwowe
AP Łódź	Archiwum Pansytwowe w Łódźi
BA, BArch	Bundesarchiv
BA-MA	Bundesarchiv-Militärarchiv
CDU	Christlich Demokratische Union Deutschlands
DP	Displaced Person
EK	Einsatzkommando
EZA	Evangelisches Zentralarchiv
LKA	Landeskirchenarchiv
LKM	Landeskirchliches Museum
NARA	National Archives Records Administration
NL	Nachlass
NS	Nationalsozialistisch
NSFO	Nationalsozialistischer Führungsoffizier
OKH	Oberkommando des Heeres
OKW	Oberkommando der Wehrmacht
SD	Sicherheitsdienst
USHMM	United States Holocaust Memorial Museum
VHA	Visual History Archive
YV	Yad Vashem
ZASP	Zentralarchiv der Evangelischen Kirche der Pfalz

Introduction
An Incongruous Institution

Bluntly put, a chaplain is the minister of the Prince of Peace serving in the host of the God of War – Mars. As such, he is as incongruous as a musket would be on the altar at Christmas. Why then is he there? Because he indirectly subserves the purpose attested by the cannon; because too he lends the sanction of the religion of the meek to that which practically is the abrogation of everything but brute Force.

Herman Melville, Billy Budd, Sailor

If God is for us, who can be against us? He who did not withhold his own Son, but gave him up for all of us, will He not also give us everything else? Who will bring any charge against God's elect? It is God who justifies. . . . As it is written, "For your sake we are being killed all day long; we are accounted as sheep to be slaughtered." . . . I am convinced that neither death, nor life, nor angels, nor rulers, nor things present, nor things to come, nor powers, nor height, nor depth, nor anything else in all creation, will be able to separate us from the love of God in Christ Jesus our Lord. (Romans 8:31-39)

Wehrmacht chaplain, sermon to soldiers on Germany's eastern front, late 1941

By any standard measure, Hitler's Germany was a Christian country. Throughout its existence, around 95 percent of its people remained baptized members of the two established churches: Roman Catholic and Protestant (Lutheran, Reformed, and a combination of the two). Germans paid substantial church taxes, which authorities of the National Socialist (Nazi) state collected and passed along to ecclesiastical bodies, just as their predecessors had done in the Weimar Republic and before that in Imperial Germany. Church buildings dominated the streetscape in big cities and villages alike, and Christian traditions and holidays structured daily life, even if they shared the stage at times with rituals invented by Nazi propagandists and neo-pagans. Although German law recognized only civil marriage, many couples still chose to have their unions blessed in a church ceremony. Almost all German children received religious instruction in school from a Catholic priest or a Protestant pastor. With few exceptions, Germans hoped for and received a Christian burial when they died.[1] At the time Hitler came to power, Jews, the largest non-Christian minority by far, made up less than 1 percent of the population.

Under these circumstances it should come as no surprise that Christian chaplains served the Wehrmacht, Nazi Germany's conscription-based military, from its creation in 1935 until its defeat a decade later. Over the lifetime of Hitler's regime approximately 1,000 men held official positions as Wehrmacht chaplains.[2] Catholic and Protestant in about equal numbers, they accompanied German troops wherever they went: into Poland, France, Greece, Yugoslavia, North Africa, the Soviet Union, and points between and beyond; on the retreats back toward their shrinking homeland; and into POW camps on four continents. Like their counterparts in the British, American, and Canadian militaries, the Wehrmacht chaplains were formally incorporated into the armed forces and held officers' ranks. Like chaplains in those forces, too, they ministered to the men in their care, performed the sacraments, comforted the sick and wounded, and buried the dead. But as part of the German war of annihilation, the Wehrmacht chaplains carried out these familiar tasks under circumstances that raised the stakes to terrifying heights. Whom or what does a chaplain serve?

Witnesses to Atrocity

A deadly incident illustrates some key themes of this study. In July 1941, advancing Wehrmacht units reached a city in central Ukraine called Bila Tserkva, about midway between Zhytomyr and Kyiv.[3] Bila Tserkva – (Біла Церква) in Ukrainian, Belaya Tserkov (Белая Церковь) in Russian, and Biała Cerkiew in Polish – means "White Church," specifically, an Eastern Rite church. Located on the Ros' River, a tributary of the Dnieper, and major rail lines, the city was an important transportation hub. On the eve of World War II, according to census records, it was home to 9,284 Jews.[4] The "big synagogue" was a landmark, as were two Jewish schools. Sholem Aleichem had lived there in the 1880s, and Yiddish culture thrived during the early Soviet period. In 1929, when the ethnomusicologist Moisei Beregovsky set out to collect Jewish songs, he began his expedition in Bila Tserkva. There he recorded hundreds of songs about love, family, and the struggle for social justice.[5]

Especially fruitful for Beregovsky was the neighborhood of Gruziia. Locals called it "Georgia" because the decrepit housing fit their image of the ramshackle Caucasus. There Grisha London, a teenaged shoemaker, performed a ballad that began, "Oy vey, in 1915, a new decree was issued." The lyrics lamented the fate of a young recruit in the tsarist army, his family forced to surrender him: "Oh every father must lead his child/like a slaughterer the cattle." Out on maneuvers on Shabbat, the singer bemoaned, with nothing to eat or drink, "you get slapped too." Viewed through the prism of the Holocaust, it is hard not to read certain lines as clairvoyant:

> Oy vey brothers, we're lost
> We are in murderous hands, oy vey.

Dire as circumstances may have been, however, the balladeer ended by asserting not doom but Jewish agency, at least for men:

> We took Jewish girls
> And wasted their lives.[6]

The song framed the travails of military service as part of the ongoing drama of Jewish communal existence.

Jewish life in Bila Tserkva was diverse and distinctive, but the destruction of Jews there was typical of hundreds of massacres the Germans carried out in the summer of 1941, throughout Ukraine, eastern Poland, and the Baltic states. In Bila Tserkva, members of a mobile killing squad, Sonderkommando 4a of Einsatzgruppe C, conducted most of the murders, with assistance from German Order Police units, Ukrainian auxiliaries, and some of the local population. The killers used techniques that were rapidly becoming standard practice: they rounded up Jews using coercion and deception; commandeered people nearby, sometimes the condemned Jews themselves, to dig pits at designated sites; forced the victims to take off their clothes, and then shot them one small group at a time, so that their bodies fell directly into what became mass graves. Afterward the killers helped themselves to the belongings of the people who were now dead.[7]

The slaughter of Jews in Bila Tserkva followed standard practice yet differed in a crucial respect from all but a handful of such killings: it drew attention after the war not only in the Soviet Union but also in the west. In 1967–68, eleven members of Sonderkommando 4a stood trial in Darmstadt, West Germany, for the murder of thousands of Jews in the southern Soviet Union. Among those called to testify were two chaplains with the 295th Infantry Division: the Roman Catholic priest Ernst Tewes and the Protestant pastor Gerhard Wilczek.[8] Their account of how, in Bila Tserkva, they tried and failed to save a group of Jewish children from death drew international headlines and remains the best known – indeed, the only – documented case of Wehrmacht chaplains intervening on behalf of Nazi Germany's victims.

For the court and in subsequent publications, Father Tewes reproduced events, relying on his memory and notes he had taken at the time. German soldiers had approached him and his Protestant counterpart to ask for their help, he said. According to the soldiers, a large number of children were locked in a school near the field hospital. The two clergymen went to see for themselves, and Tewes recalled what they encountered:

I am sure I would still recognize that building today. We found about ninety little Jewish children, among them some infants, in a hopeless situation: packed together, whimpering, crying, hungry and thirsty in the mid-day heat. Most of their parents had been shot, and some of their mothers were confined in an adjacent room. Through a window they could see their children's agony but they could do nothing to help them. Both of us agreed absolutely that against all orders, we would get involved and put ourselves on the line. The children and their mothers, like so many others before them, were to be shot by an SS Sonderkommando.[9]

Tewes described how he and Wilczek, both young men at the time – he was thirty-one – first appealed to the local commander, characterized by Tewes as "an elderly Austrian." That effort failed, Tewes reported, because the man "turned out to be a convinced antisemite."[10] Then they enlisted the support of two senior chaplains in the area.[11] Together the four persuaded Lieutenant Colonel Helmuth Groscurth to take up the cause.[12] As Tewes told it, Army High Command approved one postponement, but Security Service representatives and military officers on-site prevailed, pointing to instructions from General Field Marshal Walter von Reichenau, commander of the Sixth Army. Eventually, word came from Berlin that all the children and the women were to be killed.

On August 21, 1941, the children were taken from the school and shot. No one mentioned the women again. Whether it was Germans – Tewes noted only the possibility it was members of the Waffen-SS – or Ukrainian "volunteers" who did the job the chaplains would not say.[13] In a report dated August 1941, they emphasized that the men guarding the school were "Ukrainians," whom they suspected of acting "on their own initiative."[14] Looking back decades after the massacre at Bila Tserkva, Tewes underscored the image of himself and his fellow chaplain as powerless: "All of the people we tried to save were shot," he remarked. "Because of our efforts, it just happened a few days later than planned."[15]

Tewes's account constitutes powerful evidence that Wehrmacht chaplains witnessed the Holocaust. Witnessing is not a neutral act, a fact recognized in many traditions where it is taboo to look upon the victims of violence.[16] Those who see and watch violence are changed by it – traumatized, brutalized, mobilized, paralyzed.[17] At the same time, the presence of witnesses changes the event itself and affects how participants experience and remember it. Tewes's testimony presents Christian chaplains as tragic figures, good and decent men who tried and failed to save the lives of innocent children. His version of events was directed at an audience and shaped by its purpose, and like every narrative, it is incomplete. What Tewes left out – whether because he did not know, failed to notice, blocked, forgot, deemed inappropriate, or denied – is as significant as what he included for understanding the role of Wehrmacht chaplains during the war and afterward.

One thing Tewes omitted was context. His testimony described an isolated event, but the assault on Jews in Bila Tserkva started before and continued after the massacre of the children in the school. Germans arrived in the region in mid-July and began killing Jews immediately. The first mass shooting took place on July 14, 1941. In a park by the river, Germans shot ten Jewish men and dumped their bodies in a shallow grave. By the end of the day, they had shot and killed 200 Jews.[18] The Red Army report that provided these numbers detailed additional atrocities to follow. Soviet sources also document German and Ukrainian destruction of physical markers of Jewish presence. In 1943 the municipal government of Bila Tserkva demolished the Jewish cemetery. Workers gathered the tombstones, 300 cubic meters in total, and brought them to municipal headquarters, where they were mixed with untreated stone.[19] Soviet liberation of the city in January 1944 made the front page of the *New York Times*.[20] That same month, the Soviets created a Commission including local people to investigate evidence of Nazi crimes in the area. According to their report, of 6,000 bodies found 5,000 were Jews, many of them children and women.[21]

Germans had killed those Jews in plain sight, and eyewitness accounts survived in various forms. Already in 1941, Soviet collectors of Yiddish folklore documented a song about the murder of Jewish children in Bila Tserkva. It located the massacre at the seventh military square, on the outskirts of the city, and sounded the call for revenge:

> Oy, what should we say and what should we tell,
> when little children were buried alive.
> People, this happened on the seventh square;
> they were buried in a pit like a barrel.
>
> The assassins, the fascists, were pleased, –
> they thought all the Jews had finally met their end.
> From the still-fresh graves, one can hear a cry:
> "People, revenge – take revenge on them!"
>
> Not a single drop of their blood will go unanswered –
> we will destroy, wipe out the murderers.
> We will crush every one of them into dust, –
> they will pay for everything, for everything![22]

Jewish sources tell other stories that offer insight into the situation. In Yiddish, Bila Tserkva was sometimes known as *Shvartze Timme* (Black Tumah, or black abomination). In Jewish tradition, *tumah* is associated with withering and decay. A dead body is a site of *tumah*, not only because the corpse itself is decaying, but also because living people who come into contact with it often suffer emotionally and experience spiritual fragmentation, a counterpart of the corpse's physical disintegration.[23] The play on the city's name – transposing "white church" to "black rot" – is not only a grim joke but a reference to the history of violence against Jews as remembered and imagined there. Jews in the region viewed Bila Tserkva as the epicenter of successive pogroms: in 1648, it was said, the Chmielnicki uprising destroyed the large Jewish community; Jews rebuilt, only to be ravaged again in 1919–1920.[24] In the German narrative, the murder of Jewish children in Bila Tserkva was a tragic anomaly in an obscure place with a cumbersome Slavic name. In the story of *Shvartze Timme*, however, Christians killing Jews was the brutal norm in a place called White Church.

Perhaps because of past experience, in 1941, shortly before the Germans arrived, Jewish community leaders arranged to evacuate hundreds of children from Bila Tserkva.[25] This feat may explain why the number of children in the August massacre was small relative to the hundreds and thousands of Jewish children Germans were killing all over the region in the summer of 1941. Interviews in the Shoah Foundation collection with two survivors, Dimitri Kalinski and Isaac Piatsetski, provide valuable perspectives. Like the chaplains' accounts, these testimonies are part of a conversation with an anticipated audience and need to be analyzed accordingly. They are all the more precious because together with the song about the seventh square, they constitute the only Jewish sources I have found on Bila Tserkva in 1941.

Dimitri Kalinski was interviewed in 1998 in Nevada. He told the interviewer he was born in 1932 but did not know exactly when or where. By 1939, he said, he was in a boarding school in Bila Tserkva, where he remained "for two winters." He recalls disjointed episodes: being told in 1941 that "something's gonna happen in a month's time," and experiencing bombs being dropped near the school one night. The next morning, when soldiers appeared, Kalinski and another child set out across the river to find a teacher. They were unsuccessful, and Kalinski ended up alone, "wandering around" begging. At one house, people gave him food in exchange for looking after their cow.[26]

Kalinski remembers being "picked up" by German soldiers in "large trucks that were carrying a lot of people," though he was the only child. They were driven "quite a ways," told to get out of the trucks, and then the Germans began shooting. Kalinski implies the location was Babyn Yar: he says the adults kept saying the name and he saw Kyiv burning. He survived because people fell on top of him, he recounts; he crawled out from underneath them and "left the area." Later, Kalinski told the interviewer, he was put on a cattle train and sent to Auschwitz. The account has the marks of embellishment: did he really survive both of the most infamous killing sites of the Holocaust, Babyn Yar and Auschwitz? Kyiv was burning before the Babyn Yar massacre, but would the fire still have been visible from the ravine? The details on Bila Tserkva seem reliable though: why fabricate a connection to a place his interviewer almost certainly had never heard of? Kalinski may well have evaded the August massacre at the school only to be pulled into another of the many killing actions nearby.

The other survivor, Isaac Piatsetski, had adult memories of Bila Tserkva. Born in 1914 in Kielce, he too was interviewed in 1998, in Florida. After the Germans invaded Poland in 1939, he recalled, he fled east. Drafted into the "Russian army," he was sent to an army base near the former Polish border. In 1941, after a complicated series of moves, he ended up in Bila Tserkva, where he was arrested by the Soviets. Put to work with other refugees at a brick factory, he was given a place to stay near the train station. There he described seeing evacuations:

They were evacuating from the front zone, children – and a lot of Jewish children and Jewish families because it was a Jewish-Ukraine there. Belorussia, there were a lot of Jewish people. And the local commanders were also Jewish, and they put all the trains to their, uh, evacuation. So we met such a train which was evacuating, uh, small children from preschool age – maybe a few hundred – in a separate train.[27]

Piatsetski's account includes some flourishes. Notably, his subsequent remark, "The train ended up in Ural," was probably an assumption based on common knowledge and desire for a positive outcome. How would he know what happened to that particular train? More convincing is the offhand comment that local commanders designated evacuation trains for children, because it emerges in passing and does not serve any immediate interest.

Kalinski's and Piatsetski's accounts challenge the claim of tragic Christian impotence. At Bila Tserkva, the military chaplains lamented, they were unable to help a single Jewish child. Yet Kalinski, nine years old at the time, managed somehow to save himself. Under intense pressure from the advancing Germans, Soviet efforts succeeded in evacuating hundreds of children from Bila Tserkva to Central Asia. In short, reversing the gaze, looking at events through the eyes of Jews in the region, interrupts the narrative of German military chaplains with a pointed question: How did a massacre of Jews become a story of Christian heroism?

Power and Legitimation

Tewes and Wilczek did not stop the murder of the Jewish children at Bila Tserkva but they were by no means powerless. To the contrary, they and the other military chaplains had considerable power by virtue of the office they held and the moral authority of Christianity in their society. It is difficult to quantify that power, because it was articulated and exercised for the most part informally, and its practitioners repressed and denied it after the fact. As Michel-Rolph Trouillot trenchantly observed, "The ultimate mark of power may be its invisibility."[28] Yet its traces can be seen even in the events of August 1941 and their aftermath.

Soldiers acknowledged the importance of the chaplaincy, for instance at Bila Tserkva where, according to German sources, it was soldiers who approached the chaplains. Without the soldiers' initiative, Tewes and Wilczek might not have learned about the children confined in the school or at least they might have avoided coming face-to-face with that reality. Wehrmacht chaplains were ordained Christian clergymen, recognizable by the white and violet armbands they wore with their uniforms and other markers that ranged from subtle – the absence of the signs of rank worn by other officers – to more dramatic: crucifixes around their necks; on occasion ceremonial robes. Their physical presence in the midst of a brutal war signaled a kind of normalcy that many Germans read as legitimating. Even when the killers and the Wehrmacht units that accompanied, supported, and sometimes directly assisted them did not see an actual chaplain, they all knew Christian chaplains were part of the war effort, and that knowledge added a protective layer of moral reassurance. Those soldiers who told Tewes and Wilczek about the crying babies locked in the school could feel they had done what they were supposed to do: bring their troubled consciences to the chaplain.

Of course things may not have happened as Tewes remembered or recounted them. Perhaps the chaplains learned about the children from their own observations or from the locals among whom they were billeted. The emphasis on the conscience-stricken soldiers fits neatly with other details in Tewes's testimony that support the myth of the honorable German Army: his description of the antisemitic commander as "Austrian"; his repeated references to the SS as distinct from and opposed to the Wehrmacht; his speculation that "Ukrainian volunteers" did the actual killing.[29] Other details slide easily into insinuations of Jewish passivity, even complicity: note the image of Jewish women helplessly watching through a window as their children suffered, when in fact it was the chaplains who were passively peering in. (Why would there be a window between two rooms inside a small building?) But even with its self-serving elements, Tewes's account makes clear that chaplains had the standing to approach military commanders and the credibility to testify years later in court, as representatives of an intact Christian conscience within the Wehrmacht.

Military, state, and Party leaders regarded the chaplaincy as a moral force, even if that recognition was sometimes backhanded. Soon after the murder of the Jews in Bila Tserkva, both Tewes and Wilczek were transferred to different units. Nothing suggests this step was punitive, nor was it unusual. Nevertheless, given the tendency for chaplains to remain with the same units as long as possible, it could be that the transfers were a deliberate effort to distance Tewes and Wilczek from the men who had been with them at Bila Tserkva. Why allow seeds of conscience to take root or encourage misgivings to be shared with a sympathetic audience?

Certainly the Wehrmacht leadership was eager to forestall discussion of moral qualms. In October 1941, Field Marshal Walter von Reichenau issued his infamous directive to address "uncertainty regarding behavior of the troops" in the east. To destroy the "Jewish Bolshevist system," he assured his men, Germany was compelled to bypass the rules of war and show no mercy to "Jewish subhumans."[30] Murmurings of discontent about the active part the Wehrmacht had played in the slaughter of Jews at Babyn Yar just weeks earlier appear to have prompted Reichenau to take the unusual step of justifying himself to the men under his command and assuming the burden of moral responsibility. But the spark of conscience the chaplains showed at Bila Tserkva may also have contributed to Reichenau's directive, especially since it was Reichenau, at least as Tewes and others told it, who gave the order to have the children killed.[31]

Chaplains themselves had a sense of their authority. In his postwar recollections of Bila Tserkva, Tewes acknowledged the potential power of his position, something he said he fully grasped only later. It was in the 1968 courtroom, he claimed, that he learned he and Wilczek had been investigated:

we who had set in motion this whole thing from within the Army against the SS. I learned that the High Commander of the 6th Army, who was in charge of this southern sector of the front, General Field Marshal von Reichenau himself, had personally intervened in this matter, sharply criticized our meddling, and clearly planned to take measures against us.[32]

Yet the two chaplains were not punished, nor is there evidence that their actions at Bila Tserkva damaged their careers. Tewes's new assignment, to an armored division in Russia, was dangerous but not unusually so. In his version of events, German atrocities were a lamentable part of warfare, balanced by the perilous conditions there. "There were partisans," he observed in describing his new post in his reminiscences. "German soldiers and officers were shot in partisan attacks. Then there were the terrible reprisals, shootings of hostages, to which Jews and others fell victim."[33] In the mind of Chaplain Tewes – or at least in the way he presented his past to the world – the targets of Nazi violence had changed from innocent children to dangerous bandits.

One argument of this book is that the German military chaplaincy helped legitimize Hitler's regime and its genocidal war. Wehrmacht chaplains were effective legitimators precisely because they stood somewhat apart from the overt proponents and practitioners of violence. Although Christianity and Nazism coexisted, they were not identical, and Tewes, Wilczek, and their fellow chaplains abhorred such crimes as the murder of children. Their influence, however, depended less on individual intent than on the prestige of military chaplaincy and the venerable tradition of Christianity in Germany. Like the chaplain Melville described in *Billy Budd*,[34] the Wehrmacht chaplains were all the more effective in sanctioning force because they represented a self-proclaimed "religion of the meek."[35]

The Wehrmacht chaplains' moral authority made them key to creating a reassuring version of events for the soldiers and families to whom they ministered and also for themselves. Over the course of the war, they developed a vested interest in a narrative that normalized atrocity or elided it with German suffering. If they felt shame about their country's crimes, they could hide it behind blame of the victims, a process facilitated by propaganda that depicted Jews as a mortal threat to Germany, the sinister force behind its military foes. Chaplains were not the only people to engage in this sleight of hand: Jews were to be "exterminated as partisans," Hitler reportedly told Himmler.[36] Turning the Holocaust into a Christian morality tale served to transform Jews from victims to enemies and then to erase them from the story altogether.

The Wehrmacht chaplains enabled killing but they were not themselves hands-on killers. In thirty years of researching this subject, I have not found evidence that German chaplains personally killed Jews, Soviet prisoners of war, or civilians in occupied Poland or elsewhere. They were permitted to carry a sidearm, usually a pistol, while at the front or in occupied territory, and some of them boasted about participating in combat. In many circumstances, however, they were unarmed.

The intervention by German military chaplains at Bila Tserkva was almost certainly a singular event. Why did other Wehrmacht chaplains, who also witnessed or had direct knowledge of extreme violence – rape of Polish, Jewish, and Soviet women;[37] mass murder of Black French soldiers, Norwegian and Soviet prisoners of war, Jews in Lithuania and Belarus, Christian civilians in Yugoslavia and Greece – not raise comparable objections? Indeed, why did the chaplains at Bila Tserkva not follow up their protestation there with further actions? Both Tewes and Wilczek continued in their jobs until the end of the war, and apparently neither of them caused any subsequent trouble.

This book identifies four factors that together explain the Wehrmacht chaplains' patterns of behavior. One was the institutional structure of the chaplaincy, which rewarded cautious leadership and weeded out potential troublemakers. A second factor involved the chaplains' defensive position vis-à-vis the Nazi regime and a general crisis of relevance for the churches in the modern era. War itself, above all the confusion and moral numbing it entailed, was a third factor, and a fourth was time: the passage of time and habits and patterns formed over time. The Wehrmacht chaplaincy of 1941 – of the war of annihilation and the Shoah – would not have been possible in 1933, but chaplains would not have become what they were by then without the developments of 1935, 1939, and 1940.[38] By the same token, chaplains' actions in 1941 shaped their behavior in the years that followed and how they remembered and represented it.

Systems and Dynamics

Institutions, professions, and the systems that govern them have their own logic. Rather than asking why German chaplains were silent in the face of Nazi murder of Jews, it can be more fruitful to ask why there was no apparatus for them to protest or articulate opposition to the state.[39] What structures generated certain options for what they did and perceived they could or should do? What dynamics channeled their actions, including those that went against the rules, into legitimation of the dominant system?

A key factor was the way chaplains were selected. Appointment of military chaplains involved a multistep process that privileged men who counted as theological and political moderates. Local bishops proposed names, which the Ministry of Church Affairs, the appropriate military bishop (Catholic or Protestant), and the Gestapo then vetted. About one-third of the men considered were rejected. On the Catholic side, this meant above all keeping out priests who had been involved in youth work that contravened police restrictions. On the Protestant side, it usually meant excluding clergy with a strong record of activity in the Confessing Church, because it had opposed Nazi efforts to control who held church offices. Once selected, chaplains went through training processes and participated in professionalization events of various kinds. These shared experiences, along with a sense of duty to their calling, exerted a palpable influence on them. To be a military chaplain meant to be a soldier, to be manly, to serve one's country and one's faith.

If the office shapes the man, the leaders set the tone. Two military bishops headed the Wehrmacht chaplaincy, the Catholic Franz Justus Rarkowski and the Protestant Franz Dohrmann.[40] In position by 1935, Rarkowski and Dohrmann in effect created the chaplaincy that served in World War II. They were responsible for appointing chaplains and they represented the churches' interests to the military and military interests to the churches. Both men were traditional patriots who had served in World War I. Neither was a member of the Nazi Party, and both proved willing to speak out to protect the institution of the chaplaincy when they considered it threatened by the Party or state. This independence, in turn, gave them credibility that made them more effective as legitimators of the regime than ardent Nazis could have been.

Legitimation is a two-way street, and if the Nazi regime needed the German military chaplains, chaplains may have needed the regime even more. Their credibility and entire reason for existing depended on their bond with war and the men who fought it. Yet soldiers' taunts of irrelevance echoed around the Wehrmacht chaplains, most loudly during periods of German ascendancy, quieter but with a bitter tone in times of setback. Who needed God if they were winning? And if they were losing, had God not failed them? Meanwhile, some Nazi ideologues were openly hostile, regarding chaplains as rivals who propagated an outmoded and enfeebling world view. A series of measures introduced over the course of the war indicate that policy makers sought to curb the chaplaincy's impact and perhaps eventually phase it out altogether.

Chaplains responded with what I call "compensatory compliance": they tried to forestall criticism by proving they were essential fighters for Germany.[41] They publicized evidence that soldiers and officers regarded them as necessary to maintain morale, particularly when casualties were high. They engaged in ostentatious demonstrations of loyalty to Hitler, including special prayers and services on his birthday and other occasions.[42] This dynamic, readily apparent in contemporary sources, recedes from view in chaplains' postwar accounts. Those tend to downplay cooperation with the regime and emphasize its hostility, consistent with the chaplains' pattern of protecting their institutional interests.[43]

Like the chaplains, under Hitler the Christian churches as a whole occupied a defensive position vis-à-vis actual and imagined critics. On the one hand, Christian leaders enjoyed enhanced recognition and prestige. During wartime, the importance of the churches grew, because they sanctified sacrifice and comforted the bereaved, tasks the German leadership increasingly valued as casualties among their own people mounted. On the other hand, elements within the Nazi movement were suspicious of Christianity. After all, Christianity grew out of Judaism and called on its followers to "love your enemies" and "turn the other cheek" – attitudes antithetical to the Nazi world-view. Hitler did not destroy German churches or persecute ordinary Christians, but officials imposed restrictions and police practiced forms of harassment to keep the churches in line. Often state or Party accusations of Christian weakness sparked church leaders to redouble efforts to prove their value to the nation.

A wider, older struggle of religious leaders to remain relevant in changing times is crucial to understanding German chaplains in the mid-twentieth century. Scholars of religion have abandoned a simple secularization thesis, with its assumption that modernity replaced "traditional religion" with other loyalties. Political religion – the sacralization of a leader, a party, a cause – turns out to coexist easily with "religious religion," or, to put it differently, religion is always intertwined with political, social, and familial relations.[44] Nor did religion simply get squeezed from public into private spaces. Often the opposite occurred, as individuals became less attentive to religious practice and belief in their personal affairs but remained firmly located within Christian frameworks. In an era of "diffusive religion,"[45] Christian leaders and institutions sought out sites where they could wield influence explicitly as well as implicitly. Germany's military chaplaincy turned out to be such a site, but it was laden with risk: credibility hung by a thread and particular institutional interests sometimes trumped the churches' broader goals.

This state of affairs made churchmen nervous, and the chaplaincy typified that unease. The existing institutional arrangement seemed proof of the ongoing vitality of Christianity in modern German society, yet if chaplains could not demonstrate their value to established power structures, for instance by building morale, the churches stood to lose that platform. Church representatives worried that their target audiences – men, and specifically soldiers – were indifferent to religion. They hoped to use their institutional presence in the military to gain a place in individual hearts and minds. But if chaplains sold out the interests of their clientele, or if soldiers perceived them to have done so, the churches would lose credibility.

Military chaplaincy, in other words, was a major arena for representatives of the churches to demonstrate their relevance and perform their loyalty. When Germany rearmed in March 1935, Catholics and Protestants successfully lobbied for immediate appointment of military bishops to create a Wehrmacht chaplaincy. The chaplains proved to be reliable partners. In Spain, where the new air force's Condor Legion dropped bombs in 1937, at least one chaplain was there too, celebrating the triumph over what Nazi propaganda called Jewish Bolshevism. When Hitler purged the military leadership in 1938, not a single chaplain lost his post. No chaplains (indeed, no German church leaders) protested in August 1939 when the Molotov–Ribbentrop Pact was signed, although earlier they had been vociferous critics of Communism. Nor did any of the chaplains who accompanied the Wehrmacht in the invasion of Poland in September 1939 join the handful of bishops and military officers who spoke out against the assault on Polish civilians, including Roman Catholic priests and Jews. Likewise the massacre of French Black soldiers in 1940, the vicious reprisal killings in the Balkans, the rape of Soviet women,[46] and murder of millions of Soviet prisoners of war – all violence carried out by the Wehrmacht,[47] not special SS units – elicited no protest, at least none that has left a trace in the records – although military chaplains were present at all those places.

The Fog of War and the Force of Habit

What did Wehrmacht chaplains actually do? This simple question draws attention to the deep uncertainty of their circumstances and the complex ways that war both magnified and limited their agency.[48] Chaplains were deployed across the enormous territory conquered by the Wehrmacht and occupied by Nazi Germany. The nearest fellow chaplain or supervisor could be hundreds, even thousands of miles away. As a result, chaplains operated under remarkably little oversight. This degree of independence set them apart from other professionals under Nazism – schoolteachers, social workers, or clergy serving civilian parishes – and made the position attractive to ambitious men. In addition, the officer's rank that chaplains held provided a protective layer of prestige. No one in Nazi Germany had to be coerced into becoming a military chaplain: the number of aspirants always outstripped the number of appointments. Even Dietrich Bonhoeffer at one point considered entering the chaplaincy.[49]

Yet the Wehrmacht chaplains' position was also circumscribed in significant ways. Although chaplains had considerable leeway, isolation left them exposed and vulnerable to certain pressures. Their ability to function depended on the relationships they cultivated with the men physically closest to them: commanding officers, military doctors, and soldiers. Without a means of transportation – a motorized vehicle and fuel, a bicycle or horse – a chaplain was useless, no matter how lofty his intentions. Chaplains expended enormous amounts of time and energy in daily struggles to locate the men for whom they were responsible, to obtain supplies, or to source and distribute religious reading material. The vicissitudes of war had a particular impact on chaplains, whose ability to perform the most fundamental tasks – visit the wounded and sick, administer the sacraments, bury the dead – could be nullified by a sudden movement of the front, an ambush, or a blizzard. The stresses of what one chaplain delicately referred to as the "special nature of our war in the East" added to the burden. Under such circumstances, there was little time to read the Bible, pray, or even think. And thinking, as Hannah Arendt pointed out, is the essence of ethical existence.[50]

One obvious explanation for the Wehrmacht chaplains' behavior is missing from the discussion so far. What about conviction in the Nazi cause? Certainly some chaplains are on record as staunch Nazis. One of my earliest encounters with the topic involved a German Lutheran pastor in Luseland, Saskatchewan (Canada), who wrote to the Protestant military bishop in 1936 begging to be appointed to the chaplaincy so he could serve the Führer.[51] (Neither he nor a Baptist pastor who wrote a similar request around the same time was accepted.) Active members of the pro-Nazi German Christian movement also sought positions. In some high-profile cases they succeeded: Chief Navy Chaplain Friedrich Ronneberger and Dean of Chaplains Heinrich Lonicer were the two most prominent. However, some clergy were disqualified from the chaplaincy as being too fanatically pro-Nazi, and nothing indicates that men signed on as chaplains in order to kill Jews or other supposed enemies. The SS murder squads known as Einsatzgruppen did include former Christian clergy, most infamously the Lutheran theologian Ernst Biberstein, head of Sonderkommando 6 of Einsatzgruppe C,[52] and their murderous activities raise urgent and neglected questions about Christians as perpetrators of genocide. Such men, however, did not become chaplains, or if they did, they left no trace.

Were the chaplains Nazis? A more fruitful question asks how people who were not fervent Nazis or eager killers ended up playing an essential role in atrocity. One response can be found in the letters of Konrad Jarausch, a Protestant theologian who served with the Wehrmacht in the invasions and occupations of Poland and the Soviet Union. A devout educator and publicist, Jarausch was committed to serving his country and his faith. By autumn 1941 a master sergeant, he was put in charge of the kitchen in a camp that held thousands of sick, starving, and dying Soviet prisoners of war. Sergeant Jarausch tried his best to keep order. His hand became swollen from dealing out blows, he told his wife. And yet he felt empathy for the prisoners and became close to some of them. In his words, it was "already more murder than war." Jarausch died of typhoid fever in January 1942. His letters show neither the "clean Wehrmacht" nor Nazified killers but dutiful, if reluctant, accomplices.[53]

This book is organized chronologically, because while writing it I discovered that lines of continuity and change only became visible when I put developments in order. Following the chronology highlighted a factor often neglected in historical analyses: force of habit, at a personal and an institutional level. The Nazi period divides equally into the six prewar years from 1933 to 1939 and six years of World War II. The years of peace – or more accurately, of Hitler talking peace while preparing for war – are of key importance in showing how the chaplaincy developed to play the role it did during Germany's wars of annihilation.[54]

Even before its official launch in 1935, the Wehrmacht chaplaincy adjusted and accommodated itself to the National Socialist regime. It was built on tracks and looked back to patterns established during the previous world war and Germany's short-lived colonial empire. Christian chaplains were present in German Southwest Africa during the genocide of the Herero and Nama;[55] chaplains witnessed atrocities against civilians during World War I, and some former chaplains loudly stumped for Hitler and the National Socialist Party during the Weimar years.[56] In short, Germany's eastern front in 1941 was an escalation but not an aberration, either from what came before or from what followed, or even from the war in the west and the southeast. The habit of cooperation, part of the chaplaincy's raison d'être, proved hard to break, and the higher the stakes became, the less likely it was that chaplains – those at the top of the hierarchy and those at the bottom – would venture out of the deep ruts of their well-worn path. One compromise led to another, and each subsequent step in one direction raised the cost of turning back. When does a compromise become a betrayal? When does it turn into a trap?

Looking backward and forward from the murder of the Jewish children at Bila Tserkva highlights continuities in both directions. Study of the Wehrmacht chaplains reveals the ongoing viability of Christianity in Germany even after defeat in 1945. People seemed to need institutionalized Christianity, and it outlived Nazism, although in a weakened form. But continuities can be paradoxical. After World War II, both the German military and its chaplaincy fell out of view, only to be reinvigorated by the Cold War and the interests of NATO. In West Germany in the 1950s, creation of the new Bundeswehr was accompanied by considerable debate around how to constitute the military chaplaincy. It took two years for the new chaplaincy to be set up, and the result looked completely different from its World War II predecessor. Chaplains no longer held an officer's rank, and their purpose was not to boost morale but to be a voice of conscience within the military. In the German Democratic Republic there were to be no military chaplains at all.

Rarely did anyone mention Jews or other victims of Nazism in the public discussions about how to reconfigure the German chaplaincy. But Jews were remembered, if vaguely and uneasily, in articles like one published in 1965. In the Protestant journal *Junge Kirche* (young church), the theologian Uwe Lütjohann invoked the Holocaust as a call for Christian repentance:

> The evil in the church must be pulled out by the roots. The military chaplaincy of World War II only helps us now if we learn from its mistakes. Genuine military chaplaincy today leads us back to the law of Christ, that we love our enemies. And only a perverted definition of love can mean killing our enemies.[57]

Sources and Methods

This book is part of a wave of research on the Holocaust that surged in the early 1990s and endures decades later.[58] I build on older scholarship on German military chaplains,[59] more recent contributions,[60] and the revival of interest in the crimes of the Wehrmacht associated with an 1995 exhibition in Germany and the ensuing controversy.[61] My study also fits into a body of work that examines Christianity under Nazism. Some studies deal only with Catholics;[62] another group focuses on Protestants.[63] I consider all the Wehrmacht chaplains, Protestants and Catholics, together, as part of a wider conversation about the connections between religion, war, and genocide.[64]

Sources for this study include chaplains' periodic reports to their superiors; correspondence among church and state authorities; chaplains' letters and diaries, and eyewitnesses' postwar recollections.[65] I use all of these materials in order to see the chaplains as historical actors with personalities, values, theological and political positions. It is not my goal to recreate the chaplains' inner world, however.[66] As I have thought about this subject over many years, I have wondered whether starting the story in 1941 in Germany's east and letting chaplains speak for themselves without analyzing their accounts risks reproducing a self-justifying version of events. Chaplains were active agents in constructing their own narrative, as individuals and collectively, and my analysis considers such efforts to be an integral part of their history.[67]

Accordingly, I try to interrupt records by the Wehrmacht chaplains with sources that offer other perspectives.[68] Integrated histories of the Holocaust shift and reverse the gaze to disrupt grand narratives with the voices of victims, in particular Jewish victims.[69] This book applies that method. Outside sources are not easy to find, because rarely did anyone other than chaplains mention chaplains. Nonetheless, German troops, French prisoners of war, members of SS killing squads, captured Jews, civilians under German occupation, and Allied authorities all encountered Wehrmacht chaplains, and some of them recorded their impressions. In a letter home, a German soldier described the execution of a comrade convicted for desertion and noted the presence of a chaplain at the condemned man's side. A young Leningrad woman confided to her diary her admiration for the German chaplain who presided over the reopening of a church.[70] An SS report complained that Wehrmacht chaplains caused friction among locals in Ukraine by holding church services for different Christian denominations. Even such fleeting glances provide a valuable corrective to the view from inside the chaplaincy.

Integrated approaches to history invite attention to gender, sexuality, bodies, and the materiality of everyday life. When I started this project, paying attention to gender did not seem that important to me. But now I consider it essential. The Wehrmacht chaplains held two positions only men could hold: they were Christian clergy and members of the military.[71] Chaplains constantly invoked notions of manliness – their own and that of others – although they did not explain what they understood "manliness" to mean.[72] They were more explicit in describing Christian morality, which they tried to uphold among soldiers by railing against sex with enemy women.[73]

Representations of military chaplains in German history and culture are essential to this study. I have drawn on literary and other creative sources: novels and films, and even popular representations of military chaplains in other times and places. These materials have helped me break out of some preconceived notions about the Wehrmacht chaplains and also illuminated certain issues common to many chaplaincies. One such issue is the quest for relevance, which is evident in fictional accounts of chaplains from Jaroslav Hašek's *The Good Soldier Svejk* all the way to Mort Walker's long-running comic strip, *Beetle Bailey*.

Photographs are valuable sources, and they too require interpretation. Early in my research I happened upon a remarkable exhibit in a regional church museum in Ludwigsburg, based on the papers of Bernhard Bauerle, a Protestant chaplain with the German 16th Army. Bauerle's daughter had found a cache of his correspondence after he died, and she donated it to the museum. Two curators did a superb job of organizing that material into a thought-provoking display.[74] The contrast is striking between what Bauerle wrote and what his photographs depicted: alongside claims that "we had nothing to do with attacks on the Jews," he archived a photo of an emaciated individual, who was labeled on the reverse side of the photo, in Bauerle's hand, as *Jude* (Jew). Silence regarding German killing of Soviets is belied by images of walking skeletons gnawing on bones and corpses hanging from nooses, captioned *Kriegsgefangene* and *Partisanen* (prisoners of war and partisans). To Bauerle it seems, both aspects were important: the articulation of noninvolvement, even innocence, and the evidence of witnessing. I have puzzled over that tension and come to view it as central to understanding the Wehrmacht chaplains, who functioned, like their counterparts in other settings, under a "sign of contradiction."[75]

Every source, whether written, visual, or oral, is produced at a certain time, and what "the time" is influences what the source says, who reads or hears it, and how.[76] Many of the most detailed and certainly the most personal accounts of German military chaplains come from after the war, often long after. These materials reflect the world around them. For instance, by the 1990s, it had become unacceptable among educated people to talk about the Nazi period without mentioning the Holocaust, specifically the persecution and killing of Jews.[77] Chaplains who wrote memoirs decades after the war internalized that convention. Recognizing this process does not make later accounts worthless, but they need to be analyzed with an eye to the multiple contexts they reflect.

A concrete example illustrates my point. A few years ago, in a small archive in Berlin, I read an extensive diary by Alphons Satzger, a Wehrmacht chaplain.[78] Satzger was already known to me from wartime records.[79] A Roman Catholic, he won acclamation and an Iron Cross when in 1941, armed only with a pistol, he captured twenty-one Red Army soldiers. The diary, sixty-five pages long, was a historian's dream: articulate, detailed, and deeply introspective. It was even typed. Unlike the dry, official reports chaplains submitted to their military superiors, this document overflowed with feeling.

The author described his horror when, in early July 1941, he accompanied German troops into Lviv and witnessed the massive violence against Jews there. I knew German military chaplains must have been present at this site of carnage, but I had never before found one who mentioned it. Here was not only a fleeting reference to the violence but a detailed account of how a chaplain reacted. In vivid prose Satzger depicted his venture into the prison, where locals had found corpses of victims killed by the retreating Soviets. Antisemites seized on this evidence to launch an all-out assault on Jews in the region, dragging hundreds of them into the prison, forcing them to dispose of the rotted bodies and scrub walls and floors, and then murdering them there. The sickening stench, Father Satzger wrote, stayed in his uniform for days.[80]

That remark about the smell jumped off the page. Graphic and specific, it is the kind of detail that makes personal accounts so unforgettable. And I have no reason to doubt that it is true. But how would Satzger have known on July 4 – the day he entered the prison and the date of the diary entry describing what he saw there – how many days *later* the stench of death would still linger in his clothes? As I read on, I found other things that could only have been added after the fact: comments about the outcome of developments that could not yet have been known, details about military locations and operations that were not to be revealed, and use of terms that were not in currency in the 1940s. What is more, there was a pattern: almost all of the tell-tale signs appeared within entries that dealt directly with wartime atrocities, especially against Jews. In other words, precisely those passages that made this diary so different from firsthand accounts written during the war were almost certainly added afterward, with the benefit of hindsight and aligned with contemporary mores.[81] This is not to say the diary is a fraud. Indeed, in a note at the end, Satzger mentioned that he retyped it in the 1970s, and he did not deny he made revisions. The researcher can find much of value here, but the diary is no clear window into the chaplain's wartime soul.

Because the Wehrmacht chaplains cannot be seen without looking back from our own present, this study also reveals linkages between the past and what follows it. For my experience, September 11, 2001 is significant. When the planes struck the World Trade Center towers in New York, I had already been working on the Wehrmacht chaplains for a decade. But in the 1990s, religion was a hard sell for a historian of modern Europe. The 9/11 attacks and the response in the United States, where I lived and worked at the time, changed that: they sparked a new interest in the intersections of religion and violence, often construed in Islamophobic terms.[82] The wars in Iraq and Afghanistan added a specific focus on military chaplains, and suddenly I found that work I had done made me an "expert," called on to comment on such issues as the significance of the first Muslim and Buddhist chaplains in the US Armed Forces.[83] Decades later, the sobering tale of the Wehrmacht chaplains continues to resonate with current events.[84] Increased attention to systemic racism in the wake of the murder of George Floyd by a white police officer in 2020, and exposure of institutional complicity in genocide of Indigenous people in Canada have sharpened my approach.[85]

In the epigraph I chose from *Billy Budd*, Melville characterizes the military chaplain as "incongruous," an embodiment of the contradiction between the violence of war and the "Prince of Peace." Were the Wehrmacht chaplains any different in this regard from their counterparts in other times and places?

Since the emergence of the institution, military chaplains have served the cause of war.[86] Like German chaplains in World War II, others must sometimes have felt pulled in opposite directions by unconditional loyalty to the military and the implicit claim of righteousness. Maybe others, too, found relief in mild acts of defiance that, though they carried a risk, ended up normalizing brutal systems. The Wehrmacht chaplaincy acted as an insulating layer, protecting German soldiers from listening to their consciences or reflecting on Christian teachings. That buffer also covered the chaplains themselves and absorbed objections they may have had. The chaplaincy became a cone of silence, a tunnel. Precisely this reinforcing, silencing effect necessitates an integrated approach to research. In order to see the tunnel, you have to get inside and outside of it. Only people on the outside can get an impression of its overall shape.

The testimony of Agnes Adachi provides such a glimpse. Born in 1918 to Hungarian Jewish parents, Adachi (then Agnes Mandl) lived, traveled, and attended school in Switzerland, Austria, Germany, and France. By 1944, she had returned to Budapest, where she was baptized a Protestant Christian. Through a complicated chain of events, the charismatic, multilingual Adachi ended up working with the Swedish businessman and diplomat Raoul Wallenberg in his mission to rescue Jews.[87] In a 1996 interview with the Shoah Foundation, she sketched this horrifying scene:

There was a little child, with a star, who had evidently lost her parents, and there was a church, and out came a Catholic priest wearing inside his collar the Hungarian Nazi collar, and he had a revolver. And he saw that little kid, and he shot her. . . . I picked up the child, and she was dead.[88]

Adachi's shocking account raises a number of questions. Was the man a chaplain? What is a "Hungarian Nazi collar?" Where was the church? What was Adachi doing there? Did she shape this account for maximum impact: an innocent little girl gunned down by a devil in disguise? Could she be describing András Kun, the Catholic priest, Arrow Cross leader, and notorious killer of Jews in Budapest?[89] Considering multiple perspectives and reading for narratives, as well as evidence, cannot necessarily provide answers but it does promise insight. My method in this book is to afford sources like Adachi's – the incomplete, flawed, tainted-by-hindsight voices of victims and observers outside the chaplaincy – the same analytical attention I give to sources from chaplains and those close to them. Conversely, I try to approach accounts such as Chaplain Tewes's testimony in court or Chaplain Satzger's diary – incomplete, flawed, and tainted by hindsight – with the reflexive skepticism and theoretical consideration that many scholars of the Holocaust bring to survivor testimonies.[90]

Discerning Christianity's role in the Holocaust requires listening to chaplains' narratives and also to accounts that supplement and challenge them. The past appears different from divergent perspectives. To Wehrmacht Chaplain Eberhard Müller, whose sermon to German soldiers in occupied Soviet territory is quoted in the second epigraph, the war and the Holocaust were folded into a story of God's boundless love for His people.[91] To Agnes Adachi, who as a young woman saw Germans and their Hungarian partners destroy her family and community, genocide looked like a Christian priest murdering a Jewish child in front of a church.

1   "We Will Not Let Our Swords Get Rusty"
On the Cusp of 1933

On April 4, 1932, the Garrison Church in Potsdam opened its doors – or at least its doorway – to torch-bearing Stormtroopers who stood guard as formations of the National Socialist German Workers Party, Stormtroopers, and the SS paraded into the church. Arriving directly from a speech by Adolf Hitler, who was campaigning for election, they had come to pay homage at the tomb of Frederick the Great.[1] Twenty church members signed a letter decrying what they called the desecration of Old Fritz's grave, and a Potsdam city official complained that the church council had overstepped its authority, but no one was disciplined. For years the church had hosted similar events, supported by members of its clergy and organized by the German National People's Party (DNVP), the veterans' association the *Stahlhelm*, relatives of the deposed Kaiser, the German Association of Military Officers (*Deutsche Offizierbund*), and many others. Although this was the first time the organizer was listed as the Nazi Party, the script and cast of characters remained more or less the same.

One key figure was the Protestant pastor of the military congregation, Curt Koblanck. He had held that position since 1925, after serving as divisional chaplain and then chaplain at other garrisons during the Great War. Koblanck was actively connected to an array of right-radical groups, but by mid-1932 he was focusing his energies on the Nazi Party. In November of that year, he addressed a Party rally with a call to fight democracy: "We will not let our swords get rusty but will defend our positions," he vowed.[2]

Koblanck was no outlier. His predecessor, Johannes Vogel, a chaplain in the German Army since 1904, was even more stridently pro-Nazi. Already in 1926, Vogel spoke at a ceremony to bless Stormtrooper flags and praised the swastika as a symbol of Christianity united with old *Germanentum*. Known as a vehement antisemite, Vogel regularly preached and presided at events in Potsdam's Protestant churches throughout the Weimar period.[3] In July 1932, Pastor Vogel showed up at his local polling station wearing a huge swastika on his chest.

The spectacle at the Garrison Church raises the central question of this chapter: What was the relationship between Germany's military chaplains,

Nazism, and Nazis before Hitler came to power? The question seems simple, but it is not easy to answer. One complicating factor is hindsight. Looking back, it is impossible not to view torchlit Stormtroopers swarming into a church in 1932 as an early scene in the catastrophic drama of Nazi Germany. Indeed, Koblanck, Vogel, and the Garrison Church in Potsdam would all feature again in the twelve-year show of support for Hitler.[4] But the spectacle in April 1932 was both the beginning of something new and the culmination of preceding developments. It also merits attention as a moment in itself, contingent and replete with possibilities. Together with the other events analyzed in this chapter, it shows that the chaplaincy's embrace of Hitler's regime was foreseeable, though not inevitable.

Visible in the scene at the church are four issues that shaped the chaplains' relationship to Nazism on the eve of 1933, established patterns for the years to follow, and continue to influence how this history is viewed. One factor is that in German society, military chaplains carried significance far beyond their immediate function. Connected to the divine through prayers and sacraments, chaplains had the power to bestow legitimacy, as Pastor Vogel did when he blessed the swastika and wore it on his chest like a crusader's cross. Chaplains bound Christianity to the nation state and its past, present, and future, just as Pastor Koblanck served as the link between "Old Fritz" and the Stormtroopers at the door. To church leaders and nationalist Christians – and to chaplains themselves – military chaplains, with their congregations of soldiers, embodied hope for the revival and remasculinization of Christianity in Germany.

A second, dialectically related factor is that military chaplains on the cusp of 1933 perceived their situation as weak. With Germany's armed forces cut to 100,000 men under the Treaty of Versailles,[5] most of the old guard had needed new jobs. Instead of several thousand chaplains, as had served the Imperial Germany Army, there were now just a hundred or so. Koblanck's defiant words conjure an image of chaplains defending an exposed position, surrounded by enemies, waving their aging and tarnished swords. Shackled to the lost war and grasping for relevance in a society they feared had little interest in organized religion, chaplains and former chaplains sought new partners and new purpose.

A third point, less immediately apparent, is that chaplains actively constructed self-serving narratives, and these constitute many of the existing sources for the period in question. It was Pastor Koblanck himself who documented the procession in April 1932. Reports he and others produced in subsequent years present a teleology that culminated in Nazi triumphs. It was not predestined that military chaplains would land in the Nazi camp, and evidence shows that as individuals, their loyalties, like those of their parishioners, varied and changed. In 1932, after all, twenty people signed the complaint about Stormtroopers parading in the Garrison Church. But chaplains' own accounts of how they thought and behaved, produced in the twelve years that followed, all but erased the evidence that things could have been different. Meanwhile, histories they wrote after the war present another selective narrative, in which the early enthusiasm for Hitler has vanished.

The fourth factor, only hinted at in the short vignette here, involves the importance of personal ties. Two chaplains who saw eye-to-eye about the Nazi movement, as Vogel and Koblanck did, could silence a colleague who disagreed. Church councilors with friends and relatives among the Stormtroopers could arrange opportunities and defy congregants who opposed them, as the Potsdam group did. Affiliation with the Nazi Party and ideological kinship followed other kinds of networks, including families, friends, clubs, and church communities. By early 1933, many chaplains, Catholic as well as Protestant, had cultivated personal ties to individuals in Hitler's movement, including some in very powerful positions. These connections laid the foundation for the future partnership between military chaplains and the Nazi cause.

Magnified by the Light of Tradition

Chaplains appeared larger than life because their location at the crossroads of Christianity and the military put them in the spotlight of national myths about German strength. This position shaped their self-perception and how others saw them. Military chaplains in Germany in the early 1930s understood themselves as part of a Christian tradition rooted in the modern nation. Catholics as well as Protestants were embedded in a narrative that linked clerical service and military service around themes of history and memory, masculinity, antisemitism, and Christian exceptionalism.

German military chaplains embodied what I call "war Christianity," and this quality further enhanced their significance. More than just wartime theology, the label implies a version of Christianity that focuses on, and is indeed obsessed with, war and struggle. It defines itself in terms of war, contribution to a war effort, and sacrifice. In war Christianity, the meaning, legitimacy, and relevance of the church, the value of its teachings, and the nature of its members' religious practices are all tied to armed conflict. War Christianity by nature is dynamic and variable: it draws on collective memory because it uses, reabsorbs, and reinterprets the past. German Catholics as well as Protestants partook in war Christianity, although their history of conflict and competition often pitted them against one another.

In speeches and sermons, chaplains pointed to the past as their model for the present. They frequently invoked a glorious legacy going back to the "Wars of Liberation" against Napoleon,[6] or more immediately to the Great War. Part of a national narrative of rising power and pride in conquest, chaplains described themselves as present at the creation of German greatness. As is typical of "mythic time," they collapsed events and centuries in a self-referential teleology,[7] and omitted inconvenient facts, such as the German switch from being partners of Napoleon's France to its scourge.[8] Most of their historical allusions were to the same few scenes: General Ludwig Yorck von Wartenburg praying before battle, Field Marshal Paul von Hindenburg calling for more prayers from the home front. In neither of those canonical moments was a chaplain the main character or even on stage.

Rarely mentioned was the fact that the Prussian army chaplaincy grew out of a quid pro quo in 1713, between King Friedrich Wilhelm of the house of Hohenzollern and the Pietist pastor August Hermann Francke.[9] The king got a reliable source of discipline and morale-boosting, and the church got access to the soldiers and their souls. This arrangement had far-reaching effects: it empowered chaplains yet made them beholden to the monarch. It also generated significant differences between the confessions, in favor of the Protestants.[10] In fact, the Prussian arrangement initially applied only to Protestants, for whom pastoral care was organized by 1832 in the form of a military church (*Militärkirche*) under the leadership of a military bishop (*Feldpropst*). A Catholic counterpart was not appointed until 1849.[11] Protestants continued their ascendancy with the victory over France and unification under Prussia, and confessional rivalry persisted throughout the Weimar years.

For chaplains such as Curt Koblanck in 1932, the past provided an arsenal, a vocabulary tailor-made for the purpose of mobilizing a national religious revival. Chaplains harked back to the outbreak of war in 1914 and the outpouring of euphoria on the part of pastors, priests, and many church people.[12] Christian leaders in Germany had used all the tools at their disposal – sermons, publications, periodicals – to rally to the flag.[13] In passionate detail, publicists had extolled Hindenburg's piety and denigrated English Christians for betraying Christ (and Germany!) in favor of pacts with atheists and heathens. Preachers assured their audiences that prayers for German victory redounded to the glory of God.[14]

Evident on every page of the most widely read Protestant Church periodical (*Allgemeine Evangelisch-Lutherische Kirchenzeitung*) during the years of the Great War had been a profound hope for Christian renewal. One pastor's jubilant account of the first day of mobilization – August 1, 1914 – illustrates this longing:

That memorable Sunday also mobilized the entire people of the church, who otherwise take it easy and spend their Sundays outside the church ... Many people spontaneously got down on their knees when the prayer of repentance was recited and also with the offering of the sacrament. ... People no longer wiped their mouths so fussily after drinking from the cup, as if they were afraid of being infected. No, they celebrated respectfully, and how many of them had not been seen in church for many years.[15]

Two decades later, churchmen yearned to reignite that passion for Christian Germany.

This vision of Christianity triumphant was built on antisemitism, as Protestants and Catholics alike associated Jews with their enemies: secularism, atheism, Communism, and modernity. Chaplains emblemized the aspirational "peace in the fortress," the *Burgfrieden*, that was to bind all true Germans against their foes. At Tannenburg and Verdun, Protestant and Catholic chaplains had served alongside one another, something invoked later when praising the imagined unity of Germans under arms. But no Christian chaplains after 1918 are on record noting that Jewish clergy had likewise served the cause, ministering to the tens of thousands of Jewish soldiers in the Imperial German Army.[16] And in contrast to their Christian counterparts, Jewish chaplains had not been paid by the military or the state but by their home congregations.[17]

One of those Jewish clergymen was Georg Salzberger. In an interview he gave in the 1970s, Rabbi Salzberger alluded to the casual and contemptuous antisemitism of his Christian colleagues during World War I: "My relations with Catholic and Protestant chaplains varied. I had very good contact with some, especially with the Catholics. Jewish soldiers told me that the Protestant chaplain said at services: 'Yes the Jews: I cannot tolerate them, the Jews.'"[18]

Salzberger's account of how he responded shows his dependence on good relations with his commanding officers. He reported getting a sympathetic hearing and the satisfaction of being recognized as an equal to the Christians:

I lodged a complaint about this at Command and thereupon the authoritative officer asked what he should do and whether I wished to make an incident of the affair. "Not at all," I said, "I just want the gentleman to be told what the Kaiser said: 'No parties any more, only German soldiers.'" And this occurred. I was, together with the Catholic and Protestant chaplains, awarded the Iron Cross Second class by the German Crown Prince.[19]

With its plucky protagonist, fair-minded Imperial authorities, and happy ending, Salzberger's story conveys a strong note of nostalgia for Germany before Hitler. Still, his perspective provides a vital insight into how Nazi ideology connected to chaplains' pre-1933 habits of thought. For Christians, suspicion of Jews was a reflex, a familiar script always within reach.[20]

World War I shaped the chaplaincy in the Weimar years in concrete ways.[21] An obvious impact was on personnel. The Protestant military bishop (*Feldprobst*) Max Wölfing turned seventy a month before the war ended in 1918 and retired in January 1919.[22] His successor, Erich Schlegel, inherited the task of organizing the dissolution of pastoral care to the army and navy.

During the war, 128 Protestant chaplains with full-time officer status had served the army; 27 men did the same for the navy, and an additional 1,925 civilian clergy had served as military chaplains. Eighteen active chaplains had succumbed to illness or died in the line of duty. In 1919, most of the 128 full-time, regular military chaplains had to be let go. Schlegel wrote to them, inviting opponents of the new Republic to opt out of its service. In his words, "Who among you is deeply opposed to the new situation and does not wish to serve the new tasks of military pastoral care?" Schlegel helped those who chose to step back find civilian congregations,[23] in the process disseminating their antidemocratic views in new circles.

Across Germany, Catholic priests and Protestant pastors who had served as chaplains in World War I spoke at nationalist rallies, welcomed processions, and blessed flags in their churches. Individual clergy fanned resentment, antisemitism, and desire for revenge, at times with deadly consequences. In May 1919, Robert Hell, who had served as one of the Protestant chaplains in Hitler's division, was the Lutheran pastor in Perlach, a working-class suburb of Munich. There he experienced the end of the Bavarian Soviet Republic. When the *Freikorps* came to town, the unit leader, Hans von Lützow, found a warm reception in Hell's home. Later, the pastor's wife, worried about Communist reprisals, telephoned their former houseguest to ask for help: Pastor Hell believed his name was on a hit list. In response, a group of Lützow *Freikorps* men seized fifteen suspected Communist revolutionaries and, with Hell's encouragement, took them to Munich and shot them in the courtyard of the Hofbräukeller.[24]

Chaplains' public appearances in the wake of 1918 served various causes but many were linked to the Nazi movement. In what looks like a tag-team effort, though it was characterized as much by rivalry as cooperation, Catholic chaplains took the early shift, playing their major contributing role in the immediate postwar years in Bavaria. Protestants grabbed the baton in the mid-1920s, as the Nazi Party transformed from a regional to a national movement. In short, although individuals varied, German military chaplains as a group actively supported the rise to power of Hitler and the National Socialists.

In Bavaria, Catholic chaplains had a prominent part in this process. Derek Hastings has excavated the links between a Catholic-inflected "Positive Christianity" and expansion of the Nazi movement in Munich from 1920 to the Beerhall Putsch three years later. Surprising is the heavy involvement of Roman Catholic priests, including a number of former military chaplains, who served as Nazi speakers and publicists – "storm-troop preachers" in the vocabulary of the time. Also remarkable is the National Socialist Party membership drive of 1923 and its explicit targeting of committed Catholics. The result was an almost threefold increase in the number of Party members and a movement that contemporaries, both friendly and critical, characterized as "Catholic oriented."[25]

Did antisemitism help attract military chaplains to the Nazi movement in this early stage? To address this question, Jewish sources are essential, along with chaplains' own words from before Hitler came to power. Records of the latter type are not plentiful but they do exist. For instance, in July 1923, the *Völkischer Beobachter* reported on a speech given by the Catholic priest Christian Huber, titled "Antisemitism and the National Socialist Position on Property." In an extensive tour across Bavaria, Father Huber delivered the three-hour diatribe to numerous local Nazi Party groups.[26] As a former military chaplain, Huber embodied the "warrior Christianity" his audiences craved while preaching a message central to the Party's membership drive: "Catholicism is the born enemy of Jewry."[27] It is not clear whether antisemitism was the main factor that brought Huber into the Nazi fold, but his eagerness to preach against Jews as a Catholic priest and a chaplain-veteran made him a valuable asset to the Party at that fledgling stage and gave him the satisfaction of large and eager audiences.

All of the themes later trumpeted by the predominantly Protestant "German Christian" movement were already evident here: the National Socialist Party as the defender and champion of Positive Christianity; Christianity as a manly, "warrior faith"; and the Aryan Jesus.[28] Also noticeable is the way that enormous, open-air Nazi rallies involving former chaplains and other Catholic priests as speakers were patterned after wartime "field services" with their masses of uniformed men, flags, and crusading spirit: "*Gott mit uns*." Military chaplains must have felt right at home.

As the incarnation of Christian presence in the military, chaplains featured in another powerful storyline: the German soldier as a Christ figure. This narrative of inversion transformed fighting, killing men into suffering victims whose blood cleansed and redeemed the nation. In this tableau, the drama involved German souls seeking salvation, and the only victims in sight were the Germans themselves. The decades before 1933 had provided a number of opportunities to enact this plot. Throughout World War I, German chaplains served and witnessed massacres in Belgium and elsewhere, they numbered among observers of the Armenian genocide in 1915,[29] and they watched as their armies expelled civilians from their homes and used them as human shields.[30] By witnessing atrocities and providing pastoral care to the perpetrators, military chaplains offered justification for mass violence and genocide.

The narrative of inversion had a colonial variant, and it too formed part of the chaplains' tradition. Christian clergy participated in Germany's overseas wars and colonies: as missionaries and chaplains they supported German atrocities in the Boxer Uprising, Herero Nama genocide, and Maji Maji war.[31] The familiar narrative of European overseas missions – bringing religion to people who

SELIG SIND
DIE FRIEDFERTIGEN

Figure 1.1 "Blessed are the peacemakers," one of eight mosaics in the Berlin Cathedral depicting the beatitudes from Jesus's Sermon on the Mount. This image, designed and created in the midst of German war and genocide in colonial Southwest and East Africa, depicts a familiar inversion: white Christians portrayed as the victim and peacemaker, a Black man as the aggressor. Photographer Katharina Dorn.

supposedly lacked not only civilization but soul-nurturing culture – meshed easily with assumptions of unconditional, Christian, German righteousness. In colonialist and settler accounts of conquest and genocide in Africa, Asia, and the Americas, people of color and Indigenous peoples, victims of attack and mass death, were transformed into vicious aggressors, while the invaders represented themselves as self-sacrificing martyrs and vessels for the triumph of Christian civilization. The story of Christian military innocence and its colonial manifestations would find echoes in the genocidal culture of Nazi Germany.

In his study of Rhenish missionaries in German Southwest Africa, Glen Ryland illustrates this inversion story with an image from the cupola of Berlin's Protestant cathedral.[32] Under construction during the years of brutal German wars in East and Southwest Africa, 1904–1907, and installed in the wake of the genocide of Herero and Nama people, the dome features mosaics designed by Anton von Werner of the eight beatitudes, one on each section. "Blessed are the Peacemakers" depicts a triumphant Christ the King, a cross on his chest and a crucifix in one hand. With the other hand he restrains a muscular, almost naked Black warrior, poised to stab a prone white knight whose eyes are wide with terror (Figure 1.1).

The image is stunning in its unabashed role reversal: white German soldiers cast as victims of Africans, at a time when armed Germans had killed tens of thousands of children, men, and women, hunted them into deadly concentration camps to die of mistreatment and disease, or forced them into the desert and abandoned them to hunger and thirst; a white god extolled as the bringer of peace when his missionaries were actively luring the remaining Herero into German camps and proselytizing among them with the message that the destruction of their families and communities was God's punishment for their unfaithfulness.

This tradition, too – the colonialist narrative of the white man's burden that included the work of defeating and dominating other people – magnified the significance of military chaplains. They stood in for the divine ruler and judge, brandishing a cross that blessed His warriors and sanctified their cause.[33]

An Exposed Position

The 1932 procession in Potsdam's Garrison Church asserted Nazi power, but it also reflected divisions within German society, and those tensions cut into the military chaplaincy. One rift was confessional. How did the Protestant chauvinism of Koblanck, Vogel, and their ilk square with the presence of many Roman Catholics in the Stormtroopers, SS, and Nazi Party – including, of course, the venerated leader, Hitler himself?

A related cleft among chaplains, and within German society as a whole, was regional. How did the institution of military chaplaincy, born in Prussia and wedded to a now defunct monarchy, persist through German unification and defeat fifty years later, then manage to subsume separate, competing, and sometimes conflicting army and church authorities in Hannover, Bavaria, Württemberg, Saxony, and elsewhere?[34] In the uneven integration of these armies into the Prussian or Imperial German Army, chaplains appear to have been a low priority, making it difficult to assess their situations and how they changed.[35]

At the Nazi Party rally in 1932, Pastor Koblanck exhorted his fellow Christian soldiers to keep their swords sharp and shining. But such bravado could not hide the stain of defeat. Germany's failure to win in 1918 incriminated the churches and their leaders in betraying the military. Were the churches to blame for the fact that Germans, in Hindenburg's famous words, had not prayed enough?[36] Had Germans not believed firmly enough, either in God or in the national cause? Had they been too sinful? Were Christian clergy implicated in the treacherous home front that supposedly killed its own soldiers through defeatism and rebellion? War Christianity pointed to the past, and particularly to mythologized accounts of 1914, 1870, and 1813, to validate the position of the church as a partner, a servant, and helpmate of the nation. But history was a two-edged sword, as much the German chaplaincy's enemy as its friend.

Church spokespeople themselves provided the language that could be used against them, as they castigated each other as intellectuals and shirkers; womanly, weak, cowardly internationalists influenced by Judaism, who turned the other cheek instead of fighting like men. Anyone who has read about World War I knows the famous bellicosity of German theological circles, with their "*Gott mit uns*," denunciations of "perfidious Albion," and insistence that German victory was God's will. The shrillness of such rhetoric painted German churchmen into a corner, so that for proponents of war Christianity there was no option but victory – or apocalypse. An editorial by Wilhelm Laible of the *Allgemeine Evangelisch-Lutherische Kirchenzeitung* from October 1918 illustrates these tendencies:

If the enemies of Germany are triumphant – not only temporarily but with our destruction – then injustice, lies, money, and murder will have won. Trust in God and faith in His presence will be defeated. This is not how God has ruled the world up to now. If He continues doing as He has, He will stop world history, and the prophecy will come to pass: "When injustice gains the upper hand."[37]

Viewed this way, war Christianity was not a symptom of strength but of weakness. It developed from a specific combination of anxiety and power regarding the Christian churches in modern Germany. Like every defensive stance, it both expressed vulnerability and increased it. For decades, Catholic and Protestant church leaders alike had watched as participation, even membership dropped. They became fixated on data and statistics and agonized that the church was doomed as de-Christianization and secularization swept Germany and lured its men and its young people away from the churches.

Many scholars have emphasized that a casualty of World War I was a loss of credibility for the churches and Christianity in general.[38] Churchmen's calls to "hold on," their promises of victory and blessings over the cannons rang hollow in the face of the destruction wrought on all sides.[39] Chaplains found themselves in the center of this negative charge. The Austro-Czech Jaroslav Hašek's satiric novel *The Good Soldier Svejk* featured as one of its most risible characters the Habsburg army chaplain, an atheist, cynic, and drunk (and, a vicious touch, a convert to Christianity from Judaism), who understood that his only function was to supply men as cannon fodder.[40] Subsequent scholarship has complicated this longstanding assumption by demonstrating the vibrancy of Christian institutions in the midst of the war and after.[41] Both interpretations are essential for understanding the situation of German chaplains before Hitler.

The dynamic interplay of pride and shame helps account for the vitriolic opposition to Weimar democracy on the part of many chaplains. Not an inevitable result of their wartime behavior, it was nevertheless the logical outcome of a specific position that in order to retain its dominance had to silence and discredit others. Michael Geyer has written of "catastrophic nationalism," a drive to keep on fighting even when defeat is certain, and to try to control memory from the grave.[42] The concept describes German elites, who after World War I, in an attempt to shift blame and hold onto their power, claimed they had never stopped fighting and erected plaques and memorials and held services to remind themselves and others of their continued bellicosity. The result was a series of dangerous alliances in the Weimar period as the churches joined forces with the German National People's Party, Stahlhelm, Stormtroopers, and Nazi Party according to the principle, "the enemy of my enemy is my friend."[43]

Anxiety among church leaders generated an obsession with manliness, as churchmen defended themselves against the charge that they were not "real men." Widespread notions of manhood in Europe during the eighteenth and nineteenth centuries associated masculinity with hardness, the qualities of a soldier who fought and showed no mercy to anyone.[44] In societies that associated Christian piety with women and that accused women of "sexual treason" during the war,[45] clergy were vulnerable to charges they had become feminized. Celibate Catholic priests made especially easy targets, and Protestant clergy frequently and gleefully seized their advantage. For both confessions, military chaplaincy held out the promise of a truly manly Christian faith.

By the 1930s, German chaplains looked back to a world war that represented at the same time their shining moment and the site of their deepest mortification.[46] This tension is captured in a memo, written at the time of rearmament in 1935, from a church superintendent in Soest, Westphalia, who advocated for creation of a military chaplaincy. In support of the cause, he offered a table that showed how many Protestant theologians (chaplains, pastors, students of theology, and pastors' sons) had "fallen" in battle between 1914 and 1933. (The Stormtrooper Horst Wessel was included.) The pastor conceded that the chaplaincy during the Great War had not been perfect:

> It cannot be denied that in the last big war the church fell severely short in its duty to preach and to minister to souls. The church – and not only the church, but also the military administration – was not able to do full justice to the challenging task of the military chaplaincy. But the church should not lose the right to this task on that basis.[47]

Yet even spun as the noblest sacrifice, defeat smelled of failure. And the stigma of failure stuck to the chaplains and the churches as a whole, while it slid off the military leadership. Indeed, in his blockbuster memoir, the war hero Hindenburg, lionized by Christian leaders as piety incarnate, made no mention of military chaplains at all.[48]

Selective Narration

The sources most commonly used for studying German military chaplains are their own words. I too use their narratives but try to do so carefully. Because such materials have an agenda in terms of chaplains, the churches, and the nation state, it is important to contextualize where the narratives are coming from: they are imbricated in the nation and motivated by efforts to evade blame for its losses and failures. Pre-1933 sources are scarce, and those that exist tend to fixate on the church's position vis-à-vis the loss of World War I. After 1933, German chaplains engaged in eager revision of their personal and institutional pasts from the vantage point of the "new Germany." They presumed compatibility with a Nazi worldview and read those close relations back to the early days of the movement. Chaplains' writings after 1945 underreport or outright deny affinities with Nazism, including early ties.

The most influential history of German military chaplains over the long term remains Albrecht Schübel's *Dreihundert Jahre evangelische Soldatenseelsorge* (300 Years of Protestant Pastoral Care to Soldiers), published by the Protestant Press Association of Bavaria in 1964.[49] The time frame of 300 years, reinforced every time the book is mentioned, links the Wehrmacht chaplaincy to the Thirty Years War.[50] Its focus on Protestants only implies a special place in the chaplaincy for the heirs of Martin Luther. Rarely do those who draw on this authoritative book mention – or perhaps even realize – that its author had been a senior Wehrmacht chaplain, who was on record for praising the "courageous deed of the Führer" when Hitler introduced universal conscription in 1935, and for lauding the German attack on Poland in September 1939.[51] Schübel's book is a useful source of information, and it contains some remarkable vignettes involving chaplains. Yet he organized it in a way that presents the Wehrmacht chaplains, at least the Protestants among them, as worthy successors of Christian heroes of the past, completely separate from Nazis and immune to Nazism.

In contrast to Schübel's account, chaplains' representations of themselves during the Nazi years tended to ignore everything but the connections to Nazism. Not all roads led straight to Hitler, however. During the Weimar era, chaplains and former chaplains moved in multiple directions, and they offered their services to causes of different kinds. They could be described as institutional opportunists, attracted by power and looking for what would serve Christianity, their church, the chaplaincy, and their own need for importance – or simply provide some income. Hitler, too, when first demobilized, took a job giving speeches for the Reichswehr – that is, in the service of the fledgling Republic.[52] After 1933, chaplains, like Hitler, conveniently forgot those appearances or left out incriminating details. A historian looking back from a century later can easily overlook those non-Nazi moments or mistake their significance.

A case in point is the official world war commemorative ceremony in Berlin in 1923. On August 3, across the city, flags flew at half-mast and people laid wreaths at graves, memorials, and monuments. Many churches held services of remembrance, but the main public ceremony took place in front of the Reichstag, from 11am to 12 noon. Dignitaries gave speeches, church bells rang for a full minute, and an artillery salute followed. At noon sharp, traffic came to a halt and the city observed two minutes of silence.[53]

Military chaplains played a leading role at that event. After an army band performed songs of mourning, the rest of the hour consisted of sermons from the Lutheran and Catholic field chaplains regarding the German people's sacrifice. Then the German President spoke words of commemoration, followed by a military parade, more musical performances, and finally the national anthem.[54] The trappings were familiar rituals of war Christianity – the flags and wreaths, even the choice of hymns – but at the 1923 event, the prayers and exhortations of the military chaplains bestowed blessings on the young Republic and connected the Social Democrat Friedrich Ebert to the legacies of the past.

The Berlin ceremony, designed and approved by the Interior Ministry, was intended as a template for events throughout the country. Adopted in other settings, the rituals took on additional meanings, including performing Germanness in contested territories. In July 1924, the Silesian German city of Hirschberg, located near the new border with Poland, held its first official commemoration of the Great War. It adhered closely to the Berlin template.

Most of the formal components of the program were musical: the Reichswehr band played the usual lugubrious tunes and the familiar hymn, later standard fare at SS events, "We Gather Together" (*Wir treten zum beten*). Only two speakers addressed the assembly: the local garrison's Lutheran pastor and its Roman Catholic priest. Ceremonies in the years to follow used the same outline, with garrison chaplains regularly taking center stage.[55] In short, some chaplains offered prayers for hire, performing legitimacy for whoever invited them.

Chaplains were predisposed but not predetermined to join the Nazi cause, and individuals did not necessarily follow a consistent path. Monsignor Bernhard Lichtenberg, the hero and martyr who prayed publicly for German Jews being sent to be killed, who died en route to Dachau in 1943, and is now a Catholic saint, was a chaplain in World War I with the 3rd Grenadier Guards Regiment.[56]

Another high-profile example is Oscar Daumiller, the Protestant chaplain from Hitler's regiment. As described by Thomas Weber, Daumiller cycled through many positions over the course of his career. At a service in October 1914, Divisional Chaplain Daumiller told soldiers of the List Regiment that they were about to face "a holy war for the just cause of our people," and they should be prepared "should they be called by God to a holy death."[57] After just a few days of battle, Daumiller confided to his journal the horror he felt at all the suffering and its shattering impact on the troops. Still he comforted himself that they all showed "a longing for God" and willingness to endure for the sake of the Fatherland."[58]

Later, on the border between Belgium and France, Chaplain Daumiller and his Catholic counterpart, the Capuchin monk Father Norbert Stumpf, set up soldiers' messes to provide a space to enjoy conversation, newspapers, coffee, food, and cigars. Father Norbert, who repeatedly faced overcrowded confessionals,[59] was awarded an Iron Cross in December 1915.[60] By the end of that year and over the course of the next, many chaplains reported growing doubts among the men about religion and God. During the Battle of the Somme, Daumiller recorded news of large numbers of deserters and noted that soldiers no longer responded to patriotic slogans. "Only the word of God helps," he insisted. He wrote about his own questions as he abandoned notions of a holy war for the German national cause. He had gained a "frighteningly clear" understanding of Psalm 90:5–7, he explained, referring to the following passage:

> Yet you sweep people away in the sleep of death –
> they are like the new grass of the morning:
> In the morning it springs up new,
> but by evening it is dry and withered.
> We are consumed by your anger
> and terrified by your indignation.

Just as true, he said, was "the emptiness of our entire famed European culture. Men and entire peoples have gone bankrupt and One alone has those who finally listen to Him, the Living God." Daumiller appears to have kept these thoughts to himself, and in a service honoring the fallen of the Battle of the Somme, he pronounced the dead "heroes" and proclaimed: "There is no more beautiful death in the world than to die at the hands of the enemy."[61]

Daumiller had a successful career after 1933. Like Koblanck, he had come out publicly in support of Hitler in the election campaigns of 1932, and he too advanced up the ranks. By 1934, Daumiller was head (*Kreisdekan*) of the Protestant church in southern Bavaria. But like some other renowned nationalist church leaders, he later distanced himself from the Nazi movement and joined the Confessing Church. Another Protestant chaplain who had served with him in World War I, Friedrich Käppel, did the same. Bishop Hans Meiser would assign Daumiller to Nuremberg to organize against the German Christian movement there. According to Daumiller, the Gestapo repeatedly called him in for questioning, and they also showed up at Pastor Käppel's house in 1939 to conduct a search.

Given the temptation for chaplains to spin their personal histories, a temptation that would have been amplified in Daumiller's case because of the early association with Hitler, it is hard to know how credible some of the claims about his past are. Still, the claims themselves are significant: the Gestapo allegedly even tried to implicate Daumiller as connected to the White Rose resistance group.[62] After the war, Daumiller experienced another round of professional opportunities. As head of the Protestant church in southern Bavaria, his job included providing pastoral care for suspected Nazi criminals. This task often took him to Landsberg prison, where many of the death sentences against Nazis were carried out. As Daumiller recalled, they were hanged in "view of the cell in which Adolf Hitler had been interned."[63]

During World War II, the history of military chaplaincy, particularly in Bavaria, became a matter of keen interest to certain German authorities. A specific incident, along with the archival record it generated, reveals the paucity of knowledge about military chaplains outside Prussia and illustrates the complex entanglements of past and present at play around this topic.

In October 1941, General Friedrich von Rabenau, Head of the Army Archive in Potsdam, wrote to the Army Archive in Munich with a request for information:

It has come to our attention that in the various German contingents again and again the civilian clergy has for a period of time exerted influence on the military chaplaincy. This has been the case not only in the Catholic lands but also in Protestant ones. The last breakdown in this relationship, in fact, was in the middle of the nineteenth century. I am requesting research as to in which state or other archives the relevant documents could be located. At the moment, I am not intending to use these documents, I only want to know where they are. A response by the end of November would be appreciated.[64]

Dozens of pages of correspondence resulted, as the Munich archivist passed the request along to counterparts in state and church archives around Bavaria and beyond.[65] The responses make it clear that until the early twentieth century, in Bavaria, and likely in the other South German contingents of Wüttemberg and Saxony, there had been no distinction between military chaplains and civilian clergy. Instead, in wartime, priests and pastors served as chaplains without being officially incorporated into the military. Their status, in other words, was very different from the Prussian chaplains, who already in the eighteenth century had institutionalized the chaplaincy as a state organ, separate from the civilian church.[66] That professional Prussian model, developed in Imperial Germany, would become the foundation for the Wehrmacht chaplaincy. Nonetheless, the situation of Bavarian chaplains before 1918 also had echoes, in the hundreds of base and military hospital chaplains who served the Wehrmacht "part-time" (*im Nebenamt*) or "for the duration of the war" (*auf Kriegsdauer*).

The thick file does not reveal what issue sparked Rabenau's question. However, the timing – the letter was dated October 29, 1941 – and the fact the query came from the head of the central archive of Germany's army, a man with the rank of general, suggests the stakes were high. Throughout the summer and fall of 1941, and across an enormous sweep of territory, the Wehrmacht was involved in massacres of Soviet prisoners of war and Jews of all ages. Soldiers' grumbling about the carnage led General Walter von Reichenau to issue his infamous "order" of October 10, 1941, calling on the men of the armies under his command to show no mercy to Germany's enemies.

Also circulating that fall was the sermon by Bishop Clemens August Graf von Galen, condemning the Nazi murder of disabled people in Germany.[67] The Catholic bishop of Münster specifically noted the risk this program posed for the Wehrmacht: would a soldier who was wounded be deemed "life unworthy of life?" How would the killing of soldiers' aging and ailing parents back home affect their morale? Could Rabenau's inquiry have been part of an effort to isolate military chaplains from Bishop von Galen and other potentially defiant clergy on the home front? Bavaria and Württemberg would have been of particular interest because two of the three "intact" Protestant churches in Germany, whose bishops, Hans Meiser and Theophil Wurm, were well-known opponents of the "German Christian" movement, were located there.

Rabenau's biography, however, points in a different direction. A year after his 1941 query, Rabenau was consigned to early retirement. In 1944, after the failed attempt to assassinate Hitler, he was arrested because of his ties to the group around Ludwig Beck and Carl Goerdeler. Interned in a series of prisons and camps including Sachsenhausen and Buchenwald, on April 15, 1945, on Himmler's orders, Rabenau was executed by shooting in Flossenbürg concentration camp. Given his record as an opponent of National Socialism, could Rabenau's inquiry into the history of chaplains in Bavaria have been an attempt to use historical precedent to encourage resistance among civilian church leaders and open lines of communication between them and military chaplains?

The answer is unknown, but evidence indicates it may be wishful thinking to read Rabenau's query as a sign of defiance. Forced to retire from the army archive, Rabenau devoted himself to the study of theology. His PhD dissertation, completed in 1943, was titled, *Die Entwicklung der Grundzüge der deutschen Heeresseelsorge bis zum Jahre 1929 unter besonderer Berücksichtigung des 100.000 Mann-Heeres* (The Development of the Foundations of German Pastoral Care to the Army up to 1929, with Particular Attention to the 100,000-Man Army).[68] Military chaplains were on his mind during the deadly months of autumn 1941, but his papers, including the thesis and sermons from the war years, show his views on the subject to have been resolutely mainstream.

Rabenau's writings reflect typical antisemitic assumptions and Christian anti-Jewish prejudices, including refusal to acknowledge Jesus was a Jew, narrating intra-Jewish conflicts as attacks on Jesus by "the Jews," and denigration of Pauline Christianity. He repeated calls from the German Christian movement for a "manly" religion and a church that kept in tune with the state, ideas that were entrenched within the Wehrmacht chaplaincy. Preaching on Philippians 4:7 – "And the peace of God, which transcends all understanding, will guard your hearts and your minds in Christ Jesus" – Rabenau insisted that Christians were no "pacifist weaklings." In a letter from April 1944, he praised Jesus for his incredible "manliness and strength," and in sermons on John 18:22–36 – the story of the high priest questioning Jesus, Peter's denial, and Jesus's encounter with Pilate – Rabenau emphasized that Christianity was neither alien to German nature nor a religion of "the weak and the sick." In short, his history of chaplaincy assumed continuity from past glories to his own times, his vision of the duties and qualities of a military chaplain mirrored the current institutional ethos, and his theology fit the notion of Wehrmacht chaplains as model Christians.[69]

As individuals and institutionally, chaplains sought opportunities to advance their interests, and they told stories that positioned themselves as men of virtue, beyond blame. What constituted "virtue" changed over time, but the narrative of Christian heroism and faithfulness would prove capacious enough to absorb those transformations.

Personal Ties

In the years before Hitler came to power, personal connections linked many military chaplains, Catholics and Protestants, to the Nazi cause. Franz Justus Rarkowski, the man who served as Catholic military bishop during World War II, exemplified the ties that bound chaplains to the emerging National Socialist movement. Rarkowski, a staunch nationalist, had been acting head of the army chaplaincy on the Catholic side since 1929. He appears to have drawn close to the National Socialist Party indirectly, through military networks. Indeed, it was thanks to the support of Hindenburg and Werner von Blomberg, and through them Hitler, that Rarkowski was named military bishop over the objections of the Catholic episcopate.

Rarkowski was born in East Prussia and overlapped with Blomberg and the Protestant Naval Chaplain Ludwig Müller in Königsberg, where he served as Catholic Division and Military District priest from 1920 to 1927. Given the similar styles of Rarkowski and Müller – two rough, plain-spoken men with a martial demeanor who were mocked as simple by their theologian peers – it stands to reason that Blomberg, and Hitler, to whom the general deferred obsequiously, would approve of both men.[70]

Rarkowski's Nazification was no less thorough for being, in part, retroactive. In 1938, when Rarkowski's appointment as Catholic military bishop of the Wehrmacht was finalized after years of wrangling, he was touted as the successor of Dr. Töppen, the last army bishop of the Prussian Army, who had died in 1920. A newspaper article lauded the intimate relationship in Berlin between Catholic military and civilian pastoral care and implied it was all the result of chaplains and their advocates, going back four centuries:

Indeed, one can say that it was out of the military chaplaincy in the time of the Reformation that the almost totally defunct Catholic church life in Berlin was resurrected. Friedrich Wilhelm I, the Soldier King, was the one who, for the first time, allowed a Catholic priest into his Residence. He considered it essential, not least for reasons of military discipline, to have pastoral care for his Catholic soldiers. Over time, civilian pastoral care then developed out of military pastoral care.[71]

Catholic and Protestant leaders alike trumpeted their close and purportedly longstanding ties to the German nation and National Socialism. In 1943, when Rarkowski turned seventy, he issued a special "Word from the shepherd to all military chaplains." He drew a direct line from his efforts in a military hospital during World War I to the "humiliation and shame" of 1918 and the "new hope" awakened in 1933. The "men of 1914 and the sons of 1939" had much in common, he concluded.[72] Rarkowski repeatedly reminded "his" Catholic soldiers that he too knew war: he had volunteered for the front in 1914 and become chaplain to a division two years later.[73] During the Weimar period, he had ministered to soldiers based near contested "German borders": in Koblenz in the west, and in Königsberg and Breslau in the east.[74] However close his relations with local National Socialists may have been in those places, in hindsight, all of his earlier experience with German soldiers, Freikorps, and Stormtroopers was folded into a teleology of service to Hitler's cause.

Among Protestants, the most visible of the individuals close to Nazism was Ludwig Müller. He joined the Party in 1931, became the face of the emergent German Christian movement in 1932, and was named Protestant Reich bishop in 1933. Müller had been a naval chaplain in World War I and afterward pastor to the Military District in Königsberg,[75] facts that were emphasized every time he was introduced. A gruff, crude individual, Müller cultivated a soldierly image, often appearing in clerical robes adorned with military decorations. Though he alleged a friendship with Hitler that reached back more than a decade, Müller's strongest claim to credibility with church and Party people was his wartime experience. As a former military chaplain, he embodied the ideals of the German Christians, who aimed to transform the church into the spiritual expression of a racially pure, militantly anti-Jewish, manly German nation.

Werner von Blomberg's interest in religious arrangements in the military was likely both a cause and a result of his connection to Ludwig Müller, who was the Protestant military chaplain in Königsberg while Blomberg was headquartered there as commander of the East Prussian Military District. In *The Rise and Fall of the Third Reich,* William Shirer claimed it was Müller who introduced Blomberg to Hitler in 1932.[76] The historian John Wheeler-Bennett went even further, asserting that in 1930 East Prussia, Blomberg "found in his senior Lutheran chaplain, Ludwig Müller, a devoted follower of National Socialism, and from him the General imbibed the heady wine of the new German totalitarianism."[77] I have not seen evidence to support that contention, which sounds like typical German Christian bombast, but it is certain that Blomberg and Müller were well acquainted for at least several years prior to 1933.

The same logic that had reached back into Rarkowski's biography trans-formed other long-serving chaplains after the fact into exemplars of Nazi constancy. Rarkowski's Protestant counterpart, Military Bishop Franz Dohrmann,[78] and the hardworking Catholic Military Vicar Georg Werthmann, neither of whom had been publicly associated with the National Socialist Party before 1933, but both of whom had served in World War I (Dohrmann as a chaplain, Werthmann as a soldier), had their pasts tweaked in this way. So did many others. A Gestapo report noted that Werthmann, born in 1898, had been a soldier at the front and remained an enthusiastic proponent of the military. This information plus his support for the Hitler Youth was deemed adequate to balance his initial reticence toward the Nazi movement.[79]

A narrative of proto-Nazi support stretching back decades framed obituaries of chaplains throughout World War II. At the time of his death in 1944, Franz Albert was the oldest active German military chaplain. He had devoted thirty-eight of the forty-four years of his priesthood to pastoral care of soldiers, "in war and peace."[80] Albert, who was born in 1876 in Alsace, served as garrison pastor in Glatz in Lower Silesia (Polish Kłodzko) before World War I. There, according to his obituary, he devoted himself to pastoral care of the Reichswehr, "where he was a fearless fighter for Germanness in a region that today is a borderland."[81] Albert's trajectory fit neatly into a Nazi story, and even if he was never actively engaged in the Party, his successful career in the Wehrmacht chaplaincy indicates that he was at least sympathetically disposed.

Early bonds with the Nazi movement had a long-lasting impact on the German military chaplaincy. These linkages ensured that the leadership would be men who worked well with their military superiors, Blomberg, Reichenau, and others, and in key cases owed them their positions. The shared history and common narrative of struggle empowered individuals, among them Curt Koblanck and Franz Justus Rarkowski, who were close to Hindenburg, comfortable with Hitler, and linked to the Stormtroopers and local Party bigwigs through personal and family ties, years of cooperation, and mutual obligation. As a result, 1933 and the Nazi revolution that followed was not a barrier for chaplains but an opening onto a wealth of opportunities for personal careers and for military chaplaincy as a whole. Indeed, Koblanck had already been promoted to a high position in the emerging Wehrmacht chaplaincy in 1934. Such possibilities took concrete form with German rearmament in 1935.

The scene in Potsdam, which Koblanck and his supporters at the Garrison Church found so exciting, was perceived quite differently by a young American woman in the early Nazi years. To Martha Dodd, daughter of the US Ambassador to Germany William E. Dodd, writing in the late 1930s looking back, Koblanck and his ilk were buffoons, opportunists, and dupes:

In Potsdam itself there is a nucleus of a pro-Royalist group – retired generals, former ladies-in-waiting and their daughters, relatives, and hangers-on – who are passionate and antiquated partisans of the Hohenzollern cause. ... The word "Potsdam" in Berlin society was a word of faint opprobrium and the expression, "Don't be so Potsdam" was used to reprove people who suddenly became smug and hypocritical, or hopelessly dated in intellectual or social ideas. Many of these people, after a period of years, realized which side their bread was buttered on and swung over, half guiltily, to the Nazis.[82]

It did not have to be that way, Dodd understood, but now it was.

Figure 1.2 The Day of Potsdam, March 21, 1933. President von Hindenburg and Hitler clasp hands in front of the Garrison Church as Defense Minister von Blomberg looks on. This photograph was one of a widely publicized series by a well-known press photographer that framed the new chancellor as the heir to Germany's military and Christian traditions. Photographer Georg Pahl. BArch Bild 102-16082.

At the Nazi Party rally just months before Hitler became chancellor, garrison pastor Curt Koblanck had called on his counterparts not to let their swords get rusty. His slogan captured the conflation of clerical service and military service and the place of war – and wars, past and future – in the individual and collective sense of worth of German military chaplains. Now, once Hitler was in power, they seized the opportunity to prove themselves and their virtuous Christian manliness to their old hero Hindenburg and the younger man whose hand he would grasp so warmly on March 21, 1933. That day, Koblanck, his fellow chaplains, and all proponents of war

Figure 1.3 Hitler inside the Garrison Church on the Day of Potsdam. This occasion is said to be the only time he gave a speech in a church. Note the positioning of Hindenburg directly in front of him and the almost total absence of women among the listeners, who are attired and arranged to convey the legitimacy and power of the new leader. Photographer Georg Pahl. BArch Bild 102-16093.

Christianity watched with pride as the new regime celebrated its inauguration with a military parade and a religious service inside Potsdam's Garrison Church (Figures 1.2 and 1.3).[83]

2 "In Times of Peace the Church Arms Herself for War"

1933–1939

In December 1937, in the midst of the Spanish Civil War, Pastor Karl Keding found himself at a restaurant in Seville. To his delight, the service was excellent, he told his diary: two waiters, one of them senior, attended to the three Germans at his table:

What a difference! Fifteen years ago when I left what had become my Polish homeland and arrived in Brazil, we Germans were the most looked down upon people, and it took years to establish ourselves and gain respect. The lost war and inflation meant not only that our wallets were empty, but our Fatherland was held in contempt. It happened all the time that a waiter would walk by rather than serving us.[1]

At the next table sat several young Germans in uniform, junior officers on vacation. Did they recognize the "enormity of this transformation," Keding wondered? And it was all thanks to Hitler, "a man of our front generation," who "brought Germany back to glory!"[2]

A veteran of World War I, Keding had trained to be a pilot, although the war ended before he did much flying.[3] Now he described the thrill of going up in a bomber and the value of his pastoral presence after another plane was shot down and five Germans were killed:

It was good that I could be with the men who experienced all this that same evening in the barracks hour. There I spoke about the meaning of life and death and the steadfast hope we get from faith in Christ. I quoted Gorch Fock: "If I fall, then I will surely fall into the open hands of my heavenly Father." Quite on its own the talk turned into a time of solemn celebration. We sang the "Song of the Comrade." I made sure that we did not slide into sentimentality or get mired in sadness. Accordingly, I closed with the words: "Forward over the graves!" and the song, "I have given myself":

> "I have given myself
> with heart and hand,
> to you, my country; all my love and my life,
> to my German Fatherland. . . .

> "Fill me with power
> in my heart and my hand,
> to live and to die
> for the holy Fatherland!"[4]

Keding's diary, soon published as *Feldgeistlicher bei Legion Condor* (A Pastor at the Front with the Condor Legion), overflowed with excitement about his ministry to German forces in Spain. But he sounded a defensive note, too. His situation, though glamourous, was insecure: the Luftwaffe, created in 1935, had no official chaplains, and Keding did not actually have a job with the Wehrmacht. He had been inducted as a part-time base chaplain,[5] but those positions were abolished earlier in 1937. His six-week tour of duty with the Condor Legion was a public relations initiative, almost certainly organized by the German Protestant Church's press service in cooperation with Goebbels's Ministry for Propaganda. The goal was to counter negative reports coming out of Spain – about German casualties and German atrocities, including the massacre of civilians at Guernica. Indeed, another diary, by the German Jewish columnist Bella Fromm, described how her housekeeper, a young German Catholic woman whose husband had been killed in Spain, received a death notice trumpeting his "sacrifice" for the German Fatherland at the same time as it warned her to keep quiet about it.[6]

Additional factors weakened Keding's triumphal narrative. A Protestant in a predominantly Catholic country, he felt like an outsider, and he did not always manage to conceal his anti-Catholic prejudices. As a war veteran, he knew many soldiers had a dim view of chaplains. He had rarely encountered chaplains himself in 1914–1918, he wrote, and his comrades had mocked them as "anti-sin cannons (*SUK – Sündenabwehrkanone*), salvation on horseback, or Hallelujah on horseback." Nonetheless, he claimed, it was a chaplain's sermon that had convinced him to enlist: "Service to the Fatherland," the chaplain had preached, "is service to God" (Figure 2.1).[7]

Keding's adventure in Spain highlights the importance of the often forgotten six "peacetime" years of National Socialist rule. During this period – from Hitler's rise to power, to reestablishment of conscription, to deployments of the new German military in the Rhineland, Spain, Austria, and Czechoslovakia – a loyal Wehrmacht chaplaincy emerged. Keding's account of his weeks with the Condor Legion encapsulates several factors that help explain the chaplaincy's trajectory during these years and in the world war that followed.

One factor was force of habit. During its prewar existence, the Wehrmacht chaplaincy established patterns of behavior and organizational structures that would limit the scope for independent action in September 1939 and after, and indeed make it difficult for chaplains even to imagine breaking out of the mold. Those patterns were institutionalized in the leadership of the chaplaincy and the appointments of chaplains made between 1935 and 1939 and consolidated through developments that functioned as tests of loyalty: the exclusion of German Jewish men from the Wehrmacht just weeks after the announcement of universal conscription in March 1935, the remilitarization of the Rhineland

Figure 2.1 General Hugo Sperrle, Commander of the Condor Legion, in Spain, 1936 or 1937. A German photo service took this picture as part of a publicity campaign for the Condor Legion. The caption identified the airplane in the background as a Junkers Ju 52 but did not name the man posed on the right, whom it labeled simply "a clergyman." It is almost certainly Pastor Karl Keding, whose awkward placement in the frame reflects his ambivalent position as a chaplain. BArch Bild 146-2015-0024.

in 1936 and the Spanish Civil War that began the same year; the ouster of
Generals Blomberg and Fritsch, annexation of Austria, Sudetenland crisis, and
pogrom in November 1938 known as Kristallnacht; and the Molotov–
Ribbentrop pact in August 1939. With each event, the fledgling Wehrmacht
chaplaincy dug itself deeper into the Nazi system.

A second factor, expressed by Keding, was the chaplains' defensive posture.
Vulnerable to accusations that they had failed Germany in the last world war
and conscious of their tenuous status in the eyes of hardcore Nazis and military
men alike, chaplains regarded themselves as individuals and part of an institution with something to prove: their manliness, worthiness, anti-Jewishness,
and value to a nation of fighters. Such defensiveness made chaplains eager to
cooperate and predisposed to anticipate their superiors' wishes in a kind of
collective "working toward the Führer."[8] Confessional rivalry added to the
dynamic as Protestants and Catholics competed for favor. The Nazi leadership
repeatedly found ways to exploit these tendencies. Above all, chaplains'
perception that their self-interest, as individuals and institutionally, matched
the Nazi agenda produced a durable partnership.

Fighting the Last War

Many Catholics and Protestants welcomed Hitler's rise to power, but
Protestant church leaders were more public with their shows of support. For
them the new regime presented a golden opportunity to assert Protestant
dominance in German life. One manifestation of this enthusiasm was the mass
weddings. In the spring and summer of 1933, urban churches in particular
were the scene of crowd nuptials, at which as many as 400 couples at a time
pledged their troth in Protestant ceremonies.[9] Most of these couples had
already married in civil services, but in the spirit of national, ecclesiastical
revival, they chose to have their vows blessed before God and their
local congregations.

Protestants within Germany and ethnic Germans elsewhere pointed to the
mass weddings as evidence of the religious renewal brought about by the Nazi
revolution. The sight of tens and even hundreds of grooms in Nazi Party
insignia, SS or Stormtrooper uniforms bowing their heads beside their loyal
German wives captured the spirit that church leaders dearly wanted to see. Was
not Christianity – preferably in its Protestant variant – necessary to complete
and domesticate National Socialism? The clergymen and parishioners who
thrilled at the sight of these processions must have seen the symbolism made
explicit by publicists who called on the bride of Christ to adorn herself as the
bride of the National Socialist state.[10] Later this image would be repurposed in
the official description of the chaplaincy as the "handmaid" of the military
leadership.[11]

Generals tend to fight the previous war, and in the run-up to rearmament and the formal reestablishment of military chaplaincy in Nazi Germany, the same was true. Considerations based on past experience (or perceptions of it) fed directly into proposals for the creation of a new military chaplaincy. Looking back, however, increased the chaplaincy's manipulability. Were they the discredited female partners, the home front that had let down their warriors? A direct articulation of the problem came from Thomas Breit, Protestant church superintendent in Soest (Westphalia).

In a three-page, undated reflection titled "Protestant Clergy and Universal Conscription," Breit conceded that the churches had stumbled in the Great War. In his words, the church's past mistakes were all the more reason to apply themselves to their pastoral task, "with the utmost consideration, deepest passion, heightened responsibility, and loyalty." Military chaplaincy, he maintained, was essential to national defense: "Of course, the same holds true of this military service of the church as for the service with weapons in war: in times of peace, the church arms herself for war."[12]

For the sake of this preparedness, Breit, who was active in the Confessing Church, called for maintaining the earlier relationship of Protestant pastors to the armed forces, "i.e.: prior to ordination, all were to serve under arms, including in exercises of the reserves." But after ordination, he urged, military service should not be required. In wartime, pastors could volunteer or serve as medics, "but their first duty should be to the home front, to preaching the gospel and ministering to souls."[13]

Breit was especially concerned with ensuring pastoral care within large bases. There should be a full-time base chaplain (*Standortpfarrer im Hauptamt*), he urged, who should serve only until he reached the age of forty, to keep the ministry youthful. Supervisory base chaplains (*Wehrkreispfarrer*), in contrast, should be appointed for life. Regional church authorities should keep their eyes open for suitable young pastors and maintain waiting lists that they would make available to the military bishop. Breit closed with thanks to the leadership of the military and the Protestant military bishop and pledged, "in obedience to the Lord to help maintain the purity of the moral will of the Wehrmacht and the unblemished Christian honor of the German man and the National Socialist soldier."[14]

German-speaking Catholics, concentrated near or on the other side of the post-Versailles borders, struggled in additional ways with the legacies of defeat. In a piece published in 1938, one month after the *Anschluss*, Viktor Lipusch, a popular writer and retired chaplain in the Austro-Hungarian Army, countered imputations of failure:

When here a literary monument is erected to the Catholic military chaplaincy for its work, sacrifice, blood, and death, it is not the ambition for glory that was the

Table 2.1 *Theologians, mission workers, and sons of pastors who died in military action, 1914 to 1933.*

Chaplains	36
Pastors	92
Professors of religion	67
Assistant pastors, vicars, or candidates	568
Students of theology	1,759
Total number of theologians	2,522
Mission workers	202
Sons of pastors	4,152
Overall total	6,876

Source: Office of the Superintendent, Soest. February 1, 1940.
LKA Bielefeld 4/55, A/61.

motivation ... but alone the hope to do justice to these quiet fighters armed with the cross and to counter the often heard accusations that the Christian religion is somehow a barrier to patriotic enthusiasm and power and the Catholic clergy somehow stood aside in the massive struggle for survival of our Fatherland, or that military priests were some kind of shirkers or a superfluous burden for the fighting troops and in any case mostly stayed far away from any shooting.

Lipusch's essay, the foreword to a collection of chaplains' writings, insisted that the unadorned words of the chaplains themselves, as well as the warm responses of the men they served, would enlighten readers and reveal the true heroism of these priests.[15]

Throughout the Nazi years, Catholic and Protestant church leaders remained obsessed with trying to prove the value of Christianity in wartime. They expended tremendous effort on compiling lists of theologians fallen in battle. One detailed roster showed 2,522 Protestant theologians killed in combat from 1914 to 1933 – including postwar paramilitary units (Freikorps) and Stormtroopers. Adding in the sons of pastors – only an option for the Protestant side – brought the total to almost 7,000. The breakdown is shown in Table 2.1.

Notes specify that thirteen of those listed had lost their lives with the Freikorps or fighting "for the renewal of Germany."[16] Of the pastors' sons included, thirty-nine died in postwar fighting, including the venerated Stormtroopers Horst Wessel and Karl Freyburger.[17]

Discomfort about the lost war and insinuations about chaplains and Christianity in general as weak generated frequent harping on manliness. In the summer of 1938, in the midst of the Sudetenland crisis, the senior chaplain in Military District 5 wrote to the Protestant military bishop calling for "manly,

powerful, pious, German" music rather than the usual "soft, sweet, sentimental" fare of available hymns.[18] Chaplains looked to their leaders to model a
masculine, soldierly Christianity that they could emulate.

Leadership: The Military Bishops

Typical of Hitler's leadership, and enshrined in the so-called Führer Principle,
was a practice of concentrating power at the top and allowing selected acolytes
considerable latitude within their own spheres of influence. The resulting
dynamic promised rewards to proactive collaborators at the same time as it
fed their insecurities. Although Hitler himself did not make the chaplaincy a
top priority after January 1933,[19] this modus operandi shaped developments
here, too.

Following past practice in Germany, the proposed Wehrmacht chaplaincy
comprised two parallel hierarchies, distinguished by confession, with each
crowned by a military bishop. On the assumption that the leaders set the tone,
military bishops were put in place even before official rearmament was
announced. The Roman Catholic Franz Justus Rarkowski functioned like a
military bishop in some ways since 1929 and more extensively after German
rearmament in 1935, but he received the formal title only in 1938. His
Protestant counterpart Franz Dohrmann served as military bishop from
1934 to 1945. A look at Bishops Rarkowski and Dohrmann corroborates an
image of German chaplains as traditional Christians and old-fashioned nationalists who identified more closely with their counterparts during World War
I than with the Nazi ideologues of the 1930s and 1940s. Nevertheless, both
Rarkowski and Dohrmann served Hitler's regime faithfully and expected the
chaplains under their authority to do the same.

Rarkowski and Dohrmann had some marked similarities. Both had been
chaplains in World War I and remained connected to the military throughout
the Weimar Republic and into the Nazi era. Rarkowski volunteered for the
front in 1914 and became chaplain to a division two years later;[20] throughout
the Weimar years, he provided pastoral care to military bases all over the
country.[21] Dohrmann spent a total of thirty-six years in uniform: as divisional
chaplain under Wilhelm II, base chaplain for the Reichswehr, the armed forces
of the Weimar Republic, and finally military bishop.[22] In bearing and manner
both military bishops presented themselves to the public as soldiers, stern,
strong, and invariably wearing some form of military insignia.

Theologically, both Rarkowski and Dohrmann could be described as
traditional and conservative; neither was known to be a Nazi, although
Rarkowski loudly voiced his support of many of its elements, including
antisemitism, and Dohrmann certainly left no record of ever criticizing
National Socialism.[23] At the time of their appointments, neither man was

young. Rarkowski was sixty-five when he was finally consecrated in 1938; Dohrmann was fifty-three when he assumed the position four years earlier. Rarkowski, born in the town of Allenstein (now Olsztyn in Poland), once a stronghold of the Teutonic Knights, was an East Prussian, a fact that may have heightened his zealous nationalism after 1918. Dohrmann, a Prussian, came from Groß Lübbichow in the district of West Sternberg and made his home in Potsdam.

For all their similarities, the military bishops' personal styles and situation within their churches were quite different. Whereas Rarkowski came across as verbose and sentimental, Dohrmann was a reserved type, a man of few words, widely respected in Protestant circles. Rarkowski was appointed military bishop over the protests of the German episcopate, and he struggled for credibility with its members throughout his tenure. Dohrmann tried to remain above the so-called church struggle, but he frequently ended up criticized by both the Confessing Church and the German Christians; both sides accused him of discriminating against them when it came to making appointments to the chaplaincy. Indeed, Nazi state and military authorities chose both men over objections from within their churches, a situation that increased the bishops' dependence on supporters outside their churches.

In Dohrmann's case, a handful of outspoken, pro-Nazi clergy considered him too moderate for the new Germany. Most active in efforts to discredit the Protestant military bishop was Heinrich Lonicer, a base chaplain in Breslau, Nazi Party member, and subsequently senior Wehrmacht chaplain. Right through to the end of the war, Lonicer schemed against Dohrmann and spread rumors that he was weak and defeatist.[24] In 1939, backed by General Walther von Brauchitsch, Lonicer made a pitch to replace Dohrmann as military bishop, but the plan fell through.[25] Dohrmann, it seems, had friends in high places, although his papers do not reveal the identity of his protectors.

Rarkowski was at least as well connected politically as Dohrmann but more isolated within his church, because the German Catholic bishops refused to accept him. Their objections were numerous: Rarkowski's education was inadequate, some said, and he misrepresented his credentials; he was insufficiently intellectual; he was too old.[26] All the same, Rarkowski and his backers prevailed. According to Foreign Office sources in July 1935, the War Ministry, German officers and soldiers, the Nazi Party, and even the dead Field Marshall and former President Paul von Hindenburg all wanted Rarkowski to be named military bishop.[27] The Catholic hierarchy, however, dragged its feet. When the Nuncio Cesare Orsenigo mentioned Rarkowski's age as grounds for hesitation, Foreign Minister Konstantin von Neurath retorted that "no one expected the military bishop to take part in any cavalry charges."[28]

Neurath's involvement reveals the high-level interest in choosing the military bishops. In January 1936, Neurath wrote a "strictly confidential" letter to the Minister of War and Commander of the Wehrmacht, Werner von Blomberg. It got straight to the point: "The Nuncio, representing the Holy See, raised the question of the future military bishop ... and proposed the priest-rector of St. Boniface in Düsseldorf, Karl Büchler, for this position."[29] Neurath emphasized that Büchler had served at the front as a volunteer for four years in World War I and been awarded the Iron Cross both First and Second Class. However, he also made it clear he had lobbied for Rarkowski:

> To the question, why the Holy See did not see fit to approve the most warmly proposed wish of mine, to name as Military Bishop military district chaplain Rarkowski, who already for years has been carrying out the office of a military bishop, the Nuncio explained that the Vatican in this case certainly would gladly compromise but serious considerations prevented the fulfillment of our wish. The Vatican preferred not to reveal the reasons for this rejection and had not shared them with him, the Nuncio.[30]

Neurath noted he had it from other sources that the reason was the Vatican expected pushback, which indeed Rarkowski had already experienced for years, precisely from the military clergy who were subordinate to him: "In clerical circles, Rarkowski was not considered worthy, because of his apparently insufficient education and his lacking eloquence." He had been allowed to study theology without the *Abitur*, and he then completed his studies not in Germany but in Switzerland. The Vatican evidently was worried that Rarkowski would not have the authority needed to do the job. "Under these circumstances," Neurath concluded, "it seems to me pointless to continue to push Rarkowski's candidacy."[31]

The Church Ministry, not included in the initial discussion, also intervened. In early February, Councilor Roth, a representative of the Ministry, met with Dr. Otto Senftleben from the War Ministry and an official from the Foreign Office.[32] According to the minutes, circulated the following day, Roth raised a series of concerns about Father Büchler: he was too young (he was born in 1894!), he lacked experience with military chaplaincy, and, most notably, he had too much support: "It is striking that the Curia is so eager to promote this man and to advocate for him." At the very least, Roth added, "it must be investigated whether Büchler does not have especially strong ties to the Catholic youth organizations and what his position is vis-à-vis the National Socialist state." Roth put forward an alternate name, Dr. Eberle in Augsburg, but Senftleben considered Eberle, who was sixty, to be too old.

The general consensus at the meeting was that Rarkowski "appeared to be unacceptable as Military Bishop."[33] As a compromise solution, someone proposed that Rarkowski take the position (or more accurately, continue doing the work he had been doing for years by this point) until his retirement at age sixty-five, so in two and a half years, with Büchler as his vicar, on the assumption that Büchler would then become bishop. This plan would satisfy the Vatican.[34]

In fact, powers outside the churches played a major role in choosing the vicars to both military bishops: on the Protestant side Friedrich Münchmeyer, and for the Catholics not Büchler, but Georg Werthmann. Blomberg himself intervened to support Werthmann's appointment.[35] The Gestapo report from August 1936 demonstrated how a cautious priest's or pastor's record could be spun to fit the profile (or not). Werthmann was born on December 8, 1898 in Kulmbach. The report gave a positive account of the results of the inquiry:

> Werthmann was a front soldier and is an enthusiastic member of the community of soldiers. Before the national revolution, he often presented slide shows about his experiences in the war and on the battlefields of France. With regard to the national revolution, initially he was very reserved toward National Socialism, so that one might conclude that he was an opponent of the National Socialist state. But in the time since, he has shown himself to be very open to the efforts of the new state and has behaved correctly in every respect. In particular, in the school classes, in which he teaches Religion, he has supported the state youth.
> There is nothing negative to report about him on the political side.[36]

This ability to wait and see, keep his nose clean, and then jump in to serve the powers that be would enable Werthmann to thrive as a military chaplain, under Nazi rule and after, in American captivity, and in the newly founded Federal Republic of Germany.

Taking their time with Werthmann's and Rarkowski's appointments paid off for the Catholic church establishment, which weathered a series of attacks and by early 1938, in the midst of the Spanish Civil War, came out looking like Nazism's trusted partner. Military chaplains were at the center of this patriotic union. The press swooned at the ceremony in February 1938 consecrating Rarkowski as military bishop. The *Märkische Volks-Zeitung* printed a story with the headline, "Consecration of the Bishop in Berlin, February 2, 1938," that the Church Ministry clipped and saved: "Dr. Töppen, who died in 1920, was the last army bishop of the Prussian Army. One of his closest co-workers before the war was the young military chaplain Franz Justus Rarkowski, who now, as the first army bishop of the newly reborn German Wehrmacht is, in a certain sense, his successor."[37]

It is noteworthy that the Foreign Office under Neurath took the lead in negotiations about the Catholic military bishop; Kerrl, the minister of church affairs, complained that he had not been consulted and only found out when it was a done deal.[38] This situation reflects the priority placed on the Concordat as a foreign policy measure, not simply or even primarily an internal German affair. From the outset, German government authorities regarded the military chaplaincy, in particular its Roman Catholic component, as linked to foreign policy goals and issues, and Rarkowski's appointment also fits in here.

Rarkowski and Dohrmann were vulnerable in similar ways: both men were associated with the loss of the previous war and conscious of it. Both were subject to limitations imposed on the chaplaincy by hostile or suspicious Nazi authorities. But their situations differed too: Rarkowski was under attack from his peers, and the wider anti-Catholic initiatives of Hitler's regime, which peaked in the years 1935–1937 with the currency and morality trials, further weakened Rarkowski's position.[39] Dohrmann was caught between factions in his church. Yet in both cases, those vulnerabilities made them eager to show the chaplaincy's loyalty to the regime and dependent on military and state authorities for their own legitimacy.

Neither Rarkowski nor Dohrmann was an out-and-out Nazi. Both proved capable of protesting abuses of their jurisdictions and of Christian practices, and at times they even worked together to try to maximize their impact. Rarkowski protested repeatedly about the distribution of anti-Christian literature in the military, and Dohrmann spoke out against restrictions on chaplains' activities. Yet overall, both set a tone of cooperation and gratitude to Hitler's regime while maintaining an old-fashioned decorum. Of course, in 1933 or 1935 no one, including Rarkowski and Dohrmann, could know exactly what the years ahead would bring. Still, one is struck in reading the records of those early months by how many people, even among the leadership in both churches, had some sense of impending disaster yet persisted in endorsing the Nazi regime. Even more striking, although admittedly fewer in number, are those clear-sighted individuals like Baron Wilhelm von Pechmann, the Bavarian Lutheran and longtime president of the German Protestant Church Assembly, who eventually left the church in protest over its accommodation to National Socialism and became a Roman Catholic. Pechmann recognized the Nazi catastrophe and refused to accept it. "I know that I am free from any trace of arrogance," he wrote in September 1934, "when I say how happy a later church historian will be about each one of those who have not bent the knee before the Baal of this era."[40] The military bishops bent their knees.

Structural Issues

The seasoned chaplains who set the tone in the early years of Hitler's regime institutionalized arrangements that shaped prospects down the road. In October 1933, the military chaplaincy implemented an "Aryan clause" that went further than the Civil Service Law of July to exclude from its ranks not only converts from Judaism and children and grandchildren of converts, but men with Jewish wives.[41] They also codified a path to appointment of chaplains, including base chaplains, that gave veto power to the state Security Service (SD). In return, they got to imagine themselves at the center of a revived Christian warrior nation, with manly congregants whose attendance at religious services would be compulsory.

Arrangements in the Wehrmacht chaplaincy as it emerged in 1935 were remarkably fluid. The years 1935 to 1939 saw a number of significant changes, such as canceling of contracts of part-time base chaplains in 1937: after that, only full-time chaplains were to provide religious services to soldiers. During this period, the question as to whether chaplains would be attached to the Luftwaffe was hotly debated and eventually answered with a "no." Such adjustments and disputes added to the chaplains' sense of vulnerability.

In March 1935, the Law for Creation of the Wehrmacht introduced universal military conscription as the foundation of the new armed forces. The Military Law of May 21, 1935 announced the military duty of every "German man" – a revision that explicitly excluded Jews.[42] Official rearmament implied reestablishment of chaplaincy, but it was a piecemeal process. Initially there were not many full-time chaplains (maybe fifty), and a larger number of base chaplains, most of them part-time.

Like the German military as a whole, the chaplaincy had never completely gone away after the Great War. Under the arrangements for the 100,000-man army, including regulations from 1920, provisions were made for pastoral care to the army and navy. Together with the military bishops, who had considerable authority in their hands at this crucial point, those existing chaplains formed the nub of the new system. As to the size of the chaplaincy in the prewar years, a memo from Army High Command from February 1938 listed a total of sixty-four full-time people on the Protestant side: one military bishop (Dohrmann); twelve senior army chaplains (*Heeresoberpfarrer*); thirty-nine army chaplains (*Heerespfarrer*); one inspector (*Regierungsinspektor*); six secretaries; and five assistants. These people all counted as senior civil servants.[43] Presumably the Catholic roster was similar.

Considerable back and forth was evident as the arrangements took shape. Some experienced chaplains saw this flexibility as being in their favor. One question was: would attendance at religious services be compulsory for conscripted men? This issue had come up before 1935, and now universal conscription provided a perfect opportunity to strengthen the chaplaincy by requiring attendance. Friedrich Ronneberger, the Naval Station pastor in Wilhelmshaven, made the case to Dohrmann in May 1933:

In my experience, voluntary participation in religious events does not lead to the desired outcome. ... If we are to have a religious influence on the troops, it will not happen without a certain pressure. Young people have to be made to attend religious services, and that is especially true of recruits ... If attendance at church can be required of SA and SS, likewise of Stahlhelm, then the same must be possible for the Wehrmacht.[44]

Ronneberger, a loud and active adherent of the German Christian movement, boasted of his strong connections to leading Nazis and high-ranking military men, going back to his service during the Great War. Over the years, he, like Heinrich Lonicer, proved to be a thorn in Dohrmann's side. But his dream of forcing Wehrmacht conscripts to participate in religious services did not come about, and the heady days of Stormtroopers and SS men showing up en masse in uniform at Protestant churches ended soon after it began, in the early months of 1933.

In regard to the newly constituted Luftwaffe, advocates of the military chaplaincy again met with disappointment. The air force did not have chaplains assigned to it, although it is evident that, from the outset, chaplains performed pastoral care for its men. Pastor Keding with the Condor Legion in Spain was neither the first nor the only one to do so.

In this regard, too, Ronneberger was proactive. In December 1935, he wrote to Dohrmann explaining that in his jurisdiction, naval chaplains ministered to the Luftwaffe:

At present, pastoral care of the pilots based in Wilhelmshaven occurs through the Protestant naval station chaplain. The air force group in List on the island of Sylt is taken care of by part-time naval base chaplain Hartung. The Norderney air force group at present has no chaplain. Pastor Fischer, who is in office there ... is out of the question in the long run. He makes a very old and stiff impression and is not in a situation to give the young men what they need."[45]

Ronneberger also complained about a Pastor Cramer whose "barracks services are impossible and in the long run, this situation is untenable." Another pastor, Brahms, on Borkum, was described as "not what he seems" and unable to get along with his Catholic counterpart. Also his sermons at the oath ceremonies "always have the same theme."[46]

Ronneberger seemed to be making a pitch for more control himself, but he was rebuffed. The commander-in-chief of the navy let it be known in 1936 that "church care of the air force units at this time is not to be permitted through the naval station chaplain."[47] But Ronneberger may have got his way, because in June 1936 a memo from air force command headquarters VI (*Luftkreiskommando*) in Kiel confirmed that three Luftwaffe sites (Jever, Wilhelmshaven, and Norderney) were to receive regular pastoral care from naval chaplains in the region.[48]

In late summer 1936, a Protestant military district chaplain in Ludwigsburg reported on the proceedings of the base chaplain conference in Stuttgart in June. The occasional use of clergy who were serving in the military to provide religious services to the soldiers was very valuable, he claimed. As an example, he cited the provision of brief religious services in the field during military exercises. The situation with the air force was difficult, he continued, because according to special regulations governing the Luftwaffe, its members could no longer be invited to participate in general religious services for the military. The military bishop had promised he would try to get the Luftwaffe brought into line with the other parts of the military. The report concluded by emphasizing the "intense interest and deep need precisely among members of the air force" for what the military chaplaincy could provide.[49] The chaplains hoped to give the men what they desired and in return to benefit from association with the prestigious air force.

Christianity's "Jewish Problem"

Even before rearmament was official in 1935, those chaplains already in place were complaining about an anti-Christian spirit evident among military men. To blame, some concluded, were Jews and the Jewish roots of Christianity. In May 1934, Ronneberger took the issue up with Admiral Raeder.[50] Hitler would not approve of the insulting songs going around and the accusations that officers and their wives were reactionary, Ronneberger insisted. He attached a piece he had written, titled "Proposals for Consolidation of Church Relations in the Navy." It opened with the following sentence: "The young officer corps has no time for the Church. It sounds crass but that's the way it is." The problem, Ronneberger determined, was Christianity's Jewish roots: "Rejection of Jewry leads them to draw further conclusions that have harmful consequences for the Church."[51] In other words, Ronneberger considered antisemitism bad for the church because Jews were bad for Christianity.

Such attitudes explain why there is no record that any chaplains complained in May 1935 when German Jewish men were excluded from conscription. Indeed, it is difficult even to imagine any of the clergy in these positions conceiving of doing so. When thugs attacked Jewish veterans in the street and pro-Nazi vandals scratched "Jewish names" off memorial plaques for the World War I dead, no chaplain said a word.[52] Nor, in fact, did more than a few exceptional priests and pastors protest.

In these crucial years, chaplains consciously downplayed and even vilified Christianity's Jewish roots. At a 1936 meeting in Stuttgart, Protestant base chaplain Bernhard Bauerle urged colleagues to avoid the "language of Canaan" in preaching to soldiers.[53] In June 1938, graffiti reading "*Juden raus*" (Jews out!) could be seen painted on the Old Garrison Church in Berlin.[54] A few months later, police in Dresden conducted a humiliating and invasive search of the home of Eva Klemperer and her husband Victor, a veteran of the Great War who was born Jewish and baptized Protestant. When they found a dagger, a souvenir of Victor Klemperer's front service, they confiscated it and arrested him, further proof, as if he needed it, that his imposed identity as "Jew" erased any standing he could claim as a German war veteran.[55]

One characteristic of German military chaplains will come as no surprise: all of them were certified "Aryans" in the Nazi sense of the word. Obviously the Wehrmacht did not have Jewish chaplains, but it also excluded from the chaplaincy men who had converted from Judaism to Christianity or whose parents or grandparents had done so, that is, people who counted under the Nuremberg Laws as "mixed" (Mischlinge). In this regard the chaplaincy operated under restrictions that were never formally imposed on civilian clergy. Within the churches, debate persisted throughout the Third Reich as to whether converts from Judaism and children and grandchildren of converts could serve as Christian clergy. Such discussions went on into the 1940s, even after most of the few relevant individuals had been forced from their jobs, exiled, or killed.[56] No similar controversy affected the chaplaincy. Beginning already in 1933, regulations required all potential chaplains to produce proof that they and, in the case of Protestants, their wives, were of "Aryan blood."[57]

In the military chaplaincy, imposition of the so-called Aryan Paragraph was simply assumed. By contrast, when proposed in the Protestant Church in 1933, it became the founding issue for the Pastors Emergency League, subsequently the Confessing Church. This outcome was not because most Christians loyally stood with converts from Judaism – in fact, the small number of Protestant clergy in this group were treated shabbily and driven from their posts – but because the prohibition violated church sovereignty. Among chaplains, meanwhile, there was not even a murmur. Archival records indicate that authorities definitely enforced the "Aryan clause," although grounds to do so were rare. In 1936, Army High Command wrote to Military Bishop Dohrmann complaining that two army pastors had not yet completed the paperwork establishing their Aryan blood.[58]

The statutes for the German Catholic Wehrmacht chaplaincy came into force on September 1, 1936. Those statutes included call for provision of ancestry passes (Ahnenpässen) to prove "Aryan" lineage.[59] When it was discovered that one man with a Jewish ancestor had slipped through undetected, Catholic church authorities fell over themselves to apologize. The case was referenced in a widely distributed text of January 11, 1938 by the head of the Army Personnel Office as follows: "Recently it has repeatedly occurred that soldiers who are actively carrying out their military obligations are being promoted by their units to Private etc. or to Reserve Officer candidate [Reserveoffizieranwärtern] before they have produced clear proof of their ancestry from German blood." Should evidence emerge that "these soldiers are descended from Jewish blood," the memo stipulated, they must "without exception be struck from the list of Reserve Officer candidates." The letter emphasized that a father's petition requesting an exception for his son had been "personally and categorically denied by the Führer." Even those "Jewish Mischlinge" whom Hitler, "through an act of clemency," had allowed to hold

Party membership and serve in the army were not to become officers in the Wehrmacht.[60]

This blanket prohibition affected potential chaplains, who held the rank of officers. But the Wehrmacht chaplaincy could afford to set a high bar for "Aryan blood" and for political reliability because many men aspired to join, far more than were accepted, and this "buyer's market" held long into the war. In any case, the number of converts and children or even grandchildren of converts from Judaism to Christianity who were Protestant or Catholic clergy was tiny, no more than a few dozen people in total, so the issue was always more of symbolic than practical concern – other than to the individuals and their families in the firing line.[61]

Confessional Considerations

In a January 1937 memorandum to Army High Command outlining some of the "particular limitations with which the military chaplaincy has to struggle," Rarkowski touched on a sensitivity particular to the Catholic chaplaincy. Under the terms of the 1933 Concordat, Catholic priests, in contrast to Protestant pastors, were exempt from military service. Priests in the designated age group were to be recruited to the medical corps. But, in Rarkowski's estimation, personal experience as a soldier was required for someone to be effective as a military chaplain. He noted that the problem had also existed in World War I, when some priests who turned out to be woefully unsuitable for service at the front were deployed there at high cost to everyone involved, including the credibility of the chaplaincy. Meanwhile, other, highly capable priests were underutilized in hospital service. Rarkowski suggested that prospective chaplains participate in military training and exercises (without weapons) so they could be observed, sorted according to suitability, and prepared for subsequent service at the front.[62]

Protestant chaplains faced their own challenges around credibility. After church elections in July 1933, members of the pro-Nazi German Christian movement dominated the governing bodies of all but three of Germany's twenty-eight regional Protestant churches, and "German Christian" churchmen sought to place their friends in the chaplaincy.[63] They played up all connections to the military, starting with Reich Bishop Ludwig Müller's status as a chaplain-veteran. In April 1934, a German Christian event in Berlin advertised that music would be provided by an organist who was the "leader of the Military District Greater Berlin."[64]

Although Dohrmann tried to block it, struggle between the German Christians and the Confessing Church entered the chaplaincy in concrete ways, particularly in clashes over access to buildings. In July 1936, Dohrmann received a letter of complaint from Pastor Grimm in Düsseldorf-Gerresheim.

Grimm had been appointed base chaplain for Düsseldorf in 1935, but the Confessing Church-dominated presbyterium refused to let him use the pulpit in the church nearest the barracks (it was called Church of the Cross). Pastor Grimm had to hold some services outside and others in the sports hall, until he succeeded in getting the English Church placed at his disposal. (Grimm noted the irony of the fact it was the English church!)[65]

According to Grimm, the surge of participants at his services since the remilitarization of the Rhineland meant that the English Church was no longer big enough. But he could not get access to the Church of the Cross. The president of the presbyterium, Pastor Ufer, apparently wanted to be base chaplain himself, and would not even put Grimm's request on the agenda for discussion. Grimm, who also served as chaplain for police in the region, insisted that no one had faulted his loyalty to the Bible or the effectiveness of his work. He closed with "Heil Hitler!"[66]

According to the Military District Supervisory Chaplain Curt Koblanck, the same man who had welcomed Stormtroopers into the Garrison Church in Potsdam in 1932,[67] the problems were practical rather than political: Grimm lived too far from the barracks and had too much to do already.[68] Correspondence from the 6th Army Corps at the end of July 1936 confirmed that Ernst Ufer, born in 1899, was appointed base chaplain, part-time, in Düsseldorf. Although Ufer was known to be associated with the Confessing Church, he was preferred because Grimm resided too far from the center of the city.[69] Dohrmann confirmed the change in a note to Grimm, explaining that most important were the wishes of the troops and the chaplain's proximity to the barracks.[70]

As the outcome in Düsseldorf indicates, the German Christians did not get the hegemony they hoped for within the chaplaincy. In April 1935, Reich Bishop Müller made a tour of cities in Silesia, which his backers intended as a show of support, particularly within military circles. Representatives of the Confessing Church organized counter-events, but both sides would be disappointed. Military District 8 in Breslau issued an order from the chief of staff that, "in the interest of church-political neutrality, the Wehrkreiskommando has instructed senior base officers that they are to refrain from taking part in these events."[71]

Still, members of the German Christian movement kept finding openings. In 1939, the former leader of "German Christians" in the Rhineland joined the Wehrmacht chaplaincy. A German Christian pastor and professor of theology in Austria did the same. In addition, some members without official appointments preached to the military: for example, one boasted that he had been asked to hold weekly devotions for the troops.[72]

Appointments of Chaplains

One of the main tasks in this formative period was establishing personnel. The introduction of universal conscription and organization of a national network of military bases translated into the need for a large number of chaplains. The formal criteria included age, proximity to a base, military experience, and political reliability. Church authorities and the military bishops emphasized the first three, whereas the Church Ministry and Security Service prioritized political considerations.

The term "military chaplains," as I use it, encompasses overlapping categories of clergy. In addition to chaplains prepared for active duty at the front, a larger number of men served as base chaplains (*Standortpfarrer*). These were civilians who often assumed their duties alongside regular assignments as pastors and priests. Later, when chaplains were needed at the front, their names came up first. Some got appointments for the duration of the war as chaplains in military hospitals but remained technically civilians – *Kriegspfarrer*, literally "war clergy." Others were integrated into the military as officers with their own hierarchy: "military chaplain" (*Wehrmachtpfarrer*); "supervisory chaplain" (*Wehrmachtoberpfarrer*); and "dean of chaplains" (*Wehrmachtdekan*). Many men moved between these kinds of chaplaincy. For the sake of clarity, I refer to all these people as "Wehrmacht chaplains," unless the specific status is relevant in the context.

The process of appointing chaplains was cumbersome, and, like so much about the Wehrmacht chaplaincy, in constant flux. For instance, the period from 1933 to 1939 brought a shift from Deputy Führer Rudolf Hess's office providing political approval to the Gestapo doing so. In order to stay on good terms with the authorities, both military bishops aimed to appoint men with a firm understanding of the military and no record of any trouble with the Nazi system. The many stakeholders and the multifaceted process of approval passed along some of the vulnerabilities felt by the military bishops: worries that they were viewed as "unmanly" – manliness was frequently invoked as a criterion – or unsuitable for soldiers in the National Socialist armed forces. Military, church, and state officials all did their best to block perceived troublemakers, although each agency defined "trouble" in its own way. Two subjects almost completely absent from the discussion were religion and actual soldiers.

The unwieldy process of approval that developed required at least twenty-five separate documents. Names were proposed by regional church authorities, usually the bishop, and screened by representatives of the military, then vetted for political reliability. Military bishops made the final appointments, but by no means on their own. Formal and informal criteria were arbitrary, and considerations of proximity and age proved to be wildly flexible. Everyone involved took political issues very seriously. On occasion, adherents of the Confessing Church made it in, and frequently German Christians were declined. Clergy, Catholic or Protestant, who had openly spoken or acted against National Socialist policies or principles were always excluded. On the Catholic side, other issues involved "illegal youth work" – that is, violating restrictions on educational and social activities – and association with the series of trials against Franciscans and others for offensives around currency and morality scandals. Some slipped through and were subsequently dismissed.

Gestapo screeners scrutinized each file and prepared detailed assessments. A report in late 1942 disqualified a set of Protestant candidates as "fanatical members of the Confessing Church," whom Party leadership in their districts had judged unfavorably. One of the pastors, Herbert Haß, born in 1900, a resident of Wittstock/Dosse, got an especially long police report. The assessment was sharply negative, even though the candidate had valuable credentials. A Party member since May 1933, Pastor Haß had been Block leader in Wittstock and an active "German Christian." Since September 1939, he had been in military service.

The evaluator, however, was unequivocal: "From the point of view of character, I reject Haß. He should be treated with the utmost caution." Apparently Haß had lost interest in Party work and joined the "Confessing front," evidence of his unreliability:

As to his occupation, Haß used to be a salesman and only later became a theologian. According to statements by his mother, who lives here, he studied economics during his military service. That is a typical sign of his character. When the first vocation no longer is sufficiently rewarding, it is absolutely nothing to him to quickly jump ship.[73]

The combination of a multilayered procedure and a priority on minimizing trouble favored moderates over radicals of all kinds. If it was not anti-Nazi martyrs who found their way into the chaplaincy neither was it hotheaded Stormtroopers. Instead conventional, nationalist pastors and priests tended to make the final cut. All Wehrmacht chaplains accepted Hitler's regime, but few were themselves hardcore Nazis. They favored standard Christian rituals over Nazi cultural norms,[74] and looked back for guidance to their predecessors in earlier wars. In this way, chaplains constituted a recognizably Christian presence in the Wehrmacht and built bridges between often hostile, neo-pagan elements and the still largely churched majority.

Occasionally aspiring chaplains applied directly to their own contacts. In 1935, a Baptist pastor named Otto Jäger wrote to Reich Bishop Ludwig Müller asking for a job in the chaplaincy. Jäger's request emphasized his eagerness to serve both "Adolf Hitler's state" and "the Lord Jesus Christ." Born in 1888, Jäger received an Iron Cross in 1914. He described his experience of the war as above all an opportunity to witness for Jesus among "friend and foe."[75] Jäger invoked Müller's World War I record to make a connection: "As a devout soldier, I already heard about you on the eastern front, Mr. Reich Bishop, and your work as a military chaplain at that time, and other believers said wonderful things about you."[76]

Jäger's letter detailed an impressive career. The son of a farmer, he had volunteered in 1908 to the Garde Kürassier Regiment in Berlin. He was "born again" as a Baptist at that time, under the guidance of two men and two women, all of them members of the aristocracy. The following year he was arrested and held for three days because of a clash with "Marxism." Jäger served from July 1917 with the first armored units, and, as he told it, "the entire war was one continuous opportunity to evangelize among friends and enemies." In addition, he noted, his finances were in order, his wife "is also of pure Aryan blood," and "we have a healthy child." As evidence, he enclosed "a photograph of our vacation trip from the year before last, with the Lorelei in the background." On top of all that, Jäger offered to provide samples of his written work, including a paper on "World Events and Adolf Hitler's State in Light of Scripture."[77]

Jäger appended a reference from a Nazi Party member, the master mason J. Bendrat, who confirmed his good reputation and added a surprising assumption: "As to his attitude toward the Party, I am not informed, but I assume that he is supportive because the Baptists are German Christians." The only thing that might be held against him, Bendrat observed, was that "he is a big proponent of baptism by immersion."[78] Brief statements from local and district Nazi Party functionaries indicated there were no political objections.[79] Nevertheless, Jäger's candidacy was not even considered, most likely because, as a member of the Baptist "free church," he had no support from the Protestant establishment.

In 1936, an application sent to the superintendent of the Protestant Church in Westphalia reached Dohrmann all the way from Luseland, Saskatchewan (where my father grew up, incidentally). Alexander Wolfram, pastor of two tiny Lutheran churches, evidently wanted out of that desolate prairie region of western Canada. Like Jäger, Wolfram was a decorated veteran of World War I,[80] but he too got nowhere. Indeed, the available records suggest that such individual initiatives rarely if ever succeeded. There were too few positions and too many competing interests for such exceptions.

Every agency involved in selecting chaplains had its own priorities and criteria. Military authorities and the military bishops looked for men who would relate well to soldiers and be effective, reliable boosters of morale. Experience at the front was a plus that over time became a prerequisite; a low profile in church politics was valued as well. In 1936, the commander of the 6th Army district in Münster rejected all the clergy in Bielefeld as prospective chaplains for the division based there. In his view, the Bielefeld pastors were so polarized between the German Christian and Confessing Church camps that they would sow discord among the troops. The commander of the division likewise nixed one candidate as "unsuitable" after he heard him preach.[81] A year later, military authorities decided to do without a chaplain in Lippstadt rather than entrust the job to the local Protestant pastor, Paul Dahlkötter, who "cannot be used because of his critical political attitudes."[82]

Military and church representatives could reject candidates as they wished, but if it came to disagreements with state and Party offices, political preferences won out. For example, in 1937 the Protestant congregation at the military base in Soest, Westphalia rejected Pastor Thurmann as their chaplain, because, according to Thurmann's superintendent, "he is antisocial and his sermons are too boring." Thurmann still got the job.[83] By August 1939, following a wave of appointments, the patterns were well in place, as was a respectable, dependable corps of chaplains.

Tests of Loyalty: 1936 and 1937

Significant military events in 1936 may not actually merit the label "tests of loyalty," because there is scant evidence that any Christians in Germany questioned them and no record at all of dissenting chaplains. Consider the remilitarization of the Rhineland in March. Were any chaplains publicly or privately involved in this first foray of the new Wehrmacht and the resulting public relations success? All I know so far is that some military chaplains publicly blessed the event, though from a distance.

In 1936, the German Silesian city of Hirschberg (Jelenia Góra in Poland after World War II) moved its regular Great War commemoration ceremony from November to March, perhaps initially in honor of the first anniversary of German rearmament but then to celebrate the triumph in the west. As usual, the event featured musical performances, with members of the new Wehrmacht division gathered at the "Heroes Cemetery," where a band played the hymn *Vater, ich rufe Dich!* (Father, I Call on Thee) by Franz Schubert,[84] followed by a march from Beethoven's *Eroica*, both references to the Napoleonic wars. The only speakers recorded were the local military chaplains, now upgraded from garrison to "field" chaplains. Their speeches led up to the emotional climax of the event: decoration of soldiers' graves with branches and wreaths to the accompaniment of the melancholy favorite, "I Had a Comrade."[85]

In the wake of remilitarization of the Rhineland, after the onset of war in Spain, and in the midst of a raft of accusations and charges against German Catholic priests, monks, and nuns, the power balance shifted against the Wehrmacht chaplaincy. Kevin Spicer has described the "subtle duel" between the Catholic hierarchy and Nazi leaders,[86] and this same image can be applied to the churches in general. Although the precise timing is not easy to determine, by 1937, the chaplains' position had weakened.

In his memorandum of January 1937 addressed to Army High Command, Bishop Rarkowski had outlined some of the challenges facing the military chaplaincy. First on his list, and a recurring complaint from him and Dohrmann, were efforts to discredit religion in Nazi society. Rarkowski gave only one example: "the fact that pamphlets are allowed to be freely distributed among the military that attack not only Christianity in general but also the religious tradition of the German army and that mock the Christian hero's death of German soldiers." Among the culprits he named a publication titled *Der Soldat, der Krieg und der Tod* (The Soldier, War, and Death), issued by the Ludendorff press in Munich.[87] In the bishop's mind, German heroism and Christianity must not be torn asunder.

Another issue was even more concrete. According to Rarkowski, he was the only German bishop who did not have a company vehicle, even though his activities involved all of Germany and required him to appear in person in widely scattered places. To make matters worse, he added, he had to pay for his expensive liturgical robes and received no funds to cover many other associated costs.[88]

To bolster his requests, Rarkowski offered the services of the Wehrmacht chaplaincy to National Socialist Germany as a full partner in the transform-ation of the military – and of society as a whole. His move paralleled that of his episcopal counterparts, who offered their support in the crusade against Bolshevism in Spain in exchange for relief from anticlerical attacks at home.[89] But as military bishop, Rarkowski claimed he had even more to give:

Today the military chaplain stands in the center of the tumultuous struggles that have been ignited in every aspect of German life. ... Before the war, the military chaplaincy had a completely different character than it does today. Then everything continued in orderly ways that had been determined by tradition ... Today the military chaplain can only be true to his task when he has a deep and living connection to the spiritual situation and to the nature of the soul of the young soldiers of the time as well as to the soldierly way of life today, which in addition to honoring the old traditions, nurtures and demands new ideas.[90]

As a result, chaplains needed training, and Rarkowski proposed it should include two components:

a. An introduction to the soldierly way of life. A large part of the difficulties that individual military chaplains face in their work has to do with their lack of a sense of what the soldier's soul needs and a failure to recognize that the young soldier wants to see in the attitude and message of his priest a kind of piety that speaks to his own nature, which is oriented toward everything soldierly.[91]

The second component was to be "state-political training." Chaplains, Rarkowski explained, needed such instruction if they were to be effective in the new Germany:

The military chaplain, like everyone else, must know on which principles and with which ideas National Socialism will build the Reich. Personally he does not have a political assignment, but the young people with whom he works have gone through the political training of the organizations and live in a world shaped by a particular world-view that we must acknowledge if we are to make religious values effective in deepening the soldier's thought and will.[92]

Rarkowski's words reveal that the process of mutual legitimation, whereby the Nazi state and the chaplaincy boosted one another's standing, had tilted. Now chaplains needed National Socialism more than the regime needed them.

Over the course of 1937, key changes in the process of appointing chaplains reduced the military bishops' power. At first the office of Hitler's deputy, Rudolf Hess, had vetted candidates for the chaplaincy. Bishop Dohrmann complained that the process moved extremely slowly, so that candidates waited months, often to be rejected.[93] Beginning in 1938, the Gestapo took over the security checks, in conjunction with the Security Service and local Nazi Party offices.[94] The change occurred in stages: in early 1939, Hess's office asked that information about candidates' political stance be obtained, not from Party offices, but from the Gestapo via military intelligence offices (*Abwehrstellen*).[95] That procedural adjustment speeded things up but continued to produce many rejections.

Another far-reaching change involved abolition of part-time base chaplain positions. According to a 1937 order from War Minister von Blomberg, "Protestant and Catholic pastoral care to the Wehrmacht is to be provided only by authorized military chaplains."[96] In May 1937, Blomberg issued an order assigning responsibility for the chaplaincy to Army High Command. He united the divisions of the chaplaincy (army and navy) into one and restricted the number of chaplains serving each base to one, except with the largest bases. Most significantly, he confirmed the monopoly of the formal chaplaincy on provision of religious services to the military. From that point, assigning civilian clergy to provide part-time or extra service to military bases was to cease, and only chaplains who had been vetted in the regular process and who were part of the military chaplaincy could work in that capacity.[97] The base chaplaincies abolished in 1937 were civilian positions, and there were about 239 of them. After 1937 only permanent chaplains were on the payroll of the armed forces.

As recorded in the Hossbach Memorandum, by the end of 1937 Hitler was set on war and concerted preparations were underway. Chaplains, by all appearances, were fully on board. A major change was creation of the military office for pastoral care, *Gruppe Seelsorge*, usually referred to as "Gruppe S," Group S. Its creation was likely connected to the May 1937 assignment of responsibility for the Wehrmacht chaplaincy to Army High Command. A sketch of its duties dated October 1939 situated it in the offices of the Reserves and Army Affairs (*Amtsgruppe Ersatz- und Heerwesen*) and identified the group leader as Dr. Senftleben, author of a 1935 survey of German military law,[98] and his deputy as Dr. Julius Stahn, a veteran, lawyer, and member of the Nazi Party and the German Christian movement. There were six staff members: three senior counselors, two specialists, and an administrator.[99] Group S, and especially Senftleben and Stahn, would play a determining role in shaping the wartime chaplaincy.

Changes in the military chaplaincy coincided with deeper upheavals in church–state relations. Evidence suggests that Hitler may have reversed course vis-à-vis Christianity during 1937 or been emboldened to challenge the churches' power. Richard Weikart makes a compelling case using a famous photograph from April 1932. The image shows Hitler coming out of a church, a white cross shining above his head.[100] Hitler's private photographer, Heinrich Hoffmann, published the photograph in a collection, *Hitler wie ihn keiner kennt* (The Unknown Hitler), with the following caption: "A photographic chance event becomes a symbol: Adolf Hitler, the supposed 'heretic,' leaving the Marinekirche [sic] in Wilhelmshaven."[101]

Weikart raises the question as to whether the scene was staged and notes that Hitler, in the midst of an election campaign, was eager to counter charges that he was anti-Christian. But over time his goals changed, and so did the caption and indeed the image itself. The 1935 edition of *Hitler wie ihn keiner kennt* included the same photograph, but in the 1938 edition, the cross had been airbrushed away. Why, Weikart asked? Was Hitler now distancing himself from Christianity? The 1938 edition of Hoffmann's book also included a different caption: "Adolf Hitler after sightseeing at the historic Marinekirche [sic] in Wilhelmshaven." Whereas the earlier caption implied Hitler had been worshipping in the church, now it seemed he had been "merely viewing the architecture."[102] In the glow of the successes of rearmament and remilitarization of the Rhineland, Hitler may no longer have considered it necessary to display public piety.

Navy Chaplain Ronneberger, the German Christian who had been so hopeful about prospects for the chaplaincy in the early 1930s, now expressed his fear that behind all the changes lurked an intention to destroy the chaplaincy. In August 1937, he confided to a fellow pastor: "We in the military are deeply troubled by the massive transformations. Sometimes one cannot shake the thought that they are preparing to get rid of the military chaplaincy altogether."[103] Symptomatic of Nazism's cooling toward Christianity was a prohibition in early 1938, directed at the German Christian movement, on using a symbol that linked the swastika and the cross.[104]

In November 1938, the SS paper *Das Schwarze Korps* (The Black Corps) printed a letter denouncing two base chaplains in Mülheim as enemies of the state. Just weeks earlier, the venerable Jewish community in Mülheim and nearby Duisburg had been openly and brutally attacked in the Kristallnacht pogrom. Likely that violence emboldened Nazi activists. The letter to the editor claimed the Catholic chaplain Heinrichsbauer was implicated in the trials of Franciscans for sexual improprieties, and his Protestant counterpart

Barnstein belonged to the Confessing Church. "Is it intention or negligence," the author demanded to know,

> that Catholic priests, who under the terms of the Concordat are, by definition draft dodgers, and Confessing Church pastors, who are opposed to the Reich leadership (Minister Rosenberg), should be chosen to administer the oath to the Führer to men who come from the Stormtroopers, the SS, and the Hitler Youth, and to preach to them the message of loyalty unto death? Only those who themselves are one hundred percent behind the state and its Führer can do that job.[105]

All military chaplains could consider themselves on notice.

The Spanish Civil War

The civil war in Spain was a test for the Wehrmacht chaplaincy but not in the way one might expect. It was not a check as to how newly appointed chaplains would respond to the pressures of combat: as far as I have been able to ascertain, Keding was one of very few, perhaps the only Christian clergyman sent from Germany on assignment to the Wehrmacht forces in Spain,[106] and he was only there for six weeks and not as an official chaplain. Rather it served to test whether the chaplaincy would accept its circumscribed role, play along with the pretext of its own importance, and participate in the legitimation of German methods of warfare and cover-up of crimes. The answers were "yes," "yes," and "yes."

Germany's intervention in Spain shifted the power relations between Catholics and Protestants in favor of the Catholics. In general, in the ongoing rivalry between the confessions, Protestants had significant advantages. They faced nothing like the public humiliation of the morality trials of members of Catholic religious orders or the waves of arrests of Catholic priests.[107] Admittedly, Martin Niemöller was arrested in 1937, and members of the German Christian movement often found their love for National Socialism unrequited.[108] Still, Protestant leaders considered themselves the Nazis' preferred partners.

Developments in Spain, however, created an awkward situation for Protestant leaders. Back in 1931, some prominent German expatriates had loudly and publicly welcomed the revolution that brought a liberal republic into power. As late as 1938, they were still celebrating the end of oppressive Catholic power. There had been complete religious freedom under the Republic, they insisted. So why, they wanted to know, was Hitler's Germany siding not with its natural allies in Spain, but with its arch-enemies, the Inquisitional Catholic hierarchy and its barbaric African (Moroccan) mercenaries? The noisy protests of the long-time head of the German Protestant mission in Spain, who refused to be evacuated from Madrid and continued to express support for the Republic and demand payment of his pension from church offices in Berlin, added one more reason for military chaplains, specifically the Protestants, to be defensive.[109]

A potentially much bigger challenge for German chaplains was the atrocities their countrymen were committing in Spain. The Condor Legion's bombing of Guernica in 1937 and the killing of Spanish civilians by Germans, Italians, and Franco's forces, sparked international outrage.[110] German public relations experts in state and church offices monitored the proliferation of negative images with concern. The files of the foreign office of the German Protestant church contain an extensive collection of publications sponsored by Communist organizations and other opponents of Franco. Some flyers and books were disguised with swastikas and logos on the front, presenting them as the work of the Deutsches Ausland-Institut, the institute for Germans abroad, but the contents reveal the opposite.

One seventy-page booklet started out with a few pages of general material and then revealed its stance: "Hitler does not want the German people to learn *the truth about Spain*. They should not learn how there the blood of German soldiers is spilled for the profits of Krupp, Thyssen, Siemens, and Glöckner. . . . They are supposed to learn nothing about the atrocities the Fascist flyers commit on the Spanish people."[111] Pastor Keding and the Protestant Church's Foreign Office were proud partners in that propaganda offensive.

Keding's euphoric account from Spain included more than a small dose of German triumphalism. In his memoir, Keding described the astonishment of one of his Spanish hosts, a housewife, to find a chaplain among the Germans: "Apparently talk of the 'blond heathens' had fallen upon her pious ears. Whether I would be celebrating mass in the cathedral? . . . Things cooled off noticeably when I explained that I am a Protestant military chaplain. Having a heretic under her roof seems to be an unpleasant sensation to her."[112]

By his own account, Keding soon proved his deep Christian faith. The following day, he wrote, everyone felt uneasy. At the airfield, Keding came into conversation with a pilot. "Pastor, I am not afraid," the man told him. "Every time I take off, I say to myself that if God needs me up there, he will call me from this earth. But if he still needs me down here, he will keep me alive." Keding, still thinking of those words, turned them into a defense of Christianity and the military chaplaincy:

Could there be any more beautiful proof of the value of the Christian faith in the life of a soldier? Is there any better response to the nonsense that claims Christianity makes a man soft [*schlapp*]? . . . Here we see that the Christian virtues of humility and surrender to God's will do not end in fatalistic let-things-be-as-they-will, but in fearlessness and action.[113]

Keding talked up the possibilities of ecumenical cooperation in Spain, even while he denigrated Catholics. A Spanish priest, "in woeful German," had described his experiences with "the Reds." Keding had planned to hold a barracks hour for the Germans, but so many Spaniards appeared – men, women, and children – that he decided on a hymn sing instead:

Later the priest told me that the powerful singing of the Protestant hymns and the sermon and the men's attentiveness, made a strong impression on him and his people. In general, it seems to me that under the experience of the Reds' persecution of Christians, they have come to see the Protestant sister confession in a friendly way, in contrast to the Bishop of El Burgo, who would not at any price let me use the empty seminary chapel for a religious service.[114]

Keding praised the bravery of the Spaniards as a way to highlight the value of military chaplaincy:

Again and again we hear in every voice the hymn of praise to the Spanish military chaplains. One is assigned to every battalion. He accompanies the troops in uniform, with the rank of a sergeant, and shares all the dangers and trials with his comrades. The newspapers bring reports of the heroic deeds of these men all the time. Many times, flag in hand, they have gone ahead of the storming battalions and urged a stalled attack forward. People speak of a disproportionately high percentage of dead military chaplains.[115]

For Keding, being killed in action was the highest measure of a chaplain's worth.

Tests of 1938 and Early 1939

The tumultuous year of 1938 brought one turning point after another for the Wehrmacht chaplains as Hitler pushed Germany toward war. In hindsight, the Blomberg–Fritsch affair in January and February can be recognized as a significant test of the chaplaincy's loyalty to the regime, one they passed with surprising ease. Although Rarkowski and Dohrmann owed their jobs to the military leadership that was ousted in 1938, neither of them nor anyone else in the chaplaincy made a peep when the War Minister Blomberg and Commander-in-Chief of the Army Werner von Fritsch were forced out of office. Nor did they comment on the purging of dozens of officers that followed. By then the chaplains easily shifted their loyalties to the new men in charge.

It is difficult to find sources to ascertain the impact of the 1938 purges on the military chaplaincy, and the evidence consists mainly of silences and gaps. Dohrmann's personal papers, available in the German Federal Archive Military Archive in Freiburg, were clearly sorted and purged by Dohrmann himself. His extensive postwar notes offer his explanations of events (and laid the foundation for the laudatory volume edited by Hermann Kunst, *Gott lässt sich nicht spotten* – God Will Not Be Mocked).[116] The purges of 1938 are absent, except in a brief account of a strange incident: how Dohrmann almost lost his job. According to Dohrmann, Goebbels had press releases printed announcing his resignation as military bishop – to be replaced by Lonicer. Why it did not end up happening Dohrmann does not disclose.

Dohrmann presented this drama without a date, but a footnote in Kunst's book specifies it may have been in 1938 or 1942. That discrepancy has always bothered me. Why would the organized Dohrmann have forgotten (or have no record) of the date of such a crucial event? And even if he could not remember the precise date, how could he possibly confuse two such different periods of time? Only in thinking about Blomberg and Fritsch did I see an explanation. If the planned removal of the military bishop occurred in 1938, it was likely part of the shake-up connected with the termination of Blomberg and Fritsch, a logical assumption, given Dohrmann's close association with them. But if it happened in 1942, it could indicate that at the peak of German power, Dohrmann had expressed misgivings; in other words, it could suggest the bishop had shown resistance. Everything speaks for 1938 (and nothing for 1942, except wishful thinking), but by changing the date, or at least introducing the possibility of 1942, either Dohrmann or his biographer transformed a story of the military bishop's abandonment of his erstwhile allies into a hint of opposition to the Nazi war of annihilation.[117]

The circumstances of Blomberg's resignation made it easy for the upright Dohrmann to abandon his old friend. In her biography of the war minister, Kirstin A. Schäfer establishes that Blomberg's second wife, Margarethe Gruhn, was indeed registered as a prostitute with the Berlin police and had been convicted of offenses involving photographs of herself naked and in sexual poses with a man. Schäfer makes a convincing case that it was the scandal of his marriage, and not Blomberg's hesitation at the 1937 meeting recorded in the Hossbach memorandum, that led Hitler to force him to resign, although she notes Hitler seized the opportunity to shake up the military leadership and put himself at its head.[118] The Blomberg affair illustrates how quickly relationships changed in the corrosive atmosphere of Nazi society. Blomberg's new wife turned out to be a problem, and so did he. For the chaplains, eager to boost their position, the former war minister sank from being an asset to a liability.

Both Dohrmann and Rarkowski survived the shake-up, although they had close ties to the ousted generals.[119] Apparently the much touted value the military bishops as officers of the Wehrmacht placed on loyalty did not extend to those relationships. It is telling that in Dohrmann's account, Brauchitsch backed Lonicer, because Brauchitsch's own rise coincided with the fall of Blomberg and Fritsch.[120] A close bond between Brauchitsch and Lonicer continued throughout the war, but the new Commander-in-Chief, and

Figure 2.2 Protestant Military Bishop Dohrmann speaking at the graveside of Werner von Fritsch, in Berlin, September 1939. The ex-Commander in Chief of the German Army was hit by a bullet and bled to death near Warsaw. Visible to Dohrmann's right is Fritsch's successor, Colonel General Walther von Brauchitsch, holding his hat in both hands. Disgraced and abandoned since 1938, Fritsch nonetheless received a ceremonial state funeral and was buried in the Invaliden Friedhof, alongside Prussian war heroes. BArch Bild 183-E11084.

subsequently Hitler, left Dohrmann in place. Perhaps they feared trouble, but more likely they recognized that the Protestant military bishop, like his Catholic counterpart, was both useful and harmless (Figure 2.2).

For Wehrmacht chaplains the *Anschluss*, Germany's annexation of Austria in 1938, posed no comparable problems. They regarded this pivotal event with excited approval and enthusiastically incorporated Austrian clergy into their ranks. How differently Victor Klemperer, himself a veteran of the Great War, born Jewish and baptized Protestant, experienced that time. "Pogrom mood," he wrote in his diary in March 1938. "Any day I expect to find the body of a child in the garden. We will not live to see the end of the Third Reich."[121]

In his memoir, the Protestant chaplain Dietrich Baedeker describes how he participated in reestablishment of a Protestant military chaplaincy in Austria. He was to be based in the Schwarzspanierkirche, in the street of the same name, but the responsible authorities refused to let him use the church. Why? The building was caught up in the riptides of the times. After 1918, it had been assigned to Russian exiles from Communism, Russian Orthodox Christians who were Nazi Germany's allies against the Soviet Union. So Baedeker had to wait, but not for long. After signing of the nonaggression pact with the Soviet Union in August 1939, those anti-Communist, Russian Orthodox Christians became enemies of Germany, and the building was repurposed as a Protestant Garrison Church.[122]

Baedeker sought to transform the interior to fit the church's new role. Behind the altar hung a large oil painting of Jesus and the repentant Mary Magdalene. In Baedeker's description, it reflected the romantic, sweet style of the nineteenth century, completely unsuitable for a congregation of soldiers, because the figure of Mary Magdalene – about four by five meters large – dominated the whole space. He replaced it with a painting of the crucifixion by a contemporary of Rembrandt.[123]

Chaplains showed the same pattern in Austria as they had with Spain: keen involvement and concerted efforts to seize the changes as opportunities to expand their mission, interspersed with murmuring that they were underappreciated and needed to compensate for their deficiencies. During the subsequent crises, however, chaplains kept prudently out of sight, careful to steer clear of any flickers of Christian dissent.

Developments around the Sudetenland in late 1938 are a case in point. Amidst the tense negotiations leading up to the Munich Conference and widespread fear of war, three German Protestant pastors wrote a prayer service of confession and intercession, which they hoped would be read from pulpits across the nation. In their accompanying statement, the theologians spoke of war as God's punishment, a call to repentance, and explicitly rejected the notion of God as a "German cultural God." One intercession, with alternative language should war erupt before the service was held, read simply: "Oh God, spare (or deliver) us from war and send peace for our children."[124]

After Germany signed the Munich Agreement with Italy, Britain, and France, war seemed to have been averted. Instead of the prayers of intercession, Protestant churches held services of thanksgiving. But a month later, on October 27, *Das Schwarze Korps* published the text of the original prayer service and denounced its three authors as traitors. The editorial was scathing: "Such prayers have absolutely nothing to do with religion. They are political declarations of treason and sabotage against our people's solidarity and preparedness for war at a crucial time of our destiny. Away with it! The security of the nation demands the elimination (*Ausmerzung*) of the criminals."[125]

In response, Protestant leaders rushed to dissociate themselves from the prayers and their authors and to assert their loyalty to Hitler. Bitter debates within church circles ensued, and the lesson most clergy took from the controversy was to keep their mouths shut. Naturally, no chaplains got involved. Nonetheless, Nazi authorities applied an extra test of loyalty. In the wake of the brouhaha, they circulated among Protestant chaplains a letter critical of the regime, which purportedly had been written by a Protestant pastor with Jewish ancestry. Gestapo agents had found copies in the possession of members of the Wehrmacht. Did any of the chaplains know anything about it, they demanded? Every chaplain canvassed submitted a signed disavowal.[126]

Given all that came before, it is no surprise that during the Kristallnacht pogrom, military chaplains remained completely out of sight. But the attacks on Jews in November 1938 had a long-term impact on the chaplaincy. Those few Christian clergy who did speak out against violence toward Jews and Jewish homes, property, and places of worship were noted and blacklisted for subsequent appointments. For example, Herbert Rettig, a Protestant, was rejected for the chaplaincy in 1942. Church Ministry complaints included the following: "In the context of the Jewish action in November 1938, he showed his non-National Socialist attitudes."[127] A Catholic priest named Schosser was refused on similar grounds in 1944.[128]

By 1939, there was no reason to fear chaplains would raise questions about anything Hitler did. They had proven to be reliable and eager to serve the cause. In January, when Hitler gave a speech in the Reichstag invoking the biblical language of the prophets and calling down doom on Jews, German chaplains said nothing. In mid-March, all Christian clergy kept quiet as Germany destroyed Czechoslovakia, an act that is said to have inspired the euphoric Hitler to rush into his secretaries' office with the exhortation, "Give me a kiss, girls! This is the greatest day of my life. I shall be known as the greatest German in history."[129]

Preparations for war seeped into the chaplaincy. In May 1939, the Group for Pastoral Care released a document called "Prayers for the Führer during Military Church Services." Group S provided a formula to be used in all such invocations:

Bless our German Volk ... Plant deep in our hearts our love for the Fatherland. Let us be a heroic race worthy of our ancestors. May we protect the faith of our fathers like a holy legacy. Bless the German Wehrmacht, which is called to guard peace and protect home and hearth, and grant its members the power to make the highest sacrifice for Führer, Volk, and Fatherland. Bless especially our Führer and Supreme Commander in all the tasks that come to him. May all of us under his leadership see in the sacrifice for Volk and Fatherland a holy task, so that through our faith, our obedience and our loyalty, we reach the eternal home in the Kingdom of your light and peace. Amen.[130]

By late August, the Wehrmacht chaplains also had a new set of regulations. The text opened with a mission statement that revealed how thoroughly the chaplaincy had internalized the stab-in-the-back account of Germany's loss in the previous war: "All experience with war has taught that the spiritual power

Figure 2.3 The Wehrmacht belt buckle. The slogan "*Gott mit uns*" had been used in Prussia and Imperial Germany, including on soldiers' belt buckles in World War I. The Wehrmacht's version incorporated the swastika and a stylized imperial eagle. Initially the eagle faced left, as on this photograph, taken in February 1936, but soon it was changed to face right. Chaplains frequently invoked the slogan in sermons and letters. Photographer Dorneth. BArch Bild 183-S02633.

of an army is its best weapon. An army draws its power above all from its firm faith. For this reason, pastoral care in the field is an important means to strengthening the fighting power of the army." The second article spelled out the perceived benefits to the cause of victory: "A soldier who takes seriously his service and sacrifice for the Fatherland as a task from God ... and who trusts in God's help and believes in eternal life, can stand firm, fight bravely, and die with courage"[131] (Figure 2.3).

That same month, a circular for base chaplains and chaplains in military hospitals articulated their duties:

All of us know that in wartime it all depends on the *spiritual strength* of our people. In 1914/18 we scarcely reckoned with this fact, or we did not recognize it or attend to it clearly enough. We have learned from this mistake and we will not repeat it again. ... We have one goal before us: on the foundation of our Christian faith we want to give to the German people of our time – not least to the soldiers – the spiritual power that we all need in order to come through this war strong and with good results. God bless our work![132]

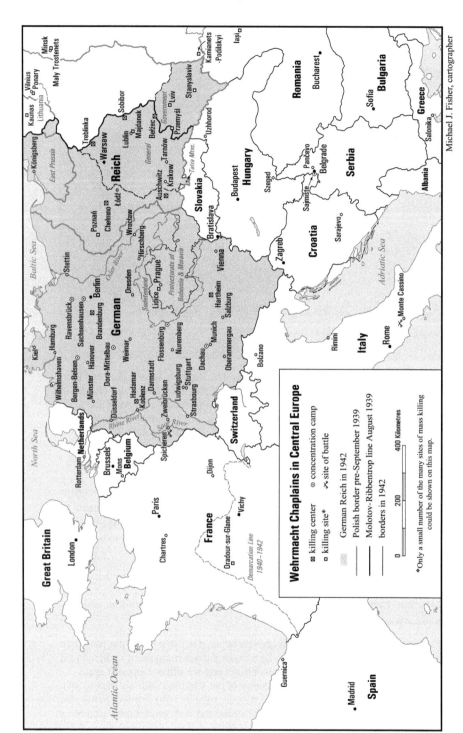

Wehrmacht Chaplains in Central Europe

⊠ killing center
⊙ concentration camp
↘ site of battle

German Reich in 1942

Polish border pre-September 1939

Molotov-Ribbentrop line August 1939

borders in 1942

0   200   400 Kilometres

*Only a small number of the many sites of mass killing could be shown on this map.

Michael J. Fisher, cartographer

Map 1 Wehrmacht Chaplains in Central Europe

On September 1, 1939, when German troops crossed the border into Poland, the Wehrmacht chaplaincy was ready. Although only four and a half years old – the same age as Hitler's new armed forces – the chaplaincy had built up a network of some 300 trained, full-time clergymen, about equal numbers of Catholics and Protestants, many of them with experience at the front in the Great War. Its leaders owed their positions to the support of the military and the state, appointments had excluded troublemakers, and chaplains had proven their loyalty under duress. In short, the chaplaincy was on track, and the track was a rut. Created within the context of Nazi rule, the Wehrmacht chaplaincy fit neatly into that system. Its goals intersected with the interests of the Nazi state in a mutually reinforcing process of legitimation. There was no need for unanimity: in this framework, skeptics could be as useful as fanatics.

Pastor Keding is a case in point. His bravado served a valuable purpose in 1937, but it appears he was subsequently disillusioned or perhaps rejected by the chaplaincy. When he resurfaced in the files, it was in 1938, to request a position in overseas missions, preferably in South America, where he had lived and felt at home because he spoke Spanish.[133] Judging from the files, he did not even get the courtesy of a reply.

3 "Gott mit uns"

Blitzkrieg, 1939–1941

The young soldier Heinrich Böll maintained a lively wartime correspondence with his parents and siblings, and his fiancée, later wife.[1] In her preface to the published letters, Annemarie Böll, née Cech, described her husband and his family as anti-Nazi and Catholic. Pastoral care to the military comes up a few times. In December 1939, Böll wrote home from the garrison in Osnabrück: "A small package arrived from the priest with 20 good cigarettes and a nice little edition of the New Testament."[2] Four months later, he received another, less satisfying, package: "From the priest I got a brochure and five cigarettes. The brochure is perfectly suited for packing soap. I'm sending you three pieces of good military soap."[3]

Chaplains expressed a grander view of their significance. On September 11, 1940, a Protestant chaplain with the 1st Infantry Division in France submitted a twelve-page report describing his activities since May of the previous year. He had surprisingly little to say about the invasion of Poland, which he had experienced, but his narrative gathered steam with his unit's entry into Belgium: "With the beginning of the offensive in the West, the deployment of the division as an army reserve group made pastoral care difficult," he noted. Long marches meant no time for religious services, so he visited the hospitals and dressing stations and met with soldiers one-by-one.[4]

The chaplain took pride in the demands for his service. On May 22–23, he found himself in a night battle south of Mons. Amidst the fighting, he held a short funeral service for Lieutenant Count zu Dohna from the staff of the 1st Division. He blessed the lieutenant's body, which some comrades helped him bring from the street into a house. The next day, during the attack of the 43rd Infantry Regiment near Blaregnies, he ministered to wounded men on the street of Mons-Bavai, and at the request of a mortally wounded German soldier, gave him Holy Communion. After the battle was over, he buried four men and held funerals for them; photographs of their graves accompanied his report. Meanwhile, he arranged for erection of a "worthy" marker on the grave of Count zu Dohna.[5]

Despite connections to his fellow officers, the report made it clear the chaplain had to fend for himself. On May 25, he and his Catholic counterpart

stumbled across members of the 43rd Infantry Regiment (9th Company) who
were fighting near Bouchain. Fortunately, they had packaged cookies with
them to distribute to the soldiers who had not received any food for twenty-
four hours. Unable to find the aid station they were looking for, they wandered
around for two hours under enemy artillery fire. Eventually they headed to the
main dressing station St. Aubert, where it was high action: "In three hours
alone, 76 wounded were admitted," the chaplain reported. He made himself
useful: "Many of them I could help with prayer and comforting words. At the
request of several wounded men, I wrote greetings and news to their loved
ones back home."[6]

In visits to a series of military hospitals at the end of May, the chaplain
spoke with many soldiers wounded in the heavy fighting at Trith, Bouchain,
and Wavrechain. He found them grappling with deep existential questions,
such as: "Does my life as a cripple still have meaning?" This issue must have
felt urgent at a time when thousands of children and adults with disabilities had
already been murdered in Germany under the deceptively labeled "Euthanasia
program."[7] The following summer, Bishop von Galen would preach his
famous sermon condemning the killing of disabled people as murder and
explicitly raising the possibility of wounded soldiers being killed as "useless
lives."[8]

Other concerns the chaplain reported hearing also indicated that Wehrmacht
soldiers were aware of the brutality they were part of and remained capable of
moral reflection. For example, they asked: "Doesn't war totally go against
serving God and God's will?" and, "How can God allow such bloodshed?"
Poignantly, given the massacres of Black French soldiers that Germans had
already engaged in,[9] some wanted to know: "Hasn't the war made me into a
murderer?" The chaplain did not report his answers. Instead, he noted that the
soldiers were grateful for every kind word. Again he emphasized his utility:
men who let themselves be helped spiritually were better equipped to bear the
pain of their wounds, he observed.[10]

Dealing with the dead became an increasingly large part of the job. Around
Bouchain, the chaplain wrote, the quickly advancing troops were unable to
bury their dead with care: "The bodies lay on the ground, needy and neglected,
in a swampy area." On orders from the Division Commander, the Catholic and
Protestant chaplains located the swamp at Wavrechain and saw to the proper
burial of nine men. At the newly erected gravestones, the Protestant chaplain
led a devotional with the soldiers who were present and blessed the graves.
During the offensive in the west, the pastor helped carry out the duties of the
graves officer, as he had done in Poland.[11]

With the Wehrmacht's triumphs in France the mood of the report changed.
The chaplain described three large services he held, with themes of "gratitude
for the wonderful victories, commemoration of the fallen soldiers, and looking

ahead to the tasks of the future." He described the period from June 5 to July 2 as a new offensive that took the division from Douai to Loudun. Again, the rapid advance meant no time for services, only individual encounters. His account of these was less uplifting than the previous round, though he tried to be positive: "These one-on-one conversations almost always revealed a raft of religious misunderstandings, prejudices, and heresies on the one hand, and on the other, a genuine capacity for understanding the Gospel."[12]

Now, in the days without combat, the chaplain faced a new set of challenges. Among the soldiers he saw severe signs of dissipation. Thank God, he maintained, "purely sexual excesses" remained the exception, though he did not spell out what forms the more common instances of intemperance took. When he personally encountered such things, he noted, "I tried through personal admonitions to bring the individual to reason." He quoted Jesus's rebuke to his disciples in Luke 9:55: "You do not know what kind of spirit you are of." According to the chaplain, whatever the sin, the men offered the excuse that everyone was doing it. At times like this, he admitted, "I found it painful that one (or together with the Catholic chaplain), two clergy was not enough to have an effective influence on the men of an entire Division." He considered this, too, to be his duty: to fight for "improvement of the inner manly character of the German soldiers."[13]

The chaplain ended on a note of triumph. On the day of the armistice, he wrote, "under the clear, starry sky of southern France, beginning with a celebratory *te deum*, I held a military church service in Loudun for the division staff and the communications division 1 in the presence of the division commander. I spoke on I Peter 5:6 with the theme, humility!" Considering the Bible verse chosen, the sermon clearly seemed to give God's blessing to an interpretation of events in France as payback for Germany's "humiliation" in the previous war. I Peter 5:6 reads: "Humble yourselves, therefore, under God's mighty hand, that he may lift you up in due time."[14]

Germany's military conquests starting in September 1939 literally and also figuratively opened up new territory for Wehrmacht chaplains. Their reports convey excitement and adventure as they seized the chance to assert their loyalty and prove their worth. They had an enormous audience of soldiers and now also sought ways to minister to Christian populations in conquered and occupied territories. In the tumult of world historical events, they insisted, they were needed and appreciated. The dramatic successes of the Wehrmacht's "lightning wars" provided opportunities to redeem themselves, the chaplaincy, and Christianity in Germany after the previous lost war.

But it was not all perfect. As Böll's letters hint, soldiers, even those closely connected to their church, often viewed chaplains as irrelevant or ridiculous. Nazi authorities continued to chip away at the chaplains' position. War generated physical demands that left chaplains no time to do the job they wanted to do, let alone to think about what they were doing. Meanwhile, Blitzkrieg was brutal on Germany's enemies, combatants and civilians. German victories in Poland involved deadly shelling of roads filled with people fleeing towns and cities. Luftwaffe bombing of Warsaw, Rotterdam, and other urban centers killed many people and destroyed homes and livelihoods. German soldiers massacred thousands of Black French soldiers in 1940 and killed Norwegian prisoners-of-war and large numbers of civilians in Yugoslavia and Greece in so-called reprisal actions. In short, although this period of the war, from the invasion of Poland to the eve of the invasion of Soviet territory in June 1941, tends to be overshadowed by the "war of annihilation" that followed, it included many atrocities of its own. The Wehrmacht chaplains insisted they remained close to soldiers: indeed, proximity was central to their claim to credibility. But if they were as one with the men they served, they must have seen, heard, and known about what those men were doing. And if chaplains did not know, they were badly out of touch.

This chapter shows that both claims hold true. For chaplains, the process of learning about German brutality, whether first- or second-hand, occurred at the same time as they practiced pushing it out of sight and building a righteous narrative about the Wehrmacht and themselves. That narrative took shape in this crucial period, and the experience of "Blitzkrieg" provided key components: stalwart chaplains, tests of physical endurance, triumphant advances, soldiers who were wild and hard yet sorely in need of pastoral care. The anti-Communist version of events, so pervasive later in the war, was unavailable in 1939–1940, after the Molotov–Ribbentrop Pact and the tag-team invasions of Poland made allies of Hitler's Germany and Stalin's Soviet Union. But familiar slogans and geopolitical anxieties still offered possibilities: chaplains, like other public voices, spun the attack on Poland as a defensive move to protect the German minority; they depicted France as secular, hostile, and wicked. As for Denmark, Norway, the Netherlands, and Belgium, all of them neutral when the Germans invaded, chaplains found justification in war itself. War proved to be consuming and distracting, physically but also spiritually and morally. So many things demanded chaplains' attention: there were wounded men to visit, sacraments to provide, sermons to preach, letters to write, regulations to follow, and graves to record. Who had the time and presence of mind to think about what it all meant?

Central to this chapter are reports written by chaplains, although these pose particular challenges for the first year of the war. The requirement to report periodically up the military chain of command was not formalized until April 1940.[15] Before that, some chaplains sent reports to their home bishops or to their military bishop (Rarkowski or Dohrmann). Some may not have prepared any written reports. The reports I have from chaplains in the Polish campaign were written after the fact, sometimes more than a year later. Because the reporting requirement was new, like the war itself, chaplains varied considerably in how and what they wrote. Some reports were wide-ranging and detailed, others were telegraphic. Some closely followed the guidelines provided, others ignored them. Some cut corners by copying previous reports and just changing the specifics. Only after the office for Pastoral Care, known as Group S (Gruppe S), was established at Army High Command, and over a period of months in mid-1940, did practices become more standardized.

The relevant regulations from Army High Command stipulated that war diaries (*Kriegstagebücher*) and activity reports (*Tätigkeitsberichte*) were records of the activities of offices, agencies, and troop units in the war and in special situations in peacetime. They served to "collect experiences for purposes of education and direction; they are essential documents for the writing of history and therefore to be carefully prepared and preserved."[16] Chaplains fell under the same reporting requirements as medical officers and veterinarians. In contrast to war diaries, activity reports were supposed to give a comprehensive overview of the activities, results, and measures taken. The form of presentation was left open.[17] Chaplains learned by doing, and their reports, passed along the chain of command, reflect those lessons. What was rewarded, what sparked disapproval, even reprimands? Chaplains understood their activity reports to be contributions to the historical record and public relations documents for them as individuals, for their church and confession, and for the chaplaincy as an institution.

The Polish Campaign: Keeping Quiet

German accounts of the attack on Poland in September 1939, both at the time and since, emphasize the rapid advance and technological superiority of the German forces, captured in the label "Blitzkrieg." One needs to look to Polish sources to see what that style of warfare entailed for the people on the receiving end. Herman Kruk, a Polish-Jewish educator and Bundist activist from Warsaw, captured his impressions in a diary entry from September 7, 1939:

People who left Warsaw today tell horrible stories. The fields around the capital are flooded with people: thousands of pedestrians – Jews and Christians, men and women, old and young, a sea of limousines, military cars.

At about 9 in the morning we had the first air raid, and it lasted all day without letup. That day was extremely hard. Dozens of times we ran from the carts to hide from the bombers. Horrible scenes took place in the forest. People look for family members who got lost in the dark of night. Women and children shudder. Men, tired from running, throw off their shoes and run barefoot. Horses are frightened by the bombing and run away with the wagons, leaving the passengers in the forest. Everyone trembles with fear.[18]

The assault sparked panic and terror of being separated from loved ones, turning the road into what Kruk called "a horrible hell":

As soon as we hear explosions, people cling to each other. People can't lie still and simply run off aimlessly. People chase after one another. In some cases people lose their senses and run away from the crowd, thinking this will save them. People run after them and bring them back. Everybody's eyes blaze. The ground shakes. The forests rise up. The rattling of machine guns is jolting, and the fear keeps rising.[19]

German coverage of the war emphasized the power of modern weaponry, maligning Poles as primitive, doomed figures, who charged German tanks with horses and let their planes be destroyed on the ground. In fact, the Polish air force exacted a high price from the Luftwaffe, and the Wehrmacht itself depended on horses, not only in the Polish campaign but throughout the war.[20] German casualties, though lower than Polish ones, were also significant. But none of these realities made it into any accounts I have found by chaplains. Likewise, they uttered no peep about the Molotov–Ribbentrop pact or the Soviet Union's invasion of Poland from the east. Nor did they mention Germans' mass murder of people in asylums and hospitals in Poland,[21] or the brutal rampages against Jewish and Christian Poles documented by Colonel General Johannes Blaskowitz in his memorandum to Hitler.[22] Instead, chaplains, if they recounted anything at all about the Polish campaign, stuck to exaltations of German triumph and lamentations over alleged Polish atrocities against the German minority.[23]

In the Polish campaign, the chaplains mostly kept quiet. Catholics among the German chaplains must have been in shock about violence against Polish Catholic priests. So far, I have seen no mention of it, and indeed I have found no accounts from Catholic chaplains of the Polish campaign beyond cursory remarks. What could they have said in the face of the wave of anti-Catholic vitriol that accompanied the German invasion? For example, Helmuth Koschorke, a prolific writer, published his experiences as a member of the police in the form of stories. Central to his tale of September 1939 were hateful Polish Catholic priests, whom he depicted as soft, well-fed, lying hypocrites, fingering their rosaries and clutching their prayer books while concealing murderous Polish "beasts" in the depths of a church in Bromberg (Bydgoszcz).[24] Protestant chaplains could feel superior, and defensiveness of Catholics intensified, but the regulations mandated cooperation across the confessional divide.

All chaplains played down German casualties. The one chaplain who went into detail about an individual German soldier killed in the attack on Poland quoted words of grief and triumph from the man's mother. Protestant chaplain Bernhard Bauerle shared a letter he received in February 1940 from a woman in Berlin Dahlem: "Thank you from the bottom of my heart," she wrote. "I am the mother of this young soldier, who gave his life for his honor. . . . I believe when Christ said to the faithful thief on the cross, 'today you will be with me in paradise,' he said it also to this soldier, who deep down was fighting for purity and for God."[25]

God came up again in conjunction with the motto on the Wehrmacht belt buckle: "*Gott mit uns*." In late September 1939, Heinrich Böll wrote to his family with a bizarre request that conveyed his disgust with Nazi wartime Christianity:

At home we have a black Stormtrooper belt. Please check and see if you can find it (as far as I know it's in the middle drawer in the kitchen cupboard) and send it to me on Monday, because it could be, with 3 percent probability, that I might be able to come on Sunday. First you have to buy an inexpensive, Reich-standard, military belt buckle with the correct inscription, "*Gott mit uns*." I will then fix the belt up correctly and be able to go out in order to get a whiff of civilians. In the long run it is terribly oppressive, day after day and hour after hour to see people in uniform, but on that subject there is a lovely French folksong that begins, "Sergeant, you are right."[26]

This is a grimly comedic passage – nonsense words, plays on words – and the leather belt kept in the kitchen drawer that connects public violence to domestic abuse, but the distaste for official jingoism still comes through loud and clear.[27]

Sources by chaplains make no mention of widespread German attacks on Polish Jews – executions of some Jewish prisoners of war,[28] hostage takings, rape, plunder, shaving of beards and other acts of humiliation – nor do they address the widespread burning of synagogues. Jewish and Polish sources show such acts were public and highly visible, like the destruction of the Great Synagogue in Przemyśl, an important garrison town (Figure 3.1). A Jewish survivor from the town, who gave his last name only (Tuchman) in an interview at Yad Vashem, described his experience in the fall of 1939:

"Tuchman" escaped the first German bombardment of Przemyśl (September 8, 1939), along with his brother-in-law. At that time, homes and other structures in the city were being bombed. . . .

A *Judenjagd* [hunt for Jews] led by the *Totenkopf* [SS] began. Tuchman was called in "to work" and almost fell for it, but decided to escape. That day, around 500 Jews were taken away.

Two rabbis were also arrested that day: Rabbi Herszel Glazer and Rabbi Zaidele Safrin. Also caught was one Kupfer, a well-known local merchant. A major plundering of Jewish stores and businesses in Przemyśl followed.[29]

The Molotov–Ribbentrop line between the German and Soviet spheres ran right through Przemyśl. Accordingly, on September 18, the Germans prepared to leave the town center:

Before they did so, they burned down the Main Synagogue, which had stood in Przemyśl for 500 years. They also burned down the Jewish temple. Two synagogues

Figure 3.1 The Great Synagogue of Przemyśl in flames. The Wehrmacht occupied
the city on September 14, 1939, but two weeks later, in accordance with the
Molotov–Ribbentrop line, turned over the territory on the east bank of the San River
to the Soviets. Before leaving, the Germans killed hundreds of Jews, including
many refugees from western Poland, and burned the Old Synagogue, which had
stood since the sixteenth century. The massive fire was visible for miles. Yad
Vashem Photo Archives, Jerusalem. 300/165.

were saved, by people requesting their Polish neighbors do so. The Poles obliged, but complained this would put their homes at risk. The store to which Tuchman had moved was also robbed.

Mounting anti-Jewish measures unleashed widespread looting of Jewish homes and businesses. As Tuchman remembered, "Anything that an aggressive Nazi demanded, including money, jewelry, gold, and other valuables like radios was to be handed over immediately, under the pain of immediate and brutal execution or punishment."[30]

Józef (Yosef) Kneppel, another Przemyśl Jew, also fled the German invasion and bombing raids, in his case, toward the Romanian border. On the way, he heard on the radio that the Soviets were approaching from that direction, and he ended up returning to Przemyśl. He found "the Germans were already gone. The so-called Old Synagogue and the Temple were in ruins. The Scheinbeck Synagogue had been turned into a stable, and the entire Jewish area in and around Kazimierz the Great Street, one of the main streets of the city, had been completely destroyed."[31]

Chaplains, for their part, rejoiced that war raised their standing, like that of the churches as a whole. Looking back on his year in occupied Poland, Protestant Chaplain Schmidt with the 75th Infantry Division highlighted the many soldiers who had visited his office.[32] But challenges persisted. In early 1941, supervisory military chaplain Mayer-Ullmann and his Catholic counterpart Kostorz met with chaplains in southeastern Poland and divisional staff of AOK (Armee-Oberkommando – Field Army Command) 17 to discuss pastoral care to the military. The main concerns involved chaplains' requests for leave, access to fuel, and budgets: "The need for absolute frugality was particularly stressed."[33]

Sitzkrieg: Godly Germans, Godless French

If the Polish campaign taught chaplains to keep their mouths shut about German brutality, the "phoney war," *Sitzkrieg*, in the west offered an opportunity to claim the moral high ground. A set of photo albums from members of the 1st Army provides a view of Wehrmacht soldiers' actions and the chaplains' evolving message.[34] The photographs, some high-quality professional images, others amateur snapshots, document German perspectives on the short-lived French offensive in September–October 1939 in the Saar and its aftermath.[35]

Separately and together, the photos tell a story to vindicate German aggression and counter accusations of German barbarism.[36] One page includes three pictures of trashed interiors. The main caption reads: "After the French retreat." A photograph depicts a kitchen with food and dishes all over the floor and cupboard doors hanging open. It is labeled, "This is how they lived in the country. A picture of the mood in the village of Bebelsheim, after the French left. October 23, 1939." Another picture shows a hallway with smashed cabinets and bureau drawers on the floor: "This is how the French made themselves at home in Herbitzheim. October 10, 1939." A third photo fore-grounds empty shelves in a pantry, with food and furniture smashed and broken dishes on the floor: "Not the stormclouds of war but blind, destructive rage turned these homes into a desolate chaos. Hartungshof, October 21, 1939."[37] Evidently, it was not only in "the East" that Germans used the language of spiritual superiority over brutish foes.

Another page, ironically titled "French soldiers as bearers of culture," was a variation on the theme. A caption spelled out the line of thought: "The former homes of the local German people have become one big mess." The photo-graph showed a jumble of bedding, broken dishes, and smashed doors. A caption about "chaos" appeared over another photograph, and a photo of a counter surrounded by smashed furniture carried this caption: "Looted, ran-sacked, and left desolate – this is how the German shops in Bubenheim were found, after the riffraff was forced to clear out of the village."[38] More photos with the same themes followed: a page titled: "Soldiers of the 'grand nation' as bearers of culture" featured a photo of clothing strewn on a bed and on the floor with a caption that hinted at sexual as well as domestic violations: "befouled and defiled German homes in the village of Biringen."[39]

Similar pages followed, often repeating the captions. One page held two photos showing how the French dealt with the bodies of dead enemies. A picture of a pile of straw bore the label: "Sergeant Schnell, 2nd company, 87th Infantry Regiment, covered over with sod in a makeshift way by the French. Imagine how the others would shriek in protest if German soldiers buried their enemies like this." The second photo shows bodies on the ground, dirt covering their clothing: "Hastily and secretly buried dead comrades after their exhumation."[40] The following page reused the captions. One photo clearly shows a body stretched out, or at least a uniform and boots. The legs are so straight and flat, it appears staged. The second photo is also a body (or an empty uniform); no head is visible on either form.[41] A page titled, "This is how the French artillery abandons their former position," shifted the theme to French mistreatment of their own dead. A picture of an uncovered body, face down in the dirt, bears the caption: "a dead French soldier in the 'great forest.'"[42]

Christianity is showcased in a number of photographs. An image of the ravaged shrine of a saint is offered as evidence of French enmity toward religion.[43] One page holds three related photos (Figure 3.2). The top one shows a wrecked interior with a table, chairs, and torn-up paper and books on the floor: "Überherrn. December 10, 1939 – ravaged rectory. Evidence of the spread of French culture. For a short time the French occupied the Catholic

Figure 3.2 A page from one of the photo albums of the 1st Army. The typed captions under each photograph distill key themes in the official German view of the war in late 1939: the French as lackeys of the English and atheist, nihilist destroyers of Christian civilization, the Germans as guardians of virtue. BArch RH 20-1/353-030.

rectory. When the Germans arrived, they found it destroyed." Below, a photo shows shot up houses: "Zweibrücken. December 19, 1939. French grenades wrought this in the service of England." The photo beside those two depicts an altar with broken objects and rubble. The caption explains: "Überherrn. December 10, 1939. Carefully aimed shots destroyed the Catholic church, new proof of the ignominy of French culture."[44]

An ominous image shows a row of crude wooden crosses: "Stiftswald, November 6, 1939 – Graves of French colonial soldiers."[45] This is one of few acknowledgments I found of men of color in the French military. It appears in the same collection as a set of photographs depicting the Wehrmacht and its chaplains as defenders of Christianity and female honor – a reminder of the German panic about supposed sexual assaults of white women by Black occupation soldiers in the Rhineland. Protestant clergy were among the most vehement propagandists in that process.[46]

Figure 3.3 This page from a photo album of the 1st Army tells a story of Germans saving Christianity from the ravages of the French. At the center of the heroic narrative is a Wehrmacht chaplain. BArch RH 20-1/351-022.

Three photographs occupy an entire page devoted to chaplains. The top of the page bears a label: "Sauberg bei Unterfelsberg, Saving the Statue of Saint Oranna." The patron saint of Lorraine and the Saar, Oranna was (and is) often prayed to by single women hoping to find good husbands. The first photo shows a group of uniformed men around a small statue of a woman with a halo. A second image shows the same men walking along a river. One of them strides ahead of the others, bearing the statue on his shoulder. The third depicts the statue upright on a makeshift pedestal, holding her cross, which is carefully framed in the center of the shot. A man stands close by, perhaps admiring her or assessing her condition. The caption identifies him: "Sauberg bei Unterfelsberg, December 13, 1939. A divisional chaplain saves the statue of Saint Oranna from destruction. The French artillery was constantly shooting at the chapel of this patron saint, located right on the border."[47] The theme of chaplains as saviors of Christianity and preservers of churches and holy sites was already live in 1939; it would surge again two years later (Figure 3.3).

The final page in the collection turned to the past. A photo showed helmeted German soldiers walking by a sign for Spicheren: "January 2, 1940. Where our fathers fought in 1870, today the German soldier of the Third Reich does his duty."[48] Meanwhile, the Wehrmacht was preparing for a new round of attacks. A Protestant chaplain with the 1st Infantry Division reported on his experiences in the winter quarters in the Rhineland and Westphalia: "After arrival of the division in the staging area in the west at the beginning of November 1939, pastoral care, on instruction from the division commander, was immediately focused on the coming deployment in the west." His preparations included providing the troops with worship services. He held fifty-eight church services during the winter months, all of them joint celebrations with both confessions: "In by far most cases all of the troops participated." The chaplain also highlighted cooperation with the surrounding population:

The civilian congregations willingly made their churches available and also on their own initiative made sure that the services would be adorned with music. When the military worship services fell on the regular Sunday church time, civilian congregations mostly participated in very large numbers. From the correspondence I had later with family members of fallen soldiers, I learned that soldiers appreciated these church services and often wrote about them in their letters home.[49]

The chaplain's ministry "reached its high point at Christmas." Although the army chaplain with AOK 6 had called for "soldier priests" from the troops to help out with Christmas services, the division commander forbade it, so the chaplain alone held fourteen Christmas services over four days in December 1939. He also reported performing eighteen funerals, two weddings, one conversion, presumably from Catholic to Protestant Christianity, fourteen barracks hours, and eight celebrations of communion. He mentioned only two weak points: "The celebrations of communion during Lent were only moderately well attended," and he was unsuccessful in putting a military hymnal in the hand of "each and every Protestant soldier," because "after receiving 3,500 songbooks in November 1939, further deliveries stalled." He noted he had provided pastoral care to a soldier condemned to death by a military court, "so that he died peacefully and steadfastly."[50]

A report from Protestant Chaplain Bernhard Bauerle echoed these themes. Bauerle was with the 16th Army, which prior to the invasion in May, was located on both sides of the Mosel from the Rhine to the French-Luxembourg border. He characterized his activity as "**Preparation for the Worst Case**" (his emphasis): "Every opportunity was seized to 'promote and maintain the inner fighting power' of the soldiers and to contribute to it by 'arming them with emboldening and comforting faith' (*Merkblatt über Feldseelsorge*, August 21, 1939, section 1)." Everywhere people welcomed the military chaplain, Bauerle wrote: "Opposition, where it came up at all, independently

and not under the pressure of propaganda, came out of mostly false notions
about what the military chaplain actually does. Again and again officers, who
themselves do not profess Christian faith, have provided the support needed
for our service."[51]

Intrepid Explorers of the North

The German campaign in the north offered new material for the saga of
Wehrmacht chaplains. Their activity reports emphasized adventure and physical hardships, particularly in the Norwegian winter. The standardization of
reporting practices in 1940 coincided with a scenario more amenable to a
traditional heroic narrative – no mass killing of Christian clergy – and although
in Norway, too, the Luftwaffe terror-bombed civilians, the death tolls did not
approach the devastation in Poland. Chaplains reported on confessional
cooperation and rivalry; they carried wounded soldiers, namedropped, and
boasted about rubbing shoulders with generals. Always keen to prove their
value, they pushed back against insinuations that they were useless and weak.
Chaplains said little about German executions of Norwegian prisoners of war,
yet their reports reveal they were not only aware but directly involved at the
execution sites.

Gerhard May, Protestant chaplain with the 3rd Mountain Division, provided
an extensive report on his activities in Narvik in May and June 1940. By that
time, he had been with his unit since the annexation of Austria and through the
fighting in Poland. He submitted his report to the Protestant military bishop in
Berlin, replete with tales of military incompetence. After months of back and
forth, he finally managed to travel with a Red Cross transport, in civilian
clothing, from Berlin to Narvik. It was mid-May before he could report to the
divisional commander and receive his assignment:

above all to concern myself with the fighting troops, the soldiers and especially the
officers, with the goal that the positions must absolutely be held. I myself considered it
necessary to show the troops that the pastor was there with them, that he was just as
damp and dirty as they were and was cold just like the soldiers of the combat unit.[52]

Later, when a Catholic priest joined the unit, May noted, the two chaplains
arranged a division of labor: "He visited the military hospitals, conducted the
burials, and stayed closer by, while I ministered to the troops in the field."
Many teams of chaplains divided the work this way, which likely reflected the
lower status of the Catholics, celibate men, who were exempt from combat
service under the terms of the 1933 Concordat.

Chaplain May boasted of the days and nights he spent, disregarding warnings of danger, to seek out the posts closest to the front. Being so far north, he
reminded his readers, "it never got dark." And so it turned out that he once

went "three days and two nights – 60 hours – without sleep, on the road without a break."[53] He visited a paratrooper company where he bonded with a young lieutenant, and the two men, "lying on our backs, watched an eagle circling overhead." The most distant group of paratroopers was surprised to see a pastor: "Some of them laugh and don't know how they should behave." Pastor May won their respect and that of all the men he encountered, he claimed, by showing no fear. As submachine gun fire whistled overhead, he remained sitting calmly on a cliff, eating his dinner. Later he empowered a group of men struggling to carry a wounded comrade across a steep glacier: "The wounded man (shot in the chest), has been tied with wire to two boards. He moans and keeps sliding down. We deeply doubt whether we will be able to get him across the glacier in one piece. ... If anyone should slip, the stretcher with the wounded man will smash into the rocks below." As the chaplain told it, his faith and strength steadied the men:

I call a halt, hang the cross around my neck, and briefly speak words of comfort to the soldiers and the wounded man. Then I say a short prayer, followed by the Lord's Prayer and a blessing on the wounded man. Some of the stretcher carriers get down on their knees. I believe all of them feel the burden of responsibility for their comrade. Then, trading off, six men at a time carry the wounded man. After three-quarters of an hour, we have crossed the glacier.[54]

A second tale recounted triumph over another foe: anti-Christian attitudes. Chaplain May described arriving at Hill 961 during a snowstorm. He found the company leader, whom he knew "radically rejects any kind of Christian ministry," huddled with two officers, shivering from the cold. May insisted he would remain on the mountain overnight: "when all of you are freezing, I can be too." Content, the company leader gave him his hand. The chaplain saw a soldier wrapped in a damp blanket, face down on the rocks, groaning and shaking so hard "the spasms lift his entire body. I haul him out of the hole and make him walk with me." After touring around the mountain to visit the individual posts, Chaplain May returned to the company leader: "We part as good comrades."

Already during the Polish campaign, May wrote, he had argued that it was not a good idea to assign the chaplain to the division staff, because then, "as for example in Poland, there is absolutely no possibility for active engagement." During deployment in Norway, too, he contended, the "hardest blow" for chaplains was that they were attached to army staff:

You cannot talk to soldiers about living courageously and dying at peace, and then, when the time comes to suffer deprivation and bear a heavy load, sit somewhere safe and sound. Our preaching then loses its credibility with the soldiers, who see us more as a kind of propaganda speaker who is hired and paid for that. If the German military is going to have chaplains, and pastoral care in the field is carried out according to the

"Guidelines" for the "furthering and maintenance of inner fighting power" of the troops, then the chaplains who offer that pastoral care have to be given the chance to live as an example together with the fighting troops.

It was essential to "win the trust of officers and men," May urged, because, "without trust, all the beautiful words mean nothing." He closed on a practical note. The fighting around Narvik proved that a pastor with the mountain troops "absolutely has to know how to ski and must have the physical strength and fitness to climb mountains." Accordingly, also in peacetime, May opined, chaplains should have opportunities to take courses in skiing and mountain climbing.[55]

One task that often fell to chaplains was offloaded in Norway. In January 1941, German Army High Command stipulated that Norwegian authorities were responsible for the labor and expense of maintaining military graves, including graves of German soldiers and enemy soldiers who fell in battle or died during World War I and also the present war.[56]

Chaplains boasted that they drew good crowds and improved soldiers' moral behavior. In February 1941, Supervisory Chaplain Winkler, writing on behalf of his Catholic colleague too, reported that the chaplains' work, always conducted "within the framework of the relevant guidelines," was warmly appreciated. An inner bond with God was the secret to deepening a soldier's sense of moral responsibility, Winkler insisted.[57] He rejoiced that everywhere people were starting to understand the chaplain was not "filling his currently widely contested office for the sake of some dubious religious denomination, but rather that in his service he recognizes only *one* goal: connecting the German soldier inwardly to God, in whose name he swears his oath of allegiance to the Führer."[58]

In their joint report for May 1941, the Protestant and Catholic chaplains with AOK in Norway noted that their efforts in Oslo, though barely visible to outsiders, brought blessings to countless soldiers. The two army chaplains held regular Sunday services for members of the Wehrmacht as well as civilians posted there. "Attendance at these services is always good," they insisted, and it would be even better if the events were announced properly. Often soldiers who want to come do not, they noted, because they did not know about it: "In the face of such deliberate dismissal of military chaplaincy, there is nothing a chaplain can do." Yet the chaplains persisted, including with unpopular work: "Along with the regular visitation of men who have been arrested and inmates in the military prison, there is also a service there once a month and on holidays."[59]

The report, though on the surface proper, had an undertone of complaint, even defiance. Although Winkler submitted it in his name and Kuffner's, evidently the latter was not comfortable with its contents. The version

I found in the file is a copy, verified by Chaplain Kuffner and sent to AOK Norway in August 1941.[60] So what was happening here? Who made this copy of the report? Was it being used against Winkler? It appears so, and evidently Kuffner was behind it, a suggestion that confessional cooperation was not perfect.

There were other issues in Norway, too. At the end of June 1941, the activity report of the 20th Mountain Army included a short appendix labeled "secret," with the heading "Prisoners of War." "The former chief of staff of General [Otto] Ruge, Colonel [Halvor] Hansson, after being held for a lengthy period in interrogation detention, has been transferred to Germany as a prisoner of war. The reason: unverifiable attempted subversive activities."[61]

The Wehrmacht also committed atrocities in Norway. In his report for the last months of 1941, Pastor Pohlmann, Protestant chaplain with the 710th Infantry Division, reported on a trip he took in the near northern sector, specifically to Luftwaffe units. On December 3–4, he provided "pastoral care at the shooting" (execution by firing squad) of "three Norwegians." On December 28–29, he provided "pastoral care at the shooting of 11 Norwegians." Meanwhile, he paid multiple visits to "the sick men in the almost empty Luftwaffe hospital at Gardemoen, and he held a military Christmas worship service there on December 26."[62] This was all under the command of General von Falkenhorst, who was sentenced to death in 1946 by the British for crimes including executing POWs.[63]

Blitzkrieg, Again, in the Low Countries and France

When the Wehrmacht embarked on another round of "lightning wars" in May 1940, and when they produced smashing successes, it must have seemed a golden opportunity for the chaplains. Many of them had been dreaming for years of triumphant Germans singing hymns and praising God in lofty cathedrals. But rather than euphoria, chaplains' reports for the period express uncertainty, even ambivalence. How did the dazzling German offensives fit into a narrative of the war built around Christian notions of righteousness, sacrifice, and justice? How to spin the attack on the neutral Netherlands, or, for that matter, neutral Denmark and Belgium? Was vanquished France an atheist enemy or a Christian partner? Given the Wehrmacht's rapid victories, were chaplains really necessary or useful at all? Chaplains' reports reflect these and other questions through contradictions and silences.

No chaplains' reports mention the bombing of Rotterdam in May 1940. In fact, there are almost no mentions of the Netherlands at all, and those I found were fleeting. One Protestant division chaplain ended up temporarily as a prisoner of the Dutch.[64] Another, Chaplain Roussig with the 12th Infantry

Division, reported in March 1941 from winter quarters in Holland, that he buried sixteen dead in the period, including four men from the Luftwaffe.[65]

Protestant Bernhard Bauerle, chaplain of the 16th Army, captured numerous tensions in a detailed report of the invasion of France. His boasts about chaplains hint at the accusations of inadequacy he sought to counter. In combat, Bauerle declared, all Protestant chaplains had done their duty "with absolute energy and joy, at the front with the fighting troops, at the dressing stations, and in the military hospitals. There were no 'shirkers' among them." None had been wounded, even though they regularly "accompanied the fighting troops into the heaviest combat." A group of them received the Iron Cross second class, and two, Bauerle noted, were decorated with the Iron Cross first class.[66]

Still their efforts and impacts remained largely invisible, Bauerle worried. As army chaplain, he was constantly on the move and managed only once in the reporting period, on August 2, to hold a "service of Gratitude and Commemoration" for the entire staff of the Field Army Command. Instead he held funerals – 250 of them for "fallen comrades" – and attempted to "gather as many comrades as possible at the grave and preach a short message to them of life and service that continues 'forward over the graves,' and to speak to them of faith that also gives meaning to the ultimate sacrifice." His most important contribution, in other words, was associated with death.

When the army chaplain – Bauerle often spoke of himself in the third person – visited the hospitals, he found the attitude of the seriously wounded men to be "incredible!" [*fabelhaft!*] After these visits, he had to spend hours writing the letters that the wounded men wanted sent to their families, based on notes he took at their bedside or as they lay on a stretcher. For the chaplain, he declared, "the most wonderful service of all is with the fighting troops." Officers and men at the front had often told him how much they valued the chaplain who "voluntarily shares their danger." Indeed, he insisted that the credibility of the "soldier-priest" depended on him putting himself in peril, like every soldier. Accordingly, as army chaplain, Bauerle instructed "his chaplains" to be with the fighting troops, and he himself sought out the various units: "the artillery under fire, infantry during the offensive, individual observation posts way at the front, or people who, with totally inadequate cover are under artillery fire." Always "gratefully accepted was a chaplain's help binding up the wounded."[67]

Wehrmacht authorities had forbidden chaplains from informing families of a death. Bauerle found a way to acknowledge that limitation while asserting the importance of the chaplain's work: "The first notification goes through the troop. But a pile of letters of thanks from loved ones shows how grateful they are when they receive a personal greeting from the pastor, who was there at the grave to give the final service to a comrade, and who can sketch for them the funeral, etc." Bauerle gave an example from the letter of a pilot's widow:

This is why my gratitude to you is so especially heartfelt, because you wrote to me about the final honor that anyone could give to the person who was the dearest to me of everything in the world. I also thank you from the bottom of my heart for the words of comfort. I value them as the greatest that you could write to me, although my faith is different than yours.

It was no coincidence that Bauerle chose to include as his sole example a letter from the wife of a man in the Luftwaffe, the branch of the military with no chaplains. Indeed, his report demonstrated an uncomfortable fact: in the Nazi system, the most potent proof of chaplains' value came from people who did not value chaplains. He made sure his readers got the message that in wartime, even neo-pagans needed Christianity: "It is noticeable, how often the loved ones ask whether their son received a cross on his grave." No one, he implied, had asked for a rune.[68]

Bauerle closed with a flourish. The chaplain, he insisted, was necessary if the motto on the belt buckle – "*Gott mit uns*" – was to be more than "an empty phrase." The work of soldiers was far too serious for "sloganizing," he wrote, "because the soldier understands that these words *must* be there to continually remind him of his responsibility before God and to strengthen his heart with the power that comes from faith." Bauerle admitted that young men, in particular, were not always "ready to heed this call," but they all appreciated being prepared for "the final emergency." He had seen the proof, he wrote, in hundreds of cases in the military hospitals, "where soldiers, who have left the church, ask the military chaplain to pray with them at their bedside and are grateful for what he has to say."[69]

The Wehrmacht belt buckle features in another source from the period, as a sign of ambivalence in the German–French relationship. In *Suite Française,* her brilliantly observed novel of France in 1940 and 1941, written in "real time," before her own arrest, transport to Auschwitz and murder, the Russian-French-Jewish-Christian author Irène Némirovsky shows the motto, "*Gott mit uns,*" as both dividing and connecting conquerors and conquered. The last scenes in the book are set in late June 1941, as the German occupiers prepared a grand celebration at the Château de Montmort. Swastika flags fluttered in the breeze, cooks prepared delicacies, and regimental musicians practiced in the village square:

Meanwhile, an enormous young German with huge thighs and a fat bottom that threatened to split his tight riding breeches entered the Hôtel des Voyageurs and, for the third time, asked to look at the barometer. It was still set at fair. The German, beaming with delight, said, "Nothing to worry about. No storm tonight. *Gott mit uns.*"[70]

The slogan signals the Germans' pompous tactlessness at the same time as it links them to the lighthearted French villagers, who share the man's "innocent delight":

And the German slapped everyone on the back with a wide grin while repeating, "*Gott mit uns.*"

"Sure, sure, *Got meedns.* He's drunk, that Fritz," they whispered behind his back rather sympathetically. "We know what it's like. He's been celebrating since yesterday ... He's a big lad ... Well, so what! Why shouldn't they have fun? They're men after all."[71]

In her study of German soldiers and the occupation of France, Julia Torrie makes the point that for Germans, France was an attractive destination and maintaining it as a "welcome respite" had advantages for the occupiers, even though doing so required some managing.[72] Comparable balancing acts are evident in chaplains' accounts, too. During the period of the "phoney war," the image of the godless French fit a narrative of Germans as defenders of Christendom. Now, however, after the fall of France, Germans were prepared to be benevolent and to enjoy the pleasures they associated with France.

Some Wehrmacht chaplains ministered to their defeated foes. A Protestant chaplain with the 12th Infantry Division described a visit to wounded men in Longue on the momentous day of June 22, 1940. Along with the Germans, there were quite a few wounded and sick French men, who had been captured in the attack at the Loire. Most of these were ensigns from the Cavalry School of Saumur, by his description, "intelligent and open-minded men, who had fought very hard." Now, he reported, they had pressing questions: "'Why has France been so unfortunate?' That is one of the questions we discussed. They themselves offered the answer: Many French people in the last generation have become completely superficial and have forgotten God. Now France in her misery must do penance."[73]

Such ideas came up frequently with captured French soldiers, the chaplain observed, and he "also found with some of them a genuine piety." However, he hastened to dial back that positive assessment:

And yet I could not get rid of the impression that the wonderful gothic cathedrals of Amiens, Beauvais, Paris, Chartres, Poitiers, and Bayonne were only witnesses of a religious energy of the past. Today, as in other areas of life, people are obsessed with possessions from bygone days. On the whole, the churches and clergy make a primitive impression and reflect a dying piety.

Still he closed with affirmation of French potential: "But I do think it is possible that the current collapse of France may release pent-up sources of religious life."[74]

Other chaplains depicted the Germans and the French as united by Christianity. A Catholic chaplain in the Vendée praised soldiers' participation

in church services as "very widespread and very joyous." It also helped
relations with the French people: "The good and respectful attitude of our
people in the local churches, the choir-like prayer that felt like it had been
ingrained through long practice, the energetic joining in to sing – all made a
powerful impression on the local people who observed us."[75] His Protestant
colleague in the Vendée echoed and extended the theme:

In all of the services of worship during the early time, the thoughts of the fallen ones
and thanks for God's help were in the center. The first service of this type took place
with massive participation in La Roche sur Yon on June 30, 1940, and made a profound
impression, not only on the comrades who were involved, but also at least as much on
the French population.

Then on to Normandy, where particularly memorable was "a purely Protestant
service, but in a Catholic church." As in the Vendée and later in Holland, the
chaplain wrote, "the people everywhere were deeply impressed by our worship
services."[76]

Jewish sources provide an important reminder that Christianity bound some
French people to the German occupiers but isolated others. After the fall of
France, while the Wehrmacht chaplains were praying with wounded soldiers
and arranging church services, a small group of French Jewish rabbis, organized as chaplains in 1939, devoted themselves to aid work among Jewish
prisoners in detention camps.[77] A handful of these rabbis, all young men in
their thirties and forties, remained connected to the Vichy regime and were the
first to provide assistance to the 40,000 "foreign Jews" incarcerated in the
unoccupied zone as of 1941.

All of the Wehrmacht chaplains' reports from France mixed positive and
negative impressions, of their own performance, the support they received, and
the men they served. In a report dated June 24, 1940, Robert Franke, Catholic
Wehrmacht dean and chaplain with AOK 16, assessed the "performance of the
chaplains of the division" as "consistently very good." With chaplains at the
military hospitals, he observed, "performance varied according to experience
and other factors."[78] Overall, Franke complained, the number of chaplains
with the division was far too small, and they could not fully carry out their
duties, even working day and night.[79] Still, he concluded, "the soldiers were
always glad to have the chaplains with them" – he added a cryptic parenthetical remark – "(whether they knew it was the chaplain or not)."[80]

Chaplain Hermann's report from late August 1940 gave a glowing account
of pastoral care to the 18th Army before, during, and after the invasion of
France. The goal was "to boost the morale of the soldiers and arm them with
emboldening and comforting faith," and the "relationship of trust between
chaplains and troops proved itself in the most difficult circumstances."[81]
During combat, chaplains did important work in the military hospitals, he

explained, with a hint that their fellow Germans were not necessarily support-ive: "Often there, because the doctors and medical personnel are so over-worked, the chaplain is the only person who can address the mental and physical needs of the comrades. (In particular with amputees and with regard to communicating with loved ones back home.)" The chaplain, perhaps con-cerned that he sounded too critical, crossed out the word "overwork" (*Überarbeitung*) and replaced it with another, meaning "extreme demands" (*Überbeanspruchung*).

Chaplain Hermann's section on burials also conveyed mixed messages. He quoted the February 1940 Instructions from Army High Command: "The chaplain's participation in the burial of fallen soldiers is, when requested, always to be given priority over other duties of the office." This was widely carried out, he assured his readers, "to the extent that the resources were available." The scarce "resources" he alluded to were a vehicle and fuel, which he noted were needed to get chaplains to those burials. An attempt to highlight the warm reception of his work came across as defensive: "Pastoral care, which was never forced on anyone, was refused in only a very few individual cases."[82]

Catholic Army Chaplain Klum had sharper things to say about the fuel problem. He too cited Army Instructions, specifically Section 5, "that the chaplaincy should serve not only the wounded and sick but, above all, the combat troops." To do so, he pointed out, chaplains had to be mobile. The shortage of gasoline obstructed the mission and undermined the chaplaincy, because it "easily led to the suspicion that chaplains are not that concerned about pastoral care."[83]

Though mindful of their mission to support the troops, chaplains' reports expressed ambivalence and even outright criticism of German soldiers. A Protestant chaplain with the 1st Infantry Division acknowledged that during the campaign in the west, he "encountered Nicodemus types, who were genuine religious seekers, among the officers and men." The reference is to Nicodemus in the Gospel of John, a man who comes to Jesus with questions. But, the chaplain continued, they were exceptions. Especially in the days without fighting, he noted, German soldiers enacted certain vices: "Homes and towns showed signs of having been plundered, and German soldiers were involved, too. Also I heard complaints that they knowingly used counterfeit money to pay for things, with an intention to cheat people." Two chaplains were not enough to deal with the men of an entire division, he complained, because "precisely with such cases, where inner rot is beginning to set in, disciplinary and legal measures cannot have a decisive impact in the long run." Instead, there had to be "a change in attitudes that comes from the inside." Change of this sort, the chaplain intoned, "as Luther teaches, never comes from the law but rather through the Gospel."[84]

The Wehrmacht chaplains worried about their soldiers and sex, sexually transmitted diseases, alcohol, and suicide. They were especially preoccupied with sexual improprieties of Germans in France.[85] In April 1941, a Protestant pastor with the 95th Infantry Division near Amiens reported on his work providing pastoral care in the military hospitals. The challenges in times of calm, he insisted, "were much greater than in times of combat. Wounded soldiers are more open to pastoral care than, for example, those with stomach illnesses or rheumatism, or those with venereal diseases, who at times like this make up the majority of the patients." His recommendation was for chaplains to present lectures, "especially lectures with slides, which delivered on site are gratefully accepted by those confined to their beds and create opportunities for pastoral care."[86]

A surprising contrast to the image of the heroic Wehrmacht is the frequency of chaplains' references to soldiers condemned to death. In his report from July 1940, a Catholic chaplain addressed "special cases." These involved execution of a German soldier: "In Brest, I prepared a man for his execution. He had been condemned to death twice and to fifteen years of prison, for murder, attempted murder, and rape. After several visits he came to see the despicable and criminal nature of his deeds and regretted what he had done. He received the holy sacrament and died calmly and at peace."[87] Note here the charges included rape.[88] In April 1941, a Catholic chaplain with the 12th Infantry Division reported on "the pastoral care provided to four soldiers condemned to death, whom we two chaplains took turns visiting and whom we accompanied with our support during their final nights and up to the execution of their sentence by firing squad."[89]

Already these early reports include a surprising number of military executions. In early 1941, a Protestant chaplain provided pastoral care to a condemned Luftwaffe deserter in Belgium. Dr. theol. Krummacher with the 208th Infantry Division elaborated: "The execution of a soldier condemned to death by military court for twice deserting was carried out without participation from the division at the high commander post in Brussels." Krummacher's report noted that "Chaplain Dr. Franzen, who is posted to Brussels, carried out the pastoral care in this case very meticulously."[90] In 1940, Germans tried to tread carefully in Belgium to avoid a repeat of the public relations debacle of 1914.[91] From the Vendée in April 1941, another Protestant chaplain reported burying fifty dead and "providing pastoral care to five soldiers condemned to death."[92]

Christian Burials

Victorious as the Wehrmacht was in 1940 and 1941, chaplains still had to face the reality of casualties. Their reports emphasized the vital presence of chaplains in providing proper, Christian burials for the dead, at least those they deemed deserving. The first deaths of chaplains at the front also occurred in this period. In August 1940, the Protestant chaplain with the 18th Army announced that during operations in France, two Catholic chaplains fell, and two Protestant chaplains were wounded.[93] Less than a year later, Chaplain Robert Franke, who supervised Catholic pastoral care to the 16th Army in June 1940, suffered a fatal accident. The obituary took note that he died in military hospital, after receiving last rites.[94]

Catholic and Protestant chaplains alike emphasized the importance of administering the sacraments, notably last rites and also communion and absolution, including general absolution. The 5th Panzer Division played a prominent part in the campaign in the west. Its Protestant Chaplain Gleditsch described his activities from May 10 to July 12, 1940:

In general I visited the troops in the morning, to the extent that was possible, and the main dressing stations in the afternoon. ... Toward evening I turned to burying the comrades who died at the dressing stations, in the process of which I organized the layout of the graves, held the funeral services, and registered the personal information, number of the identifying marker, and location of the grave.[95]

In the process, he observed, "I often encountered deep religious yearnings that went beyond what I expected."

Pastor Gleditsch made sure to mention that services during the campaign in the west were carried out according to the "Guidelines on Pastoral Care to the Military," that is, not divided by confession but with Protestants and Catholics together.[96] Still, he and his Catholic counterpart followed the by-now familiar division of labor:

After the end of the last period of fighting, on June 26, once the ceasefire with France came into effect, the Division put on a large military celebration with a religious consecration in Brest, for the units located there. I presided over the service of Thanksgiving to God, and Father Gehrmann performed the service to honor the dead.

Chaplain Gleditsch listed the men he had buried and where: there were around fifty of them, with the largest number being fifteen in Ailly-le-Haut-Clocher on June 6 and another ten there on June 5.[97]

Dealing with dead and dying soldiers was at the heart of chaplains' self-presentation. In July 1940, a Catholic chaplain with the 5th Panzer Division submitted his activity report covering "the time of action in the campaign in Belgium and France." He highlighted "the particular situation of the armored division," the vanguard force of the Blitzkrieg. Constant, relentless combat created special circumstances for pastoral care, he explained. Much of his work was concentrated in the hospitals and dressing stations, where he reported "excellent cooperation with our medical companies." His practice was to first walk through to see to the wounded and inquire about their wishes: "In the process, many pastoral care conversations with the wounded started naturally." He felt welcome and needed:

I always had the *Sanctissimum* with the holy oil for the sick with me and often in serious cases was able to administer the holy sacraments. In two months I only met one man who did not wish to receive the holy sacrament. Much in demand, especially among the less seriously wounded, was reading matter, including religious literature.[98]

Of course, he never had enough or an adequate selection.

The chaplain highlighted the "positive mood that one found everywhere at the main dressing stations." News from the front was eagerly received, and "everyone's desire was to return to the troops as quickly as possible." He considered it to go without saying "that after providing pastoral care to the wounded Germans, we also saw to the spiritual needs of the wounded Belgians and Frenchmen"; the word he used was *selbstverständlich* (of course).

Usually after visiting the wounded, the chaplains took care of funerals. "These were performed by both chaplains together, when Catholic and Protestant comrades were to be buried together. In the entire campaign I counted 49 dead (48 German and French officers and men, and one child, who was wounded by a grenade splinter), whom I sent to their eternal rest. Their names are listed." But by far the majority of the fallen had to be buried without a priest, the chaplain lamented, even though officers and soldiers alike valued Christianity: "The strong inner bond of the troops is clear from the fact that in the 11 Catholic services I held, often with numerically very small units, I administered 1,020 holy communions. In total, 95–98% of all those present received the holy sacrament."[99]

Other records from this period confirm that chaplains did make an effort to bury at least some French and English soldiers with dignity and recognition of their shared Christianity. An official photo album with high quality images of the 1st Army at the front, from November 1939 to January 1940, has jolly scenes, like two smiling men on bikes with a cart between them, labeled "Walsheim, November 18, 1939. Two grunts found a keg of beer, which they now cheerfully bring to their bunker in a child's wagon."[100] A chaplain appears on a more somber image: coffins draped in flags, with a clergyman in robes standing on front of them, his hands clasped as he addresses a group of helmeted Germans. The fact they kept their helmets on is a clue, but the caption makes it clear who was in those coffins: "November 9, 1939 – Burial in Kreuznach of three Englishmen who were shot down."[101] Another image shares the caption, showing German soldiers in their helmets carrying the coffins, about to lower them into graves.

At this stage of the war, Wehrmacht chaplains ministered openly to at least some of Germany's enemies. The album of the 1st Army devotes two pages to an event in January, 1940: "Burial of the English First Lieutenant Everitt." One photo shows men in a cemetery, draping flags on a coffin, with crosses visible in the background. Another, a face-on view of soldiers next to the coffin, is captioned: "Weißkirchen, January 11, 1940. Honor guard at the tomb of the English First Lieutenant Everitt, who was seriously wounded when he came into German captivity and died shortly after he was captured."[102] Additional photos of Everitt's funeral show a lot of German soldiers present, to witness and provide musical accompaniment, as "the fallen English First Lieutenant is buried with military honors." And yes, the chaplain was there, too. A page with four photos includes one with the caption: "Sermon of the army chaplain at the grave of the English First Lieutenant Everitt." The cross around the neck identifies the chaplain and foreshadows the markers on the graves on the adjacent photograph (Figure 3.4).[103]

Such images of German chaplains turned evidence of casualties the Wehrmacht had caused into an assertion of moral superiority to the supposedly secular, degenerate English and French. Another numbered series of photographs depicts more graves, a mix of German and French soldiers. One image is a snowy cemetery, with no people visible: "Near Wedelsheim, December 31, 1939. Snow covers the graves of our heroes, who fought and died for Germany's glory and security." Below it, two pictures of barbed wire and snow share a caption: "Spicheren, January 15, 1940. Graves from two wars – Under the stone cross to the right rear is a French soldier who fell in 1870; the cross in the foreground marks graves of French soldiers from this war; the rectangular wooden grave marker indicates the resting place of a Moroccan." Notice the half-moon symbol (Figure 3.5).[104]

French and German dead mingle on another page, too. One photo depicts snow-covered shapes under a tree with a board nailed on it to form a cross: "Near Saarbrücken, December 31, 1939. Here lie two Frenchmen, who died in the October fighting in the High Forest." Next to it is another caption and image: "Zweibrücken, December 31, 1939. Snow covers the graves of our heroes, who fought and died for Germany's glory and security." Presumably the curator of the album intended to contrast the unkempt graves of the un-Christian French with the orderly German cemetery.[105]

Greece: War as Tourism

Wehrmacht chaplains' reports from Greece overflowed with excitement about being in the cradle of antiquity. Hans Radtke, a Protestant chaplain with the 12th Army in Greece, collected a full set of guides for the German soldier, printed in Athens to help the invaders maximize their opportunity for tourism. He pronounced them extremely useful. Passionate about antiquity, Radtke seized the chance to visit sites he had read about since childhood.[106]

Figure 3.4 A photo album of the 1st Army devoted two pages to the burial with full military honors of English Lieutenant Everitt in January 1940. Lieutenant Everitt was killed by German machine gun fire near the border with northern France. According to the War Diary of the Royal Norfolk Regiment, P. A. J. Everitt was the first British Patrol to cross into Germany during World War II. The grand ceremonial funeral, featuring a Protestant Wehrmacht chaplain, was a display of German martial piety. BArch RH 20-1/352-033.

Figure 3.5 The 1st Army albums include many photographs of graves. This page is unusual because it shows graves from 1940 and 1870, for German and French soldiers, and also for one Moroccan soldier. Cemeteries and graves became increasingly important sites for the Wehrmacht chaplains. Many served as graves officers for their units, and those with access to a camera took pictures of graves to send to bereaved families. BArch RH 20-1/352-034.

Catholic Chaplain Schloss, with Military Command Southeast, reported for April–June 1941, the period "of the operations against Yugoslavia and Greece." He mentioned a series of meetings in early April with Orthodox churchmen, including Archbishop Kyrill von Plovdiv in Sofia, from whom he and his Protestant counterpart requested permission to use Orthodox churches for military church services. Permission was granted. In the afternoon he buried Alfons Kauka, a soldier who died in a fatal accident, in the military cemetery in Sofia. He also performed a funeral there for the SS man Lauritsch, followed by a tour of the city with "Stormtrooper leader Drexl."[107] In Greece, as in other areas further from the center of Nazi power in Berlin, chaplains' contact with SS and Luftwaffe increased.

Chaplain Schloss was kept busy with funerals for German and Bulgarian soldiers and officers and also some civilians. Conversations with officers and men in the military hospital in Dupnica demonstrated that the work of the chaplains, "in particular in caring for the wounded," was universally welcomed: "A captain told how he had been wounded near the Catholic chaplain of the 18th Army who immediately bound up his wounds."[108] In Sofia, Chaplain Schloss was able to acquire hosts and holy oil and bury more soldiers before heading to Athens. There he met with the Catholic Archbishop Philopucci to arrange for use of the churches in that city for military worship services. Again, he found "absolute agreement and cooperation." He personally set up pastoral care for Catholic prisoners of war in Piräus and in the Polytechnikum, and he welcomed chaplains Walter and Goes to the military hospitals in Athens. A conference he convened for chaplains in the region closed with a tour of the Acropolis, led by Chaplain Dechamps, "an art expert."[109]

Traveling constantly, Chaplain Schloss visited countless hospitals and dressing stations, including in Kyustendil, where among the ninety-five wounded and sick soldiers and officers, an SS major lay: "He proved to be especially happy and grateful for my visit." In the military hospital in Dupnica, he was up until late into the night with the seriously wounded men, "carrying out their religious and private wishes (correspondence with loved ones)." There he also made his first visits to wounded Greek soldiers, some of whom had had their feet amputated. He made sure to visit the sick, including those with typhus and scarlet fever. His appearance attracted special attention from a large ward full of wounded officers, he noted. Elsewhere, he encountered a seriously wounded medical student who was feeling down because he had lost his left arm. The chaplain tried to raise his spirits by telling him that in Dupnica, he had met a professional painter who had lost his *right* arm but stayed positive and even cracked jokes to cheer up his roommates.[110]

Chaplain Schloss managed to get to Thessaloniki, Larissa, Thebes, and many other places. In Thessaloniki, he visited sick and wounded German soldiers in the "Hirsch Lazarett," a military hospital in the building named for the Jewish philanthropist Baron Hirsch. When they arrived in Thessaloniki, the historic center of Sephardic Jewry, the Wehrmacht had seized the hospital for their purposes. German military authorities also took charge of registering Jewish men in the city for forced labor, a process that got into full swing in 1942. Likewise, Wehrmacht officials spearheaded the inventorying, appropriating, and distributing of the possessions and businesses of the 45,000 Jews in Thessaloniki.[111] The chaplain did not mention any of these enormous and public programs of plunder, of which he was a direct beneficiary.

In May, Chaplain Schloss took charge of pastoral care for some wounded English soldiers and an officer in Ekali. Like his colleagues in France, he seemed to consider it obvious that German chaplains and doctors would treat at least some wounded enemies, in this case Greek and English men. In a hospital on Crete, he visited the Protestant military bishop and the Catholic Chaplain Witte, who were ill with dysentery. Another Catholic chaplain, Anton Gerritschen with the 50th Infantry Division, was killed by an enemy grenade. The obituary noted Father Gerritschen was the fifth Catholic military chaplain to die "in the struggle for Germany's glory and freedom." It praised him as "one of our best, a selfless priest after the heart of God, a faithful idealist and a manly brave soldier."[112] Chaplain Gerritschen was buried with military honors at the new military cemetery in Dupnica.

Together with a military judge, Army Chaplain Schloss traveled to Rila to participate in the tribunal regarding a German pioneer named Weiß, who had been charged with desertion. "To me and the others he came across as a feeble-minded and cowardly person," the chaplain wrote. Was it usual for a chaplain to participate in the investigation and not just at the execution of an accused soldier? Just days after the deliberations involving Weiß, the chaplain prepared another man, in prison in Corinth, for execution. Hofer, the man in question, was a veteran of World War I. Now he met his fate "calmly and fully prepared." The chaplain visited him regularly and provided him with reading material up until he was sent on to Vienna, presumably for the sentence to be carried out.[113]

Under the heading of "problems and requests," Chaplain Schloss listed familiar challenges. It was very difficult to get around, and he needed more timely information in order to stay in touch with troops at the front, he noted. Chaplains Schraff and Witte in Bankja had told him they could not fulfill their duties, because they had neither field kits nor a vehicle. He closed by summing up his activities: "giving the sacraments to healthy and sick soldiers, facilitating their wishes, writing letters for the wounded who could not write, and providing advice and encouragement, for which everyone was grateful."[114]

Protestant Chaplain Radtke characterized the situation in Romania and Bulgaria as marked by constant movement and immense distances, which made his job difficult. The time immediately before the operation against Greece had been especially fruitful, he wrote, because in the face of "uncertainty about their fate in the battles ahead," soldiers were receptive to pastoral care. "Also in this period, many people wanted to take communion." Like his Catholic counterpart, he emphasized how grateful everyone was for the chaplains' presence. They had been able to bury the majority of the dead, he reported, with the exception of the Panzer divisions, where they only got to half of them.

The conquest of Crete had posed particular challenges, Radtke wrote. During the fighting, five Protestant chaplains, Radtke included, were active on the island. Chaplain Schütz served the paratroopers, while the mountain troops had their own divisional chaplain. Radtke noted with pride that a Protestant chaplain, Dr. vom Berg, who had held the first military church service at the Oster Gate twenty minutes after Germans conquered the citadel in Belgrade, had also been active in the days of combat on Crete.[115]

The sightseeing and action in southeastern Europe came with side effects for soldiers and the chaplains who served them. A Catholic army chaplain reported to Military Bishop Rarkowski about the first quarter of 1941: "The saddest of all experiences in Romania," he grumbled, "was the noticeably rapid and massive increase in the number of sexually transmitted diseases, which in the Balkans are particularly severe and treacherous."[116]

Army Chaplain Schloss summed up the key points from the reports chaplains down the chain of command had submitted to him. He observed that attendance at religious services and celebrations was on average very good among the fighting troops, so-so among rear units, especially among the staff, and downright bad in many cases. It was starkly obvious, he maintained, that wild sexual behavior increased wherever religious life had fallen off and soldiers had time on their hands. As an antidote, he suggested "private meetings with the military chaplain and more emphasis on the barracks hours, making them compulsory." On the bright side, he mentioned he had held a religious service with three seriously wounded Italian soldiers, "who were delighted to have an Italian-speaking Catholic priest to hear their confession." And he continued to be thrilled about all the beautiful buildings where he and his fellow chaplains could hold services and the large congregations they attracted, including generals and many soldiers.[117]

In Yugoslavia and Greece the familiar anti-Communist claims did not hold, because those were not Communist territories and anyway, the first half of 1941 was still the Molotov–Ribbentrop period. Yet the Wehrmacht was embroiled in atrocities against civilians there, with reprisal killings and killing of, and encouragement or allowing the killing of, Serbs, Jews, and Roma by the Ustasha. Chaplains were definitely present and aware, as expressed by the Protestant chaplain with the 1st Mountain Division in Greece, in August 1943, where German soldiers killed 317 civilians in a village. In his official report he wrote that "the mass killing of women and children during operations against the bandits" was creating a "difficult inner burden on the conscience of many men."[118]

Ready for New Challenges

Chaplains' reports make it clear that they were actively involved in preparing for the invasion of Soviet territory in 1941. According to Protestant chaplain Dr. Bergfried, one of the highlights of his summer was a church service in Pančevo (Pantschowa), in South Banat, where he, "for the first time, openly informed our men of their impending deployment against Soviet Russia."[119] Just months earlier, the Wehrmacht, with assistance from local ethnic Germans, had publicly massacred thirty-six Serbs in Pančevo: they hanged half of them and shot the others at the town's Orthodox cemetery.[120]

At least some chaplains appear to have been aware of plans for the invasion several months before it occurred. In March 1941, a meeting of chaplains in the area of the 17th Army in Upper Silesia took place in Breslau. Protestant Supervisory Chaplain Mayer-Ullmann and his Catholic counterpart Kostorz traveled there together. In his report for March, dated April 3, 1941, Mayer-Ullmann described the purpose of the meeting as: "to clarify questions about pastoral care before the special deployment, and to exchange experience based on previous special deployment."[121] A few weeks later, the two supervisory chaplains were on the road again, traveling to Czarny-Dunajec, Rabka, and other sites in southern Poland to connect with chaplains attached to hospitals who were now being commandeered to divisions. Evidence that military authorities considered their assignment a priority is the extra gasoline ration Mayer-Ullmann and Kostorz received for the journey.[122]

Chaplains were well prepared in other ways, too. The process of selection weeded out potential troublemakers, and spring 1941 seems to have brought particular attention to who was being appointed as base chaplains. Pro-Nazi "German Christians" who had demonstrated insufficient obedience to state authorities were shut out of the chaplaincy along with outspoken adherents of the Confessing Church. In March 1941, the Gestapo gave a German Christian pastor in Berlin points for his opposition to "the Old Testament and the Jews," but disqualified him because he had alienated his congregation and ignored police restrictions on public meeting times.[123] The vast majority of rejections, however, continued to be political. Indeed, even what seemed to be personal reasons often turned out to be related to political behavior: a priest disqualified because he had allegedly boxed the ears of two small boys, had in fact disciplined members of the Hitler Youth.[124]

Police reports screened Catholic clerics most carefully for evidence of illegal youth work. Here, too, the concern was to exclude from the chaplaincy priests whose ecclesiastical involvement suggested inadequate commitment to National Socialism. Thus the Reich Church Ministry rejected a Dr. Tilmann in March 1941, because he had been a leading light in Catholic youth work in the Leipzig region and continued to write and publish works exhorting young men to keep the faith.[125] Scores of other Catholic applicants were turned down on similar grounds.[126]

The authorities who approved chaplains' appointments were concerned with more than ideological purity. Their primary goal was to boost and sustain the fighting spirits of the troops. In the words of the 1941 guidelines from Army High Command's office for pastoral care:

As in earlier wars, in this war too the military chaplaincy is an important handmaid of the troop leadership: educating the men to enthusiastic willingness to give their utmost,

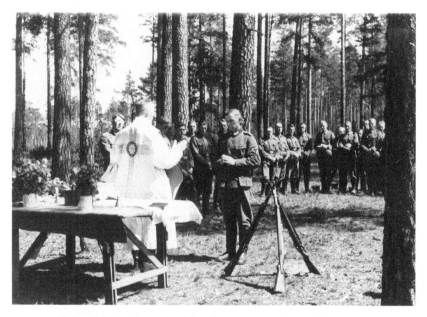

Figure 3.6 A Catholic chaplain celebrates mass with soldiers in the field, East Prussia, June 2, 1941. Walter Henisch, a renowned Wehrmacht photographer, took this picture. His skill is evident in his use of light: the priest seems to shine from within, and his radiance illuminates the faces of the men around him. After the war, Henisch insisted he had done his job and pursued his art without involving himself morally. His son, Peter Henisch, disagreed and wrote a novel, *Negatives of My Father*, that probed the conflict between them. BArch Bild 146-2005-0193.

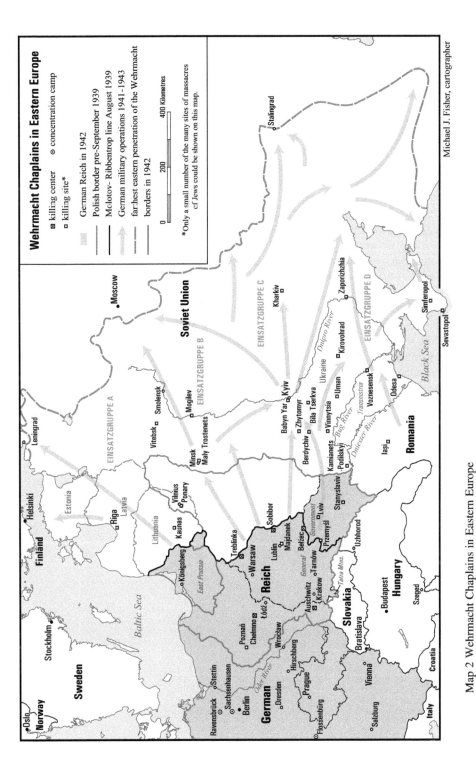

Wehrmacht Chaplains in Eastern Europe

⊠ killing center ⊙ concentration camp

□ killing site*

⊡ German Reich in 1942

—— Polish border pre-September 1939

—— Melotov–Ribbentrop line August 1939

⇒ German military operations 1941–1943

⇢ far-hest eastern penetration of the Wehrmacht borders in 1942

|0   200   400 Kilometres|

*Only a small number of the many sites of massacres cf Jews could be shown on this map.

Norway
Oslo

Sweden
Stockholm

Finland
Helsinki

Leningrad

Moscow

Soviet Union

EINSATZGRUPPE A

Estonia

Latvia
Riga

Lithuania
Kaunas
Vilnius
Ponary

Vitebsk
Smolensk

Mogilev

EINSATZGRUPPE B

Minsk
Maly Trostenets

EINSATZGRUPPE C

Baltic Sea

East Prussia

Königsberg

Treblinka
Warsaw
Łódź
Poznań
Chełmno

Reich

German
Ravensbrück
Stettin
Sachsenhausen
Berlin
Dresden
Hirschberg
Prague
Flossenbürg

Wrocław

Auschwitz
Kraków

Oder River

Lublin
Majdanek
Sobibor

Bełżec
Tarnów

Przemyśl

General
Government

Lviv
Stanysłaviv

Tatra Mtns.

Slovakia
Bratislava

Salzburg

Vienna

Italy

Croatia

Hungary
Budapest
Szeged

Uzhhorod

Kamianets-
Podilskyi

Iași

Romania

Babyn Yar
Kyiv
Zhytomyr
Berdychiv
Bila Tserkva

Vinnytsia
Uman

Ukraine

Dnipro River

Kirovohrad

Zaporizhzhia

Kharkiv

Stalingrad

EINSATZGRUPPE D

Bug River

Dniester River

Transnistria

Voznesensk

Odesa

Black Sea

Simferopol

Sevastopol

Map 2 Wehrmacht Chaplains in Eastern Europe

Michael J. Fisher, cartographer

including their very lives; training warriors who are ready to sacrifice, and by so doing, contributing to the spiritual strength of the German soldier at the front.[127]

Revised guidelines and renewed restrictions on chaplains were themselves part of preparation for a new phase of the war. Bishop Dohrmann's files are full of orders from Armed Forces High Command and Army High Command imposing new limits on chaplains, many of them clustered in the first half of 1941. For example, as per an order of mid-June 1941, chaplains could only bury soldiers whose papers clearly showed church membership.[128] On the Catholic side, a crackdown on unauthorized production and distribution of religious literature intensified at that same time.[129]

After two years of war, chaplains were still on the defensive, although they had taken every opportunity – in Poland, Norway, France, Yugoslavia, and Greece – to prove their value to Germany's fighting power. In the process, through their words, their actions, and their selective silence, they had crafted a narrative of German rectitude and Christian fortitude, for themselves and for the nation (Figure 3.6). Not everyone was convinced. In May 1941, Heinrich Böll wrote of the betrayal he saw embodied by a young soldier, his leg amputated, in civilian clothes with the little band of his Iron Cross in the buttonhole of his collar.[130] Over the past dull and desperate half year, Böll told Annemarie, he had neither gone to mass nor received the sacraments; he had barely prayed. Rushing from work to training to roll call, numb with exhaustion, he had been too tired and depleted to gather a thought.[131]

4 Saving Christianity, Killing Jews
June–December 1941

On June 22, 1941, the Wehrmacht and key Axis partners invaded Soviet territory. In the weeks and months that followed, the swath of territory from the Baltic states to southern Ukraine – lands occupied by the Soviets under the Molotov–Ribbentrop arrangement in eastern Poland and parts of Romania, plus the western Soviet Union – was the site of terrible massacres. Nina Gelman survived the German rampage that summer as a nine year-old Jewish girl in Zhytomyr. Her recollections, offered in a Russian-language audio interview decades later, show how brutally public the attack on Jews in the region was.

In her interview, Nina Gelman included details to emphasize she was both Jewish and Soviet. She described her family as simple and poor. Her mother Figa (Fajna) stayed at home, while her father Ephraim worked, occasionally in Moscow. They had five children. Gelman remembered that her father wore a large ceremonial hat, "according to the old Jewish customs." Mostly Jews and Ukrainians lived in Zhytomyr. The family had a poor Ukrainian friend, with whom they got along well. Nina's mother and father spoke Yiddish at home, but Nina spoke only Russian. Her brothers spoke both languages. In early summer 1941, Ephraim was shot and murdered by the Nazis.

Before the Nazi invasion, Zhytomyr was a pleasant, green city. There was a forest nearby, where the family picked raspberries. "Zhytomyr was a Jewish city," Nina explained. "I remember that until the war, my mother, along with granny, would go to the synagogue, and I recall that they would not take me with them . . . I remember that."

The Jewish community of Zhytomyr was executed en masse in July 1941. Nina managed to hide and survive in villages located close to the nearby towns of Stanyslaviv and Berdychiv. To perpetrate the murders of the Jews of Zhytomyr, people were first arrested and then forced onto trucks. Shooting pits had been prepared just outside the city. After one such "hunt," Nina, together with her mother, grandmother, and younger sister, was taken by the Nazis and transported to the pits. Upon arrival, she noticed German guards standing around with automatic weapons and shouting. Along with all of the other victims, the three women were made to stand sunk up to their knees in the pits. Nina stood beside her mother, who stood next to her sister. She recalls how everyone was crying, and how young her mother still was. There came a shout of, "shoot them all!" With that, everyone in the pit was shot. Most died on the spot. Nina was not hit, so played dead until the murderers had left.

A Ukrainian woman in the vicinity of the pits saw her. This woman and her husband took Nina in, cared for her, and fed her, before hiding her in their barn. She was unable to stay there for long, however, and later on, while walking down a main country road, she saw Wehrmacht soldiers riding on tanks. She walked for 45 kilometers, crying, distraught, and thirsty. A woman on a photo she shows to the interviewer saved her. Nina called her "Auntie Dunia." This "auntie" calmed Nina down and allowed her to stay in her home. When gunshots could be heard outside, "Dunia" and her husband would talk over it to help the girl. They were very kind people who saved her life.

Much later, during perestroika, Nina and her husband returned to Zhytomyr for a visit. On the road to the forest, they saw a large monument to the victims. She did not go into the forest during this trip.[1]

In the last six months of 1941, the SS Einsatzgruppen murdered hundreds of thousands of Jews, and local pogroms added to the carnage.[2] German soldiers captured, then killed or let die, enormous numbers of Soviet prisoners of war, 2.2 million by the end of that year alone.[3] The killers used many different methods: they shot their victims in forests, pits, forts, and cemeteries; drowned them in marshes and rivers; beat, starved, and exposed them to disease in camps, ghettos, and labor gangs. But the killings had one thing in common: they were visible. And they were seen – witnessed, filmed, photographed, and described in letters, diaries, reports, poems, and songs – by victims, their families, and neighbors, and by the perpetrators and their friends.[4] Frequently the Germans marched Jews through the streets on the way to killing sites as a public spectacle to win local support or intimidate opposition into silence. In the case of POWs, families and communities who searched for captured Red Army soldiers in order to feed them helped bring the destruction into the open.

Along with murderous and public violence against Jews and Soviet POWs, the German invasion in the summer of 1941 brought a widely publicized effort to rescue Christianity from Communism. Wehrmacht soldiers and officers, accompanied and in some cases organized by military chaplains, posed in front of newly reopened churches to symbolize the rededication of sites that had been used as cinemas, assembly halls, and warehouses. In southern Ukraine, the German occupiers expended considerable time and energy on reinvigorating religious life in the Mennonite communities they encountered there, many of whose members spoke German.[5] Wehrmacht chaplains featured in these efforts, too, as they did in other initiatives to restore Christian communal life among the region's *Volksdeutschen* (ethnic Germans). Meanwhile, the invading Germans and their local accomplices annihilated Jews, recruiting Mennonites and other Volksdeutschen as collaborators and killers. This chapter probes the relationship between these projects of destruction and revival and situates them in a wider analysis of Christian chaplains and the role of Christianity in Nazi genocide.

Presence and Absence of Chaplains

Military chaplains were both present and absent in the German religious campaigns entangled with the invasion and mass killings of Jews in the summer of 1941. A series of photographs taken by a photo service employed by the Wehrmacht in August and September 1941 illustrates the chaplains' simultaneous visibility and invisibility, their high and low profiles. I found these nine photographs at the German Federal Archive in Koblenz when I first began researching military chaplains. The images, filed together as a group, came up when I searched for the keyword *Militärseelsorge* (pastoral care to the military), and my original intention was to use them as illustrations showing chaplains in action. But the photographs themselves require analysis, and they raise many questions about the nature of Germany's Christian campaign of 1941 and the stakes for publicizing it. They also serve to focus discussion in this chapter.

This set of images, taken by professional photographers serving the Wehrmacht's propaganda companies,[6] reflects the gaze of power and access. As a result, the photos highlight the function of the events they depict for the Germans who initiated, choreographed, recorded, and publicized them. Only one of the photos actually shows a chaplain, and even in that case, although he is featured in the caption, he is barely discernible in the image itself. Yet the photo service or military press employees who wrote the captions, labeled the negatives and prints, and organized them for distribution clearly connected the scenes of church buildings and religious services in the occupied east with the Wehrmacht chaplains. They also made sure that anyone looking for images of chaplains would find these photographs, as I did decades later.

One photo each shows Christian services in Vitebsk (Viciebsk), Troyitsya, and an unspecified location in occupied Ukraine or Belarus in August and September 1941. The remaining six photographs, all taken by Heinz Mittelstädt, depict stages of the same event, the opening of the Orthodox Cathedral of the Holy Transformation in Zhytomyr in central Ukraine in August 1941 for a German military church service (Figure 4.1). Until he was called up, Mittelstädt, who was twenty-seven years old in 1939, had worked as a journalist with the *Königsberger Tagblatt*.[7]

Zhytomyr was the site of both celebrated church openings and mass slaughter. There, in the late summer of 1941, Germans restored several of the city's

Figure 4.1 German soldiers enter a church in occupied Ukraine to take part in a worship service. Wehrmacht chaplains had long hoped to make participation in religious services mandatory for the troops. They did not succeed, but this photograph, taken in August 1941 to publicize the opening of churches in territories newly conquered from the Soviet Union, indicates that the image of pious German warriors had propaganda value. Note the small group of local civilians, including children, under the watchful eye of a uniformed German. Photographer Heinz Mittelstädt. BArch Bild 183-B09573.

grand churches to Christian worship. At the same time, they destroyed the city's synagogue, murdered thousands of Jews, and established a deadly camp for captured Red Army soldiers. In August 1941, Zhytomyr was at the center of Nazi violence. Indeed, Wendy Lower maintains it was here that the Germans crossed the line to genocide.[8] Led by the brutal Higher SS and Police Leader Friedrich Jeckeln, the region saw numerous massacres of Jews, ranging from large open-air shootings to intimate local killings. A major POW camp was another place of carnage, all of it widely known and highly visible.[9]

Wehrmacht officers describing German atrocities in occupied Soviet territory took their most terrible examples from Zhytomyr. A January 1942 "Report of the Commander of the 9th Army Corp, Schirwindt, and of Major Roesler on the Mass Executions of Soviet Citizens" described the killing of

Jews in Zhytomyr. The author, Major Karl Roesler of the 528th Infantry Battalion, expressed shock at the unprecedented violations there:

I have seen many unpleasant things, having been a member of the Free Corps in 1919, but I never saw anything like this. I cannot begin to conceive the legal decisions on whose basis these executions were carried out. Everything that is happening here seems to be absolutely incompatible with our views on education and morality. Right out in the open, as if on a stage, men murder other men. I must add that according to the accounts of the soldiers, who often see spectacles of this kind, hundreds of people are thus killed daily.[10]

What Major Roesler witnessed in late July 1941 was a mass shooting of Jews into a trench dug along a railway embankment. He did not identify the victims as Jews, but in the report he emphasized the large numbers of corpses of "both sexes and all ages." He also noted that he took a photograph of the scene.[11] Another observer in the region, an eleven-year-old Ukrainian boy, witnessed a similar mass shooting of Jews and found the evidence persisted even after the fact: "When on the next day I went to see, two large pits had been filled in ... and two large pits were there, *and the earth was breathing – that was certain.*"[12]

References to the "stage" and the "spectacle" bring to mind another notorious killing in Zhytomyr, the execution on August 7, 1941 of two Jewish men, Wolf Kieper and Moshe Kogan. It was a brutal display,[13] watched and photographed by a huge crowd of German soldiers. A photograph taken by one of those soldiers provides a close-up view of Zhytomyr in August 1941 that contrasts the polished shots of the church openings (Figure 4.2).[14]

Kieper and Kogan were judges, and the Germans accused them of being Cheka agents responsible for the deaths of more than 1,000 ethnic Germans and Ukrainians. Loudspeakers mounted on vehicles of a Wehrmacht propaganda company urged local residents to come and see, and hundreds of local Jews were rounded up and forced to watch the hanging.[15] They were photographed too, in a scene of collective denigration. Although Kieper and Kogan were singled out, their fate was far from singular: after the public show, the 400 forced witnesses were taken outside the city and shot (Figure 4.3). Altogether, during July and August 1941, Germans transported 4,000 Jews from Zhytomyr – almost one-quarter of the city's Jewish population – a few kilometers to Dovzhyk and murdered them there.

A report prepared by the Reich Security main office regarding activities of the Einsatzgruppen mentions the hanging on August 7, 1941, "of Kioper, the Jew, in the central square of Zhytomyr, accused of having promoted resistance and Zionism." According to the report, "many locals attended and jeered. This 'Aktion' concluded with the shooting of 402 Jews." Also noted was the shooting a week later of fifteen "functionaries" north of Zhytomyr.[16]

Figure 4.2 This photo is one of many, amateur and professional, of the public execution of two Jewish men in Zhytomyr, in August 1941, shortly after the German invaders arrived. Here the privileged status of the unknown photographer allowed him to get close enough to capture the faces of the condemned men and their executioners as well as some of the soldiers gathered to watch, dozens of them piling onto a nearby roof for a better view. USHMM 17540, courtesy of Jewish Historical Institute, Ringelblum Collection, Warsaw.

Figure 4.3 This scene, too, was documented in many photographs. The Germans who staged the public spectacle of the hanging of Kogan and Kieper forced their victims to watch. They rounded up 400 Jewish men from the surrounding area, tormented them for hours in the market square, and then brought them to the horse cemetery outside the city and shot them. It is not clear precisely which part of that deadly process is documented here. USHMM 33399, courtesy of Sheva Zilberberg.

From Mass Killing to a Narrative of Redemption

During the summer and fall of 1941, Germans actively shaped events and experiences in the newly conquered "bloodlands" into a story of Christian redemption.[17] Chaplains were characters in that story but they were also among its narrators and promoters. This process was uneven – soldiers, chaplains, and their conversation partners back home sometimes expressed surprise at observations that did not fit the frame. Many Soviet people appeared to be devout, for instance, and many Germans proved indifferent or hostile to Christianity. As for Nazi German authorities, rather than pursuing a crusade against "godless Communism" with constant zeal, they were capricious: they made and then broke a nonaggression pact with Stalin's USSR; they championed then obstructed the opening of churches, they encouraged then forbade communing with fellow Christians in occupied territories.

Wehrmacht chaplains rushed to stay on this zigzagging path and to protect their office and their faith. Only after the war ended and the Cold War set in did the narrative of saving Christianity lose its contradictions and rough edges to become a smooth, hard carapace over the bloody mess of genocide. To analyze the role of the Wehrmacht chaplains in the "fateful months" of 1941 requires looking through, under, and at that shell.[18]

The narrative of saving Christianity depended on the presence of chaplains, if not in the flesh then symbolically. The Nazi press expert who decided to file the photographs of church openings under the heading "pastoral care to the military" reflects this linkage. Germans told one another and themselves a story of Christian dedication and evangelization in the "wild East,"[19] and military chaplains were key figures in this narrative, because they embodied the assumed Christian nature, even essence, of German warfare. Whether or not chaplains were physically on hand, their existence somewhere and the institutional reality of military chaplaincy made them virtually present wherever the Wehrmacht went.

Soviet documents confirm that the church openings were actual events, not merely performances of German propaganda. At the same time, by switching the perspective, they serve as a reminder of the importance of not simply taking the official German records and the chaplains' recollections at face value. In January 1942, Janis Mistris, a political commissar with the Red Army's 201st Latvian Rifle Division, participated in the Soviet counteroffensive in the Battle of Moscow. One of the villages his division liberated was Riabushki, along the Borovks-Narofominsk road in the Kaluga Oblast. Mistris reported to the head of the political administration of the western front and head of the political department of the 33rd Army on the "monstrous atrocities committed against our wounded, captured Red Army soldiers and commanders in the localities liberated from the German occupiers." Along with details about mutilated corpses found, including a lieutenant who had been thrown alive into a hot oven, Mistris relayed "stories told by the local residents." One of them involved a reopened church: "In the village of Riabushki, Germans staged in the church a memorial service (*panikhida*) in honor of Tsar Nicholas."[20] In general, Soviet sources paint a much more complex picture of the church openings and the various roles played by local actors. Many contemporary reports, as well as interviews with survivors of the German occupation, describe the church openings as local initiatives, permitted but not necessarily led by the Germans.[21]

Sources of various kinds situate military chaplains in immediate proximity to atrocities. Perpetrators themselves recorded the presence of chaplains and other Christian clergy at killing sites. A report from Einsatzgruppe D, the German mobile killing squad assigned to slaughter Jews and other purported enemies of the Reich in southern Ukraine, mentioned chaplains unfavorably.

Military chaplains, the author complained, had followed German motorized units into the region in 1941 and since then, effectively re-Christianized many local ethnic Germans. The report tagged Catholic priests as the worst offenders and named a certain Father Pieger as their ringleader.[22]

More common are references to chaplains in perpetrators' accounts after the war. Such descriptions follow a pattern of invoking the presence of Christian clergy to justify killing or to intimate that the killers and those close to them had uneasy consciences. In autumn 1941, SS-*Sturmbannführer* Karl Hennicke was head of Office III (SD) of Einsatzgruppe C. After spending the early summer in Lviv killing Jews, Einsatzgruppe C proceeded to Zhytomyr in July and continued on to Kyiv in September, in time to participate in the massacres at Babyn Yar. By the end of the year, the men of Einsatzgruppe C had murdered 95,000 Jews. Looking back, Hennicke described extensive conversations with a Christian clergyman about the killing: "I myself was about 200–250 meters away from the actual shooting place. I stood with a group of Wehrmacht officers, among whom there was a Protestant pastor. We spoke at length about these shootings."[23] For Hennicke, it must have been comforting – and perhaps mitigating – to note that he had discussed the murders he and his men committed with a Christian clergyman who raised no objections and in fact was present and in uniform.[24]

Hennicke's self-serving recollection matches other sources. Gisbert Kranz, a young Catholic soldier on the eastern front, remembers that a military chaplain was the first to tell him that Germans were murdering Jews in eastern Poland and the Soviet Union. Kranz encountered the chaplain, a priest from his hometown, by chance in 1941. Kranz's memoir does not give the clergyman's name.[25] Definitive evidence exists to locate chaplains at specific sites of killing. As is well known, at least four Wehrmacht chaplains observed events surrounding the killing of Jewish adults and children at Bila Tserkva, Ukraine, in the summer of 1941. Eyewitnesses recorded their presence and activities, although these accounts were only publicized long after the war was over.[26]

Some of the evidence of Wehrmacht chaplains' presence at sites of mass killing is circumstantial. For instance, military guidelines required chaplains at the front to situate themselves in the areas of heaviest fighting. According to the Guidelines for Pastoral Care in the Field, signed by Field-Marshal Wilhelm Keitel: "In combat the military chaplain will be found in the hottest part of the battle and at the main dressing station, unless – and this will be the exception – he has received a special assignment from divisional command."[27] Although formalized only in May 1942, this instruction reflected what was already standard practice. At the same time, it disciplined those chaplains who may have tried to steer clear of the most dangerous situations and stirred up suspicions of shirking. Chaplains called this regulation the "Uriah law," after the officer whom King David in the Bible sent to the most dangerous part of the front to be killed so the king could have his wife, Bathsheba.

Intended to maximize the chaplains' morale-boosting function and, at least according to chaplains' perceptions, to increase their rate of mortality, the so-called Uriah Law also forced them to observe the brutal reality of German warfare, including the destruction of Jews and Soviet POWs, at close range. Though they rarely mention this proximity to the action in postwar accounts, in sources from the time chaplains often raised it with pride. In late July 1941, one month after the Germans invaded Soviet territory, the Catholic Military Bishop Franz Justus Rarkowski issued a "word to his flock" of Catholic members of the military "on the great and decisive war in the East." Six of his chaplains had already "sacrificed their blood and their lives for the Fatherland," he boasted, when he learned on July 12 that divisional chaplain Josef Weber "met a hero's death in the struggle against Bolshevism."

Just weeks earlier Weber had visited Rarkowski in Berlin, en route from the war zone in southeastern Europe, his arm in a sling because of an infection contracted there. People urged him to rest, but he insisted "as a priestly comrade he belonged with his comrades." According to Rarkowski, Weber's "soul was on fire with concern for the German people," whom he had served for years across the Czech border, where his "genuinely German, powerfully manly, and deeply priestly personality made him risk his life on the frontlines fighting for the German way of life." Rarkowski described Weber as an orator who "burned like fire" with passion for the German Reich as for the Kingdom of God and praised him by association with Hitler:

In the struggle that the Führer began exactly twenty years ago at the head of a small force, and that he is now leading as Supreme Commander of the Wehrmacht on behalf of the entire European cultural world against Bolshevist barbarism, this priest, whose name must never be forgotten, has fallen on the field of honor.[28]

Chaplains boasted to their superiors that men in the Luftwaffe and SS, who had no official chaplains of their own, sought their services. In July 1941, the Catholic dean of chaplains (*Wehrmachtdekan*) Gmeiner reported from Romania that "pastoral care found particularly receptive ground among units of the army and the air force that had not had a chaplain for a long time."[29] By the middle of July, murder of Jews in the region by Einsatzgruppe D and Romanian troops was in full swing.[30] Chaplains far from the sites of the Holocaust made a point of recording that they too saw action. A Protestant colleague at the northern naval base of Zapadnaya Litsa reported his excellent "cooperation with the SS men in the area."[31] Another Protestant, Chaplain Pohlmann with the 710th Infantry Division in Norway, reported on his service to air force units, which included pastoral care at the execution of fourteen Norwegians in December 1941. Pohlmann did not specify whether he ministered to the condemned men, the shooters, or both. He also paid repeated visits to the small number of sick at the air force hospital Gardemoen and held a military church service there for Christmas.[32]

The simultaneous presence and absence of chaplains at sites of killing was refracted in their own accounts, in which German atrocities, in particular killings of Jews, and chaplains' knowledge of those acts, were both revealed and concealed. Many chaplains' activity reports situate individual clergy squarely in areas of major massacres of Jews, although they do not explicitly mention those events. The Protestant chaplain with the 15th Division in Belarus submitted a twenty-six-page report covering the period from the beginning of July 1941 until the end of January 1942. Based in Mogilev, he was in the center of the territory ravaged by Einsatzgruppe B, and specifically Einsatzkommando 8, during the months of most active and open killing of Jews. Mogilev was also the site of an important conference in autumn 1941 formalizing the equation of Jew = Bolshevik = partisan, which cemented the Wehrmacht's involvement in the Holocaust.[33]

The chaplain's report did not use the word "Jews," but its emphasis on Bolshevism as a mortal threat reflected the Germans' assumption that Bolsheviks were Jews:

The number of wounded has risen sharply. Among the troops this first serious encounter with a brutal and bitterly fighting enemy has aroused shock and awe. Any expectation of an easy struggle, where it existed, has disappeared and the full gravity of the conflict with Bolshevism has become clear. At the same time, the men's inner attitude has remained confident and firm, although the difficulties of these first battles came as a surprise to many and already brought numerous painful losses, including among leaders of the units.[34]

Even before the center of the city had been "fully cleansed," the chaplain continued, it had become necessary to set up a second "honor cemetery" right in Mogilev. The mounting number of German deaths, he intimated, occurred under the sign of Christianity ascendant, as the Germans too experienced re-Christianization. Every grave was marked with a cross of birch, so that crosses dominated the entire space: "Only in one single case was the erection of a runic symbol requested instead, the first and to date only time the cross has been refused as a grave marker."[35]

Covering the Truth with Words

Some chaplains communicated awareness of German atrocities but in vague, oblique ways. Such references easily slid into elucidations of the Germans' own suffering, sacrifice, and inner righteousness.[36] One such cryptic formulation occurs in a report from a Catholic chaplain, looking back to 1941 and early 1942. He listed nine problems he faced during the reporting period from his vantage point with an armored division in the east. In addition to cold, mud, danger from partisans, and lack of adequate hosts and wine, he mentioned "the unique nature of the action and the relations with the enemy."[37]

Dr. Eberhard Müller, a Protestant chaplain attached to the same armored division in the summer and autumn of 1941, chose similar words. He described the many, searching conversations he had with his men, "even on the particular problems that are part of this struggle against the Soviet Union." The next sentence indicates that those discussions addressed the brutality of German troops in the east: "Again and again," he wrote, "everyone comes back to the question of the future of the German spirit and of religion."[38] In an extensive and unusually detailed report, Müller admitted that he too was challenged by the conditions. He focused on the Germans, including himself, not their victims: "Work with the wounded was especially difficult, though also rewarding. It was not easy, after spending the entire day on the battlefield, to have the necessary concentration. The sheer number of wounded makes one numb and discouraged." His antidote was "constant engagement with the Word of God" and a focus on "particular Bible verses." Müller observed that most of the severely wounded, no matter how brave they appeared on the outside and how much they expressed their belief they were "suffering for Führer and Reich," were terrified of death. Their "indifference and defiance," he worried, were often a cover for fear and alienation. It had been painful to experience this, he wrote.[39]

He found it especially hard to minister to dying comrades, Chaplain Müller admitted. But it was a "sacred duty" and "rich in blessings" for him to pray aloud with them and "prepare their souls for eternal life." Whenever possible, he maintained, he buried the dead himself. Writing about himself in the third person, he insisted that every human body be treated with respect: "He always made it clear to the comrades that they owe it to the fallen not to just stick them in the ground as if they were livestock, but rather to bear witness at their graves to the divine value of a human being."[40] By autumn 1941, they would all have seen many bodies dumped like garbage.

German chaplains dealt with atrocities in a range of ways. Some focused on their own hardships, some practiced denial; others found their own indirect ways to document their presence and knowledge of the slaughters carried out by the forces they served. After the war, the Protestant chaplain Bernhard Bauerle insisted that the Wehrmacht had had nothing to do with the murder of Jews. In the same manuscript, however, he described how he had witnessed the slaughter of Jews in Kovno and Dünaburg (Kaunas and Daugavpils in Lithuania) in 1941. Photographs and accounts from those massacres make it clear that members of the Wehrmacht were present and active,[41] and Bauerle's own papers include a photo of a living skeleton, labeled simply, in his handwriting, "Jew."[42]

Rather than articulate their own responses, some chaplains recorded their knowledge of mass murder of Jews using the words of others, including other chaplains. A Catholic priest at the Soviet front contrasted his (silent) opposition to the Holocaust with the enthusiasm of his co-religionists. He recalled his shock at hearing Hitler in a radio speech proclaim that, "Jewry must be destroyed, and not only in Germany. The hour of reckoning has come." The priest himself witnessed a forced transport of Jews from a marketplace piled high with bodies; he saw trains jammed with people he knew were to be killed. But what surprised him most was the discovery that "various people welcomed the destruction of the Jews." In his words, a fellow priest told him at the time, "There is a curse on this people ever since the crucifixion of Jesus when they cried: 'Let his blood be on our heads and the heads of our children.'"[43]

In diaries and memoirs chaplains tend to be reticent about their participation in Nazi ideology. The outspoken Hermann Wolfgang Beyer, whose diary has been analyzed by Dagmar Pöpping, appears to be an exception.[44] But often vague memories about their own roles coexisted with precise recollections of colleagues who shared the regime's views. For example, the diary (published after the war) of Josef Perau, a Catholic chaplain, betrays little about his response to Nazi ideas. But its description of Protestant colleagues affirms that at least some chaplains openly endorsed Nazi goals. Chaplain Perau's entry of July 27, 1941, from Tomaszow-Lubelski (southeastern Poland), identified his Protestant counterpart as a "German Christian," a member of an explicitly pro-Nazi group within the church.[45] That pastor, Perau wrote, announced to the entire officers' mess that he had made sure all of the "asocials" in his congregation were sterilized. According to Perau, the Protestant chaplain also favored moving all Poles out of Poland and replacing them "with farmers of the Germanic race."[46] Still, Perau seems to have chosen the less obvious atrocities to discuss. Tomaszow-Lubelski, an important Hasidic center near Lublin, had seen massacres of Jews since the early days of the war in 1939, including an incident where disabled Jews were put in a cellar and drowned.[47]

Chaplains in the armies of Germany's Axis partners shared information about mass killing of Jews with their countrymen. It seems impossible that German chaplains would not be at least as well informed as their Slovak and Italian counterparts. Slovak Bishop Michal Buzalka learned about mass shootings of Jews of all ages and both sexes from his chaplains serving in the east. In October 1941, he relayed that information to Giuseppe Burzio, the Vatican *charge d'affaires* in Bratislava.[48] In May 1942, Pirro Scavizzi, a Roman Catholic chaplain with the Italian military in the Soviet Union, wrote to his old friend Eugenio Pacelli, by then Pope Pius XII, that the Germans had already annihilated the Jews of Ukraine and unless someone stopped them, they would soon do the same to the Jews of Poland.[49] Evidence points to Romanian Orthodox chaplains who themselves killed Jews. Ionuț Biliuță has linked Romanian Orthodox chaplains with killing of Jews in Transnistria,[50] and Adrian Cioflâncă indicated a chaplain participated in killings near Iași.[51] Jouni Tilli showed the fanatically pro-Nazi posture of Finnish military chaplains.[52] Meanwhile what about Croatian chaplains? Hungarians? Did the Wehrmacht chaplains ever communicate or coordinate with them?

Genocidal Culture

Genocidal cultures reward and support the perpetrators of violence and their beneficiaries.[53] The German notion of "Kultur" – Germans as a "people of culture" in contrast to the supposed "primitive peoples" of Eastern Europe and the southern hemisphere and the cold "civilization" of the west – added force to this particular genocidal culture and provided a familiar vocabulary. The Germans rampaging through Soviet territory rarely bothered to pretend to be there for the good of the local populations; their goal was not to spread their "Kultur" to others but to impose it on spaces to which they presumed their superiority gave them the right. Of course, Germans were not the only actors, and the people they encountered exercised agency and tried, however they could, to assert their own interests.

In such volatile circumstances, Christianity served multiple purposes. One such function for the German invaders was to establish and maintain hierarchies. The photograph shown in Figure 4.4, taken for a Wehrmacht publicity campaign, bears the following caption: "On the Soviet front: Religious service in a prison camp on the eastern front. The Soviet prisoners stand in a circle around the clergyman as he gives his sermon. August 1941." The preacher is not identified, but the context and the inclusion of the photo in a collection curated under the title, "Pastoral Care to the Military," indicate he was a Wehrmacht chaplain.

A more apt caption might be: "captive audience." The scene captures a dilemma of imperialist, social Darwinian conquest: the supposedly superior forces are outnumbered, and the more putatively superior they are, the more imbalanced the numbers are. Colonial images often reflect this scenario: a large crowd of people of color in thrall to one white man. Yet such images of power also communicate vulnerability. Where even is the chaplain in this photograph? He is surrounded, indistinguishable from the men around him. What is to stop them from subsuming or crushing him? The power and assumed rectitude of the conquerors' position is what, in the Germans' imagination, would stave off revolt and even make it unthinkable.

Figure 4.4 Soviet POWs in August 1941. The photographer, working for a Wehrmacht propaganda company, labeled this scene a "worship service in a prison camp" and indicated that the men pictured were listening to the German chaplain's sermon. I have not been able to find the chaplain in the photo. The location is specified only as "south Russia." Photographer Helmut Möbius. BArch Bild 183-B13608.

In this unstable situation, the Christian campaign served a vital sorting function for the Germans, dividing the conquered population into friend and foe. It worked to this end alongside extreme violence and terror, which likewise created immediate and rigid categories: Who would collaborate, who would not. Who could be lured into a partnership, who had to be intimidated into submission, and who would be destroyed.[54] Christianity automatically excluded Jews, and countless Jewish sources make it clear that Jews understood the role of churches as sites of ostracism and exposure. Jews "passing" as Christians describe the dread at having to enter or even just seeing church buildings and fearing they would not know how to act. Also excluded were non-Jewish Communists ("Bolsheviks"), who by the antisemitic logic of Judeo-Bolshevism were more or less the same as Jews. In this script, conquered Christians became Nazi Germany's allies against "Jewish Communists." Many of them joined in, and antisemitism often provided common ground.[55]

The religious campaign also allowed the Germans to make distinctions among Christians, to pick their favorites and set up hierarchies that facilitated ruling. Anna Sudermann, a Mennonite schoolteacher in Khortytsia near Zaporizhzhia in southern Ukraine, had a happy experience of religious and cultural revival after the arrival of the Wehrmacht in August 1941. In her memoir, she describes encountering Wehrmacht soldiers who came to fetch water at the local well. To their surprise, the men found a household of women, all of whom spoke excellent German. Even better, they had a piano. Soon Sudermann, her sisters, and the soldiers were singing German hymns and folksongs together. Our home became an "oasis" for the men, Sudermann wrote, where they could escape the "pains and dangers of combat."[56] Her account echoes the Bible stories of the patriarchs Isaac and his son Jabob, who in different ways, both found their wives Rebekah and Rachel drawing water at a well.[57] While the German soldiers in southern Ukraine sang hymns with Mennonites, they forced local Ukrainians into labor units. In Chelm in south-eastern Poland, Germans transferred church buildings from Roman Catholic Poles to Orthodox and Greek Catholic Ukrainians.[58]

Two of the photographs by Heinz Mittelstädt capture the process of cleaning the church in Zhytomyr. The original captions are brief. One reads: "German-Soviet War – German soldiers and Bolshevik prisoners cleanse the interior of the church of trash" (Figure 4.5). The other: "Debris and trash are removed from the church" (Figure 4.6). These images, composed to show the imposing pillars and the ornate detail of the doorway, invoke another familiar narrative – the New Testament story of Jesus "cleansing" the temple. Recounted in all four gospels,[59] it would be familiar to anyone with a cursory knowledge of the Christian Bible. Given that religion was taught in every German school by Catholic priests and Protestant pastors, even children from non- or barely observant homes heard Bible stories.

In this story, Jesus returns to Jerusalem before Passover and visits the temple. He finds the outer courtyard busy with people selling services and things: currency exchange, animals for the upcoming sacrifices. He flies into a rage, fashions a whip out of rope, and attacks the traders, overturning their tables, scattering their goods, and driving them into the street. In the different gospel accounts, he lambasts the merchants for turning "his father's house," a "house of prayer," into a "den of thieves" or a "marketplace." For the latter, the Luther Bible used the German word, "*Kaufhaus*," the same word used for a "department store," code in Germany at the time for a Jewish business. The Gospel of John, which used the word "*Kaufhaus*," explicitly named Jesus's targets as "Jews." This Bible story was popular in Nazi Germany, and the version from John appeared unaltered in the "dejudaized" New Testament published by the "German Christian" movement in 1941.[60] In at least one case, we know that a Protestant chaplain preaching in a reopened church chose as his text the story of Jesus "cleansing" the temple.[61]

Figure 4.5 Zhytomyr, August 1941: Soviet POWs carry piles of material in a church under the supervision of armed Germans. Photographer Heinz Mittelstädt. BArch Bild 183-L26913.

Figure 4.6 Soviet prisoners carry a large object out of the church under the eye of a German soldier, Zhytomyr, August 1941. Photographer Heinz Mittelstädt. BArch Bild 183-B09438.

Accounts in the press and in soldiers' letters borrow vocabulary from the gospels and popular representations to describe the church openings they witnessed. The terms "cleansing," "purging," "driving out," and "house of prayer" recur frequently, and the notion that the Soviets desecrated churches by using them to house animals is ubiquitous. Of the gospel accounts, only John mentions the presence of animals (Matthew and Mark refer to sellers of pigeons or doves), but animals were a standard feature in narrative and pictorial depictions of the scene. Chaplains' accounts stress how filthy the buildings were and invariably say they were used as barns, machine sheds, or granaries.[62] Other sources, however, point to different uses – cinemas, performance spaces, assembly halls. These purposes make more sense given the size, shape, and location of the church buildings. The debris piled in the arms of the men in the photograph shown in Figure 4.5 resembles hay or straw, and anyone familiar with common representations of the story would likely assume that is what is shown. Only after reading outside sources and looking again did I realize the piles consist of more "urban" material: torn or shredded paper and possibly film.

Christianity as a Gift ... To Whom?

Five of the photographs from the opening of the cathedral in Zhytomyr include the same sentence at the beginning of the caption supplied by the photo service. It reads as follows: "On the Soviet front: (Ukraine). German soldiers restore to the oppressed Ukrainian people the gift of their faith in God." The language is patronizing – why was faith in God the Germans' gift to give? It also reveals without openly stating it the identity of the enemy who purportedly stole that faith: Judeo-Bolshevism.[63]

Local newspapers and the Christian press back home carried accounts of the churches rededicated and services held for soldiers and local populations. One short piece did not name the community but specified it was in Ukraine. It was a congratulatory message: "The village has its church again. The people will never forget the day when the German military liberated them – and their souls."[64] The accompanying visual, a sketch, showed grateful Ukrainian peasants: women in headscarves and a bearded man.

Catholic Military Bishop Franz Justus Rarkowski, always eager to improve his standing in the eyes of Nazi authorities and his fellow bishops, gushed to "his chaplains" about their roles as liberators of Christians from Bolshevism and its ubiquitous alter ego, Judaism: "Comrades! Who would question that we Germans once again have become the people at the heart of Europe, and in a sense that goes far beyond geographic or geopolitical considerations? ... Many European countries ... understand that the war against Russia is a European crusade." It was no exaggeration, Rarkowski continued, "when

I say that you in the East are like the German Knights from long ago." As proof, he invoked the campaign of re-Christianization: "You have experienced how people in the borderlands occupied by the Bolsheviks rejoiced as you came into their cities and villages, and they greeted you as liberators."[65] His words indicate that he had seen photographs and sketches or imagined them: "In the eyes of these people you could read their gratitude for saving them from brutal tyranny, for freeing them from a hell of torture and fear." He contrasted the false and deceptive light of the Soviet star with the "bright light of Christian faith in God."[66]

For the chaplains and their men, the opening of churches and the public performance of Christian rituals served as both a symbol and a source of German unity. In contrast to the vulnerability of the chaplain outside, surrounded by prisoners of war, the church represented a fortress, physical and spiritual; in the words of the psalmist, enshrined and Germanized by Martin Luther's hymn: "A Mighty Fortress is Our God."[67]

The photograph shown in Figure 4.7 reveals something not stated in the celebratory texts about the church openings. The Germans intended the

Figure 4.7 Uniformed Germans seated in the newly re-opened church in Zhytomyr, August 1941. The photo raises many questions: who are the children and women standing squeezed between military men? What is on the sheets of paper that some men hold? Songs? Prayers? Photographer Heinz Mittelstädt. BArch Bild 183-B09383.

beneficiaries to be themselves, not local Christian populations. Note the mass of uniformed men filling the church, and the small huddle of civilians, children and women, surrounded by men in uniform, off to the side. The captions of the preceding photo in the series and this one also make it clear for whom German authorities opened this church: "After the fundamental cleaning of the church of all dirt and filth, German Pioneers decorated the church with fresh greenery and flags. The next day, a Sunday, for the first time in twenty-three years, a worship service was held." Among the "dirt and filth" removed from the church were the Soviet prisoners who had been conscripted to do the heavy labor. Then: "A view of the decorated church during the worship service for the German soldiers. Zhytomyr, August 1941."

In the context of the German war of annihilation, opening of churches occurred alongside crimes against "houses of God." Three years after the destruction of hundreds of synagogues during the November pogrom in Germany, traces of uneasy consciences echoed in the disqualification of prospective chaplains who had been critical of those events. During the invasion of Poland, the Germans ruined countless synagogues and churches, with bombs and fire;[68] they commandeered church buildings for profane purposes, and at Chełmno incorporated a church into the killing center.[69]

The invasion of Soviet territory also brought German assaults on synagogues, but one has to consult Jewish sources to learn about them. Lucy Gross Raubvogel, a Jewish teenager in July 1941, described how in her town of Peremyshlyany (Przemyślany), in German-occupied eastern Poland, the synagogue was both a target of destruction and a killing site:

Our large synagogue and all of its annexes were burnt. The flames were rising up high, parched window frames and benches on which our grandfathers, fathers, and brothers used to sit now crackled. Fire turned into an awesome element. A throng of peasants gathered around the fire with their sacks ready to plunder; a mass of devoted Christians, their children and the Germans who recorded this overwhelming sight on film. The wind carried sparks from one building to another, the fire crackled and soared into the sky mercilessly, and the bones of the first victims crunched. An enthused mob of shrieking peasants, just like locusts, pounced on everything that belonged to the Jews. They plundered, stole, and in some incredible ecstasy they destroyed within minutes what had sometimes survived the generations.[70]

Two other survivor accounts from Peremyshlyany add important details about the fire. Karolina Berger, then a twenty-four-year-old woman, watched the fire from the top of the main hill. She later found out that five Jews had been burnt to death in the synagogue. Among them was the son of a popular rabbi from Bełżec. As she recalled, "this was the only son the rabbi had who could speak – the rest of his children were mute."[71] Pepa Altman, a girl at the time, described killing and physical destruction as immediate and inseparable: "The Germans came to us. On the first day they began to murder Jews; they burnt down the synagogue, throwing 20 people into the flames." She too noted that one of the dead was "the son of a famous rabbi from Bełżec."[72]

Soothing Uneasy Consciences

There were murmurings of unease, including among German soldiers. Why else did the military leadership – most famously Field Marshal Wilhelm Keitel, chief of Armed Forces High Command, and General Walter von Reichenau – deem it necessary in September and October, in the wake of mass killings at Kamianets-Podilskyi, Babyn Yar, and elsewhere, to issue orders to show "no mercy" to Jews and Bolsheviks? Many private statements by soldiers, civilians, Germans, and non-Germans register a foreboding that God would punish the German nation for their crimes.[73]

In his diary a young SS officer responded to the massacre he witnessed of Jews of Zhytomyr:

Liquidations, executions, purges. All these words, synonymous with destruction, seem completely banal and devoid of meaning once one has gotten used to them. It is a vocabulary which has become general usage, and we use such words just as we talk of swatting disagreeable insects or destroying a dangerous animal. These words however are applied to men. But men who happen to be our mortal enemies.[74]

Hence a need for reassurance, and who better than an all-powerful, merciful God to provide it. This photograph of the church service in process (Figure 4.8) almost spells out *"Gott mit uns!"* Note the enormous number of crosses represented and their prominence in the composition of the photograph – on the flags and the altar, in the shape of the aisles, embedded in the bricks, and of course built into the cathedral itself.[75] The skill and status of the photographer, Heinz Mittelstädt, are evident. He was able to move freely inside the space, to get in close to the German officers as he did in the previous image, and to go up onto the balcony for this grand view. The Germans were not uniform in their beliefs and behaviors or in their responses to the church openings. And they did not comprehend, let alone control, all of the local forces at play around the revival of religion in occupied Soviet territory. Yet this image and others like it communicate uniform, indeed uniformed unanimity. Christianity was an important site of intimidation and, closely related, of incitement and recruitment to collaboration.

It is difficult – perhaps impossible – to measure the chaplains' impact on Wehrmacht troops. We know that some Nazi killers, like Franz Stangl, commandant of Sobibor and Treblinka, seized on the involvement of Christian clergy in attacks on people with disabilities and Jews as a way to justify their own roles in murder.[76] But Stangl was not a soldier, and he recorded no encounters with military chaplains. After the war, at least some German

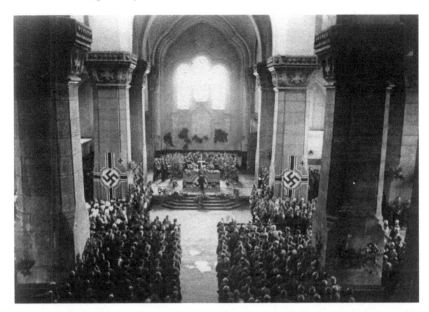

Figure 4.8 An imposing view inside the church in Zhytomyr, with uniformed men filling all the spaces available. This is the only one of the nine photographs in the series on pastoral care to the Wehrmacht that actually shows a military chaplain. He stands in the center of the image, directly in front of a swastika and a cross. Photographer Heinz Mittelstädt. BArch Bild 183-B09404.

veterans remembered with bitterness that the chaplains assigned to promote their spiritual life had raised no voice of protest against murder of civilians. Looking back after forty years on his experience on the eastern front, the theologian Hans Richard Nevermann wrote that throughout the entire war, no officer, no comrade, and no chaplain ever had anything to say about German atrocities other than that the war was terrible.[77]

Many soldiers' letters and diaries say nothing at all about chaplains, an indication either that chaplains were too few in number to have much impact or that they seemed irrelevant. Still, we know from various sources that men did approach Christian clergy, including chaplains, with questions of conscience.[78] Reflections from a Catholic priest stationed in the Crimea illustrate the issues that faced clergy who ministered not only to death but to killers. As he recounted after the war, a wounded man confided to him about his past:

He had been ordered to take part in a shooting commando in Sevastopol. The guy was completely ruined by this experience. Line up the Jews, clothes off, naked before his eyes, women, children, men, and then the machine guns. He had to man one of the guns himself. "I can say I did not hit any of them. I always shot in the air." But the experience, how the people fell backwards, earth over them, and then the next row, until the anti-tank trench was full ... 40,000 people.

"'What should I have done?,'" the man wanted to know. He had a wife and family. Should he have refused? The priest was beside himself. "And I am expected to respond as a priest!," he exclaimed. His answer echoed both the rationalizations and the performance of conscience familiar from many post-war German utterances:

I do not know how I would have reacted in that situation. Am I supposed to tell the soldier that he was a coward and should have stood up against it? He would immediately have been put in the same row and shot along with them. Is that what God wants? For us that was the first time that we heard anything about the shooting of Jews. The commanders of the Wehrmacht who were in charge should have refused to have anything to do with it.[79]

A Reward for German Men

The picture in Figure 4.9, also taken in Zhytomyr by Heinz Mittelstädt, is quite different from the others in its framing and vantage point. The scene of one uniformed, German man surrounded by Ukrainian women invites reflection on the role of gender in this setting and the ways that, in the reckoning of the conquerors, Christianity, like access to women's bodies and the comforts of domesticity,[80] was their reward and their right. At the same time, the presence of Ukrainian women and children but no adult men underscores another form of divide and rule. The Germans' "gift" of faith to the Ukrainian "people" was exposed here as a gendered bequest: Soviet men, captured and starved, were used as forced labor to "cleanse" the church, and they were also part of the "dirt and filth" that was purged from it. Ukrainian women, sometimes allowed inside, were to receive religion like a numbing drug, another form of submission, disguised as solace.

And yet this image, too, is open to multiple readings. Can you look at the German man's face and not see discomfort? I cannot. The women looking over his shoulder – are they devout? Curious? Hostile? Planning to spit in the food they will be forced to prepare for the Germans billeted in their homes? Throughout the region, no doubt also in Zhytomyr, local women were dragooned into labor units that brought food right to the killing sites.

It is important to keep in mind that these photographs reproduce the Germans' gaze. In his discussion of popular piety and the church openings in Ukraine, Karel Berkhoff provides a very different picture, of villages and small towns where practically everyone celebrated the return to church:

Figure 4.9 The original caption provided for this photo by the Wehrmacht propaganda company emphasized German benevolence: "On the Soviet front (Ukraine). German soldiers give back to the downtrodden Ukrainian people the gift of their faith in God. Word of these events spread throughout the entire region of Zhytomyr. Ukrainians came from far and wide to experience the worship service." Photographer Heinz Mittelstädt. BArch Bild 183-B09408.

The buildings were painted white and church bells improvised from iron rails were installed. Whenever the original church had been demolished before the war, ordinary buildings were used. People who had hidden icons, communion cloths (*w antyminsy*), church books, utensils, towels and garments now brought them to the surface. In the town of Vasylivka, south of Zaporizhzhia, a magnificent iconostasis was put back together from parts saved by various people.

Looking back on those times, one Ukrainian recalls above all the women praying and weeping.[81]

Many accounts of church openings refer to the tears of local women. One German soldier wrote to a friend describing what he assumed were tears of joy, the rapture of receiving the gift of piety.[82] Tears are also ubiquitous in Mennonite descriptions of their encounters with the Germans and with Christian services in the summer and fall of 1941. Hans Werner writes that his mother told him everyone cried so hard they could not sing.[83] Another woman, a young girl in southern Ukraine at the time, writes in her memoir of women weeping uncontrollably as they prayed.[84] The tears speak to a depth of religious feeling that deserves to be acknowledged.

It is also worth contemplating other reasons why Soviet women in the summer of 1941 might cry in the presence of uniformed Germans. Large numbers of women experienced sexual violence at the hands of the invaders.[85] Many had sons, family members, and friends who were killed or captured by the Wehrmacht in the initial onslaught.[86] In numerous towns and cities, including Zhytomyr, mass killings of Jews occurred in public, terrifying and traumatizing events for eyewitnesses.[87] Women also bore the brunt of having Germans occupy their homes, being forced to cook and clean up after men who felt entitled to do whatever they pleased, even if it was fouling their beds when the weather made going outside inconvenient.[88]

A picture taken in Belarus by a photographer identified as Benno Wundshammer foregrounds local women embodying four stages of life – girl, young adult, mature mother, and elderly grandmother (Figure 4.10).[89]

Figure 4.10 Civilian women and girls and German soldiers, their heads bowed in prayer, at a church service in Vitebsk in August 1941. Although the photo was taken as part of a publicity campaign for the Wehrmacht in the newly conquered Soviet territory, the mood seems less joyous or triumphal than uneasy and exhausted. Photographer Benno Wundshammer. BArch Bild 146-2018-0001-1.

The other people shown are all men in German uniforms, in keeping with the brief caption provided: "Military church service in Vitebsk, August 1941." This image presents Christianity as the foundation for a partnership with the people of the conquered territories, specifically the women. It would not be an arrangement of equals: in this scenario, prayer and worship were to empower and strengthen the men while they rendered the women docile and subservient. By August 4, the date on this photo, the Germans had occupied Vitebsk (Viciebsk) for three weeks after hard fighting in early July. They had forced the 16,000 Jews who remained in the city into forced labor, and by the end of the month into a deadly ghetto. Sonderkommando 7a and Einsatzkommando 9 had already carried out numerous shootings of hundreds of Jews at a time, and EK9 was headquartered in the city.[90] According to the survivor Giorgi Valerianovich Shantir, son of a Jewish mother and an ethnic Russian father, "the first Vitebsk Jew to be murdered was a woman. She was hanged on Freedom Square, right across from the town's historical museum."[91]

Christian scripture offered numerous models of pliant women who were useful to men: the Virgin Mary, who gave birth to the savior of the world and devoted herself to nurturing and promoting him; sisters Mary and Martha, who each fulfilled important needs of Jesus, one listening and admiring him, the other cooking and cleaning; or the unnamed "sinful woman," who washed Jesus's feet with her tears and dried them with her hair (Luke 7). The women in Figure 4.10 remain unnamed, too, and no information is available as to their identities. But from many other sources, we know that German soldiers occupying Ukraine recruited young girls and boys to perform various tasks for them, from minding the geese and other livestock they appropriated until time came for slaughter to walking on fresh mass graves to tamp down the dirt.[92]

Adolescent and young adult women were especially vulnerable to rape, forced sex work, concubinage, and other forms of coerced intimacy. Middle-aged and elderly women had to house soldiers billeted in their homes, provide meals, including serving food and drinks at sites of mass killing, wash clothes and bedding, empty chamber pots, and more. German military chaplains paid attention to all of these relationships and tried to influence them toward some notion of propriety through sermons and conversations with soldiers and officers.

Other moral challenges involved sex. In mid-July 1941, Dean of Chaplains Gmeiner's activity report described the guidelines he had issued to the chaplains in the 11th Army, advancing since Operation Barbarossa into the southern USSR:

Chaplains are particularly called upon in teaching sessions and hospital visits to handle the problem in this region of deployment (sexual diseases) in appropriate ways. Chaplains are instructed to direct the main thrust of religious care at the focal point, "Strengthening the Morality of the Troops," and thereby to contribute to the fighting power of the troops. In particular the chaplain should emphasize the theme of "German loyalty," with special stress on marital fidelity and being faithful to German girls.[93]

As Gmeiner intimated, to German soldiers conquered women represented not only temptation but risk. Less familiar to cursory readers of the Bible than the Virgin Mary but not totally obscure was the story of Jael, from the Old Testament book of Judges, Chapter 4. When General Sisera, fleeing from his enemies, sought refuge in her tent, she gave him a glass of milk and let him come in to rest. But while he was sleeping, she killed him by hammering a tent peg through his head. Such scenes haunted Wehrmacht soldiers, officers, and chaplains. They relied on women in the conquered territories for food, sex, and other domestic and intimate comforts, but food could be poisoned, sex could transmit diseases, and men sleeping and bathing were vulnerable to attack, as were drunk men. Commanders expressed the hope that participation in religious services would curb their men's recklessness and promiscuity; chaplains took the opportunity to preach the value to German men and the war effort of equating discipline and purity with godliness.

Another photo, by a military propaganda company photographer identified only as "Elle," and dated September 1941, conveys the mingling of Ukrainian women and German men in the reopened churches (Figure 4.11). The white-kerchiefed women stand out and appear to outnumber the bareheaded men, whose uniforms are barely visible from the photographer's vantage point. Whoever wrote the caption strove to give order to the jumble of faces, eyes looking in every direction: "On the Soviet front: Reverentially soldiers and civilians listen to the Latin prayers spoken by the German military chaplain. Troiza, September 1941." Presumably the place was Troyitsya, in the region of Stanyslaviv (Stanisławów, now Ivano-Frankivsk) in Galicia. This region too was characterized by rapid and deadly anti-Jewish measures in late summer 1941.[94] Were those women "reverential"? Or confused? Ambivalent? Terrified? It seems impossible to generalize, although no one seemed willing to close their eyes.

One can contemplate Michel de Certeau's distinction between strategy and tactics, as tools of the more and less powerful respectively, as a way to interpret this image and its contradictory and ambivalent content.[95] Here Christianity functions, like sexual violence in Regina Mühlhäuser's analysis, as a strategy of the conquerors to occupy and control the territory.[96] For local women and also for individual soldiers, it was a tactic, a way to try to salvage self-respect, find comfort, and perhaps ease their consciences. Wehrmacht chaplains moved back and forth between these functions.

Figure 4.11 This photo differs markedly from the others in the series. The church is small and simple, and the local women are in very close proximity to the Germans and at the same level. Yet even here, closer inspection reveals the German soldiers to be grouped together; the few men mixed in with the women are not in uniform. Photographer Elle. BArch Bild 183-B09823.

God's Unconditional Love

The Protestant chaplain Dr. Müller with the 7th Armored Division provides a glimpse into the strategic and tactical use of the narrative of saving Christianity in the midst of a brutal war. The end of 1941 found his unit fighting along the Königsberg position near Gzhatsk as the Red Army advanced. He sought a silver lining in the military setback:

In general the difficult winter time has been extraordinarily fruitful for the work of the military chaplain. It was evident that continued engagement since October under the most difficult conditions has stretched not only the physical power but the spiritual power of everyone. Where in special moments and often for days on end everything shook and each individual no longer bore the consciousness of superiority, where death stood so immediately before all of our eyes, and our bodies and souls were exhausted by snow and cold, at those times the eternal star came into view and each one was thankful for the gifts of God's Word and the Lord's Table.

The harder the situation became, he insisted, "the more the question of faith came into the center – admittedly not in the foreground – of the spiritual scene." It was the chaplain's task "to meet the comrades with the living Word, with worship, communion, Bible study, discussion, and prayer in a way that will be decisive." In the position at Lama, Müller reported, it had been possible to hold a worship service for some units that were in transition:

These services belong to the most beautiful and profound experiences of the Russian campaign. Almost everyone there partook of the Lord's Supper. In the process, one could see how the faces of the men became revitalized and full of peace. Many of those who participated at that time have since fallen in the bitter fighting.[97]

Again Chaplain Müller provided the texts of some of his sermons: Romans 8:31–39; Matthew 9:23–27; I. Corinthians 13:13; Luke 22:39–46. All are core texts of Christianity: Jesus raises the dead and prays for strength; the primacy of love is affirmed. The passage from Romans promises God's unconditional love:

If God is for us, who is against us? He who did not withhold his own Son, but gave him up for all of us, will He not with him also give us everything else? Who will bring any charge against God's elect? It is God who justifies. Who is to condemn? ... Who will separate us from the love of Christ? ... As it is written, "For your sake we are being killed all day long; we are accounted as sheep to be slaughtered." ... I am convinced that neither death, nor life, nor angels, nor rulers, nor things present, nor things to come, nor powers, nor height, nor depth, nor anything else in all creation, will be able to separate us from the love of God in Christ Jesus our Lord. (Romans 8:31–39)

The chaplain framed the men's questions – and his own – in Christian terms that provided comfort even as they cast the Germans as victims:

Again and again the question came back to Christ. And the darker the situation was and the more serious the look in the spiritual future, all the more wonderful was it to bear witness for Christ as the light of the world. As individuals the comrades were all moved by the same questions: How can God allow this killing? Why are we humans so crazy? Where will we get the inner strength to bear it all?[98]

Christianity served as a reward and an alibi, at the time and after the fact. Chaplains facilitated the process, but they were by no means its only beneficiaries. In 1941, Sara Letkeman was an ethnic German teenager in occupied Ukraine. Decades later, she told her son, the historian Hans Werner, that she had been horrified by the murder of Jews in the region. However, her vague references to the genocide always came coupled with praise for the Nazi German restoration of her Mennonite community's religious life. Werner, following the cultural critic Steve Stern, calls this maneuver "memory as salvation."[99] It is a common feature in Mennonite accounts of the war years, particularly in the many memoirs by women. What the Nazis did to the Jews was terrible, they concede, but they saved us from Stalin and gave us back our faith.

In his memoir, *Odyssey wider Willen* (Odyssey against My Will), Peter Hildebrand goes a step further with this approach. He embodies the Mennonite conscience in the person of an elderly, frail, and sensitive aunt, who was crushed by her knowledge of the murder of local Jews, including people she knew.[100] In his narrative, the burden she carried in turn expiated the rest of the Mennonite community, including him and other men of his age who were positioned to see and participate more directly in killing of Jews. The language of knowledge and witnessing of atrocities as a burden for the perpetrators, beneficiaries, and onlookers, appears in many accounts, including the memoir of the schoolteacher Anna Sudermann. "It was a heavy burden," she writes of her knowledge of the Nazi German assault on Jews.[101] The most famous articulation of this idea – killing and awareness of killing as a burden on the killers – is of course from Heinrich Himmler, Reich leader of the SS, in his 1943 speech to SS officers at Poznań (Posen), but it was a staple of Nazi discourse: acts of violence recast as self-sacrifice. The Christian frame and female voice translated and magnified that inversion from an individual rationalization to a communal narrative.

Reversals, Inversions, Absences

The vocabulary of sacrifice gained currency at the end of 1941, because for the first time in its existence, the Wehrmacht faced major setbacks as the Red Army seized the offensive. From Lataschino on the Lama River, Chaplain Dr. Müller warned of the moral dangers of retreat. If conquest had encouraged hubris, retreat revealed spiritual weakness:

Anyone who joined the Wehrmacht in 1935 had never had to practice determined resistance. During the retreat it came to some rather unattractive scenes. Many lost their nerve. No one bothered with many of the wounded. Selfishness and craving for security together with a certain mood of panic triumphed over the sense of duty, starting with the units in the rear.

Müller used his platform "in worship services and Bible studies to lead the comrades in the right direction when it came to understanding and dealing with this retreat." He tried to impress upon the men the gravity of the situation and restore their trust:

We are fighting for everything. Against the monstrous power of Russia, against the territory, and against the weather. If a mistake was made by the leadership and if so, what it was, is not the question for a pastor to explore. In what has happened we can see a sign from God who is warning us not to be arrogant because of our continued victories. War, and this has to be learned at home, too, is not won with printer's ink but with blood. To be able to hold fast, also in a temporary retreat, is the crown of all soldierliness.

His work bore fruit, Müller boasted, "because I never preached a cheap 'hurrah' patriotism but always emphasized the seriousness of the struggle."[102]

Meanwhile, other reversals were already underway. Even as the military propaganda effort geared up its promotion of the pro-Christian, anti-Judeo-Bolshevik campaign, the Nazi leadership was applying the brakes. In early August 1941, around the time the nine photographs were taken, Hitler issued a decree that curtailed efforts to save Christianity: he ordered the Wehrmacht neither to promote nor hinder local religious practice. Nor were German soldiers and officers to worship alongside the local populations. Military chaplains protested what they perceived to be a blow to their mission,[103] and their reports and correspondence as well as personal accounts from a range of witnesses and participants make it clear that such activities continued.[104] What ended, however, was the publicity. As far as can be ascertained, the nine photographs in the series discussed here were all taken after Hitler issued his order, but they may not have been published or at least not widely circulated.

Why did the German leadership pull back from this publicity campaign? There are several possible explanations, and all may hold true. First is the security threat. Such close proximity to conquered populations was highly risky. Second is the idea of a tipping point. The rapid advance of German and other Axis units into Soviet territory in late June and throughout July 1941 created new dynamics and generated its own momentum, as caution gave way to euphoria. Third, under these conditions, the overt rationalizations provided by the church openings and widespread publicity around them proved to be no longer necessary. Perhaps they had never really been needed. The systems and narratives of domination that they presented were already in place. Habits of mutual instrumentalization between conquering forces and

Christianity had a long history, and they allowed for massive mobilization of religious energies to a number of ends: in occupied Ukraine, where Greek Catholic chaplains would later serve the men of the Waffen-SS Galicia Division;[105] in Croatia, where Roman Catholic priests held active and deadly roles in the highest echelons of the Ustasha;[106] in Romania, where Orthodox missionaries to Transnistria emerged as chief plunderers of the Jews and other victims of expulsion and murder.[107]

And yet, for a devoted believer, Christianity provided at least some possibility of finding distance from the regime and its horrors, though it could be a cold consolation. A description of church openings in 1941 comes from Konrad Jarausch, a German staff sergeant with a reserve battalion. Jarausch, a Protestant theologian, publicist, and religion teacher, corresponded almost daily with his wife, Elisabeth, who had also studied theology. (Their son, also named Konrad Jarausch, became a historian and published his father's letters.)[108] On August 14, 1941, Jarausch (Sr.) wrote to his wife from Minsk.[109] As his unit advanced from occupied Poland, he had been keeping his eyes open "for signs of churches and crucifixes," he told her. In many destroyed villages he saw church towers and wondered: "Did any kind of ceremonies take place in these buildings?" In Minsk, next door to the Lenin House, he noticed a red-brick church, "Romanesque in style," that reminded him of a church in the Berlin working-class district of Wedding, "except that everything was more marked by poverty, and the tower was smaller." The exterior had not been heavily damaged, but the building had been repurposed under Soviet rule:

There were no crosses or Christian iconography of any kind. Plastered on the fence posts outside were theater and cinema announcements. The main entry had been blocked off with a kind of glass wall that looked like a storefront widow. A side entrance led me past a ticket counter. Inside, carpenters and others were at work. They were whitewashing the walls and refinishing the floor.

Using his rudimentary Polish, Jarausch struck up a conversation with a few people standing around, but he did not know what to make of their reactions: "I could get the basic facts ... – the Bolsheviks had converted this 'beautiful, wonderful Kyrka [church]' into a movie theater. It is now supposed to be turned back into a church. Were they expressing some kind of religious sentiment? Who can say?"

Later Jarausch found himself at the "cathedral" on the market square, a "modest building of the late baroque period." In this case, the building's "religious character" had been reestablished:

A crucifix made of pieces of birch stood on the altar, flanked by flowers. In front of it stood a smaller cross that had been saved through difficult times. One of the side chapels had also been restored. An old woman knelt at a pew. Otherwise only German soldiers were milling about. There were posters announcing both Catholic and Protestant field services.

Jarausch's observations were cut short by a siren that emptied the market square: "another planned explosion, this time right next to the church." Perhaps that interruption deepened his uncertainty. Could "a new Christian spirit rise up from the rubble," he wondered? "Or are the reopened churches yet another part of German war propaganda?"[110]

On September 20, 1941, now further east with German forces advancing into the Caucasus, Sergeant Jarausch wrote another letter. "It's Sunday morning," he told his wife, but nothing about the day seemed special or holy:

At the most there are a few women with cleaner clothes standing on the street who cast glances at the soldiers. The world is so barren without God both here and at the other side of the front. I have often thought so when watching yet another one of our prisoners lie dying. No priestly words. Carried out like a corpse. Such deaths occur by the millions. This is truly the work of the devil.[111]

Surrounded by killing and dying, the deeply religious Jarausch, who himself died of typhoid fever in 1942, makes no mention of military chaplains in scores of detailed letters. In the Nazi German war of annihilation, chaplains preached, read the Bible, and prayed, but for the soldiers who died, and perhaps he also meant for all those who died at German hands, there were "no priestly words."

Through the encounter with atrocity, Christian chaplains went from being the voice of rectitude to getting legitimacy from military leaders and the war itself. Klaus Scholder tells of a Protestant pastor who, as a junior officer with the 11th Armored Division, took part in the invasion of the Soviet Union. He witnessed a mass shooting of Jews in Berdychiv and appealed to his commanding general for guidance. What was he supposed to do, the general answered. After all, he explained, the police battalion in charge was not under his command.[112] That pastor continued to serve in the Wehrmacht, as did those who photographed the hanging of "partisan bandits" in Yugoslavia, or watched as Germans burned villages along with their inhabitants in Greece, or ministered to condemned German soldiers before their executions, or witnessed the murder of Jewish children in occupied Ukraine in the summer of 1941.[113]

5 "The Power of Christian Truth and Christian Faith"

Genocidal Culture, 1942–1943

Let your face shine on your servant: save me in your unfailing love.

(Psalm 31:16)

In an interview years after the war, a priest named Heinrich Pachowiak related a story he had heard when he was assistant to the Catholic Wehrmacht chaplain stationed in Chartres. One evening General Otto von Stülpnagel, Military Commander of occupied France, invited the senior Catholic chaplain to dinner. When the two were alone, the general asked, "What do you think of the practice of shooting hostages?" The priest dodged: "Sir, you are under orders. What can you do?" But, as the story went, the general would have none of it: "Not like that, Father! I want your opinion as a Catholic priest!" The chaplain then replied, "In that case, I have to tell you it cannot be justified." "My opinion exactly," said the general. Stülpnagel resigned, was transferred to a distant post, and later joined the July 20 plot against Hitler.[1]

As recounted, this incident suggests the moral power chaplains might have wielded and connects that possibility to the touchstone of July 20, 1944. I was moved when I read about it, though aware it was likely a product of wishful thinking. Still, the story intrigued me, with its heroic version of Stülpnagel, who indeed resigned in February 1942, and the figure of the pusillanimous but ultimately righteous chaplain. Like so many of my sources, it is not easy to verify, given the private conversation, reported second- or even third-hand, and the fact that Otto von Stülpnagel committed suicide in 1948. Only much later did I realize this vignette, quite apart from its veracity in detail, reflects a turning point in the Holocaust. Stülpnagel did oppose mass executions of French people as a policy of reprisals. And he did clash with Hitler over the issue. But the general's reasons were pragmatic – he did not want to jeopardize French collaboration – and the compromise he implemented – limited executions, primarily of Jews, and mass deportations of so-called Jewish Bolsheviks to the east – initiated the destruction of Jews in France.[2]

In an essay published in 2000, Raul Hilberg offered a view of Stülpnagel's decision that was strikingly less noble than the image in the priest's account. He also omitted the chaplain:

There was a hostage problem, and there was an army general who did not feel comfortable shooting a lot of Frenchmen. Three Frenchmen shot for a dead German was okay, but a hundred? He had to keep the peace. So he suggested the following: how about Jews as substitutes? Who would think of that!? And indeed, the first trains going out to the death camps from the periphery of Germany left the same month, March 1942 – one from France and another from Slovakia.[3]

Stülpnagel apparently did consult a chaplain, identified in a laudatory work by another Catholic priest as Senior Military Chaplain Hofer.[4] Did Father Hofer know about or even approve the trade, dead Jews for live Christians? I cannot say, although the pattern is familiar. The chaplain in the story functions as a mirror, allowing both men to see themselves as virtuous while it blocks out their victims. And the narrative, its telling and retelling, transforms the encounter from an act of betrayal of Jews to an assertion of Christian honor. This transformation – turning the callous military commander, who discovered that sending Jews to their death would solve his problems, into a humanitarian hero, and the compliant priest at his side into a clarion voice of conscience – is a move typical of genocidal culture.

Genocidal culture rewards, supports, and protects the perpetrators of violence and their communities. It obliterates its victims and produces its own justification. Chaplains functioned as figures in and agents of the narratives that held the system in place. By 1942 chaplains were part of the killing machine, as Germans, as Christians, and as representatives of an institution that linked the churches and home front with the war and the men who fought it. Their role was to execute genocide of the mind.[5] Not merely silent, they were aware and active; they manipulated language and deployed Christian rituals and symbols to construct a story of justification, with devastating consequences.

In this period, the Wehrmacht chaplains turned inward, and in the process they legitimated the violence and at the same time obscured it from view. They provided a frame of Christian stories and symbols and showed the people inside the system what they wanted to see. Reflected by the chaplains, military leaders could see themselves as righteous rulers, akin to biblical judges and kings. German soldiers could see themselves as noble warriors and suffering Jesus figures. Their families, in the chaplains' mirror, appeared as Pietàs, like the Virgin Mary cradling her dead son, crushed by grief yet strong in the faith that sacrifice would bring salvation. Chaplains looking into that same mirror could see themselves illuminated by the light of Christ.

Chaplains' ministry to soldiers had two parts: top down, dealing with the hierarchy, as partners and morale boosters; and bottom up, caring for the souls of the soldiers as pastors, and for their bodies, as surrogate nurses. Though surrounded by non-Germans and dependent on them, chaplains rarely acknowledged their existence and only in a very few exceptional cases included them in their "universe of obligation."[6]

The years 1942 and 1943 may seem less dramatic than 1941, but this period is even more telling of how entangled chaplains were in the violence. Now atrocities were routine, and genocide was not a sudden explosion but a deadly heat wave with no end in sight. Over the course of 1942, Germans carried out hundreds of murderous "actions" against Jews, in forests, fields, and cities from Paris to Sevastopol. The following year brought the brutal "second sweep," as Germans retreated from Stalingrad through territories they had already ravaged, killing the remaining Jews and massacring others in the name of anti partisan efforts. Wehrmacht units were directly involved – assisting with round-ups, guarding the perimeter of shooting sites, catching and handing over to the SS people who had escaped. Even when soldiers were not immediately participating, they were never far away.[7] The Wehrmacht was even more directly implicated in many other forms of mass killing, all over German-occupied and dominated territories.[8] It was the military hierarchy that presided over arrests and transports of Jews in France in early 1942; it was not special SS units but the regular military that carried out the murder of Soviet POWs,[9] executed reprisal killings against Serbs, Jews, and Roma in Yugoslavia,[10] and imposed death through starvation and disease of hundreds of thousands, eventually millions, of civilians in besieged Soviet cities, most famously Leningrad.[11] Everywhere chaplains stood by their men.[12]

The Sign of the Cross

Christianity was woven into the fabric of Nazi German war and occupation. This reality and its implications become visible only when seen through the eyes of the Germans' victims and targets. Nama Bakshi (née Sholom) was born in 1928, in Karasubazar in Soviet Crimea. In a 1998 interview, conducted in Russian in Simferopol, she described growing up a Krymchak (part of a Jewish ethno-religious community of Crimea deriving from Orthodox Judaism).[13] Her neighborhood was made up of Germans, Armenians, Estonians, and Krymchaks – "everyone was mixed." Before the war, she maintained, following Soviet conventions, there had been "no difference in religious/national ethnicities," but from the beginning of the war, "the different ethnicities became scared of each other." Her father, Efrem, was a shoemaker. Her mother, Guliush, was severely asthmatic and stayed at home. In the Soviet times, Nama recalled, her family had kept a low profile, not "making it widely known that they were Jewish (but neither had they hidden it)."[14]

When Germans, whom Nama characterized as "SS Gestapo death squad soldiers," initially arrived in her neighborhood, they "kicked out the residents and took over their homes." To identify that a house was now occupied by a German, they "drew a cross on it." Other accounts from occupied territories also show the Germans marking buildings and even people they claimed with a

Figure 5.1 Paulette Feiler, a French Jewish girl in hiding, at her first communion in 1943. The crucifix, prominently displayed here, is a reminder that the cross could be both a form of protection and a sign of erasure for Jews.

cross.[15] The symbol of Christianity, in other words, became shorthand for the German occupying presence. It came loaded with centuries of meaning. As a sign of conquest, it evoked Constantine and the crusades; as a marker of death, it harked back to medieval plague crosses on the doors of people stricken by disease. The ultimate symbol of the crucifixion, the cross called up the accusation of Jews as deicides. It also functioned as a gesture and manifestation of blessing and protection from evil (Figure 5.1).

Bakshi did not comment on the symbolism but she understood the assault on communal solidarity. The "Mountain Jews," she says, "because they feared for their lives," collaborated with the Germans and gave out Jews and their occupations and addresses. Her mother took steps to try to protect the family. When a "German Gestapo soldier" moved in, she changed their last name from "Sholom" to the more Russian-sounding "Shalin," hoping to conceal their identity. Nama's survival testifies to her success. Because there were so few Krymchak Jews, Nama posits, the German residing in her home did not realize the family was Jewish. If he had known, Nama is sure he would have shot them all on the spot.

Nama Bakshi's account includes many details meant to show the interviewer that her family, though integrated into Soviet society, was firmly Jewish. Still, the picture it paints of multiple overlapping and sometimes conflicting identities and groups in the region contrasts with the Germans' simplistic view of the people around them. Bakshi's words also highlight the abyss between the enormous impact the German presence had on occupied peoples and every aspect of their lives and the privileged ease with which the Germans could ignore, deny, and erase their victims.

And yet for the Germans, "the enemy" was ubiquitous, in the form of POWs, Jews – always the object of major attention, whether alive or dead – and local populations that embodied "the partisan threat," yet upon whom the Wehrmacht, including its chaplains, relied for everything from preparing grave sites to getting their laundry done.[16] In order to see these people, I have integrated sources from those targeted for destruction in German-occupied

---

Figure 5.1 (cont.) Feiler's father, Beiral Feiler, originally from Russia, was one of the foreign Jews executed by order from General Stülpnagel at Mont-Valérien in December 1941 for resistance activities. Her mother, Roche Leja Feiler (née Gimelstein), managed to arrange for Catholics in Seiches-sur-le-Loir to take in Paulette and her sister Dora, before she, originally from Lithuania and also not a French citizen, was arrested, deported, and murdered in Majdanek. The priests and nuns in charge of the girls informed them their mother was "no longer here," and they were to be baptized. Both sisters survived the war. USHMM 38215. United States Holocaust Memorial Museum, courtesy of Denise Bensaid.

and -controlled areas. Their perspectives reveal aspects of the Wehrmacht that its own sources conceal. For instance, a Russian Jewish survivor quoted a memorable line. In an interview conducted in Moscow in 1987, Giorgi Shantir, a boy in Vitebsk (Viciebsk) during the war, recalls hearing a German soldier declare with "sadistic joy": "*Krieg ist gut*" (war is good).[17] For the occupiers, it often must have felt that way.

Countless Jewish accounts identify German soldiers as present and active in assaults on civilians. Lidiia Andrushchenko remembers German soldiers entering the ghetto in Zvenyhorodka (Zvenigorodka) in central Ukraine and killing Jewish children with their bare hands. A teenager at the time, Andrushchenko (née Kogan) might be accused of not recognizing the difference between Wehrmacht soldiers, SS men, and other uniformed Germans. But her account, presented in Russian in an interview conducted in Ukraine in 1998, differentiates quite clearly among Germans and even observes variations in the behavior of individuals. She describes a mass escape of Jews in 1942 from the Nemorozh labor/concentration camp, where she too was a prisoner. They were fleeing a killing action: "The Germans were shooting almost everyone." A policeman bicycling to the killing site spotted Lidiia. He stopped, and she was sure he was going to kill her, but instead he grabbed her arm and commanded, "Run." Only sixteen at the time, Lidiia thinks the policeman took pity on her and let her live. Meanwhile, he nabbed an elderly woman who was also trying to escape and took her to the woods to kill her.[18]

People living under occupation had a lot to say about Germans in uniform, but not specifically chaplains, who could be hard to spot. (They wore a standard uniform but without epaulets.) More than twenty research assistants have listened to USC Shoah Foundation interviews and other oral testimonies for me, in multiple languages, and we have found only a tiny number of references to Wehrmacht chaplains. Still, even if they do not identify chaplains explicitly, Jewish, Russian, Polish, French, Serbian, and other sources reveal the Wehrmacht's dependence on people in occupied territories. Where did chaplains sleep, eat, and bathe? Who washed their uniforms, their underwear? Who grew their potatoes, cleaned their toilets, fed their horses, polished their boots? A plethora of sources show Wehrmacht soldiers lording it over conquered people: helping themselves to their belongings, using children to herd pigs and geese, raping women, soiling their beds rather than going outside in cold weather, and leaving local women to clean up the mess.[19] Taken together, these materials reveal chaplains' lived experiences as shaped and shadowed by the "violence of occupation" in the forms of forced labor, requisitioning, deprivation, abuse, and killing of subject populations.[20]

An account from a Ukrainian man, a boy during the war, reveals the close contact between the German military and the surrounding population. Aleksander Ivanovich Iakimenko was born in 1930 near the village of

Malyn (Malin) in Zhytomyr Oblast. In 1941, he witnessed the mass murder of the Jews of Malyn by an Einsatzgruppe, in a pit on the outskirts of town. The eleven year-old had been taking his family's cows out to pasture when he heard shooting. He followed the din to its horrifying site: people being unloaded from trucks, Germans and police shooting, the screams and groans of the dying. Some Germans yelled at him and he ran away, in the process coming across a Jewish boy he knew from school. That boy was running, too, and seemed, as Iakimenko put it, more afraid of him than of the Germans.

Two years later, the Wehrmacht was back in force. Now the teenaged Iakimenko and his family had more sustained contact with the Germans. In an interview years later, Iakimenko described the situation, although he did not talk about what it was like to live with men like those he had seen killing his classmates. In 1943, four Germans (signal men, not soldiers) settled in the Iakimenko home. Among them was a young man who in the evenings played sorrowfully on a harmonica and wept. Sometimes he gave the family chocolate and sugar:

One evening, this signal man visited Iakimenko's mother, telling her that "tomorrow you and yours [in reference to his father – he called him by a word pertaining to his long moustache], will be *kaput*." He warned them that they should escape that very night if they could. Aleksander's mother went to their neighbors to warn them, and that night they left town. The neighbors had horses, and with three other families, used them to escape. The Iakimenkos fled to a village in a nearby forest named Бабью Лозу (Bab'û Lozu), where they remained until liberation.[21]

Reports from chaplains themselves rarely mention non-Germans, but a few glimpses are telling. Their accounts tend to occlude specific victims at the same time as they inflate the category of "enemy." A case in point involves the Catholic chaplain Alphons Satzger, who won fame and special recognition from General Erich von Manstein for singlehandedly capturing twenty-one Red Army soldiers.[22] In the fighting around Sevastopol, Father Satzger had stumbled across a cave with the men inside. As the story goes, the priest was alone, armed with nothing but his wits and a small pistol. Only in Satzger's original text does he mention that "several Russian prisoners of war" had been helping him bring wounded Germans from the line of fire to a dressing station.[23] In other words, his shining moment of selfless bravery was their perilous forced labor assignment.

Hans Radtke, a Protestant chaplain with the 12th Army in Greece from 1941 until 1944, offered another glimpse of the Wehrmacht's victims. A life-long antiquity buff, Radtke collected souvenirs and guides. One pamphlet was playfully titled: "Ein kleiner Spaziergang durch Saloniki. Andenken vom Einmarsch der Deutschen Truppen in Saloniki" (A Little Stroll through Salonika: A Souvenir of the Arrival of German Troops).[24] The lavishly illustrated booklet said nothing about Jews or, for that matter, anyone in contemporary Greece. But Chaplain Radtke knew there were people on the receiving end of German crimes. In his papers he included a photograph, with no comment, showing emaciated bodies, clothed but jumbled together in a mass grave. It was contained in an envelope labeled: *Hungerleichen. Athen – Kokkinia. 1941* (Starved corpses. Athens – Kokkinia, 1941). Radtke duly noted the photographer's name: Pastor Schian.[25] Were military chaplains sharing information about crimes against civilians? To what end? Radtke's voluminous collected papers give no clue. For him and his fellow chaplains, Germany's victims – Greeks in mass graves, Jewish orphans like Lidiia Andrushchenko, bereft survivors such as Nama Bakshi and Giorgo Shantir, and traumatized witnesses like Aleksander Iakimento – had no place in the story of their war.

Handmaid of the Troop Leadership

Guidelines from Army High Command designated the chaplaincy an "important handmaid of the troop leadership."[26] Chaplains understood their place in the pecking order and sought to serve the military hierarchy in this spirit. Systemic violence thrives on hierarchies that simultaneously empower certain people and make them beholden to those above them. Such chains of command transmit expectations, issue rewards and punishments, and diffuse responsibility. In Nazi Germany's genocidal culture, chaplains looked up with unwavering loyalty yet always worried their superiors were looking down at them. This dynamic bound them to the system and led to repeated performances of their zeal.

Chaplains sought to bolster their standing by leveraging ties to people in more powerful positions. Accordingly, their reports, submitted up the chain of command, indulged in frequent name-dropping. In 1942, Protestant Supervisory Chaplain Hermann Lonicer bragged about three camp services he held in honor of Hitler's birthday, all violating the prohibition against coerced attendance.[27] His counterpart with the Panzerarmee Afrika pushed the envelope as well, with an initiative to organize chaplains for the Luftwaffe: he had secured a Protestant chaplain each for the 19th Flak Division and the Ramcke Parachute Brigade.[28] One of his activity reports made much of the death of the Panzer Army's Captain Dr. Brauer, who was buried in September 1942. The chaplain based his funeral oration on Psalm 31:16: "Let your face shine on your servant: save me in your unfailing love."[29] Numerous chaplains boasted to military superiors that men in the Luftwaffe and SS, who had no access to chaplains of their own, sought their services. Another Protestant reported in early 1943 that the Luftwaffe units in his jurisdiction always asked him to preside over burial of their dead.[30]

The higher-ups were not always receptive. In 1942, a period of military success and Nazi confidence, the Wehrmacht chaplains faced a series of measures to curtail their independence. Invasion of Soviet territory in 1941 had brought a spike in prestige, with the public relations campaigns around re-Christianization that accompanied mass murder of Jews. Now leaders who had worried about backlash from the churches could relax: the war effort might not need Christianity after all. Meanwhile, chipping away at the chaplaincy served to keep chaplains in line as they focused on defending their prerogatives.

In the spring of 1942, Field Marshall Wilhelm Keitel issued new guidelines that defined military chaplaincy as a purely "religious matter," not to include "training, intellectual/moral and political education of soldiers."[31] Restrictions on what chaplains could do inside the Wehrmacht were coupled with prohibitions on work outside: "Military chaplaincy is for members of the Wehrmacht only. Providing services related to the church for the civilian population of enemy territories or in occupied areas and carrying out religious propaganda toward them is not permitted."[32] The guidelines emphasized the chaplain's role during combat and left little space for other forms of ministry. Religious services must be "brief" and strictly separate from military occasions. Chaplains could only bury members of the Wehrmacht who had explicitly requested a religious funeral.[33] More rules followed: for example, chaplains could not visit men in their barracks.[34]

Other measures weakened the links between chaplains and the people back home. In July 1942, Army High Command stipulated chaplains could only write to family members of dead soldiers after at least ten days had passed since the troop leader or medical personnel had informed the family, and only if the deceased had expressed the wish that such correspondence occur.[35] A few months later, Armed Forces High Command threatened serious consequences for clergy who disobeyed.[36]

Among themselves or to trusted superiors in the military, chaplains described encountering disinterest, even hostility, from Wehrmacht officers. In March 1943, Protestant Military District Chaplain Karig, in District 9, submitted a report to the Protestant military bishop. He described several meetings of chaplains in Kassel, Eisenach, and Frankfurt/Main. Karig's presentation was titled "Possibilities and Difficulties in Pastoral Care to the Troops by the Reserve Army." He pulled no punches in calling out unsupportive officers:

Attendance at church services suffers in part because the officers all, or almost all, never attend church services. Even when we had religious funeral services for officers, no officers participated. Church services on Heroes' Memorial Day take place almost everywhere without participation by the Wehrmacht, because the scheduling of the military celebration and the radio broadcasts makes it impossible for members of the Wehrmacht to attend the religious services.[37]

On some bases, he noted, special military church services could not be held, because the finance offices had not provided funds for coal to heat the churches.[38]

Karig's presentation exposed a familiar dynamic. Chaplains, faithful servants of the brutal German war and occupation, still found themselves on the defensive. They tended to say one thing for public relations – we are doing great, everyone recognizes our value – and another for audiences they assumed to be sympathetic: we are stretched to the limit and constantly undermined. Both narratives ignored the millions of people Germans were killing, the lives, families, and communities shattered, to present the Wehrmacht chaplains as pious heroes and selfless martyrs.

Chaplain Karig returned to the perennial issue of church attendance. Under the "special circumstances of the war," the troops were not coming to services, he reported, and uncooperative officers were to blame: "Only where the troop commander or unit leader makes it very clear that participation of soldiers in religious services is desired and where he supports it – of course without putting pressure on those with other beliefs – only then do we see soldiers actively attending church services."[39] Karig was overtly defensive about the contribution chaplains made to morale and the antagonism they faced from their superiors:

The extraordinary challenges of the struggle in the East . . . may have opened the eyes of many an officer . . . to the fact that any weakening of the religious basis of our people means clearing the way for Bolshevism. By contrast, every promotion of Christian faith among the soldiers contributes mightily to the German army's power to fight back and strengthens the German *Volk*.[40]

Chaplains brandished their importance for morale like a shield: breaking them, they intimated, would allow a new "stab in the back." In November 1942, when a seminar for prospective chaplains was canceled, the Protestant Church chancellery protested to Armed Forces High Command. Countless letters from the front showed that soldiers' needs for pastoral care were not being met, they noted. Further decrease in the number of military chaplains would lead to "increasing unrest among their loved ones at home, who are deeply grateful for the pastoral care of their husbands and sons at the front."[41] Catholics echoed those warnings. That same month, the Archbishop of Breslau raised what he deemed "a matter of urgent military concern": the dearth of religious reading material at the front. "For hundreds of thousands of genuine Christian Catholic soldiers in the most difficult times of severe trepidation," he wrote, "only the power of Christian truth and Christian faith can create spiritual security and strength."[42]

Chaplains found that efforts to prove their value resonated best during military setbacks. In January 1943, amid the debacle at Stalingrad (Figure 5.2), Military Bishop Franz Dohrmann addressed Protestants in the Wehrmacht. More than 100 years ago, before the Battle of the Nations, General Yorck had prayed, he told them,[43] and now too, prayer would bring "manly clarity." The bishop quoted Romans 8:28: "We know that all things work together for good to those who love God,"[44] and Matthew 24:13: "He who endures to the end shall be saved."[45] In the words of the Lord's Prayer, "Deliver us from evil," he found assurance that, "Power and salvation reside in our communion with God." Citing Romans 8:31, Bishop Dohrmann asked rhetorically, "If God is for us, who can be against us?"[46]

The military oath was a key moment linking the chaplaincy, the military hierarchy, and individual soldiers. From the mid-1930s, Wehrmacht and base chaplains had fought to administer the oath of obedience or at least to be

Figure 5.2 A Wehrmacht chaplain presiding over the burial of Colonel Riebel, commander of a tank regiment, near Stalingrad, August 1942. Note the traditional Christian crosses that mark the graves of two other Germans and frame the scene, photographed by a skilled professional. Information in the Bundesarchiv photo collection refers to the man being buried as "Oberst Riedel," but it is almost certainly Gustav-Adolf Riebel (1896–1942), Commander of the 24th Panzer Regiment, who died August 23, 1942 at Krasnoarmeisk. Photographer [Hermann] Dieck. BArch Bild 101I-217-0498-26.

present (or invited) for the swearing-in ceremonies. Now, in the wake of Stalingrad, they trumpeted their role in holding soldiers to their oaths and billed themselves as a bulwark against desertion. At the February 1943 meeting of Protestant base and military hospital chaplains in Military District 12, which included Mannheim, Koblenz, and Trier, the Protestant district military chaplain opened with this theme. "It is the task of the military church service to bring to the soldier the message of the Gospels, where he will meet the living God," he intoned:

And here he will be bound to his duty, which culminates in the commandment to love God and our neighbor. The soldier will forever stand and fall, therefore, not only before his human superiors but before the eternal judge. It is this ultimate responsibility that finds expression in the oath of allegiance.[47]

In the chaplain's view, Christian clergy were necessary to literally instill the fear of God in soldiers.[48]

Always anxious about their standing, during the middle years of the war, chaplains became ever less willing to stick their necks out for people who could be a liability. Earlier in the war they had sidestepped prohibitions and provided religious services to local populations in occupied Poland,[49] to captured soldiers, and forced laborers. They had expressed no problem with burying enemy soldiers in Belgium and Greece,[50] and in 1941, maintained at least the pretense that they were bringing the "gift" of Christianity to Ukrainians deprived by Communism.[51] Into 1942, 1943, and 1944 some German clergymen continued to try to provide pastoral care to imprisoned Poles,[52] Dutch Catholics,[53] French women,[54] and prisoners at Ravensbrück.[55] But none of the priests who did so were military chaplains, who reserved their time, attention, and the sacraments "for members of the Wehrmacht only."

Loyal partners as they were, chaplains still had to navigate between pleasing their military superiors, answering to government and church authorities, and doing what they believed right. Sometimes these imperatives pulled in different directions, and a few individuals acted on beliefs that opposed the system. In one well-documented case, military authorities rushed to get in front of the situation when someone raised the alarm over a chaplain's behavior. In May 1942, the Commander in Military District 5 in Stuttgart wrote to Army High Command in Berlin to present the complaint. At issue were two masses celebrated in April 1942, at a military hospital near Karlsruhe. The chief physician, Dr. Kramer, had given his permission and instructed the nursing staff to prepare the space as the clergyman requested. According to the complaint, those requests were the problem:

For both events, the Catholic priest and part-time chaplain Müller had the large portrait of the Führer that hung in the hall of the small military hospital in Wilhelmshöhe taken down with the explanation that it would be distracting if he were to set up his altar in front of the portrait and celebrate mass framed by the picture.

This behavior upset people in the hospital. According to the report, the finance officer had informed the head physician of what transpired, but Dr. Kramer failed to take immediate action.[56]

As soon as he heard about the matter, the military commander hastened to add, he had initiated an investigation and arranged for the transfer of Dr. Kramer, who was demoted to a position as assistant physician (*Hilfsarzt*) at a military hospital in Warsaw. Because the doctor had served at the front and been wounded twice, that punishment was deemed sufficient. As for Chaplain Müller, he was fired immediately. According to regulations, military authorities could not discipline a part-time base chaplain, but the commander, after hearing from the Gauleiter in Baden, decided he had to lower the boom.[57] In this affair, each authority that got involved upped the ante and left the others scrambling to prove they had taken measures against the priest and others who had not reacted with sufficient severity.[58]

Gauleiter Robert Wagner, in a letter sent to the commanding general in Army District 5 and Commander in Military District 5 and in Alsace, General of the Infantry Herbert Oßwald, urged the harshest penalties possible: the doctor should be expelled from the army and the priest arrested. In the Gauleiter's ominous formulation: "with regard to punishment of the clergyman Müller, the civilian authorities have already been instructed to take the necessary steps." Wagner also demanded to know if military space was going to continue to be used for church services.[59] The keen interest at the highest levels indicates how seriously German authorities took this minor deviation by a lowly civilian, part-time base chaplain. It also speaks to the infrequency of such incidents. For the record, I have not found any examples of defiance, even as mild as in this case, involving Protestant military chaplains.

"A Man among Men, a Comrade among Comrades, a Soldier among Soldiers"

Turning inward, chaplains fixated on German soldiers as if they were the only people in the world. The mirror both reflected and deflected. Of the almost 200 chaplains' reports I read covering the period from January 1942 to June 1943, not one mentioned mass murder, rape, assault, or cruelty as sins of soldiers, nor did they warn of God's wrath and judgment. Instead, chaplains promised soldiers rewards in heaven. Though they decried drunkenness and promiscuity within the Wehrmacht, they lauded the purifying effect of war. In the words of the Catholic Chaplain Graf in August 1942: "Countless men have found themselves reborn in these death mills, their souls prepared for eternal life. How true it is, as the old saying goes, 'When people go to war, the gates of Heaven are opened.'"[60]

Chaplains presented soldiers' deaths as redemptive suffering, an imitation of Christ that was cleansing to the soul. Protestants and Catholics alike drew on an interpretation of war as the ultimate sacrifice, to be welcomed and embraced. Chaplains focused on the tasks of caring for the wounded and burying the dead, with all that entailed – retrieving and identifying bodies, corresponding with family members, and keeping track of graves. They preached courage to their men, sometimes in large assemblies that included general absolution, more often in small groups or individual encounters. In countless reports, Wehrmacht chaplains described the gratitude with which soldiers, including committed National Socialists and anti-Christian *Gottgläubige*, received their ministry.[61]

At the heart of Christianity are potent symbols of sacrifice, triumph, and resurrection – the cross, the body and blood of Christ. These are performed and enacted in the forms of communion, confession, and absolution. Protestant as well as Catholic chaplains celebrated the sacraments and pronounced forgiveness and absolution, including general absolution, at religious services throughout the war and in all regions. Catholic Chaplain Wirtz noted in an activity report that he offered general absolution in every mass he performed before battle during the invasion of France.[62] The Catholic Chaplain Tomaschek, with the 2nd Mountain Division in Norway, reported doing the same:

Right up to the hour of the attack, the Divisional Chaplain advanced with the various battalions, distributed general absolution, and visited the companies in their sectors. During larger operations he remained at the main dressing stations, where the wounded from neighboring regiments were also brought. Here his training as a medic proved valuable in helping the wounded, comforting the dying, and burying the dead. ... Prior to combat general absolution was given, and the troops and troop leaders gratefully received it. The priest-medics in the companies were authorized by the chaplain and the commanders to do the same, and with the "oleum informorum" that was prepared for them, they were able to be a priestly help to their comrades.[63]

Chaplains focused on serving their men unconditionally, their bodies and their souls. They understood their job to be boosting soldiers as fighters, and their constant worry was how to connect with them. In his new year's pledge for 1943, Chaplain Graf articulated this hope: "May the Lord God, in this new year of struggle, grant me again the right words, so that religiously as well as patriotically I achieve the good that, in these tumultuous times, the front soldier expects from a chaplain."[64]

As chaplains turned inward they constricted their view of morality. They exhorted men to "proper" behavior, meaning curbing their drinking, stealing, sex, and general debauchery.[65] Embedded in a system of massive crimes with no end in sight, chaplains zeroed in on individual sins and misdemeanors, especially sexual "immorality."[66] In early 1942 in France, a Catholic chaplain tried to instill "decency" in soldiers in a Wehrmacht prison in Dijon;[67] meanwhile, his counterpart in the east organized discussions in the barracks on the Commandment against adultery:[68]

In conjunction with the long-distance marriage of a sergeant, I held for the assembled non-commissioned corps of the Division (forty-two men) a talk with spiritual content ... on the meaning of marriage and the 6th Commandment. ... In the process, questions were raised that the men, as a result of the necessarily long absence from their loved ones, experience as especially urgent, and which every single one of them in Russia has to cope with.[69]

Soldiers, Wehrmacht chaplains frequently complained, were not as receptive as they should be. In a report dated January 3, 1943, a Protestant chaplain with the 218th Infantry Division in Russia lamented the situation: "Particularly on Christmas we saw how our church service suffered under the human, all-too-human soldiers' way of celebrating. Alcohol was a powerful master at Christmas this year. For this reason, I canceled the planned celebration of the Lord's Supper."[70]

Yet chaplains worried that their scolding would alienate soldiers. Protestant supervisory chaplain Bernhard Bauerle advised the pastors under his tutelage how to avoid that outcome: "Recently I met a young fellow-clergyman in uniform," he wrote in August 1942:

He started to whine: How hard it was for him as a theologian among the men! When he spoke to them about the Word of God or pointed out their immoral behavior, they laughed in his face ... I told him, "I wouldn't be impressed by you either or let you minister to or convert me as long as you're such a pathetic soldier! First put your honor and all of your energy into making yourself a real, topnotch soldier and a good comrade. Leave the preaching and missionizing alone for the time being, by God! Maybe later they'll let you tell them something and take you and what you have to say seriously."[71]

The customer, in other words, should always be considered right.

Chaplains looked past the unbridled power soldiers wielded over conquered people and the corruption and brutality it brought.[72] Instead they grumbled that the men challenged their authority. Complaints about hostile soldiers, officers, doctors, and nurses pepper their reports and correspondence,[73] creating the impression that neo-pagans dominated the scene. However, Supervisory Chaplain Hunzinger, reporting from Belarus in March 1942, observed that of the 1,241 soldiers he had buried in the reporting period, 96 percent belonged to a Christian confession; only 38 (3 percent) were *gottgläubig,* and 5 reported as having no religious affiliation.[74]

Still, soldiers raised in the Nazi worldview had models for how to disdain Christianity with its Jewish roots. One chaplain reported that antagonistic men asked him embarrassing questions about Christianity: for example, about the witch trials or the mission to the Jews.[75] A deluge of antisemitic publications gave Germans in uniform permission and a vocabulary with which to deride the churches. According to Catholic Military Vicar Georg Werthmann, there was always plenty of anti-Christian and anti-religious literature available to soldiers; Christian publications, in contrast, could be difficult to get, and chaplains were always asking for more.[76] As one Protestant chaplain put it, "Those who didn't know God before are not going to find Him in the war."[77]

As a group, chaplains were neither zealous Nazis nor amoral robots. Yet by this point in the war, even their questions and warnings tended to fold back into self-justifications. For example, at a front training session for Protestant chaplains in the east, Protestant Dean of Military Chaplains Schackla began with a stern admonition:

The sermon for soldiers is not a national speech, nor is it political propaganda or a newsreel decorated with Bible verses. ... How do we know that God is on our side or what God has planned for our people? How do we know that God will punish another people now and in the future? (This was the mistake of many sermons during the Great War!)[78]

Soon after this bold start, however, Schackla steered back to safer terrain. Sermons needed to be less heavy-handed, he stressed, and must concentrate on supporting German soldiers: "After all, as military chaplains, politically and as soldiers, we live together, experience together, and act together with the men." Chaplains, Schackla emphasized, were spiritual morale boosters, and war was "an eminently spiritual endeavor."[79]

Schackla offered a typology of the German soldier of the day. One type "struggles inside with his experiences of the war and is full of countless, tormenting questions." Another type had been numbed by all of that: "The souls become deaf and dumb." For many soldiers, he observed, there were no firm foundations: "The 'empty space' that exists in place of religious values for some of these men is filled with belief in fate, for others with superstition."[80] Still others, Schackla continued,

seek earnestly in the atmosphere of war itself for a new "religion" to help them live and also die. Yet others, who still bear within themselves a religiosity built on Christian beliefs, are thrown into doubt by the experience of war. From the intellectual side, they ask questions such as, "Does a God of love really rule the world?" etc.

Almost everyone, Chaplain Schackla noted, was "completely caught up in the experience of war." In these tumultuous times, the success of pastoral care at the front ultimately depended on the chaplain's personality.[81] As chaplains, Schackla proclaimed, "we by no means stand there first and foremost as a Christian among Christians, but rather as a man among men, a comrade among comrades, a soldier among soldiers."[82]

When rebuffed by soldiers, chaplains responded by asserting their manliness, like the Catholic priest with the First Mountain Division south of Kharkiv, whose report in May 1942 described his active role in a skirmish with 500 Russians.[83] They aligned themselves with their men and blamed women, above all enemy women – Polish, Jewish, French, and Russian women – for embodying temptation and leading good men astray. In many references to sexually transmitted diseases, not one chaplain's report mentioned the women who were infected by soldiers and who, unlike the men, did not have the benefit of dedicated treatment. Chaplains' discourse erased women living under German occupation and replaced them metonymically with the disease itself. In the throes of genocide, chaplains obsessed with the nineteenth-century Catholic idea that war and morality were linked, that the decline in German morals endangered the nation. Protestants echoed the notion that sexual promiscuity was to blame for the war.[84]

Away from the immediate peril of combat, soldiers perceived chaplains less as a source of consolation than as instruments of military discipline, affiliated with their superiors by the officers' rank they carried, compounded by education and class.[85] One of the few soldier's letters I have found that mentions encountering a Wehrmacht chaplain in this period of the war saw him accompanying a condemned man to his execution. In a private letter from France, the German corporal J. S. offered a glimpse of an unidentified chaplain. A member of J. S.'s battalion was court-martialed and sentenced to death for stealing, and the corporal was assigned to the firing squad. J. S. saw a Catholic chaplain escort the condemned man to the place of execution and watched the soldier take leave of the priest. The prisoner addressed his final words to the commando: "Comrades, do your duty."[86] This is likely the same case described by the Catholic military chaplain Graf:

On November 25, I had to instruct a young twenty-year-old man to prepare for the end of his life, in other words, to be with him in his final steps. The man had been charged with a series of thefts (from packages to soldiers/*Feldpostpäckchen*) and sentenced to death by the Division Military Court. After a most exemplary preparation for death, strengthened by receiving the sacraments, he died with a manly attitude, having recognized his wrong and repented.[87]

I had always associated the Wehrmacht's killing of its own men with a later stage of the war.[88] Yet it comes up in many of the reports for 1942, and not just in the east. One chaplain spoke dispassionately of an "epidemic of self-mutilation that appeared suddenly in our division too, on the part of people who wanted to remove themselves from service at the front. It disappeared just as quickly as it had come, once a number of death sentences were pronounced and carried out under orders from the commander of our division, by our own troops."[89] The chaplains' fundamental task of smoothing the situation meant getting the man to confess his sin (the military offense) so that he died quietly yet isolated from his comrades.[90] Were any such cases expressions of soldiers' bad consciences?[91] If so, chaplains did not engage them on that level.

"We Are the Homeland"

The quintessential Catholic image of a mother and her dying son also holds a special place in Protestant imagery. The chaplains' mirror reflected the suffering of the son as an imitation of Christ that also served the state. In the mythical body of Christ, the greatest joy is born in suffering.[92] Chaplains of both confessions invoked the image of a loving mother to express the ideal relationship between home and fighting fronts. In his April 1942 collection of Sunday greetings, the Protestant Bernhard Bauerle provided this sentimental anecdote:

A young comrade lay severely wounded in our military hospital. He had lost a leg and an arm and in addition suffered serious injuries to his back. He was in all probability not to be saved. His mother has come to us from Danzig to care for her son as only a mother can. ... Yet in spite of everything, she is happy and grateful that she is able to care for her son, something that thousands of other mothers are not able to do. "It is our Passion season," she says quietly. "We have always celebrated it, but now we ourselves are in the middle of it." This is how German mothers experience the agony of seeing their sons dying. They can still be grateful, even when their hearts are almost breaking.[93]

Catholic Military Bishop Franz Justus Rarkowski offered his own florid versions of this gendered narrative. Replete with clichés, his sermons and pastoral greetings overflowed with pathos, as illustrated by a 1943 "Word to all Military Chaplains": "There is something wonderful about the word 'fatherland.' Wherever the German language expresses the most intimate human closeness, it uses the word 'mother.' But the most holy, the most valuable, that which brings everything together and at the same time forms the heavenly crown over it all, we call 'fatherland.'"[94]

Chaplains claimed to hold the key to a mutually reinforcing bond between the Wehrmacht and home. As Pastor Hunzinger put it in 1943, to German men at the front, military chaplains and their familiar religiosity were a "piece of the homeland" amid the disorientation of war. The phrase comes from a presentation by Hunzinger made to a group of fellow Protestant chaplains in March 1943. For soldiers "out there in the field," he told his colleagues, "we are the homeland."[95]

Still, there were cracks in the narrative, and the relationship with the home front was steeped in ambiguity. For starters there were practical problems linked to Germany's worsening military and economic situation and the decreased access to booty that went with it. One recurring complaint was about lack of essential supplies. High on the list was wine, required by Protestants and Catholics for celebrating the eucharist. Over the course of 1943, the Catholic military bishop's bulletin addressed this theme repeatedly. In May, a piece called "Obtaining wine for mass" instructed chaplains to ration their supplies because orders would only be filled with a certificate from the Catholic military bishop. Was the subtext that chaplains were drinking too much of the wine themselves? Precise amounts were stipulated: "In the celebration of mass, an amount of only 3.3 centiliters can be used. For each priest, mass ten times per week will be calculated, adding up to an annual need of 17 liters, about 23 bottles."[96]

In October 1943, the Bulletin warned chaplains to be cautious when ordering wine from small firms, many of which failed to deliver. Chaplains in military hospitals were encouraged to personally check the unloading station to see if the shipment had arrived.[97] The implication seemed to be that the firms might cheat chaplains or soldiers or others might purloin a shipment of wine left unclaimed for too long. Meanwhile, there seemed to be no shortage of alcohol for German SS and police killers "drunk on genocide," as Edward Westermann has shown.[98]

Chaplains repeatedly insisted how much they were appreciated. In spring 1942, Protestant Chaplain Damrath reported from North Africa that he was very busy writing to family members of fallen soldiers: "The exchange of letters keeps growing due to the demand."[99] Another chaplain, in Soviet territory, reported that "numerous letters demonstrate that the vast majority of loved ones are grateful when their fallen one has received a Christian burial."[100] True as such claims no doubt were, the fact was the ambiguity in chaplains' relationship with the home front went both ways. Pastor Bauerle had to remind his colleagues to use caution when corresponding with people at home: "We should avoid theological formulations, which, among other problems, are no longer comprehensible. If among 100 recipients, 99 respond with gratitude and only one takes 'offense,' the offense of that one counts for more than the appreciation of the 99!" Bauerle also recommended that letters written by chaplains in their capacity as "graves officers," should not be signed "Divisional Chaplain," but rather simply "Graves Officer."[101]

Death was the main topic of conversation between chaplains and soldiers' families, and this reality generated its own tensions. Chaplains offered comfort and meaning but they were also the bearers of bad news. Protestant Divisional Chaplain Roussig reported from Demjansk, where arduous conditions had forced him to learn to ride a horse, that over the course of 1942 he wrote more than 800 letters to family members reporting on funerals and providing information about the location of their loved one's grave.[102]

Not everyone was comforted to hear their beloved had served God by dying. Navy Chaplain Friedrich Ronneberger published a "book of comfort" (*Trostbuch*) titled *Und fielen vor dem Feinde, und werden leben* (And they fell to the enemy, yet they will live). The slim text elicited a bitter response from one set of parents:

What's the use of this booklet? Where are we supposed to find solace? We can't even find out how and where our poor son died. . . . and we don't know where his body lies. And we're supposed to believe in God? . . . People say God is all merciful, perfect! Ach, if there were an all-merciful God, it is impossible that he could watch people suffer as they do. . . . Does life still have any meaning? . . . What we are experiencing is also happening to countless other people, on both sides, who all are innocent and yet must suffer. Why?[103]

To the home front, chaplains projected an image of righteousness and sacrifice, against rumors of the "decadent West" and "wild East." In the process they downplayed, normalized, and denied German crimes. For example, as proof of his usefulness, one chaplain, a Protestant, presented testimony from the family of an SS man whom he had buried: "Only after we received your detailed and comforting letter," the parents wrote, "did our hearts find some consolation, because we knew that our darling had received a proper burial from you in the memorial cemetery."[104] Did the chaplain's assurance that he buried their son as a Christian also lay to rest the fear that they had raised a murderer?

In unexpected ways, the immense destructiveness of the war seeped back into the chaplaincy. The only case I have seen of a chaplain with Jewish ancestry was exposed in 1943. In May, Army High Command informed the Ministry of Church Affairs that Heinrich Adolf Wolf, a Catholic military chaplain since 1940, was a *jüdischer Mischling ersten Grades* (first-degree Jewish mix).[105] A spokesman for the Ministry hastened to pass the blame: at the beginning of the war, Army High Command had presented a list of names to be approved for the chaplaincy, and there had been no time to obtain proof of "Aryan blood." It could not happen again, the bureaucrat promised, because the Gestapo check would unmask "non-Aryans."[106] I have not yet found what happened to Wolf, but at the very least, he lost his job and almost certainly much more. No other sources by military chaplains that I have seen mention Chaplain Wolf, nor is there any evidence to suggest any solidarity or support for him within the ranks. He simply disappeared.

Wolf's case is a reminder that in the intertangled world of Christianity and Judaism in Central Europe, there were always exceptions. Among these were a few chaplains who took risks on behalf of Germany's victims and paid a price for breaking ranks. One chaplain who got into serious trouble left only a scant trace in German records. In October 1943, a Catholic base chaplain lost his position, and more, as a result of contact with a Jewish woman. According to a file entry initialed by many officials, including Senftleben from Group S: "The Catholic Chaplain in charge of Military District 18 reported on October 8, 1943, that the part-time base chaplain Schumacher in Markt Pongau was arrested by the Gestapo and sent to a concentration camp. The reason for the arrest: prohibited interaction with a Jewish woman [*verbotener Umgang mit einer Jüdin*]." The priest's superiors were quick to dissociate themselves. On October 14, 1943, just days after Father Schumacher's arrest, the Catholic military bishop requested permission to remove Schumacher from the part-time base chaplain position in Markt Pongau.[107]

Before 1938, Markt Pongau (today Sankt Johann in Pongau), near Salzburg, was not home to many, if any, Jews. Even if some individual Jews had lived there, by late 1943 they would long have been rounded up and killed. Since March 1941, the town had been the site of a large POW camp, Stalag XVIIIC "Markt Pongau." When I first came across this case, I wondered if perhaps Father Schumacher had somehow encountered a Jewish woman in that context. The archival records offer few details, not even the chaplain's first name. But looking at other kinds of sources, notably victims' accounts, allows informed speculation as to what occurred. Most likely the woman was in fact a Christian, "Jewish" under Nazi law and practices but a convert to Christianity, like Erna Becker-Kohen.[108] Becker-Kohen's experience nearby in Tyrol at exactly the same time offers a scenario for what was possible in Markt Pongau.

In October 1943, Becker-Kohen, who grew up Jewish in Frankfurt am Main but was baptized into the Roman Catholic church, was living with her five-year-old son Silvan in Tannheim, a village in the Tyrol. A priest, Father Lukas from Ettal in Bavaria, had directed them there, and they found lodgings with a "pious old woman," Frau Binosa. In a text compiled from wartime diaries, notes, and postwar reflections, Becker-Kohen highlights the division in the village between "loyal Catholics and National Socialists" and describes the comfort she and her little boy took from visits to the "local baroque church," the Parish Church of St. Nikolaus, where she attended Mass "almost every morning." Becker-Kohen's papers marked her as a Jew, with the middle name of "Sara," and she was desperate to avoid coming to the attention of the local mayor, whom she described as "a German" and "a committed National Socialist."[109]

One day, riding her bicycle on a narrow mountain road, Becker-Kohen collided with a lumber truck and was badly injured. People at the nearest house called for help, which arrived in the form of a military doctor. Terrified that he would send her to the hospital, where she would be exposed as a Jew, Becker-Kohen insisted she be brought to Mrs. Binosa's. There, neighbors cared for her and Silvan as her broken bones healed. Becker-Kohen and her son survived the war, and her account of those times includes many names of priests who constituted her main network. She also frequently observed that certain priests became fearful. News of a fellow priest nearby being sent to a concentration camp for contact such as they were maintaining with Becker-Kohen would have traveled quickly.[110]

Another woman's experience, at a later date, but in Markt Pongau, further substantiates the hypothesis that the Catholic base chaplain Schumacher had been assisting someone on the run. It is an extraordinary story, like many accounts of Jews who survived against all odds, and the details, told in an interview decades after the fact, alternate between hazy and crystal clear. In 1944, a Jewish woman named Xenia Stephens, together with a non-Jewish Polish man, tried to escape Nazi control by way of the Tatra Mountains. A woman ski champion who worked for the Polish underground was going to help them navigate the terrain, but this plan fell through, because the skier was being watched by the Gestapo. Xenia and her companion went to Vienna, where some SS men were trying to recruit him. He told the SS officials she was his wife (she was not) in order to convince them to let her join him. They did not believe it but eventually labeled her a Cossack, which allowed her to get a pass to go to a Cossack camp in Italy. Instead, she stayed in Vienna where she worked in a factory until she fled with two friends into Tyrol. In April 1944, they ended up in Sankt Johann im Pongau.

While walking in the town, which she describes as a "mountainous ski resort," Xenia and another woman were hit by a German soldier on a motorcycle. The soldier, unaware she was Jewish, called an ambulance. Like Becker-Kohen, she was frightened and refused to go, but she was so badly injured she did end up in the hospital. The Germans in charge did not suspect she was Jewish, and she recalled receiving "fantastic care." From her hospital bed, she learned the war was over, and when American troops arrived in Sankt Johann im Pongau, they hired Xenia Stephens as an interpreter.[111]

"Greater Love Hath No Man Than This"

Casualties among chaplains, as within the Wehrmacht as a whole, rose sharply starting in late 1942, as the Germans faced massive losses in North Africa and at Stalingrad.[112] The narrative of sacrifice, blood washing away sins, and death as purifying got full play. The Catholic military chaplain's bulletin (*Verordnungsblatt*) published more and more obituaries, some of them rich in detail and national rhetoric. They illustrate a morbid truth: in the Wehrmacht chaplaincy's quest for credibility, dead chaplains proved at least as useful as those who were alive. In death, chaplains embodied the often-quoted Bible verse, John 15:13: "Greater love hath no man than this, that a man lay down his life for his friends."

In mid-November 1942, an obituary appeared for Heinrich Gerling, chaplain with an Infantry Division, who had served in the campaigns in Poland, France, and the Soviet Union. Gerling died in October 1942, "in a field hospital on the Eastern Front after previously being mortally wounded in the loyal fulfillment of his pastoral care duties." Born in 1912, he had served in the chaplaincy since the beginning of the war. The write-up included a quotation from Gerling's quarterly report for 1940 that "expressed his personal understanding of the task he set himself" as a chaplain in the field: "It goes without saying that danger will never stop us from fulfilling our priestly duty."[113]

In April 1943, Dr. Leonhard Laumen, chaplain with an Infantry Division, died in a reserve military hospital in Düsseldorf. He was thirty-six years old and decorated for his service as a chaplain since 1940. Laumen became ill in 1941, but according to the obituary, "with unsparing hardness against himself, he persisted with raw energy, despite his damaged health, to be active alongside his comrades."[114] Less dramatic was the obituary for Ludwig Rues, who died in October 1943, "in a Reserve hospital on the home front after severe illness." Born in 1912 and called to the military in July 1940, Father Rues served first as a medic until February 1942, then in military hospitals in the rear of the eastern front until his death.[115]

Military Chaplain Dr. Hubert Scheidt, who "fell in the East," was posthumously promoted to supervisory chaplain, effective one week before his death on November 7, 1941.[116] In March 1943, Carl Anton Esser, chaplain with a Security Division, died in the Reserve Hospital in Cologne Hohenlind. Born in 1900, Esser became a part-time base chaplain in 1936 and a military chaplain in 1941. He had been attached to the Security Division in the east since November 2, 1942.[117] These details, included in the obituaries to demonstrate the centrality of chaplaincy to Wehrmacht operations, allow us to situate chaplains with some of the most murderous units of the war.[118]

The author of the obituaries, likely Military Vicar Werthmann, was eager to emphasize death in battle or at least to render all deaths heroic. He chose which details to include accordingly. In late November 1942, Jakob Kaiser, "Military Chaplain with an Infantry Division, met a hero's death in the line of duty providing pastoral care in the East, through a direct hit by a grenade." Father Kaiser had an Iron Cross from 1939; born in 1907 near Aachen, he had been called to the Wehrmacht in 1940, become a chaplain in June of that year, and been assigned as a divisional chaplain in 1942.[119] Johannes Mies, chaplain in a military hospital, died in January 1943. Although Mies met a less warrior-like end, his obituary stressed another essential point – the importance of having chaplains to give last rites to the dying. Mies died "in a military hospital on the Eastern Front, after a fellow priest had given him last rites."[120]

In mid-January 1943, with German casualties reaching thousands each day at Stalingrad, one issue of the Bulletin carried three obituaries, spread over two full pages. Thirty-year-old Josef Pöschl died "a hero's death in the East on November 4, 1942, in the course of fulfilling his duty providing pastoral care." He had entered military service in 1940, presumably as a medic, become a chaplain in 1941, and been transferred to an infantry division from service in a hospital unit. Another priest, also born in 1912, died later that month at a main dressing station in the east, "after previously being seriously wounded." Albert

Bartsch began his service as a "medic soldier," became a chaplain in 1941 and a divisional chaplain in 1942. The third man was older and a veteran of World War I. Friedrich Schneider died at the age of forty-nine in December 1942, "in Stuttgart, well-prepared, after a short illness." The Catholic Schneider entered the Wehrmacht chaplaincy in 1939, served as base then division chaplain in the Polish campaign, was decorated, and became military district chaplain in Stuttgart.[121]

Chaplains' inward focus cast their own suffering as redemptive, their hardships as a sacred sacrifice. In mid-1942, Hermann Raible, a Catholic chaplain with the 15th Infantry Division, submitted his quarterly activity report. Chaplain Raible began by describing his physical tribulations:

March 15: A telephone call from divisional command summoned me to take part in a ceremony ... to honor our dead war heroes. A huge blizzard brought snowdrifts three feet high. The team and sleigh that was to bring me to Suschewo got stuck after twenty yards and had to be shoveled out. After an exhausting march of more than two hours in the bitter cold, I arrived at divisional headquarters. Because of the storm, the ceremony had been canceled.[122]

He also alluded to the personal and spiritual challenges of dealing with soldiers:

March 19: ... I traveled to Fedosowa for the execution of Private G. S., condemned to death for desertion ... When informed that he had been given the death sentence, S. fell apart. I spent the entire night in the cell with him, and he soon calmed down. He showed remorse for his disgraceful deed, and after receiving the holy sacrament, wrote two letters of farewell.[123]

In May 1942, Father Raible was briefly hospitalized. He wondered if heavy sweating had strained his heart. Perhaps his illness helps explain the show of emotion, unusual in such reports,[124] in his final paragraphs:

June 1: The last part of this activity report is supposed to summarize the situation at the main dressing stations where I have been providing spiritual care. It is a terrible scene of blood, wounds, and death. It is an enormous strain on one's nerves to see nothing day and night but blood and mangled human bodies, to hear nothing but moans of pain from wounded soldiers and the death rattles of dying comrades ... No one except the priest assigned to the clearing station has the opportunity to spend those last hours – the most difficult time – with these dying comrades; no one else can transmit to the loved ones at home so many important final words and wishes.[125]

During the three-month reporting period, the priest noted, he had given last rites to 209 men who died at the clearing station, and to a large number of seriously wounded soldiers, many of whom died on the way to hospital. He mentioned the countless letters he received from family members, telling him how comforting it was to know their loved one had been with a priest in his final hours. But the anguish of his words – "nothing day and night but blood and mangled human bodies" – suggests that Raible, who had been with the 15th Infantry Division throughout 1941, in areas, including Minsk and Mogilev, where Germans massacred enormous numbers of Jews and Soviet POWs,[126] might also have been thinking of Germany's victims. Even if so, however, he reverted to well-trodden ground by invoking the Wehrmacht's holy sacrifice: "May the souls of the dead heroes, whom I have been privileged to help lead to the heart of God their Father, find eternal rest from their suffering. And may their hearts' blood, spilled for the homeland, be the everlasting bond for the building of a free and great Germany!"[127]

An essential move in the justification and facilitation of German atrocities was inversion, switching perpetrators and victims. Inversion is familiar to Christians and built into Christian faith, because Jesus, the innocent victim, conquers death. In Christian tradition Jews were standard targets; as supposed killers of Christ, they figured as deserving destruction, embodiments of evil and an ossified religion that was reduced to devouring the blood of Christian children to try to revive itself. Christianity was a powerful tool and a force in its own right, complicit in the destruction of existing religious and communal traditions, and a central component in the genocidal culture that replaced them, justifying violence, magically transforming perpetrators into victims and victims into perpetrators, providing a narrative of salvation and redemption through blood. Individual Germans in occupied France or Ukraine in 1942 did not have to believe or even think about those narratives: all the pieces were in place.

The middle period of the war, which saw the widest reach of German military domination, the beginning of its unraveling, and the peak years of killing, implicated chaplains in a genocidal culture, whether they were on the Soviet front, or in occupied Poland, France, or Greece. Even at the height of German power, chaplains were on the defensive, scrambling to prove their worth. The Wehrmacht chaplains served multiple constituencies: the military hierarchy, soldiers, Germans back home, and the chaplaincy as an institution. Their commitment to their clients and their position in a system saturated in violence facilitated eradication of the people outside those relationships, that is, "the enemy." As destruction on a massive scale became the everyday reality of a brutal occupation, chaplains increasingly turned inward and focused on giving solace to men waging a war they described as hell for everyone. In their narrative, an epic unfolding of God's plan, no one was to blame. The Catholic priest Ernst Tewes, one of the chaplains who had tried to halt the killing of Jewish children in Belaya Tserkov in 1941 but supported the "anti-partisan" massacres of the following year, summed the situation up with this passive formulation: "the furies of war had been unleashed."[128]

6   "What Should We Preach Now?"
1944–1945

Over the course of 1943, the war turned against Germany.[1] By the end of the year, the advancing Red Army was hammering the Wehrmacht,[2] and the Soviets had started trying – and hanging – Germans and collaborators in the territories they liberated.[3] Italy had surrendered, and Allied bombs were pounding German cities. Still, the Wehrmacht's retreat was slow, uneven, and extremely violent. The killing frenzies that accompanied it destroyed hundreds of thousands of Hungarian Jews, partisans in Italy and Yugoslavia, civilians in Belarus, and concentration camp prisoners on death marches. At the same time, more "Aryan" Germans became targets of Nazi violence, including tens of thousands of soldiers accused of desertion and defeatism.[4] Wehrmacht chaplains operated amid all this carnage.

Under the volatile conditions of what is now known as the last year of the war,[5] the chaplains found their job both more difficult and, in some ways, easier. Surrounded by uncertainty and devastation, chaplains were stretched to breaking point. Air raids, retreats, and shortages plagued their efforts, and their critics seized the moment to crack down on them. For years German chaplains had insisted that their presence raised the Wehrmacht's fighting spirit; now, as failure loomed, they were exposed, easy targets for blame. Yet as the cause they served faltered, German military chaplains also experienced spikes in prestige. Wounded men and bereaved families looked to them for comfort; commanders called on them to warn soldiers they were bound by a sacred oath. From the beginning, the Wehrmacht chaplains had craved relevance and chased credibility. Now they got both, at a high price.

For all their woes, the Wehrmacht chaplains operated in a world of Christianity triumphant. To grasp the significance of this claim, one has to look at sources from outside Christian circles. Consider the account of Emilia Kotlova, a teacher from Kyiv who, in January 1945, wrote about her experiences to Soviet journalist Ilya Ehrenburg. In 1941, Kotlova managed to evade the massacre at Babyn Yar and escape with her two little girls to Zhytomyr. Over the next three years, she was repeatedly denounced, arrested, interrogated, and beaten, by Germans and also by Ukrainians and Russians. Again and again, she told Ehrenburg, her life and the lives of her daughters depended on her convincing people she was not a Jew.

Kotlova eventually found work in a village school. Conditions were desperate: she and her children had no heat, no blankets, and nothing to eat but potatoes. Their precarious existence got worse when religious education became mandatory in the schools, as Kotlova explained:

> How was I supposed to know anything about religious education? ... And the priest's son (the principal) knew straight away that I was not Russian (in their way of thinking, Orthodox). ... At the village council, they asked me about my religious faith. I nearly answered Jewish instead of Orthodox. Even though it was so revolting to me that it made me cry, I had to keep silent. The priest's son, a first-class hooligan, began interrogating me. Who was I? Why didn't I recognize any holidays or even know their names? Why didn't I go to church and teach the children to pray?

Kotlova likely included the story of her failed religious test in order to demonstrate to Ehrenburg that she was a good Communist and loyal Soviet citizen. But there is no reason to doubt that the incident occurred, and the details are compelling. Many other sources confirm the picture that even in Soviet territory, whether German-occupied, liberated, or in the rear, Christianity not only survived the Nazis but thrived.[6]

According to Kotlova, the principal reported her to the Gestapo, and she was summoned to appear at their office in Zhytomyr. She continued to deny she was Jewish and, after brutal questioning, was released on the condition that she return with her passport. Having no alternative, she went back to the village, where the principal and others assumed she had been killed. Now, she told Ehrenburg, "out of nowhere, I showed up in the village. Everyone ran out to see the 'hanged woman,' and it was only then that they became convinced that I really was a Russian."[7] In short, to the people around her, the fact Kotlova was still alive was itself proof that, whoever and whatever she was, she could not be Jewish, because in their experience, Jews – and Judaism – were dead. Christianity, in contrast, they knew to be very much alive.

The vitality of Christianity provided an anchor to the Wehrmacht chaplains during the tumultuous period from the Soviet liberation of Kyiv in November 1943 to VE Day a year and a half later. Tentatively at first, then more boldly, they began to position themselves for the possible defeat of their country. The intense uncertainty of the last stages of war brought new troubles, and familiar tasks – writing reports and sermons, vetting prospective chaplains, and awarding military honors – posed new dilemmas. Yet the vigor of Christian traditions and institutions gave chaplains ways to assert themselves with Nazi authorities. It also shaped their prospects for the future and limited the damage they faced. Though their nation might be vanquished, their religion remained intact, and rather than dividing them from their military adversaries, Christianity promised common ground.[8]

In January 1944, a year before Emilia Kotlova wrote her letter, Theodor Laasch, the Protestant superintendent of pastoral care in Military District 11 (Hanover), sent an unusual New Year's message to base chaplains in his region. Laasch's missive was silent on German atrocities and terse about the military situation, and it mentioned Allied bombings only in passing. Perhaps he was being prudent: clergy were prohibited from discussing politics or security issues in public, and private comments could leave him vulnerable to accusations of defeatism. But the superintendent proved willing to broach a different risky topic: internal divisions, specifically Nazi hostility toward military chaplains. Laasch's text, a mix of caution and boldness, reflects the contradictions chaplains faced during the last year of the war. On the one hand, Nazi authorities, increasingly frantic about security, doubled down on efforts to restrict the chaplaincy and established a corps of ideological rivals: the National Socialist Leadership Officers (NSFOs).[9] On the other hand, the deteriorating military situation and attempts to boost morale by any means opened new opportunities for chaplains' ministry.

Laasch's greeting set a positive tone. "Most of the reports about the Christmas celebrations and your other activities sound favorable," he assured his pastors. They did have critics, he conceded, and they should be patient and keep trying "to gain at least the respect of the other side." Should they be rebuffed, however, chaplains must stand firm: "When our service is willfully obstructed, we will demand our rights." Laasch proposed a plan of action: base chaplains should keep inviting people to church services, especially on holidays, and they should personally remind commanders that they were required to relay those invitations to the troops.[10]

Laasch paid particular attention to the military oath. In some cases, he had learned, clergy had been shut out of soldiers' swearing-in ceremonies. His response, though addressed to the pastors, aimed a two-pronged threat at Christianity's Nazi foes. Germany needed chaplains now more than ever, Laasch warned, hinting ominously at the mounting number of deserters:[11] "I would like to remind you that precisely as the war continues, it is necessary to instill in the men the holiness of their oath of loyalty." Moreover, he intimated, military chaplains had powerful friends who guaranteed them access to the troops. In his words, headquarters "has ordered that every man be given the possibility of participating in religious instruction about the soldiers' oath."[12] The superintendent closed with a poignant reminder that chaplains shared the wartime sacrifice of all German people:

Our thoughts are with our honored Military Bishop who, together with his family, lost everything in the bomb attacks on Berlin, though he was unharmed. His house, the old field manse on Frommel Street, is completely burned out. Also the church where he preached, the Old Garrison Church, fell victim to the flames.[13]

Sources on military chaplains in 1944–1945 are scarcer than for previous years. Germany's rapidly moving fronts, mounting casualties, and disruption of lines of communication all made it hard for chaplains to write and to send, receive, and save correspondence. When chaplains did write, what could they say? In Nazi Germany, *Wehrkraftzersetzung* – undermining the war effort – was a crime.[14] The Gestapo, always on the look-out for defeatists, was on high alert after the July 20, 1944 attempt on Hitler's life. The issues of most pressing concern to chaplains, soldiers, and their families were dangerous to write or talk about openly. As a result, many of the sources I use in this chapter deal with mundane matters. But read closely and considered alongside other kinds of materials, they reveal a lot about the relationship between chaplains and Nazi authorities and shed light on the place of Christianity in the death throes and killing frenzies of Hitler's empire.

Atrocity and Christian Presence

As Hitler's forces were pushed into a shrinking territory by the advance of the Red Army, their acts of violence spiraled out to new victims.[15] Chaplains could not avoid the evidence of German crimes. Murder of the Jews of Hungary in May, June, and early July 1944 was centered at Auschwitz, but it also occurred along the route that marked transports of Hungarian Jews, many of them young women, to the labor camps and factories of annexed Austria.[16] Chaplains, including base chaplains, shared that space. Brutal anti-partisan warfare in Belarus, Yugoslavia, Italy, and Greece took place in the presence of chaplains, too. Likewise chaplains saw at close range the smashing of the Warsaw Insurrection and destruction of the city in August 1944, the practice of scorched earth, destroying as much as possible when the Wehrmacht retreated, and the death marches that brought the Holocaust home to German civilians.[17]

Numerous victims' accounts attest to Christianity's ubiquity in the midst of violence. Michael Jackson was born in 1920 in Torun (then in Czechoslovakia, now Ukraine), to a "very observant" Jewish family. Perhaps his upbringing sensitized him to issues of religion: in a 1997 interview, he noted many encounters with Christianity. In December 1943, after months in a labor unit in occupied Yugoslavia, Jackson was transferred to Stanyslaviv (Stanisławów, now Ivano-Frankivsk), Ukraine. Before they were sent east, he recalled, a representative of a church (he did not know which one) paid a visit. The clergyman said that whoever converted would be taken out of the labor camp and sent to another one with no "yellow bands." In Yugoslavia, the marker for Jews was a yellow armband marked by "Ž," for *Žid*, Serbo-Croatian for "Jew." According to Jackson, only one person agreed.[18]

That incident served several purposes in Jackson's narrative: it demonstrated his own steadfastness, marginalized those Jews who accepted conversion, and exposed the perfidy of Christian clergy. In the process, it also draws attention to the existence of Christian efforts in the midst of mass murder to evangelize Jews. Indeed, Christians across Europe could feel that their religion's moral teachings and claim to superiority had been vindicated by the annihilation of its oldest rival, Judaism.[19]

From a very different location and vantage point, another survivor, Tomas Stern, confirms a key fact: some Christians, aware Jews were targeted for destruction, used that knowledge to try to win converts. In 1944, when Stern was ten years old, he and his parents were forced into the ghetto in Szeged, Hungary. "They took all the Jews to the ghetto," he recalled:

Although there were a few hundred they did not take because ... several priests from different Catholic churches came and told them that, if they converted to Christianity, they would not take them to the ghetto, they would not have to wear the yellow star. There were Jews that got scared and converted to Christianity and they were taken to buildings where they, let's say, had more freedom and they lived there until they [the Nazis] deceived them too and took them to concentration camps as well.[20]

Stern's account also needs to be read analytically. Although he was almost certainly correct to assume that those Hungarian Jews who accepted last-minute offers of baptism ended up transported to labor and killing sites anyway, he could not have known this outcome as a ten-year-old who saw or heard about the priests' overtures. Eagerness to show the futility of apostasy probably influenced his narrative. Still, Stern had no reason to invent proselytizing Christian clergy, and their existence is confirmed in other settings, including displaced persons camps.[21] Such efforts reflected a recognition that the future, like the present, belonged to Christianity.

Although Jewish accounts of the period rarely identify chaplains, they do include striking evidence of close contact between the Wehrmacht and its victims. Iuliia Fleischman (later Penziur), was born in 1936 near Uman in Ukraine, where her parents worked on the *kolkhoz*, the collective farm. In an interview conducted in Russian in 1997, she described the Germans who were billeted at her aunt's house near the end of the war. Iuliia's older sister Liza spoke German and communicated with the soldiers. As Iuliia recalled, one of the soldiers had said to Liza, "Look at my hands, I have callouses on my hands. I am a worker, I don't need war. I don't want people to kill each other." This man said about the other soldier in the room, "Look at him, he is a fascist. Look how many gold rings he has on his fingers; he needs the war. Hitler kaput and Stalin kaput." That exchange, with its dichotomy between the good, Communist German and the greedy Nazi is standard Soviet fare. But it highlights the fact that German soldiers and officers, including chaplains, lived in conquered people's homes, and it provides a glimpse of the resulting fear. Her mother, Iuliia recounts, lived in terror that the "fascist soldier" would discover the family was Jewish.[22]

Ernest Light, born in 1920 to an Orthodox Jewish family in Uzhhorod, in Subcarpathian Rus', remembers another kind of close encounter with Wehrmacht soldiers. In an interview conducted in 1996 in Pittsburgh, Light described how he and his family gathered for Passover in April 1944, less than a month after the German occupiers arrived in Hungary:

> The night, on the Seder night, we were all sat, the table was set. And, I think it was on the second night, not on the first night, and while we were eat – preparing, all was . . . the wine and everything was set. And, we were reciting the Haggadah. And suddenly, a young lady from across the street – it was a good looking woman – walk, walk, ran into our house and says, "Please, hide me. A German soldier try to abduct me."

They let her into a side room and returned to the ritual.

During the Seder, Light explained, "you don't lock the door, you kept the doors open." On that night, "Elijah the Messiah is supposed to come," but the idea is anybody who enters during the Seder, "you should feed him, you should – he should participate in the Seder too." Suddenly, Light recalled, there was a second interruption: "A German soldier with a gun on his shoulder walks in. He walked in and we didn't flinch or anything. My father kept on reading. And everybody sat in their positions and not moved at all." For two or three minutes, Light said, the man just stood there. Light's fragmented narrative reflects the bizarre scene: "It's . . . it's very difficult . . . to describe it, what the feelings were or anything. But nobody – completely just . . . like nothing – nobody reacted to it." Then just as suddenly, as he had appeared, "the man turned around and walked out."[23]

For Light, who by his own account struggled after the war with his Jewish beliefs, this incident may have provided a way to give some meaning to the horror of the Holocaust. What made the German turn around, he wondered? Perhaps it was the sight of the family calmly reciting prayers that convinced him they could not be hiding anyone. Maybe the Germans had "strict orders not to alarm the population," so people would not run away. Or maybe the soldier was "a human being. He saw people sitting there, it's a family affair, and something flashed in his eyes, maybe – I'll never find out. I'll die with – without knowing what it was, but anyhow, it was a very – it was a something that . . . I never forget when I sit down, even now, to the Seder."[24]

Many in-depth accounts from victims exist for the last phase of the war, whereas sources from chaplains address the matter of German crimes obliquely, if at all. Chaplains may have talked among themselves, but their coded records offer few clues as to what they said. In late April 1944, the chaplain with Army Group E submitted a report to the Protestant military bishop on a meeting in Athens earlier that month. Details were scant, and the titles of the presentations only hint at what chaplains were dealing with by then. For instance, Dean of Chaplains Hunzinger gave a talk on "Demands of Military Chaplaincy in the Balkans."[25] Did those "demands" include watching Wehrmacht men round up thousands of Jews in Athens, Ioannina, Kastoria, and Volos in March 1944, all to be sent to Auschwitz for killing?[26] Catholic chaplains in the territory of the 1st Army held their own seminar two months later. The itinerary included a talk by Wehrmacht Chaplain Kurschatke, titled "The Divisional Chaplain in Combat – Experiences on the Eastern Front."[27] By then "combat" in Germany's east meant the scorched earth assault euphemistically called "anti-partisan warfare."

A May 1944 report from Dr. Schuster, chaplain with Army Group Center, described a recent training seminar for Protestant chaplains in Belarus. His account captures in a muted way something of the carnage that surrounded his colleagues and him. All the men struggled over long distances to get to the meeting. In an effort to anticipate the needs of the participants, the itinerary included presentations on "The Work of the National Socialist Leadership Office (NSFO) in Its Relationship to the Service of the Military Chaplain" and "The Events of the War and the Gospel of the Almighty and Merciful God." A roundtable with four pastors addressed "The Particularities of Base Pastoral Care and Service with the Security Divisions."[28] The Wehrmacht's security divisions were the main executors of the anti-partisan massacres.[29]

Around the same time, Protestant chaplains with the 18th Army and Army Detachment Narva held a seminar at the front in Riga. Participants could not have reached the seminar without encountering prison and labor camps, one of which, Kaiserwald, was located in a suburb of Riga. By the early days of June 1944, these places were swollen with inmates shunted from "liquidated" ghettos across the Baltic region and Jewish forced laborers from Hungary.[30] Judging from the titles, none of the presentations acknowledged Germany's victims directly, but two "experience reports" on "Pastoral Care during evacuation actions" would have had to deliberately avoid mentioning them. Likewise, senior chaplain Bauerle would have had to willfully ignore dead enemy civilians in his speech on "standardizing pastoral care at the front."[31]

Only in postwar writings do chaplains provide explicit accounts of witnessing atrocities in this period. Even these glimpses are fleeting, and a common theme is chaplains' powerlessness. The Catholic Josef Perau described watching a roundup of forced laborers in Belarus in 1944. Germans fenced off a space where they robbed and killed their victims (who, given the date, were likely non-Jews). Chaplain Perau saw Germans walking on dead children and dragging corpses "like sides of beef" through the muck. He said he appealed to a medic, who told him, "Father, leave this to us. I already shot a couple of helpless children myself, out of pity. Once we have won the war, Germany will become a people of culture again." Then Perau saw a general, he wrote; he wanted to throw himself on him and demand justice. But he was "no prophet," so instead he expressed his disgust privately and tried to prevent soldiers from plundering.[32]

Former Protestant chaplain Hans Leonhard published his memoir much later, in 1994, but his account of witnessing atrocities strikes a similar note. In a short section titled "War's end" he portrays his encounter with a death march:

From Tarnów our Lazarett was moved to Saybusch [Żywiec], and from there I came to Neustadt [Prudnik] in Upper Silesia to another military hospital. There I experienced how the inmates of the concentration camp Auschwitz were driven out; there's no other way to put it. We had two buildings on either side of the street on which all day long the column straggled by: men, women, old and young in their thin striped prison uniforms, often nothing but a few rags on their feet, in the icy cold of January 1945.

Like Perau, Leonhard described an abortive effort to intervene:

One old man could not go on. An SS man beat him on the head with a club. Two others tried to support him, but he fell to the ground. The other two were also starved to skeletons. The SS man, who was very young, coldly pulled out his pistol and shot him dead. He was just left lying there. The entire road to the next town ... was littered with corpses ... I tried to talk with one of the SS men. It wouldn't have taken much, and he would have shot me, too.[33]

In Perau's and Leonhard's narratives, the chaplains' self-justifications – I was powerless, I would have been shot – are inseparable from their up-close depictions of German violence.

Stretched Thin

The conditions under which the Wehrmacht chaplains worked, always taxing, deteriorated in the last stage of the war. Unstable fronts and escalating casualties meant chaplains had more to do with fewer supplies and no relief. In a report on his trip to Krakow in March 1944, Catholic Military Vicar Georg Werthmann outlined the situation: across the entire General Government, only ten military chaplains were providing pastoral care to about 200,000 active soldiers and another 80,000 who were wounded or ill.[34] Given vehicles and fuel, Werthmann granted, the chaplains might be able to reach all those men, but then what? They had no books, no Bibles. "Our military chaplains do not understand how it is that paper is available for every other purpose," Werthmann grumbled, "but then the paper shortage is invoked as an excuse for the lack of religious literature." Most serious, in his view, was the dearth of hymnals. Werthmann pitched the songbooks, and Catholicism in general, as key to ensuring the loyalty of new recruits. "Maybe the demand for songbooks is not as large on the Protestant side," he wrote, "but that could be explained by the fact that from their youth on, Catholics have a prayer book. Recently a lot of soldiers have come from the western and eastern border areas, which are overwhelmingly Catholic."[35]

Reporting from occupied Belarus, Protestant Army Group Chaplain Schuster voiced similar concerns in the form of a pep talk: "I tried to awaken the chaplains' understanding for the increased demands that are being made on them. Our segment of the front is twice as long as the western front in the First World War, and the number of pastors is so small that for more than 10,000 men there is just one military chaplain."[36]

Anti-partisan warfare, the accompanying atrocities, and the collapse of the distinction between combatants and civilians created additional challenges. Werthmann addressed these too, although with a coolness that forestalled ethical considerations. Security Divisions, he noted, had "special assignments in the East." By 1944, any German who had seen reports from the front would recognize that code for mass killing operations. According to Werthmann, three factors shaped pastoral care to these units: the size and vulnerability of their territory, the nature of security work, and the age of the men (older). As an example he cited the 286th Security Division, which he visited in the Mogilev-Orsha-Borisov (Mogilew-Orscha-Borissow) region. In his words: "Part of the area is threatened by bandits, part of it is plagued by bandits, and part of it is actually controlled by bandits."[37] Following official guidelines, Werthmann used the word *Banden*, which could also be translated as "gangs" or "criminal bands," so as not to dignify anti-German resistance fighters with the label "partisans." He spoke only of the physical hardships chaplains faced: fuel shortages, poor roads, and insurgents. Overall, he concluded, "pastoral care with a Security Division is tiring, dangerous, and mostly fruitless." Hence it was unacceptable when chaplains with health problems were transferred to such units: "Here the best is just barely good enough."[38]

Most of what happened to chaplains in the last phase of the war was typical of all members of the Wehrmacht. But chaplains' sense of their professional and spiritual standing added meaning to their experiences. For a Protestant chaplain above the Arctic Circle in occupied Norway, July 1944 was quiet. It was stimulating to be in "purely Lutheran" territory, he wrote to a colleague back home in Speyer: "Sometimes I've been able to play the organ in a little country church. You can get to know some nice literature and deeply moving music here."[39] Meanwhile, in an entry dated Belarus, July 19, 1944, Josef Perau expressed the mixture of spiritual fulfillment, resignation, and fear hinted at in other chaplains' words from that time:

Yesterday I marked the seventh anniversary of my consecration as a priest, without a mass, without community. I don't even have a New Testament anymore. Yet separate from all of that is the gift from God that is given to us through the laying on of hands. "My lot has fallen wonderfully to me. My cup, how richly it has been filled for me."

Perau and his Protestant colleague took their team of horses to visit the general on his birthday. They returned to an influx of wounded soldiers, and Perau attended to a dying man:

He had a serious head wound and he lay there, making the death rattle; with him he had his soldiers' hymnbook and a medallion of Saint Theresia with the baby Jesus. I buried him up at the Orthodox church, next to a stone cross that marked the grave of a priest. The current priest came by and prayed briefly over the body of the nineteen-year-old, which I had adorned with red carnations.

There was no time to linger. Perau and two volunteers ended the little ceremony to find their base camp being broken up. They joined the march westward.[40]

Chaplains invariably framed their narratives in terms of sacrifice, but to observers, they could seem as interested in self-preservation as anyone else. Looking back from the vantage point of 1952, an ethnic German pastor recalled encountering a chaplain as the Soviets swept into Poland:

Military chaplain W. Graßey from Feuchtwangen, Middle Franconia, together with his assistant, was able to escape in a car and told me what was going on when I saw him in the afternoon of January 18 in Mühlenrode [Sobieski]. Although officially they were still spreading favorable news, he told me the truth about the situation. "Our soldiers fought like lions," he said, "but the Russian came with so much armored infantry and such superior artillery that they succeeded in breaking through."

To the pastor's reproach about abandoning his post, the chaplain replied, "The only reserves there to defend the Warthe position were the two of us, me and my boy. So if you can, get out of here today."[41] In other cases too, chaplains on the run urged ethnic Germans in Ukraine, Yugoslavia, and elsewhere to flee the advancing Red Army.

On all fronts, including at home, chaplains were in demand, even by Nazi officials. In June 1944, the military plenipotentiary for the Reich Protector of Bohemia and Moravia wrote to the Protestant military bishop requesting that Pastor Kurt Freude be appointed base chaplain for Mährisch-Ostrau (Ostrava) and Friedeck (Frýdek).[42] Later that year, the Catholic district base chaplain in Innsbruck asked that all part-time base chaplains be retained in their positions. He was working at full capacity, he explained, with one or more soldiers' weddings almost every day and nearly as many funerals.[43] But hectic times also brought exhaustion and despair. Perau alludes to the discouragement chaplains encountered among the men they served: "North of Langhaken we held a church service with a penal company. It was not easy to connect with the resigned and embittered men."[44] The penal units (*Strafbataillonen*) were made up of soldiers and civilians condemned for some offense and assigned the most dangerous missions. By the last year of the war, these battalions, supervised by the military police, were bulging with forced recruits.[45] Their hostile reception deepened Perau's gloom, expressed in his entry for April 17, 1945: "Everywhere there is unrest. We are afraid that soon 'the night' is coming, 'when man works no more.'"[46]

Adding to the stress for Perau and his colleagues was the falling number of active chaplains. When chaplains for various reasons became unable to serve,[47] under army policy they were not replaced. Both military bishops and all the supervisory chaplains fretted about those vacancies. In late 1944, Bishop Dohrmann's office prepared two reports. The first presented a sobering overview: the approved number of Protestant military chaplains was 550, but only 121 were currently active in permanent positions. Sixty-nine positions were vacant, and 331 chaplains held temporary appointments (a. K., *auf Kriegsdauer*, for the duration of the war).[48] These latter were mostly base and reserve chaplains.

The second report revealed that the gaps were almost all on the ground. All but one of the seventeen "military deans" (*Wehrmachtdekane*) were in place, and likewise all but one of the fifty-seven supervisory chaplains (*Wehrmachtoberpfarrer*). But at the level of military chaplains (*Wehrmachtpfarrer*), almost as many positions were vacant as filled: sixty-seven versus seventy-one. To make matters worse, of those seventy-one active military chaplains, twenty-two were missing, captured, or had left the service but still technically held their positions.[49] In short, by early 1945, there were forty-nine Protestant military chaplains in the field. No wonder soldiers' letters rarely mentioned them.

Contrast this situation with the British Army chaplains. One hundred of them landed with 156,000 Allied personnel on D-Day; twenty were killed in that campaign.[50]

Wehrmacht chaplains at the front, meanwhile, devoted more and more time to dealing with death. In February 1944, a Protestant reported to his military bishop on a meeting of chaplains in Rome. The program was adjusted so that the Wehrmacht graves officer with Army Command 10, a Captain Dr. Haß, could give a presentation on tending to graves. According to the author, "This was particularly valuable, because most of the divisional chaplains have taken over the work of the graves officer." As a result, there was time for only one of the other planned presentations, on presumably the second most urgent topic: "sexual questions."[51]

The divisional chaplains' new role as graves officers reflects the tensions of this period. The job was time-consuming and would become ever more so, and it reinforced many soldiers' morbid view of chaplains. Yet it offered chaplains precious connections to the men and their families. It may also have facilitated a return to marking Wehrmacht graves with Christian crosses rather than, or in addition to, the swastika and Iron Cross.[52] In his April 1944 activity report, Protestant Chaplain Rosenthal with the 14th Infantry Division east of Vitebsk (Viciebsk) explained that doing this work was a way to look after his men: "When the troops are situated in the midst of hard battle and they can no longer really care at all about their dead, it is a particular service to take over the job of performing burials, identifying the dead, and offering various kinds of help." Rosenthal highlighted a large service he held at military cemetery number 2 in Vitebsk. Although it honored a dead major and captain, he explained, "In a deeper sense it became a memorial service for all the dead of the Division in the past bitter fighting."[53]

Vitebsk was indeed the scene of heavy fighting in spring 1944, but the vast majority of graves there were not German. It was a historically Jewish city, with Jews making up half the population in the early twentieth century. In July 1941, the Luftwaffe bombed it, and in October, the Germans murdered thousands of Jews who had been confined to a ghetto: the number is unknown, but estimates run between 8,000 and 16,000. Another round of killing Jews followed two years later, as the Germans returned on their retreat westward. Vitebsk was also a center of partisan activity, and German Security forces were ruthless in their assault. Some sources estimate that 240,000 people – one-third of the population of the Vitebsk Oblast – were killed over the course of the war.[54] Giorgi Shantir, the boy who remembers hearing a German soldier pronounce that "war is good," witnessed the final round of killing Jews and burning their bodies in Vitebsk in autumn 1943. Among the dead was his mother, Ida Isaakovna (née Soloveichik).[55]

Rising casualties hit chaplains too, with oddly conflicting results. Dwindling numbers meant chaplains struggled to meet their responsibilities, but for public relations purposes, sometimes the most useful chaplain was a dead one. Deaths constituted compelling evidence of heroic sacrifice and provided a forum to extol military chaplaincy. Over the course of 1944, the Catholic military bishop's bulletin, the *Verordnungsblatt*, printed more and longer obituaries. The diligent Vicar Werthmann wrote most, maybe all, of these. He lavished special attention on chaplains who had served in the Great War. These men had a doubly legitimating function: their many years of service attested to Catholicism's steadfast patriotism, and their sacrifice for Hitler's war normalized the new German Fatherland.

One such chaplain was Franz Albert, whose death "after a short illness" the Bulletin announced in May 1944. The obituary cast Albert's death as an inspiration: "The words, with which he, deathly ill, greeted the Host that was extended to him in farewell – *Miles salutat Regem Christum!* [a soldier greets Christ the King] – are a call to duty to all of us and an expression of his faithful, priest-soldierly spirit."[56] Another chaplain, Johannes Gehrmann, died in a military hospital in Warsaw in April 1944. The obituary showcased his soldierly bona fides and emphasized that he perished in the line of duty: "In the course of a pastoral visit to troops at the immediate front he was seriously wounded."[57]

Werthmann packed a lot of boasting into the obituaries. In June 1944, he visited Catholic military chaplains with the 2nd and 4th Armies. At the "heroes' cemetery of Minsk," he laid a wreath on the grave of Chaplain Walter Kauder from Army Group Center, who had suffered a fatal accident.[58] Kauder's obituary did not include the cause of death, presumably to leave open more heroic possibilities.[59] Nor did it mention a much larger "cemetery" on the outskirts of Minsk: the killing center of Maly Trostenets (Maly Trascianiec in Belarusian), where Germans murdered an estimated 206,000 people, most of them Jews, between May 1942 and May 1944, the month Chaplain Kauder died. Established on the site of a former *kolkhoz*, Maly Trostenets was the third or fourth largest killing site in the Holocaust (after Auschwitz, Treblinka, and either Bełżec or Majdanek, depending on the data used). Killers there shot their victims or suffocated them in gas vans. As the Red Army approached in June 1944, the Germans bombed and burned the site, leaving no survivors.[60]

A July 1944 memo from Armed Forced High Command to the Reich Church Ministry shows that church efforts to capitalize on casualties annoyed the top brass. This document also hints at why it is difficult to obtain exact numbers of military chaplains or statistics regarding how many were wounded or killed. Confessional rivalry appears to have played a role:

From a report of the Protestant Church Council it is evident that from time to time in the Catholic churches of the Archdiocese of Freiburg during the regular Sunday service exact numbers are announced of priests and theology students who are in military service as well as priests who have fallen. Such announcements are absolutely not wanted, and Armed Forces High Command requests that you instruct the relevant church offices accordingly.[61]

Undaunted, the obituaries' authors spun every chaplain's death into proof of courage under fire. In October 1944, the Catholic military bishop's bulletin announced the death in a reserve hospital in Dresden, "after a short, severe illness," of Dr. Eduard Zimmermann. According to the obituary, Zimmermann served in World War I and joined the Wehrmacht chaplaincy in 1934, even before rearmament was official. He held a series of high-ranking positions within the chaplaincy until he fell ill in 1942. To prove his bravery, the obituary quoted his military superiors:

Despite continuous enemy fire, he did not allow himself to be deterred from holding religious services with the troops in the Reserves or from providing pastoral care to the many wounded in the unit and main dressing stations. He thereby performed extraordinary service under enemy attack.[62]

The final issue of the Catholic military bishop's bulletin, from January 1945, reported two deaths, one from disease, the other at the hands of partisans. Both were presented as the price of military valor. On November 15, 1944, Catholic Naval Chaplain Rochus Schneider died in an air force hospital in Denmark, "after a short, severe illness with diphtheria, which he contracted in the course of duty." A chaplain since 1939, Schneider was the recipient of a War Merit Cross (*Kriegsverdienstkreuz*) 2nd class with swords. According to his obituary, his enduring contribution was putting together the Catholic Hymn and Prayer book for the navy.[63] The second obituary portrayed a less lofty career but more bellicose death. Karl Sauer joined the Wehrmacht in February 1940 as a medic and became a military chaplain a year later. In August 1944, he was transferred to the southeast. There, on November 29, 1944, "in the course of carrying out his duties at a field hospital, he fell victim to a bandit attack."[64]

Vetting Chaplains

The process of appointing chaplains, which required clearance from the military, Church Ministry, and Gestapo,[65] had been fraught all along, but the push and pull of this period of the war added further complications. Yet it was here that chaplains took the first, small steps to distance themselves from the Nazi state. All of the appointments made in 1944, it appears, were part-time base chaplains, that is, civilian clergy who took on the responsibility in addition to their own parishes. These were vital positions: base chaplains outnumbered front chaplains at least three to one, and their less frenetic circumstances meant they often had more opportunities to engage with soldiers. Still, the Church Ministry and Security Service (SD) blocked most of the men proposed as base chaplains in 1944. Those rejections were a backhanded tribute to the chaplaincy's relevance: if the authorities cared so much, perhaps military chaplains really did matter. Cautiously chaplains began to test the limits.

A common reason for rejecting prospective chaplains was political, a category that encompassed party and church politics. The Security Service looked as far back as the early years of Nazi rule and found the slightest grounds to object. Typical was a report from January 1944 that turned down the curate Franz Josef Wohl. "A passionate proponent of the Catholic youth movement," the report complained, Wohl had organized performances of prohibited secular plays and, in 1935, "denied political leaders entry to a public event of the Catholic association of apprentices." He was also accused of stopping schoolchildren from using the "German greeting" by insisting it was "inappropriate" to greet a priest with "Heil Hitler." For good measure, the report added a sin of omission: "To date he has not demonstrated the slightest interest in promoting the *Volksgemeinschaft*."[66]

Negative reports rarely invoked current political misdemeanors. Either clergy had learned to toe the line or bishops realized there was no point in nominating troublemakers. Ferdinand Peus, the Catholic base chaplain for Moers, near the Dutch border, was an exception. In May 1944, Peus lost his position as chaplain. According to a police report, he spent three weeks in prison in January 1944, because he had his assistant's daughter copy a pamphlet he had written, "The Religious Situation of the Soldier Today," then gave it to clergy serving in the Wehrmacht to distribute.[67] A note from Army High Command to the Catholic military bishop instructed that Peus be fired.[68] After the war, Peus was lauded in his hometown as a hero of the resistance.

In only three of the 250 cases I examined did the reason for turning down a candidate have anything to do with Jews. Two of those cases were from 1944. That year, a Protestant and a Catholic were each rejected because of sermons they had given six years earlier, criticizing the November 1938 pogrom known as *Kristallnacht*.[69] In fact, prospective chaplains were at least as likely to be denied because their exuberant pro-Nazism made them divisive. In 1944 some soldiers complained about a Protestant pastor in a military hospital who held a lecture series they derided as German Christian propaganda. The preacher replied that he was on assignment from the Nazi Party.[70]

Ethnic politics also came into play. Since the Sudetenland crisis in 1938 and the attack on Poland a year later, Nazi authorities had favored clergy from the German minorities, and the vetting process reflected that preference. In May 1944, a Security Service report on a prospective Catholic chaplain noted that Alois Dyllus from Teschen (Český Těšín) had "openly agitated for Germanness during the Polish time."[71] The Church Ministry quickly confirmed his appointment.[72] Two other files that sailed through originated in Czechoslovakia. According to the police report from September 1944, Catechist Blahut had "sought to join the Sudeten German Party" but was not accepted due to his profession.[73] His colleague had been a more overt champion of Germanness: "Catechist Sperlik previously belonged to the Christian Socialist People's Party and was a member of the board of the League for the 'German East.' His pro-German position earned him the enmity of his Czech colleagues. In June 1944, Sperlik was awarded the Merit Cross 2nd class."[74]

Leading chaplains tried to exploit the popularity of the German minorities, the *Volksdeutschen*, with Nazi authorities. In May 1944, Military Vicar Werthmann reported on his visit to Prague and Holoubkau (Holoubkov) and emphasized the contribution of military chaplains to strengthening Germanness:

The peaceful surface conceals a quiet yet very intense struggle between the German and Czech people. ... Without taking on a church political role, the full-time and part-time military chaplains there are not only exponents of a religious-pastoral calling, they are also naturally representatives of Germanness in the areas to which they minister.[75]

According to Werthmann, everyone at the military posts he visited was convinced of the chaplains' value: "The Commander underscored the immense significance of the military chaplaincy for the inevitable battle between peoples in the Protectorate."[76]

Werthmann singled out for praise the Catholic military district chaplain for Bohemia and Moravia, Father Schinzinger. Active in the Protectorate since 1939, he was lauded for his intimate knowledge of the "church political situation in his jurisdiction."[77] But something went wrong. By the time Werthmann returned to Prague in December, General Rudolf Toussaint, commander of the Military District of Bohemia and Moravia, had removed Schinzinger from his post. Werthmann's guarded remarks reveal only that the chaplain had overstepped his bounds: "Schinzinger had personal ambitions in the area of church politics: he got involved in civilian church issues and tried to influence them, although that was not his responsibility."[78]

Schinzinger's fall fit a pattern in the last phase of the war. As Germany's military fortunes wavered then sank, Nazi authorities worried about the reliability of the many ethnic Germans they had recruited (and created).[79] Prospective chaplains from territories that were reverting to Polish or Soviet control came under particular scrutiny. A Security Service report from December 1944 addressed the case of the Catholic vicar Emil Peter Chmiel, from Neu-Berun (Bieruń Nowy) in the district of Pleß (Pszczyna). The verdict was not positive:

During the Polish period, Vicar Chmiel, who is a member of the German People's List, Category 3, was regarded as a Polish-oriented clergyman. During the time he was working in Bobrownik [Bobrowniki] he was accused of violating the prohibition against giving sermons in Polish and of refusing to hear confessions in German. In a further incident, he was accused of using expressions hostile to the state and saying to a Polish auxiliary policeman, "Let Hitler have it!" [*Gib dem Hitler richtig!*]

Because he had been active in the National Socialist Flyers Corps since 1940, Chmiel got off with a warning from the Gestapo.[80] But now the Church Ministry rejected him.[81] Protestants faced similar hurdles. In January 1945, the Church Ministry nixed a Lutheran pastor named Peter Weiland, a German from Pressburg (Bratislava), for a post as base chaplain in Engerau (Petržalka). The grounds were familiar: "Pastor Peter Weiland is regarded by the local National Socialists as politically unreliable."[82]

The biggest barrier to appointments was the Church Ministry, where the bottleneck was largely due to one person: State Secretary Hermann Muhs. A lawyer, vociferous member of the "German Christian" movement, and long-time Nazi activist, Muhs became top man in church affairs in 1941, when the minister, Hanns Kerrl, died. Hitler never named a replacement. Muhs lorded it over his enemies old and new – opponents in the Confessing Church but also rivals from competing German Christian factions. The process of appointing chaplains gave him a stick that he used to beat the military bishops.

Throughout 1944, Muhs fought with Dohrmann and Werthmann over eight prospective base chaplains. On the Protestant side, he objected to the appointment of Pastors Rehmann, Wicke, Demuth, and Bastert. According to the police report, Wilhelm Rehmann in Mönchen-Gladbach was an active member of the "Confessing front," who had hired "seriously compromised" people to work in his church, including "a former Separatist and a stateless person who had been a Communist Party member."[83] Arnold Wicke, proposed as base chaplain in Dietersdorf, was disqualified as "a fighter for the Confessing Church cause." The police report noted he had received a warning in April 1938, because he scheduled a confirmation class for a group of girls during a speech by the Führer.[84] Emil Demuth, though not active in the church struggle, had been assessed unfavorably by regional Nazi leaders.[85]

For the Church Ministry, one of the weakest ministries, and for Muhs personally, being able to slap down all those nominees was an assertion of dominance. Muhs showed his hand with a case that on the surface seemed benign. He raised "serious objections" to the appointment of Hermann Bastert as chaplain for the military base in Soest. According to the police report, Bastert was not a Party member, but since Christian clergy were rarely accepted into the Nazi Party, he could hardly be faulted on that score. He did belong to the National Socialist People's Welfare, the Reich Air Raid Defense League (a paramilitary organization), and the Reich Veterans' Association. And although he had ties to the Confessing Church and headed the Westphalian Ladies' Aid, Bastert had not played a negative role in church politics.[86] In short, his record was innocuous.

Muhs's concern, however, was not Bastert but Dohrmann. A month earlier, the bishop had informed the Church Ministry that he had gone ahead and named Bastert base chaplain, "with an understanding that the appointment could be canceled at any time." He had no choice, he maintained, because there were no other suitable clergymen, and in any case, Army High Command had approved.[87] Muhs exploded. He admitted that Bastert might have been assessed differently but defended his mandate by asserting the political consequence of the chaplaincy: "Pastoral care to the army in its various forms is an extremely significant part of the National Socialist training of people. I must emphasize that it is unacceptable to bring people into this role who have a poor reputation with the highest Security Police officials in the Reich."[88] The Church Ministry did approve some appointments, including two base chaplains in June 1944, but those were rare exceptions.

Meanwhile both military bishops, while they continued to wrangle with Muhs and his surrogates, proceeded to install base chaplains on their own.

Dohrmann and Rarkowski (or Werthmann) almost certainly cooperated in this enterprise, and both communicated directly with their contacts in the military.[89] It was no straight line from chafing under the rule of the Church Ministry to ignoring Muhs's objections, but in fits and starts the chaplaincy exercised increasing independence.

In the case of the four Catholics, the Church Ministry emphasized political unreliability. Franz Neumann, while vicar in Jablonetz (Jablonec nad Nisou), "had an unfavorable influence on the mood and attitude of the German population, above all the schoolchildren, whom he tried to alienate from the National Socialist movement." Moreover, "he has shown no interest at all in political life or the events of the war."[90] Erich Juraschek "held Sunday services on Ascension Day in contravention of existing regulations." Nevertheless, the Catholic military bishop appointed Neumann and Juraschek as base chaplains.[91]

Likewise, the two priests Anton Kowalleck and Dr. Paul Hornig took up the duties of chaplains despite the Church Ministry's objections.[92] Kowalleck was deemed too close to the Center Party, and Hornig had spent three weeks in prison in 1942 for violating the censor. While serving as a prison chaplain in Bautzen in 1939–1940, he had carried an inmate's letters out of the institution.[93] Hornig's case may have had direct political implications, because Bautzen's two prisons were notorious sites of incarceration of Communists, Social Democrats, and other opponents of the regime, among them Ernst Thälmann.[94] Nevertheless, Army High Command backed Hornig's appointment.[95]

Recriminations around appointments of base chaplains dragged on through the summer. In August 1944, the military office for pastoral care known as Group S, the Church Ministry, and Armed Forces High Command all weighed in, each claiming victory. A lengthy memo from High Command asserted the importance of military intelligence in the vetting process but ceded priority to the Security Service reports. The explanation echoed, and in parts quoted, Muhs's earlier proclamation:

A pastor, who is even the slightest bit politically compromised does not belong in the military chaplaincy, even if the judgment is based on considerations that lie many years in the past. It is unacceptable and for the leadership intolerable, when on the one hand, we strive to strengthen our fighting power by deploying officers who are driven by firm National Socialist principles and then, on the other hand, military chaplains are let loose on the soldiers who lack a clear political stance in the current circumstances.[96]

Group S relayed the message, backing the Church Ministry against the military bishops, and took the opportunity to expand its own purview. Base chaplains could not be appointed over the ministry's objections, it instructed; in cases of conflict, Group S would decide.[97] Satisfied, the Church Ministry announced that a number of men "to whom we had objected and who had been named against our will (eight cases) have been removed from those positions."[98]

Did the chaplaincy lose? Even if all eight men officially left their positions, who would control whether they continued to offer pastoral care to soldiers and families in their districts? With regard to the vetting process, the disruption of the last year of the war cut both ways. By mid-1944, many names proposed by the military bishops did not even make it to the next level.[99] Meanwhile, evidence suggests that Muhs, and others looking to be punitive, contemplated unleashing a new round of accusations of impropriety against Catholic clergy, and maybe Protestants, too. An unlabeled file within the Church Ministry collection contains items related to cases against clergy, though not specifically military chaplains. For example, in one 1944 case, a doctor of theology was charged with crimes against boys at the school he taught at in Graz, including inciting them to masturbate.[100] But these schemes never got off the ground. Between early 1944 and spring 1945, the situation changed, from Nazi authorities having the upper hand, to a tug-of-war, to chaplains and the churches as a whole exercising their independence. Looking back, they could claim they had been Hitler's adversaries all along.

Rewards, Restrictions, and Opportunities

As the bodies of Nazi Germany's victims piled up along the routes of the Wehrmacht's retreat, chaplains began to contest another issue: military decorations. The seesawing status of the chaplaincy in 1944–1945 is evident around this matter, too, as is the chaplains' uneven transition from partners and supplicants to outsiders vis-à-vis Hitler's regime. In September 1942, military authorities had ruled that chaplains could not receive the Iron Cross. However, the War Merit Cross could be awarded to chaplains, even to non-members of the military, including base and military hospital chaplains.[101] Throughout 1944 and into the early months of 1945, chaplains and their representatives continued to seek this distinction, but Nazi officials blocked them. Increasingly, the military bishops and supervisory chaplains tried to bypass state and Party organs, often with the backing of their friends in the officer corps.

Supervisory chaplains initiated the requests for medals in order to reward individuals for meritorious service and also to boost the status of the chaplaincy. But in early 1944, the process suddenly changed. In February, the Protestant chaplain in Nuremberg East informed Bishop Dohrmann of a recent ceremony awarding the War Merit Cross 2nd class, "without swords," to three part-time base chaplains, in Würzburg, Coburg, and Bamberg.[102] A month later, Army High Command wrote to both military bishops noting that from now on, proposals to award military service decorations to part-time base chaplains and reserve military hospital chaplains were to be submitted though the Protestant or Catholic military bishop to Group S, which would pass them on to the Army Personnel Office for a decision.[103] Undeterred or perhaps uninformed, supervisory chaplains continued to propose names.

One such proposal originated in April 1944, with Hermann Bunke, the Protestant chaplain for Military District 3, Berlin-Spandau. Bunke proposed awarding a War Merit Cross 2nd class, without swords, to base chaplain Hans Dannenbaum. Born in 1895, Dannenbaum already had a Friedrich August Cross 2nd class from 1914 and an Iron Cross 2nd class from 1941. His supervisor, Bunke, served as chaplain to the military prison at Spandau, where he ministered to many condemned Wehrmacht soldiers before their executions. In violation of regulations, Bunke frequently carried messages between the men and their families. His impassioned letter of nomination highlighted Dannenbaum's work in that same vein:

Pastor Hans Dannenbaum has been part-time base chaplain in Berlin since January 1, 1940. In addition to his pastoral care at church services and the functions of his office, he has cared for the soldiers who end up in the military investigation prison at Tegel and provided pastoral companionship to the condemned men in the final night before their execution. ... Pastor Dannenbaum has applied himself to his assigned task with his full energy and with visible success.[104]

It is hard to imagine that Bunke's pitch would land on sympathetic ears. In fact, it seems almost a deliberate provocation, in spring 1944, as Wehrmacht arrests of their own men for charges of desertion were reaching new highs, to propose decorating a pastor who ministered to condemned German soldiers. Both Bunke and Dannenbaum had a history of clashes with the German Christian movement,[105] and they would have known that their enemies would spare no effort to bring them down. But Bunke was experienced and well-connected. Did he overestimate his standing or have misplaced faith in German military honor? He seems to have expected that representatives of the Wehrmacht would reward Dannenbaum and him for their service to soldiers. Instead, his request cost him his position and occasioned a special training session for all military district chaplains, in order to ensure, as Muhs put it, "that only truly suitable clergy find their way into the Army Chaplaincy."[106]

Even after the debacle with Bunke, chaplains tried to acquire military awards, but their opponents kept pushing back. In January 1945, Army High Command requested that several medals be revoked. At issue were three War Merit Crosses 2nd class, without swords, that had been awarded on September 1, 1944 by the commanding general in District 11 (Hanover) to part-time base chaplains Kittle and Alberts, and military hospital chaplain Leclaire. All had been declared "null and void."[107]

The chaplains tried again. In March 1945, the Protestant military bishop proposed three part-time base chaplains from Military District 10 to be awarded the War Merit Cross 2nd class: Pastors Oskar Meyer in Lüneburg, Anders Tange in Schleswig, and Horst Scheunemann in Lübeck.[108] Army High Command punted by sending the case on to the Command of Military District 10 in Hamburg, "with a request for further consideration."[109] But by then the point was moot. March 21, 1945, the date on the draft, marked two weeks since US forces had crossed the Rhine at Remagen. Soviet troops were on the road to Vienna, and two-thirds of the population of Hamburg, pounded by months of air raids, had fled the city. The letter never got sent, and Pastors Meyer, Tange, and Scheunemann were spared the trouble of concealing or disposing of those medals, which suddenly became a liability. So who won that round?

As the back-and-forth around military awards shows, the last year of the war brought chaplains under scrutiny, yet the chaotic conditions created opportunities for them to act autonomously. Military and political leaders increased pressure on the chaplaincy, and the bishops and supervisors passed it on to their men on the ground. At every level, leadership was crucial, because the person who took charge at a tipping point could have a dramatic impact, often far out of proportion to their formal power.

Leadership posed particular challenges on the Catholic side as Military Bishop Franz Justus Rarkowski was increasingly sidelined. In 1944, Rarkowski was seventy-one years old and reportedly had health problems, which may have included cognitive issues. Certainly after the war, Werthmann and others claimed Rarkowski had not been mentally competent.[110] According to his postwar biographer, Rarkowski moved out of Berlin in early 1944 and retired a year later. He lived out his life in obscurity in Munich, where he died in 1950 and was buried in the crypt of the cathedral vicars.[111]

Georg Werthmann, who held the position of vicar general to the Catholic military bishop from 1936 to 1945, enjoyed widespread respect during the war and a much more positive reputation afterward than Rarkowski.[112] No doubt the contrast with his boss became an advantage for him, although it was challenging at the time. A loyal servant of the chaplaincy, including the bureaucrats who oversaw it, Werthmann maintained a network of former chaplains after the war; he also testified for the defense at the denazification hearing of Karl Edelmann from Group S.[113] No one seemed to remember that Werthmann had first been appointed as the Nazi authorities' choice. After West German rearmament, he again served as vicar general to the Catholic military bishop.[114]

More than ever, in the midst of retreat and collapse, chaplains' situations were influenced by the decisions, abilities, and whims of individual commanders – men who were busy recalculating their own interests.[115] Field Marshall

Ferdinand Schörner offers a case in point. Known for his sycophantic relationship with Hitler and his proclivity for pulling sick soldiers out of hospital and sending them back to the front,[116] Schörner is considered among the worst of the German generals of World War II. Yet like the chaplains, during the heavy fighting and soaring German casualties of the last year of the war, he demonstrated a mix of continued loyalty to the Nazi cause and increasing independence. In late summer 1944, Schörner ordered numerous soldiers executed for cowardice and other reasons, and in early 1945 he posted lists of their names. Later he said he had fabricated those lists, but many of the names on them were not invented. Yet Schörner kept his Army Group intact, and his casualty numbers were lower than others. He ordered immediate retreats without waiting for orders or sanction, and although he disobeyed Hitler, he retained his command.[117]

Mass executions of German soldiers by their own military leadership created a demand for chaplains' services that was both an opportunity and a trap. Chaplains appeared relevant but risked being associated with weakness. Eager to prove themselves "real men," they found the means to do so pried from their grasp. By 1944, chaplains were prohibited from using the word "manly" to describe how men condemned for treason, self-mutilation, and desertion met their deaths.[118] Like all clergy, chaplains were excluded from the German Home Guard, the *Volkssturm* of 1944 and 1945, as Hitler rallied the forces of German manhood in defense of the fatherland.[119] They also faced restrictions on wearing uniforms.

Chaplains sometimes encountered opposition when they tried to optimize demands for their services. In February 1944, the Protestant base chaplain in Chemnitz, Pastor Börner, reached out to certain members of his congregation: "The undersigned has learned that you are concerned about someone in your extended family who is missing," he wrote. "With the support of the Commander in Military District 4, the next military church service will be especially dedicated to prayers for our missing. ... You and yours are warmly invited." He asked recipients to pass the invitation on to "other families who share the same fate."[120]

Someone forwarded the letter to Group S, where it triggered a hostile response. Addressed to the Protestant military bishop, that communication relayed a reprimand from the National Socialist Leadership Office at Army High Command:

Quite apart from the fact that it is not the task of the military chaplain to provide pastoral care to the civilian population, it sounds rather odd to mention the Military District Commander's support. Indeed, it looks like unwarranted advertising. Base Chaplain B. is to be clearly instructed to stick to the duties of his position.[121]

Harsh as it sounds, the scolding may have had little impact. Pastor Börner sent his invitation in February, whereas the Group S letter was dated April 28,

1944. He could have held numerous prayer services during those two months. Moreover, Group S files contain a draft of their missive but no indication it was actually sent. In short, this correspondence reveals as much about the NSFO's impotence as its influence.

Group S's files include a number of drafts slapping down chaplains' late-war initiatives. In May 1944, one such letter, addressed to the Protestant military bishop, complained about base chaplains overstepping their authority. The Gau leadership had reported Pastor Bruns in Oldenburg for using letter-head of the "Protestant Base Chaplain of Military District 7/1" to invite family members of the war dead to services on Heroes Memorial Day. Bruns's correspondence, the Party personnel insisted, was "strictly confessional" and unconnected to his role as chaplain: "Please inform Pastor Bruns that he is not to mix his work as a civilian pastor with his duties in pastoral care to the military."[122] Catholics received similar rebukes. In July 1944, the Catholic military bishop passed along an order reiterating that clergy at the front were not allowed to provide pastoral care to soldiers.[123] Of course, repeated remind-ers of this sort are evidence that clergy who were not military chaplains continued to carry out such functions.

In rapidly changing circumstances, chaplains found restrictions against them were eased, often informally. Formal instructions frequently followed after chaplains de facto ignored rules or expanded their ministry. For instance, in October 1944, the bulletin (*Verordnungsblatt*) stipulated that "the Catholic Military Bishop allows Mass to be said in the morning and evening, when necessary by military chaplains at the front, clergy in the reserves, and priests who are soldiers, and when not possible in the regularly permitted times."[124] Three months later, the following announcement appeared: "The Minister of the Air Force has determined that if the severely wounded or dying in the medical emergency posts request the presence of a clergyman, there are no objections to fulfilling this request. But this should only be done with the express wishes of the severely wounded or dying individual."[125]

Chaplains boasted that men in the Luftwaffe and SS, who in principle had no access to chaplains of their own, increasingly sought their services.[126] In September 1944, the SS Personnel Office made an urgent request for Pastor Karl Langer to be made available to serve as chaplain to the SS Storm Brigade "Wallonia." That same month, the Wallonian unit was upgraded to a Division of the Waffen-SS. According to the SS communication, Langer, who was currently serving as chaplain of the reserve military hospital in Branitz (Branice), Upper Silesia, had personally requested the new assignment.[127]

Some SS units enlisted non-German chaplains, who had their own reasons for participating.[128] Nationalist Ukrainians followed religious calculations to try to benefit from the volatile moment and German desperation. With the approval of Himmler, twelve Greek Catholic priests signed up as chaplains to

Figure 6.1 Greek Catholic priest Vasyl Laba celebrating mass during the swearing-in ceremony of the 14th Waffen-SS Division "Galicia" in Heidelager, occupied Poland, on August 29, 1943. Dr. Laba, an accomplished theologian who had been a field chaplain in the Austrian army during World War I, was chief chaplain with the SS Division "Galicia." After the war, he became the first rector of the Ukrainian Catholic seminaries in Hirschberg, Bavaria, before immigrating to Canada where he served as vicar general of the Ukrainian Catholic Eparchy of Edmonton. Photographer Weyer. BArch Bild 101III-Weyer-033-16A.

Figure 6.2 A choir of Ukrainian soldiers in the Waffen-SS "Galicia" Division sing for the mass and swearing-in ceremony, August 29, 1943. This photograph and the preceding one are part of a series of 76 images of the division, most of them taken during the swearing-in ceremony at the SS training complex Heidelager, in Pustków in occupied Poland. Heidelager was adjacent to a forced labor camp, and training of recruits included involvement in killing operations there and at nearby ghettos for Jews. Photographer Weyer. BArch Bild 101III-Weyer-033-16A.

the Waffen-SS "Galicia" Division. Their service encompassed three years of battle as well as two years, 1945–1947, in POW camps in Italy. The Greek Catholic Church, including Metropolitan Sheptyts'kyi, gave its support on the condition that its priests function throughout the Division, which became the only SS-sponsored formation of Eastern Europeans to include Christian chaplains (Figures 6.1 and 6.2).[129]

Why did influential Ukrainians, including churchmen, support the Waffen-SS project so late in Germany's failing war? National self-interest was a factor: some Ukrainian leaders, convinced that the alliance between the Soviets and the western Allies would not survive the defeat of Germany, sought to lay the foundation for a military that would protect an independent Ukraine after the war.[130] Yet the "holy oath" that men in the Galicia Division swore, in the presence of Chaplain Laba, was not to Ukraine but to Hitler.[131] Likewise, the Bosnian Muslims in the 13th Waffen-SS Mountain Division

"Handschar" swore an oath pledging loyalty and "obedience unto death" to "the Führer, Adolf Hitler." Similar calculations about independence and the future were likely at play for the Bosnian Muslim imams who served the Waffen-SS Division Handschar. In neither case did it work out as planned. In October 1944, the senior Bosnian chaplain, Abdulah Muhasilović, led a mutiny of 100 men who walked away from the SS, heading home to Bosnia.[132]

"One Does Not Dare Use Lofty Words of Joy"

For the Nazi leadership, July 20, 1944 was a pivotal moment: whom could the regime trust? Postwar accounts likewise identify the attempt to assassinate Hitler as a turning point. The most famous account of desertion from the Wehrmacht, Alfred Andersch's *Die Kirschen der Freiheit* (The Cherries of Freedom), calls the date he went over to the Americans in Italy his personal July 20, 1944. (The actual date fell in June.) Military chaplains did not appear to make any decisions comparable to what Andersch described. Instead their transition away from Hitler reflected the same mix of institutional loyalties and old habits as their adaptation to the Nazi regime had.

Individual chaplains did get into trouble, but it is difficult to determine exactly what they did and whether their actions were connected to the events of July 20. Two days earlier, the Catholic chaplain of Military District 1, Königsberg (Kaliningrad) reported the arrest of one of his clergy:

I am writing to inform the Catholic Military Bishop that in the evening on Saturday, July 15, 1944, the Gestapo arrested the Catholic part-time base chaplain Kunkel in Königsberg Pr. . . . apparently on charges of treason. The arrest on the basis of the crime mentioned is for this office . . . a surprise, because the aforementioned . . . carried out the heavy responsibilities of the base chaplain with a special joy and tactful skill.[133]

The only chaplain on record supporting the attempted coup was the Protestant Johannes Schröder, in a radio address from Moscow. Captured at Stalingrad, Schröder was one of three military chaplains recruited into the Soviet-sponsored Free Germany Committee.[134] Together with his counterpart Matthäus Klein and the Catholic Joseph Kaiser, he contributed to the committee's messages to the German people.[135] The Soviets paid particular attention to religion, and the chaplains' involvement underscored the compatibility of German nationalism and Communism. For instance, one broadcast featured a conversation between Monsignore Kaiser and Walter Ulbricht, in which Ulbricht praised the heroic struggle of the Church in Nazi Germany.[136]

Chaplain Schröder's first address after July 20 was directed to the women of Germany. "Our worried thoughts are with you, German wives and mothers," he assured his audience. "Brave German men" had risen up against tyranny, and in response, Hitler was bringing the war home: "Prisons, jails, and concentration camps are overflowing. Germans are shooting at Germans – and now *German soil* is to be turned into 'scorched earth' in a suicidal war of annihilation!" Schröder beseeched his listeners to hear in his voice "*your* husbands and sons" and to "listen to the hundreds of thousands of German soldiers in POW camps, yearning to come home." Hitler had turned the "cross of honor of the German mother into a cross of pain," the pastor intoned, but now the tears and sacrifice had to end. Help stop the war, he implored: shut down the factories and stay put, "in the borderlands, in your homes, on your farms." Keep your families together, he urged: "save yourselves and your children!"[137] In a sermon the next month, Schröder emphasized that Stauffenberg, Witzleben, and the others were committed "*Christians.*"[138] A subsequent broadcast spoke directly to chaplains:

You have the trust of the men at the front, as well as the women and men at home. ... Help them through word and deed, so that freedom and peace will return. *Awaken* their *consciences, liberate* their hearts from all *fears,* strengthen their *courage* and *devotion* for the *just struggle of the nation* through *faith* and *fear of God.*[139]

Were any chaplains listening?

Josef Perau mentioned July 20 only in passing. In a diary published after the war, he included this entry, dated July 22, 1944:

We had quiet days in Malinka. Yesterday, however, the number of wounded rose. I buried two comrades at the edge of the bushes behind the school. We marked the graves with stones from the field and planted blooming thyme in between. There is still time to make crosses for the graves. Meanwhile news reached us of the conspiracy and assassination attempt on the Führer.

The atmosphere, he noted was "almost electric with tension, although on the surface our lives at the moment seem rather idyllic." Perau described feeling comfortable, his physical needs satisfied:

I slept until 8 AM in the straw in a shed. When I got up and went out into the sunny morning, a Polish woman was standing there, and she filled all my dishes with fresh milk. The company has butchered another calf.
After a good breakfast, I let an old granny do my laundry.[140]

Chaplains showed fortitude in bypassing and even defying orders that limited their freedom of operation. But with regard to Germany's victims, most weighed in on the side of the perpetrators, sanctioning and even blessing their acts through silence, words, and actions. One obvious manifestation of this condoning function was providing group absolution for soldiers – a practice that continued to occur frequently enough to elicit a warning from the Catholic military bishop in August 1944:

Through General Absolution the sacrament of confession with all its mercy should be made available in extraordinary circumstances to all the faithful, who do not have an opportunity to give an individual confession to a priest. For this reason, in every believer before receiving General Absolution regret and repentance must be awakened, as they are necessary before every confession. In addition, everyone who receives general absolution is under the strictest obligation, on the opportunity of the next confession, to confess all serious sins that have not yet been confessed.

It is strictly forbidden and a serious sin, if anyone who is in a condition of serious sinfulness deliberately does not go to confession, in the expectation that he will be able to participate in a general absolution.[141]

For German chaplains in 1944, the concept of people in a serious state of sin was not abstract. But chaplains kept their responses to murder, rape, and cruelty to themselves or inside closed circles of trusted friends. They seem to have been especially muted about the killing of Jews, because the few mentions of protest in police reports came from years earlier. A fatal crackdown on a group of Catholic priests, including two chaplains, in 1944 fits this pattern. Herbert Simoleit provided pastoral care to the local military base in Stettin (Szczecin). Friedrich Lorenz, a veteran of World War I, was divisional chaplain for the Pomeranian reserves in 1939, and in that capacity he had learned about the German slaughter of Polish Catholic priests. In 1942, Simoleit and Lorenz connected with Carl Lampert, who had spent the previous two years in the concentration camps of Dachau and Sachsenhausen. The three priests started a "Wednesday Circle" with soldiers from the base, who gathered to discuss political and military affairs.

A Gestapo informer joined the group and denounced all three priests. In 1944, a military court charged them with sedition. Simoleit had been most outspoken in condemning the slaughter of Jews. The official charge recorded his outrage at the actions of German murder squads: "The accused . . . sharply criticized measures of the SS, and in this regard, said the following: 'On one single day, SS men in Estonia shot 3,500 Jews in mass graves.' He spoke of the cruelty of the brutish SS murders and said in closing it was clear that the God of love would not reward such atrocities with victory." Simoleit and Lorenz were beheaded on November 13, 1944, and Lampert was executed a week later.[142] I have not seen evidence that other chaplains protested or commented on the killing of these men, their peers.

In this frenetic period, most chaplains focused on a limited sphere of moral concern – the men they served and their families. Formal sermons declined in importance.[143] Who had the peace of mind to reflect and compose? And who was there to listen? So it is especially valuable to have a set of sources that shows how one chaplain's message changed over the last year of the war. Theodor Laasch, Protestant superintendent of chaplains in Hanover, sent all base and military hospital chaplains in his district periodic circulars that included inspirational messages and ideas for their own sermons and correspondence.

In his circular for Advent 1943, Laasch tackled the themes of doubt and despair. By the fifth year of war, he wrote, many soldiers had become "stubborn and numb" and had "beaten to death God and their conscience." And yet he marveled at the moving encounters between chaplains, officers, and men. In the hardest times at the front, he wrote, nothing could replace Christian faith. Laasch's readers would have recognized his jab at the new Nazi ideological officers, the NSFOs: "The German soul cannot be satisfied by the pathetic, empty substitutes it has been offered but hungers instead for the Bread of Life that our Lord Christ Jesus alone can provide!"[144]

Chaplains also faced material deprivations. "Let it not affect our joy," Laasch wrote, that the "hope of remuneration for military hospital chaplains has been disappointed." Nonetheless pastors should use their New Year's messages to help soldiers "cross the threshold to 1944 with twofold certainty." First, "that our people out there on the front and here at home are giving it their all." And second: "God cares about you! Like a mother who holds each child in her heart and loves each child in a special way, according to its nature, so does God love each of us, and to each of us on the day of baptism, He promised His faithfulness."[145]

Six months later, Laasch raised a practical matter. How were chaplains to interact with the NSFOs? Established in December 1943, those ideological officers were now in place. Were they competitors, enemies, or partners? Laasch modeled how chaplains could work with the commissars and bypass them at the same time. He used relaying some reprimands as an opportunity to highlight chaplains' achievements and expose the pettiness of Nazi functionaries. Like other representatives of the military chaplaincy, he wanted "practical clarification and delimitation of the terms 'world view' and 'religion,'" but there were no guidelines, he observed, nor were any likely to be forthcoming.[146]

Concrete instructions did emerge on one topic: Wehrmacht soldiers executed by military justice. Laasch passed along the rule that they were to be erased: "Armed Forces High Command has ordered that those who are condemned to death and executed on the basis of a military court judgment are no longer to be entered in the list of the dead in the military church books, nor in a separate list of the dead."[147] He also communicated the criticism of one chaplain's action in a way that set it up as an example to emulate:

A chaplain wrote the following to the sister of a man condemned to death by a wartime court, about her brother's last hours: "Meanwhile we prayed together. That gave him so much strength and peace that he went to his death with an almost calm lightness of spirit and died bravely as a soldier and a Christian." To that the NS Leadership Office at Armed Forces High Command had the following to say: "The pastor's observation that the executed died 'bravely as a soldier,' reflects a gross tactlessness, because it is not appropriate to equate the stance on the way to the place of execution, perhaps strongly influenced by religious words, with the brave death of a soldier at the hands of the enemy." The Military Bishop therefore asks that expressions of that sort be left out of such letters.[148]

More complicated were discussions around burial of soldiers. Laasch reported that General Command in the district had expanded the principle for Heroes Memorial Day (that military celebrations were not to be connected with religious celebrations) to the burial of individual soldiers, "and the religious celebration may only begin after the troops have left the graveside." Laasch noted that he was trying to have this order revoked and was hopeful he would succeed. He referred to a manual from 1943, allowing "burial of members of the Wehrmacht who die in the field to be carried out as a unified celebration," and stipulating that "these guidelines are to be applied in spirit to military chaplaincy on the home front." In other words, Laasch argued, "the legal foundation supports our practice to date." Moreover, he had been made keenly aware from daily interactions with "comrades and citizens" that "changes would lead to immense alienation on the part of soldiers and their families."[149]

Laasch's next circular, in November 1944, had an altogether different quality. He offered no defiance, no assurances, no references to God or scripture, only practical information. First, he noted that clergy active in the military would not be drafted into the *Volkssturm*.[150] He also passed along a critical message from the NS Leadership Office:

The chaplain carries out his duties in agreement with the commander, with whom he arranges the time and place for pastoral care. It is not in keeping with this stipulation when chaplains initiate events connected to pastoral care, such as Bible study for soldiers, soldiers' evenings, religious song evenings, and so on, without those being announced by the troop leader. To the extent that events of this sort are not purely part of pastoral care, they trespass into the arena of care of the troops and are prohibited.[151]

A punitive measure accompanied this notice. By order of the Reich Führer SS, the position of divisional chaplains in the Volksgrenadier divisions formed in autumn 1944 was to be cut.[152] Finally, guidelines for burial of members of the Wehrmacht were to be applied to the burial of navy and air force auxiliaries who were killed or died in the course of duty.[153] In other words, there was to be no Christian burial for them, either.

Laasch did not wait the usual six months before sending his next communication. Three weeks later, he issued what would be his final circular, dated December 2, 1944. It bore the marks of recognition that this was the end, of the war and perhaps the world:

This year General Command did not issue any orders regarding the Christmas celebrations in military hospitals. The order from last year applies.

The Gauleiter has instructed district Party leaders to hold gift exchanges in the military hospitals. Presumably these will be held in conjunction with the official celebration in the military hospital.

Aside from that, chaplains in military hospitals are issuing invitations to optional participation in a church Christmas celebration, best held in a room of the hospital (otherwise in a nearby church).

There would be no Christmas greeting from the military bishop, Laasch wrote, because the Military District printer could not make the copies: "Another local printer was prepared to print it, but told me with regret the next day, that the office in charge of assigning paper deemed the greeting of the Military Bishop to be 'not important to the war.'" Laasch found a few copies of a Christmas tract titled "The Bells of Home" (*Glocke der Heimat*), so he sent as many of those as he could. For the others he included the text of a Christmas sermon he had written. "Perhaps you will be surprised by the text. But this time one does not dare use lofty words of joy."[154]

Unfortunately, Laasch's text is not in the file. One can speculate that he found a similar answer to the question raised by the unnamed chaplain, "what should we preach now?" as his counterpart, Wehrmacht chaplain Dr. Hugo Gotthard Bloth. In a sermon delivered in Prague in late February 1945, Bloth invoked the apocalypse:

In the Book of Revelation we read that the day is coming when Satan will be thrown down to earth. – I spoke with someone who saw how on the 13th and 14th of this month, Dresden went down: Fire fell from heaven, like leaves, hundreds of balls of light – perhaps this occurrence is the beginning of that time of Satan that will one day break forth. But the Scripture says something else, too: You will not wait long, because "he does not have much time." As Luther says, death too is only a short, easy sleep! "It is only a short time and victory will be won." ... This is the final reason for joy and an incomparable promise of victory! Amen.[155]

In a letter dated Easter Sunday, 1945, a Wehrmacht soldier wrote to his wife and child with a simpler message: "The festival of Easter reminds us of Jesus Christ, who took from Death its power and by rising from the dead brought humanity salvation and resurrection. All Christians can rejoice at His promise, no matter what circumstances we find ourselves in."[156] Those familiar Christian binaries – death and resurrection, apocalypse and renewal, Satan and Christ – must have occupied the chaplains' minds as they looked ahead with deep uncertainty.

1945 and Beyond

In September 1944, Elfriede Braun wrote to Bishop Ludwig Diehl in Speyer about her husband Erich, a Protestant pastor, now a POW in American hands. She quoted from his letter to her, written a month earlier, presumably from Italy:

"On May 14 in the evening ... we were captured ... In the first days we buried the dead, friend and foe. We set up a small German military cemetery, and I was allowed to bless the fallen with a short sermon and prayer. On May 20, we were sent to an American prison camp. ... Here we are well looked after and have good food."[1]

For German military chaplains, as for their compatriots, although the war ended in May 1945, the world did not. Defeat, collapse, occupation, and internment – all generated problems and barriers but also possibilities and, significantly, opportunities. As Pastor Erich Braun's experience near Monte Cassino showed, Christianity held out the prospect of common ground with the victors; even before the war had ended, chaplains embodied this potential.

Christianity served the Wehrmacht chaplains well in the tumultuous postwar era. It offered individuals a redemptive narrative for their own role in the war and Holocaust and that of the military and nation they served. The common ground of Christianity proved advantageous in dealing with the Allies, including chaplains among the western Allies, and some former Wehrmacht chaplains emerged as trusted spokesmen for German soldiers and mediators with the victors. Defeat opened some new roles for chaplains, in particular ministering to German POWs, incarcerated Nazis, and accused war criminals. Even the interpretation of Nazism as a political religion, widespread among the western Allies, worked in favor of chaplains, who found they could present themselves as a Christian bulwark against paganism – and against Communism. Their experiences and adjustments during the cataclysm of 1945, and the interventions they made and inspired in popular culture, disseminated a positive version of their part in the German wars of annihilation and prepared them surprisingly well for a new conflict: the Cold War.

Two biological phenomena provide metaphors for the ways in which the German military chaplaincy continued through the upheaval of defeat and collapse and the enormous transformations of the years that followed. One is the tardigrade, a tiny, aquatic invertebrate discovered in 1773 by a German zoologist and Protestant pastor, Johann August Ephraim Goeze. The tardigrade, given that name and also a nickname (little waterbear) by Goeze, can withstand extreme heat, cold, and pressure, and survive for decades, maybe centuries, without water, by retracting its head and legs and going into what is known as "tun state," a kind of intense dormancy. Such retreat inward, or withdrawal to virtual invisibility, gave the Wehrmacht chaplains protective cover in the postwar period. The second metaphor involves fragmentation or splitting, a form of reproduction common in molds and lichens that produce tiny filaments called *hyphae*. These get food and nutrients from the bodies of other organisms. If they are able to grow and fertilize, a piece of hyphae breaks off and grows into a new individual. Then the cycle continues. Likewise, the chaplaincy proved able to generate ties, if fragile ones, that could connect and develop in a range of settings.

"Do This in Remembrance of Me"

Pastor Bernhard Bauerle's personal motto was "duty above all."[2] Bauerle, who had served with the 16th Army in southern Russia, intimated that he and other chaplains had chosen to remain with "their men" in Soviet POW camps and gulags even when given a chance to return home.[3] As long as German soldiers were in captivity, Bauerle pledged, a chaplain belonged with them. During the war, he had preached a "manly Christianity" and instructed junior chaplains to avoid the embarrassingly Jewish "Old Testament" in their work with soldiers. When he returned to his family from a Soviet camp in the 1950s, he brought a crust of bread that he insisted be placed on the table at every meal so no one would forget what he and his men had suffered. As a pastor who had given Communion thousands of times, the words of Jesus must have rung in his ear and lent sacramental gravity to his own ritual: "Do this in remembrance of me" (I Cor. 11:25). Viewed this way, the hardships of the last decade became for Bauerle, and chaplains like him, not time and vitality squandered in the service of a murderous regime, but suffering and sacrifice in the name of Christ.

Bauerle's experience points to some of the possibilities and limitations of the postwar situation and hints at their dialectical entanglements. Soviet power and the chill of the Cold War were at once devastating and a golden opportunity, because the hostile climate allowed chaplains, like Christianity as a whole, to move from the side of the persecutor to the persecuted without in fact changing position at all. The discourse of sacrifice, so potent during the war as a way to maintain Germans' focus on their own suffering and the toll war took on their soldiers, now provided a ready-made narrative of legitimacy: chaplains as tragic heroes who had put their lives on the line to preserve a Christian presence amid the hell of war and who now embodied that part of Germany – its eternal soul? – that had always remained true to Christian civilization.

Yet there was something hollow about Bauerle's ritual with the bread, and indeed his life and career after the war, its triumphs shot through with bitterness and failure. He assiduously collected his sermons, letters, and reports from the front, but the boxes of paper languished for decades in the attic, discovered by his daughter after his death and donated to a local museum. There they were displayed in 1995, not as a show of German grandeur but as the basis for an exhibit that exposed with gentle honesty the depth of Christian complicity in Nazi crimes.[4] To generations who grew up eager to confront their parents and grandparents with accusations of moral failure and keenly aware of the active involvement of "ordinary Germans" in the Holocaust, Bauerle's crust on the table might symbolize nothing more than the cranky narcissism of a self-righteous old man.

Looking back forty years after the war, a veteran from the Rhineland, Wolfgang Schrör, provided another reality check to Bauerle's grandiosity. He accused the Wehrmacht chaplains above all of irrelevance:

Like my classmates and friends, I was not enthusiastic about becoming a soldier. But we did not have a choice. As luck would have it, I was assigned to a unit based in Berlin, whereas most of those from my class were put together in a different unit. So unlike them I was alone. My first experience was that among my fellow soldiers, there was dead silence around the subject of God. One Sunday, when we were asked who wanted to attend church, and I was the only one to say yes, I got assigned to clean toilets. In my entire time as a soldier I never met a single priest. We had no conversations about the meaning of the war, and I have to admit that more and more I lost a sense of God. We only cared about one thing and that was survival. After a short period as a POW, in June 1945 I came back home.[5]

One argument of this book – that chaplains served to legitimate the Nazi German war effort – finds a denouement in this final chapter, as the erstwhile legitimators sought new sources of legitimacy for themselves. What impact did chaplains have on German interactions with the Allies? What repercussions did chaplains' actions and reactions have on other Germans – in their families, churches, and communities, and in the construction of new, post-Nazi institutions? How did (former) chaplains present their wartime roles, and how have others represented them?

In early June 1945, Bishop von Galen of Münster welcomed the Wehrmacht home with these words: "We want to offer deepest thanks to our Christian soldiers. In good faith that they were doing what was right, they put their lives on the line for our country and our people. Even in the chaos of war, they kept their hearts and hands clean of hatred, plunder, and unjust acts of violence."[6] In private, and on rare occasions in public, German chaplains promoted the image of the Wehrmacht as a military like any other, whose men, like most of their enemies, were Christians who had merely tried to do their duty.[7] They continued to invoke a favorite Bible verse that drew all members of the Wehrmacht, dead and alive, into association with Jesus: "Greater love hath no man than this, that a man lay down his life for his friends" (John 15:13). Underpinning the Wehrmacht chaplains' emphasis on duty was an assumption, sometimes implied but often articulated, that they had had no options under Nazi rule: they had followed the only path open to them as Christians and as Germans.

One needs to switch perspectives in order to imagine the existence of other paths. In an interview with Svetlana Alexievich, a Soviet war veteran and nurse named Nina Vasilyevna Ilinskaya recalls a German soldier's shock at being treated with decency. "I remember a battle," she began: "In that battle we captured many Germans. Some of them were wounded. We bandaged their wounds; they moaned like our lads did. And it was hot . . . Scorching hot! We found a teapot and gave them water." They were exposed and under fire, she continued, and an order came to "quickly entrench and camouflage" themselves:

We started digging trenches. The Germans stared. We explained to them: so, help us dig, get to work. When they understood what we wanted from them, they looked at us with horror; they took it that once they dug those pits, we would stand them by those pits and shoot them. They expected . . . You should have seen their horrified looks as they dug . . . Their faces . . .

And when they saw that we bandaged them, gave them water, and told them to hide in the trenches they had dug, they couldn't come to their senses, they were at a loss . . . One German started crying . . . He was an older man. He cried and didn't hide his tears from anyone.[8]

Was either the weeping German man or the Soviet woman aware that they had just reenacted the parable of the Good Samaritan?

Allied Chaplains

Legitimation is a two-way process and that reciprocity is key to understanding postwar developments around the chaplaincy. If chaplains needed to find new sources of legitimacy, they also discovered that their prospective conversation partners had needs of their own. To the churches in occupied Germany, to local and would-be national German leaders and spokespeople, to military men on all sides, and to the Allied powers, chaplains were potentially both a liability and an asset.

In the wake of the war, chaplains from the western Allies took the stage in what had been Hitler's empire. Like a reflection in water, they were similar yet opposite to the Wehrmacht chaplains. An extraordinary document from the 82nd US Airborne Division, titled "Tombs of the Unknown," shows Allied chaplains in action in the final days of the war. Their tasks were not so different from those the Wehrmacht chaplains had carried out: preaching, burying the dead, giving meaning to the war. But the message of their words and deeds was the opposite: not "Gott mit uns," but the right of human beings to be treated with respect, even after death. A public ceremony, as described by the US military chronicler, asserted and performed this contrast:

On the morning of 7 May, at 1000 Hrs, a very dignified and impressive public burial was held in LUDWIGSLUST, GERMANY. Chaplains of the 82nd US Abn Div officiated. The ceremony, attended by 5,000 "invited" German citizens of the town of LUDWIGSLUST and officers and men of the 82nd US Abn and 8th US Inf Div, was held in the town's park.

Eight German officers "were brought from our PW cage" to witness the performance. After "10 minutes of soft music by the 82nd US Abn Div Band" and a few words from the local mayor, the Division Chaplain spoke:

We are assembled here today before God and in the sight of man to give a proper and reverent burial to the victims of atrocities committed by armed forces in the name of and by the order of the German Government. These 200 bodies were found by the American Army in a concentration camp 4 miles North of the City of LUDWIGSLUST.[9]

The US chaplain proved remarkably knowledgeable about Nazi German atrocities: "The crimes here committed in the name of the German people and by their acquiescence were minor compared to those to be found elsewhere in GERMANY. Here there were no gas chambers, no crematoria; these men of HOLLAND, RUSSIA, POLAND, CZECHOSLOVAKIA, and FRANCE were simply allowed to starve to death." He also understood that the regime and its violence were rooted in local communities:

Within 4 miles of your comfortable homes 4000 men were forced to live like animals, deprived even of the food you would give to your dogs. In three weeks 1000 of these men were starved to death; 800 of them were buried in pits and in the nearby woods. Those 200 who lie before us in these graves were found piled 4 and 5 feet high in one building and lying with the sick and dying in other buildings.

His judgment was clear:

This is not war as conducted by the international rules of warfare. This is murder as is not even known among savages.

Though you claim no knowledge of these acts, you were still individually and collectively responsible for these atrocities, for they were committed by a government elected to office by yourselves in 1933 and continued in office by your indifference to organized brutality. It should be the firm resolve of the German people that never again should any leader or party bring them to such moral degradation as is exhibited here.

The US chaplains embodied their country's commitment to respect each person:

It is the custom of the United States Army through its Chaplains' Corps to insure a proper and decent burial to any deceased person, whether he be civilian or soldier, friend or foe, according to religious preference. The Supreme Commander of the Allied Forces has ordered that all atrocity victims be buried in a public place and that the cemetery be given the same perpetual care that is given to all military cemeteries. Crosses will be placed at the heads of graves of Christians and Stars of David at the heads of the graves of Jews; a stone monument will be set up in memory of these deceased. Protestant, Catholic and Jewish prayers will be said by Chaplains WOOD, HANNAN and WALL of the 82nd Airborne Division for these victims as we lay them to rest and commit them into the hands of our heavenly Father in the hope that the world will not again be faced with such barbarity.[10]

The actions of Allied chaplains reveal the range of possibilities within military chaplaincy. In the Netherlands in the fall of 1944, Canadian Jewish chaplains encountered liberated Dutch Jews and sought to help them.[11] In December 1944, "somewhere in France," Rabbi Max Eichhorn and two other American Jewish chaplains organized a service for Erev Hanukkah. The XV Corps chaplain, Colonel Gustave Schellhase, a Lutheran, preached "with oratorical brilliance," Eichhorn wrote to his wife, and a choir "(all Protestant)" sang.[12] Rather than unquestioning obedience, French, British, US, and Canadian chaplains offered challenges of various kinds to their military superiors. In some cases, they interceded on behalf of Germans, urging gentler treatment of the vanquished.

At least on the US side, chaplains, Christian and Jewish, took initiatives to organize religious services, so that the many dead they encountered in Nazi German camps and prisons could be honored, buried, and mourned (Figure 7.1). Sometimes Allied chaplains took the lead in requiring local Germans to partici- pate. In an interview in 1998, a US Army veteran recalled the impression one such event made on him. Frank Yturbide, a Catholic from California, was drafted into the US military in 1944, "June or somewhere in there," and shipped to Europe. In April 1945 his Division, the 104th "Timberwolf," reached Dora- Mittelbau (Nordhausen) concentration camp. Yturbide's commanding officer ordered local German authorities to "come to work and place the bodies and help with all the dead, and the sick and what have you." Yturbide was one of the soldiers enforcing the mass burial of bodies by German civilians at gunpoint. Severely affected by the suffering he saw, he still cried about it fifty-five years later. He also highlighted the significance of the American chaplain:

Well of course he was very helpful to the prisoners, and ... usually a man of the cloth, you know, is used to death and what have you and they ... don't cave in and start crying like some of us did. However, I saw this priest ... but I saw him with tears in his eyes. He did assist some ... or tried to assist ... There were more than one, incidentally. There were several [chaplains].[13]

Figure 7.1 Two US military chaplains, a cantor, and a crowd of men at a reburial ceremony near Stuttgart, 1945. Moses Rontal (wearing a fedora), a cantor from Radom, survived Auschwitz and Dachau. His wife, Luba Kovarski, and daughter Yehudit were murdered in the Holocaust. Cantor Rontal officiated at the first postwar High Holiday services in Stuttgart. The man next to him (in a trenchcoat) can be identified from other photos as Rabbi Morris Dembowitz from Brooklyn. Chaplain Dembowitz's activities included overseeing the exhumation and reburial of Jewish victims. USHMM 80562. United States Holocaust Memorial Museum, courtesy of Moses and Ruth Rontal.

A group of American chaplains devoted themselves to work among Jewish displaced persons, bending and defying orders when necessary in the interest of humanitarian relief. One of them, Rabbi Abraham Klausener, even went AWOL in order to give his full attention to the DPs. Rabbi Max Wall, one of the chaplains who officiated at the 82nd Airborne's public burial ceremony, also helped DPs,[14] and Rabbi Judah Nadich submitted reports to General Eisenhower that directly informed army policy toward Jewish survivors.[15] What must these chaplains have thought of their German counterparts and their protestations of impotence?

Rabbi Nadich was the senior Jewish US Army chaplain in the European theatre of World War II. He grew up in a "very pious" Jewish home, and his father ran the only kosher grocery and butcher shop in a "completely Jewish" neighborhood in Baltimore.[16] In an interview in 2000, Nadich recalls hearing stories about the "terrible situation" in Europe from the few German Jews who escaped Germany to Baltimore in the 1930s: "We were very much aware of what was happening because of the radio and the daily press ... We thought we knew quite a bit. Of course even more was revealed afterwards, but we knew the Jews were being mistreated badly in Germany."[17]

In May 1942, Rabbi Nadich decided to enlist. He "felt that [he] wanted to be a part of this fight against Hitler" and saw the chaplaincy as his opportunity to help. After D-Day and the liberation of Paris, Nadich was ordered forward to Army Headquarters in Paris. There he served as the contact of the American Jewish Joint Distribution Committee and witnessed and aided the recovery of the Jewish community. He also presided over the first service at the reopened Grand Synagogue in Paris, a "very moving moment" for him and all those who participated:

It was as though we were saying to the Nazis, "You did not win after all." ... Of course there was a great deal of emotion among the Jews who attended because they had, I am sure, never thought of the day when the Germans were in control of Paris that they would live to participate in another Jewish service ... I delivered the talk under very emotional circumstances, it was all I could do to keep from weeping.[18]

After the war, Rabbi Nadich went through a serious religious and personal crisis, something I have not seen any of the former Wehrmacht chaplains describe for themselves. When he returned to the United States, he told his interviewer,

I did not think I could be a rabbi again, serving a congregation as I had before I had enlisted in the army. I was wrestling with the thought, the question that bothered me – how could a good God have permitted what I saw with my own eyes? How could He have remained silent when innocent men and women and children were tortured and killed? Placed in gas ovens that I walked into myself, and asphyxiated, and then their bodies thrown into large furnaces, and the ash was to be taken for use to fertilize the soil of German farmers.

It took a year until Rabbi Nadich decided he could return to the pulpit:

because I had figured there's good in the world and there's evil in the world, and we don't understand the workings of God. And so I've got to make peace with the idea that evil exists in the world, that God isn't necessarily responsible for the evil, and that it is He who empowers some human beings to be good people and to fight against the evil in the world.[19]

The contrast between Rabbi Nadich's soul-searching and the Wehrmacht chaplains' refusal to engage the past as it really was fits a pattern evident in many personal accounts of the Holocaust: victims and survivors blame themselves, whereas perpetrators and their enablers deny their responsibility.[20]

The Wehrmacht's Best Face

Allied commanders sometimes looked to chaplains as potential liaisons with surrendering Wehrmacht units. Or perhaps it was more that the chaplains

stepped forward on the assumption that they would present the best face of the
Wehrmacht. In May 1945, US Army photographers captured some of these
encounters on film.[21] As Lauren Faulkner Rossi has shown, the Catholic
Military Vicar Georg Werthmann played a key role in establishing dialogue
with the Allies.[22] Werthmann was significant in conveying an impression of
the Wehrmacht chaplains as above politics, although his boss, the Catholic
Military Bishop Franz Justus Rarkowski, had been a boisterous cheerleader,
and Werthmann himself had been the Nazis' preferred candidate for the job of
vicar. Werthmann perpetuated the useful impression that Rarkowski, who had
been sidelined since early 1945, had been an outlier with no real power.[23]

Some chaplains leveraged their influence to help old friends. Former Vicar
Werthmann defended Karl Edelmann, a senior official in the Wehrmacht's
Group S, before a denazification tribunal. At the Nuremberg Trials, former
Navy Chaplain Ronneberger testified in defense of Admiral Erich Raeder.
Ronneberger's testimony, provided to a notary in Wilhelmshaven and submitted to the International Military Tribunal in April 1946, provides an extended
example of the chaplains' self-serving postwar narrative. Ronneberger opened
by establishing that he had known Raeder for more than thirty years, since
October 1915, to be precise, when they met as officers on a ship under the
command of Admiral Franz von Hipper. "Already then," the pastor maintained, "I could clearly see his deeply Christian attitude and attachment to the
church, and in that respect, nothing has changed over all the years that have
gone by." It went without saying, Ronneberger continued, that at Raeder's
home "they said grace before meals."[24]

The crux of Ronneberger's spirited defense is that Raeder supported the
military chaplaincy and therefore could not have been a Nazi. In 1937,
Ronneberger noted, the admiral had instructed a chaplain to "preach the
Gospel of Christ with all seriousness and without compromise, and never
grow tired of doing so." On the eve of the invasion of Poland, Raeder had
issued a statement condemning neo-pagans and the movement to leave the
church. According to Ronneberger, Raeder also endorsed the "Christian services in the Wehrmacht" and warned he "would not tolerate" them being
rejected or undermined. Raeder was a dedicated Protestant Christian,
Ronneberger insisted, who was not afraid to let Hitler know that he attended
church every Sunday. Raeder's public pronouncement of faith had
strengthened the Christians in the officer corps, Ronneberger contended, and
turned "the Nazis" against him.[25]

Meanwhile, the chaplain continued, "the National Socialist Party let the cat
out of the bag" and showed its anti-Christian hand: "Military chaplaincy was
supposed to be liquidated. And if it were not for Grand Admiral Raeder, they
would have succeeded." In Ronneberger's account, Raeder, along with
Generals Fritsch and Brauchitsch, had defended the chaplaincy against the

predations of Bormann, Himmler, Goebbels, Rosenberg, the Gauleiters, and General Hermann Reinecke.[26] The first big blow had been shutting chaplains out of the swearing-in ceremonies for soldiers, Ronneberger claimed, and he went on with the usual litany of Nazi infringements: restrictions on distribution of religious literature, ban on chaplains entering the barracks, prohibition on writing to families of the fallen, and so on.

Ronneberger's list included one proscription I have not seen mentioned elsewhere, which seems clearly intended to appeal to his audience: chaplains had been forbidden "to bury fallen enemy pilots," he wrote. For his own part, Ronneberger hastened to add, "I carried out those burials in the usual manner until the very end."[27]

The former Navy chaplain and enthusiastic supporter of Hitler managed to sneak a personal note of self-promotion into his defense of the admiral. Raeder had refused to enforce the Propaganda Ministry's orders regarding notifications to families of the fallen, Ronneberger explained. Instead, he made sure that loved ones of sailors killed in action received a copy of Ronneberger's book, ... *und fielen vor dem Feinde*, with the following inscription: "May this book of comfort help you bear your heavy loss, strong and brave through your faith in God."[28] The impact of Ronneberger's testimony cannot be determined, but Raeder was sentenced to life imprisonment, not to death. He was released in 1955.[29]

Those German chaplains held in Allied detention found they could use their standing as men of the church to mediate between German POWs and their captors. The Protestant Johannes Schröder, captured by the Soviets in 1943, was recruited into the Free Germany Committee and allowed to broadcast sermons over the radio and convey greetings from prisoners to their loved ones back home.[30] Some chaplains established ties to their counterparts in the French, British, and US forces and then worked with those contacts to press for better treatment of Germans.[31] Fabien Théofilakis has done important work to analyze relations with the French side.[32] Allied chaplains, Jews as well as Christians, often proved generous and open. In France, the German chaplain Franz Stock was allowed to run a seminar for theology students in a German POW camp near Chartres.[33] The American priest Fabian Flynn and other Passionists worked extensively with German prisoners, including in Father Flynn's case as a confessor at the Nuremberg Trials. There he lobbied to give German chaplains access to the accused.[34]

Military chaplains' rehabilitative efforts were reinforced by German prison chaplains, who labored to save the souls, reputations, and even lives of imprisoned perpetrators. Björn Krondorfer has examined the SS boss Oswald Pohl, his conversion to Catholicism in 1950, and his confessional text, *Credo*. The book, modeled after Augustine's *Confessions*, listed only one author, Oswald Pohl, but Pohl received extensive help from Karl Morgenschweis,

Figure 7.2 German pastor Dr. Heinrich Vogel speaking at an ecumenical church service in the Osterkirche, Berlin-Wedding, Sunday, June 30, 1946. The church was reportedly packed, and many members of the US, English, and French militaries participated, along with German clergymen. A British

the Catholic chaplain of Landsberg prison.[35] Krondorfer shows that the "womanly" image of Christianity, against which the Wehrmacht chaplains had struggled throughout the war, came in handy in its aftermath. It allowed a former warrior to present a "'softer' male self – a suffering man who is also receptive to a new morality," and hence deserving of clemency.[36]

Religion did more than help men like Pohl portray themselves as harmless. Religious language also empowered them and gave them respectability and a way to distance themselves from Nazi ideology (Figure 7.2).[37] For Pohl and the chaplains, too, affiliation with Christianity enabled them to criticize the Allies while laying claim to the "virtues of humility and tranquility."[38]

Postwar Reconstructions

Billy Budd, in Herman Melville's eponymous novel, describes a military chaplain as being as "incongruous as a musket would be on the altar at Christmas." This characterization fits the Wehrmacht chaplains, entangled as they were with a genocidal military. Yet always being out of place allows for a certain adaptability. Such was the case with German military chaplains, who in the 1950s found a place, albeit a changed one, in the new military of West Germany, the Bundeswehr. Their outsider position facilitated the role of legitimator in very different regimes, and the Cold War was a boon for the Wehrmacht chaplains, who in a certain light appeared as the face of Germany's enduring Christian humanity. It helped that establishment of the Bundeswehr in 1955 and its chaplaincy two years later coincided with release of the last German POWs from the Soviet Union.

So was the military chaplaincy just another instance of failed denazification? Not exactly. There were certainly continuities in personnel and image, fanned by the Cold War and enabled by sympathetic western Allies, who also helped perpetuate the myth of the clean Wehrmacht.[39] The divide between individuals and institutions proved convenient for public relations: the failures of the chaplaincy could be blamed on a few individuals – the usual "bad apple" was Rarkowski – and individual acts of heroism, however modest, could be projected onto the institution as a whole.

Figure 7.2 (*cont.*) army chaplain gave the main sermon, and shorter sermons were offered by the French Army chaplain George Casalis and German pastor Vogel. As in this case, Allied chaplains often helped build bridges to Christians in Germany. The tapestry in the background shows a scene from Luke 24, the supper at Emmaus, after Jesus's death and resurrection, a fitting symbol here of Christian community. Photographer [Bruno] Heinscher. BArch Bild 183-S74360.

Yet within those continuities, major change was afoot. Remilitarization of the Germanys in the 1950s eschewed the old, national model of military chaplaincy. In West Germany, creation of the new Bundeswehr unleashed intensive, at times bitter, debate around how to constitute the military chaplaincy. This issue proved the final straw that separated the Protestant Church of Germany into its western and eastern parts: opposition to any religious chaplaincy led East German authorities to finalize the break. It took two extra years after the creation of the Bundeswehr – until 1957 – for the new chaplaincy to emerge, and it looked completely different from its World War II predecessor. No chaplains were permitted in East Germany,[40] and the new chaplaincy in the west was tied not to the nationalist fatherland but to the international framework of NATO.[41] Chaplains were no longer to hold an officer's rank. They were to be closely connected to civilian church authorities and serve for a limited term. Most significant, their main task was not to promote morale or boost the fighting power of the troops but to be a voice of conscience within the military.[42]

Distrust of chaplaincy remained strong in some circles in the postwar period. It seems significant that one of the men active in building the new Catholic military chaplaincy for the Bundeswehr had not been a chaplain in World War II but had been in World War I. Friedrich Wolf died in 1970 at the age of eighty-seven. Here is what Georg Werthmann wrote in his obituary:

When we remember him in the periodical *Militärseelsorge* [Pastoral Care to the Military], it is not only because during the First World War he was active as a Divisional chaplain. In the years of the creation and expansion of the Catholic Military Chaplaincy for the Bundeswehr, Prelate Wolf made the cause of military chaplaincy his own. ... In his clear, positive attitude toward the Bundeswehr and toward military chaplaincy, he did not let himself be deterred by anything.[43]

Adenauer's government also took an interest in chaplains. The Blank Agency, headed by Christian Democratic (CDU) politician Theodor Blank, was responsible for matters relating to the Allied occupation forces. It also oversaw preparations for rearmament.[44] According to one of its bureaucrats, Franz Lubbers, chaplaincy was part of planning for the Bundeswehr all along. From a vantage point of forty-five years later, Lubbers recalled a conversation when he took up his position in September 1951:

I was tasked by Representative Theo Blank, in addition to the expected military/legal assignments, with establishing a military chaplaincy. For Blank this was an especially important responsibility. I still remember his words, "Without good pastoral care for the soldiers, I cannot imagine a future German fighting force." These words accompanied us through the entire project.[45]

Lubbers summed up the differences between the new chaplaincy in the Bundeswehr and the Wehrmacht chaplaincy as follows: the basis of the new arrangement was the churches' voluntary partnership, whereas the terms of the old arrangement were almost all decided by the state. The churches' independence from state influence was protected as never before. At the same time, the state recognized soldiers' legal right to pastoral care and provided "generous personnel and material resources" so that chaplains would be well equipped to do their work. Also the state dropped the waiver of church taxes for soldiers, and made those funds available for the churches to use for social issues. In addition, the new chaplaincy would contribute to the Bundeswehr's training and educational programs.[46] A collection of photographs showing relaxed, smiling chaplains accompanied Lubbers' and other similar texts.[47]

The creation of a soldier's oath for the Bundeswehr sparked extensive discussion. In 1952, the Protestant theologian Werner Elert took up the issue in a multipart article in *Deutsches Pfarrerblatt* (German Pastors' Bulletin), the main periodical for pastors.[48] Elert argued that keeping one's oath and honor were inseparable, and in support of this point he quoted, of all people, von Rundstedt at the Nuremberg Trials. When asked why he had not simply quit, Rundstedt had responded, "I was a solder and not a traitor."[49] Elert complicated his analysis by introducing the men of July 20, 1944 as heroes:

Whoever experienced that critical day as a civilian will remember that with the first reports all of Germany exhaled, and then followed the regret that it had not succeeded. If the emotional judgment inside the Wehrmacht on that day was even halfway like the civilian mood, this would prove that the oath to Hitler ultimately had been found to be only a terrible burden, nothing more than moral support for the soldiers, who were bound to him by law through their soldiers' oath.[50]

To Elert, the counter to the oath to Hitler and its pledge to unconditional obedience must be "duty," the duty of the soldier to *Volk und Vaterland*, which he insisted had an ethical dimension.

Elert ended the discussion with a section titled "Concerns about a New German Soldiers' Oath." Given the possibility of rearming, he observed, the issue had current relevance. He said there would have to be an oath – every military had one – but it must not demand unconditional obedience. The core question, he contended, is what would be the soldier's duties? In his analysis, the dismantling of the monarchy had opened the door to Hitler, the "Judeocide," and Germany's "unspeakable misery." Even in the Weimar Republic, he maintained, "there was still an ethos that transcended the individual, to which the duty of the soldiers was linked: the general obedience to a shared mother tongue and other values that bound people together through a common history, fate, and constitution, and the duty to protect the Fatherland." But that bond had been shattered by the Führer principle, Elert contended, and by the oath of unconditional obedience to Hitler, who put himself in the place of Germany, "and thereby sparked the conflict within the Wehrmacht and its catastrophe."[51]

The outcome was to require soldiers to take a public oath, "to loyally serve the Federal Republic of Germany and to courageously defend the right and the liberty of the German people." To underscore the departure from the oath to the Führer, the public oath-taking ceremony occurs on July 20.[52]

Between the 1930s and the 1960s, the German military chaplaincy was revamped or remade at least four times (and two or three additional transformations have followed in the subsequent half-century). In the process it passed more than once between the spotlight and the shadows. Reinventions of the chaplaincy were enabled and even driven by transnational, international, and global networks involving Christianity, the churches, world war, Cold War, NATO, and popular culture.[53] Military chaplains were both a reflection of and a factor in Germany's changing place in those networks. One transformation saw the German military chaplaincy change from high-profile servant and witness of National Socialist warfare to quiet, internationalist partner in European and western integration.

Memories of German suffering in World War II, widespread disillusionment with organized Christianity, and taboos surrounding discussion of the crimes of the Wehrmacht prevented open, critical evaluation of the chaplains who served in Hitler's military. Nevertheless, efforts to create a completely new kind of military chaplain in the context of a democratic Germany represent tacit admission that old ideas about the chaplaincy were no longer tenable. According to an article by an unnamed author analyzing changes in the German chaplaincy, looking at the failures of the past was essential to shaping a new kind of chaplaincy. Wolf Graf von Baudissin was a key figure in this process. Here is how the new role was described:

Soldiers are expected to perform their duty as "citizens in uniform" educated on the basis of peace ethics and committed to peace. Military chaplaincy is to support them in this respect. It is to act neither as an appendix to the military apparatus nor as part of the command structures of the armed forces but as a "watchman" (Karl Barth) integrated in the civilian church to the maximum possible extent. The free organization of military chaplaincy in the Bundeswehr is aimed at preventing chaplains from inciting soldiers to fight and kill, as chaplains often did in the past, in line with Prussian tradition.

Rather than boosters of morale, chaplains in the Bundeswehr were to be counselors, responsible for helping decision makers as well as individual soldiers develop an ethical stance within and toward the military. The Bundeswehr chaplains were to nurture and sharpen the soldiers' conscience, a collective task requiring "the support of Christians and the public."[54]

In history, things rarely if ever happen the same way twice. Given the scale of suffering and mass death brought on by Nazi German warfare in World War II, Marx's aphorism that "history repeats itself, first as tragedy, then as farce,"[55] seems glaringly inappropriate, and yet in some way it fits. World

War II, like World War I, brought in its wake a fracturing of the credibility of churches in Germany, despite a brief surge of prestige.[56] This time, however, just as defeat was more total, so was the decline of institutional religion. Germans voted with their feet, in the Soviet zone and subsequently the German Democratic Republic, by abandoning church membership in droves; in the west, and later the Federal Republic of Germany, they showed massive indifference.

And yet something of the old chaplaincy endured too, if tinged by cynicism and humbled by an awareness of inadequacy. Like tiny hyphae, the remnants of the old found new sources of life. The idea that there is a place and a need in the military for pastoral care, not as a morale booster but as a check on brutalization, could be inspiring to Christian believers. *The Rebirth of the German Church*, written after the war by the American Lutheran theologian Stewart W. Herman,[57] did not specifically address chaplains, but they might have borrowed his title, or that of a later book by another American theologian, Franklin Littell: *The German Phoenix*.[58]

Tragic Heroes

In reaction to the role military chaplains played in the genocidal war of 1939–1945, a new chaplaincy emerged in the Federal Republic in the 1950s and was affirmed after German unification in the 1990s. It was designed to side with those who question authority rather than those who uphold or enact it. In practice, however, rejection of the Wehrmacht chaplains and their legacy existed alongside strongly positive popular representations of the Nazi-era chaplains, in memoirs and church publications and also in novels, movies, and exhibits produced in Germany and abroad.

Former Wehrmacht chaplains played an active role in trying to control their image, and to that end some of them published memoirs and histories. Few in number – a trickle, not a flood – these tend to emphasize certain themes. They invariably depict chaplains as untainted by Nazi influence and above internal church conflicts.[59] They emphasize duty, underpinned by an assumption, sometimes implied but often articulated, that chaplains, like soldiers, had had no choice: they were bound by their calling. Other recurring themes were the chaplains' powerlessness and their sacrifice.

Memoirs, written and read after the fact, highlight the contradiction between German chaplains' loyal service at the time and their efforts afterward to distance themselves from Nazism and its crimes. The diary of Roman Catholic Chaplain Josef Perau, published in 1962, in the depth of the Cold War, illustrates this moral and temporal tension. A site of interaction between the wartime past and his present a decade and a half later, Perau's text illuminates a point along the spectrum of changing attitudes.

Perau depicted the grueling conditions under which he and his counterparts labored. In an entry dated early April 1945, from Kahlberg (in East Prussia), he described holding a mass for "White Sunday" (Pentecost) in a church that "the Russian" had not yet "shot to pieces." Like many of his countrymen, Perau favored this odd metonymy, reducing the Soviets from plural to singular. He commented on an evening spent with two fellow theologians, the joy of companionship intensified by the perilous surroundings: "Every meeting with friends can be the last. The glance and handshake when we part say more than words."[60] Later that month, Perau picked up his account from a flimsily constructed bunker, where he and his comrades had "no protection from heavy caliber fire, let alone bombs."[61]

There is no reason to doubt the conditions described in these entries, but some passages appear to have been added or padded with the benefit of hindsight, as is the case with Perau's sketch of one momentous loss: "We learn that General Lasch has surrendered Königsberg. The Führer has condemned him to death, and *Sippenhaft* has been invoked. A 'heroic downfall' is being demanded."[62] ("Sippenhaft" referred to the practice of arresting family members of the accused.)[63] This segment, in hostile hands, would have branded Perau a defeatist.

Perau made sure to express disapproval of what he presented as fanatical Nazism. His insistence on the distinction between extremism and faithful service and his specificity (naming names) are markers of entries he wrote or revised after the war. Consider this excerpt, dated April 19, 1945: "Today Captain Goerke from the Information Section paid us a visit. He saw to it that we chaplains got a small radio. We heard Goebbels's speech for the Führer's birthday. I wasn't able to stand the shameless sophistry to the end and went outside. There are still 'believers,' even here."[64] Did Perau really walk out while the radio was tuned to Goebbels's speech? Did he openly express disdain for countrymen who believed in the Nazi cause? He may have done so, but why would he have recorded these acts in a diary someone could find? Even if he did not care about his own safety, he would not be so reckless about others. By the time he published his diary, however, the ground had shifted. Looking back, Perau understood that he could not talk about this phase of the war as if he did not recognize and reject what Goebbels represented.

The diary of Alphons Satzger, Catholic chaplain with the 132nd Division, written in the 1940s and retyped and revised in 1970, offers a bewildering glimpse at one priest's efforts to give voice to his knowledge that Germans massacred Jews while refusing to talk about it. The entries for October 1941 are a chilling litany of murder mixed with religious justifications: "Kirowo [Kirow], October 2–3, 1941: … It is said that yesterday 4,500 Jews, women and children, were shot by the SD. Horrible!"[65]

October 6, 1941: "Novo Ukrainska [Novoukrainka]: In the morning I visited the pope of the region. He spent 17 years in prison. He is so happy that he found his church still standing."

October 7, 1941: "Novo Ukrainska: 8:00 pm: Worship service in a former Russian church. 600 participants! All of them received Holy Communion. Beautiful participation!"

Sunday, October 12, 1941: "Wosnessensk [Voznesens'k]: ... But what endless space! No trees, no forest! Here too all the Jews were shot by the SD: men, women, children!"[66]

October 13–14, 1941: "Wosnessensk: City tour. A former statue of Lenin with a cross! The Italians and Romanians are turning this war into a crusade!"

October 15, 1941:

Andrewoka [Andriivka]: At night we get the news that Odesa has fallen. So our Division no longer needs to attack. The Romanians, who do not deserve any praise, took a long time to conquer the city. The officers accept bribes and keep the best of everything for themselves. The Romanians tear through the land like robbers, grabbing the cows from the pastures and plundering. The Romanians shoot the Jews, too: they have to remove their clothes! The clothes are then given out.[67]

All of these entries sound like they were written after the fact. Even the multiple exclamation marks seem so alien to the 1940s style.

The death notices of chaplains published after the war also fit into this pattern of wanting to have their cake and eat it too. Written by Georg Werthmann, these obituaries appeared in the Catholic periodical, *Militärseelsorge*. They list with pride the wartime positions the men held and employ a muted version of the familiar wartime language to extol their accomplishments. The summaries of postwar careers make clear on a case-by-case basis something that is stated explicitly in the report of a reunion of Catholic Wehrmacht chaplains who were in Soviet captivity: all who returned were taken back into employment of the Church. Much is left unsaid, however, and one wonders how to interpret the missing and present details. For instance, was a priest who spent the entire war in northern Italy ministering to German-speaking congregants and who remained in Bozen/Bolzano after the war part of the Vatican "ratline"?[68]

In the postwar climate, chaplains benefited from staying under the radar or, like the tardigrade, going into "tun state." Later accounts could be more creative in their version of events, since fewer people had the knowledge to call out misrepresentations. The result was some unabashedly apologetic memoirs, notably Dietrich Baedeker's *Das Volk das im Finstern wandelt: Stationen eines Militärpfarrers, 1933–1946* (The People Who Wandered in Darkness: Stations of a Military Chaplain), published in 1987. Hans Leonhard's memoir, *Wieviel Leid erträgt ein Mensch?* (How much Suffering

Can a Person Bear?), published seven years later, was more self-reflective, even self-critical. But the titles of both books reveal Christian messages of redemption. "The people who wandered in darkness" were still the "chosen people," and anyone with even rudimentary knowledge of the Bible could add the triumphant rest of the sentence: "have seen a great light."[69] As for Leonhard's plaintive title, it struck a tragic note of mourning, but for his own and Germany's losses.

As during the war, chaplains continued to fight for credibility, and now they used their memoirs to this end. Leonhard's account of a visit to a military hospital is a case in point. He told how he entered a ward full of men with sexually transmitted diseases. "So you're a pastor?," one patient jeered. "We don't need one of them. You just want to tell us those stories about cattle breeders and pimps."[70] The phrase came from Alfred Rosenberg who had dubbed the Old Testament a collection of "stories of pimps and cattle traders."[71] Accustomed to hostile reactions, Leonhard answered the taunt with a challenge: "Tell me just one such story," he recalls saying to the man. "If you can tell me even **one**, I'll leave the room immediately and never bother you again." All the patients looked at their comrade. "I can't think of any right now," he finally said.

The others laughed, but the man did not let up. "You probably want to tell us something about praying," he accused Leonhard. "Well, a real man doesn't pray." The plucky chaplain countered with another question: "Were you at the front?," he wanted to know. There was a pause before the man muttered, "We from the reserves have done our duty, too." According to Leonhard, that admission ended the exchange. The chaplain sat down with the rest of the men and talked about the Old Testament and about prayer. The next day, his memoir reports, they all showed up at the church service.[72]

A skeptic can raise doubts about the veracity of Leonhard's account, with its stereotypical antagonists – the stalwart Christian chaplain, the Nazi reservist infected by cynicism and disease – and its overdetermined happy ending. Indeed, it seems safe to assume that Leonhard, writing almost half a century after the fact, used familiar narrative patterns, contemporary vocabulary, and wishful thinking to give coherence to his memories. Still, the general outline of the encounter resembles many other descriptions of German chaplains' work in World War II, as recorded in their diaries, letters, and wartime reports to military and ecclesiastical superiors and in their postwar representations.[73] Like Leonhard's memoir, those sources show chaplains bidding for credibility – in the eyes of the men they served, with the authorities to which they answered, and with their readers and public opinion, long after the fact.

A handful of chaplains enjoyed considerable acclaim in the decades after the war. In July 1970, former Catholic Division Chaplain Johannes Kessels was awarded the Federal Cross of Merit (*Bundesverdienstkreuz*). "We are proud of you," crowed the Mayor of Essen, who gave the laudatio. Catholic Military Vicar Georg Werthmann explained that Kessels, who was Director of Caritas in the Bishopric of Essen, had received many such honors from church and state: the Golden Ring of Honor of the City of Bochum and the Golden Cross of Honor of the German Caritas Association. His wartime claim to fame seemed to put him at least adjacent to the heroes of July 1944:

Prelate Kessels became renowned as the courageous Division chaplain, who in 1944, at his own expense, had a manuscript by Reinhold Schneider, "The Kingdom of God," illegally printed by a Polish printer, as a brochure in 5,000 copies. He distributed these to his fellow priests and to friends. When National Socialist authorities learned of this action, Reich leader Bormann started an investigation of Kessels, and it is only thanks to fortunate circumstances that he was not sent to a concentration camp.[74]

In his analysis of postwar Europe, Tony Judt shows how political silence around the crimes and failures of World War II in western Europe coexisted with cultural probing of precisely those issues.[75] With the Wehrmacht chaplains, a comparable process occurred but in the opposite direction. At the level of formal institutions, the old ways were tactfully but decisively rejected, while in the cultural sphere, they were venerated, albeit quietly. This seeming contradiction allowed the chaplains to save face within Germany and also internationally, and, more important, it opened up a space where significant change could occur without running up against public pushback.

The Wehrmacht chaplains were beneficiaries of a popular culture that depicted them as tragic heroes. Indeed, they contributed to this narrative themselves. In 1950, the German theologian and acclaimed writer Albrecht Goes published a short novel called *Unruhige Nacht* (The Restless Night). It is a poignant account of a Protestant military chaplain in October 1942, in the Vinnytsia region in occupied Ukraine, called upon to minister to a German soldier who has been condemned to death for desertion. Goes's book was widely read and praised for its depiction of the struggle to maintain Christian ethics amidst the evil of the war.

In 1952, an English translation, *Arrow to the Heart*, was filmed for TV by the BBC, followed three years later by a popular German TV movie, *Unruhige Nacht*, and in 1958 by an acclaimed film with the same title. Translated into English, French, and Italian, Goes's book remains an esteemed antiwar text and an influential source of impressions about the Wehrmacht chaplains. Glowing reviews on Amazon.com seventy years later praise it as "beautiful and moving" (2014) and "a classic!" (2020). The author, who died in 2000, published dozens of books, including poetry, speeches, a German edition of *The Diary of Anne Frank*, and a dialogue with Martin Buber. Goes won many prestigious prizes, including the Federal Cross of Merit in 1959 and the Buber-Rosenzweig Medal in 1978.

The chaplain in Goes's celebrated account is clearly aware of Nazi German atrocities. In his words: "Despite all efforts to maintain secrecy, the murder of the mentally ill did not remain concealed. As for the pogroms against the Jews, various people beyond the circle of those directly involved knew more than they could bear."[76] This sentence is especially significant because the Germans murdered thousands of Jews in Vinnytsia, starting already in July 1941. One of the most famous photographs of the Holocaust, showing a man at the edge of a mass grave already full of bodies, with a uniformed German holding a gun to his head while a large group of other Germans in uniform look on, was allegedly given the title by the German soldier who collected and perhaps shot it: "The Last Jew in Vinnitsa" (Figure 7.3).

Goes himself served in 1941–1942 as a soldier and then chaplain in a military hospital and prison in Vinnytsia. He is sometimes described as not officially a Wehrmacht chaplain, but he did indeed have a formal position, and the book was based on his experiences and observations. This authenticity, along with Goes's powerful writing, gave credibility to his portrayal of chaplains as devout Christians who tried to do good in an impossible situation. At the same time, it normalized his erasure of Germany's victims, including all the Jews in Vinnytsia (Figure 7.4).

The image of the noble chaplain popularized by Goes drew on what might seem an unlikely source: Italian cinema. Roberto Rossellini's 1943 movie, *L'uomo della croce* (The Man with a Cross) presented its protagonist, an Italian military chaplain, as purely heroic. Inspired by the life and death of an actual chaplain, Reginaldo Giuliani, who was killed on duty, Rossellini's movie, like Goes's novel, was set in occupied Ukraine in 1942. Rossellini's filmographer, Peter Bondanella, describes him as more concerned with the aesthetic than the moral issues associated with Fascism, until the war began to go sour for Italy and his own safety was jeopardized.[77] But Rossellini was a close friend of Mussolini's son Vittorio Mussolini, and *L'uomo della croce* was the third film in a trilogy made with active support from the Italian armed forces.

Rossellini started work on his movie about the Italian chaplain in 1942, as part of a project to glorify the Fascist war effort and celebrate duty, self-sacrifice, nation, and church. There was no moral ambiguity here! Rossellini's film ends with the redemptive death of its hero; the Italian chaplain's forehead is covered with blood, like Christ bleeding from the crown of thorns, a classic symbol of martyrdom. A final title, shot against the cross on the dead chaplain's uniform, reads: "This film is dedicated to the memory of the military chaplains who fell in the crusade against those without God, in defense of their country, in order to bring the light of truth and justice even to the land of the barbaric enemy."[78] Bondanella emphasizes that Rossellini did not posit Christianity as the opposite of Communism but as a moral standard that

Figure 7.3 This iconic photo, probably taken in the summer of 1941, captures the intensely public nature of German killing of Jews in Vinnytsia and countless other cities, towns, and villages in eastern Poland and Ukraine. Here members of the SS and Reich Labor Service simultaneously commit, watch, document, and celebrate murder. Yad Vashem Photo Archives, Jerusalem. 2626/4.

Figure 7.4 A still from the climactic scene in the 1958 movie, *The Restless Night*. Chaplain Brunner (Bernhard Wicki) ministers to the condemned Wehrmacht soldier Baranowski (Hansjörg Felmy) before his execution. Compare this image to the preceding photo, showing another execution in Vinnytsia. Here the German perpetrators and Jewish victims have been expunged, and Christian Germans claim the roles of innocent victim and bestower of mercy. Director Falk Harnack. Cinematographer Friedl Behn-Grund. BETA 601954.

transcended all politics. This is exactly how German chaplains, including Albrecht Goes, spun their postwar narrative: as Christian heroes, they were and always had been above politics.

Goes would almost certainly have been familiar with Rossellini's film. Italian neorealist cinema was very influential, including Rossellini's 1948 movie, *Germany Year Zero*. Also widely discussed after the war was another Italian chaplain, Carlo Gnocchi, an Italian priest who served with an elite Italian mountain unit, on the Greek–Albanian front, and then the Soviet front. After the war, Father Gnocchi earned renown for his charitable work with orphans and disabled adults. He was declared venerable by Pope John Paul II in 2002 and beatified in 2009.[79]

The image of the heroic, Christ-like chaplain carried over beyond Europe. In November 1951, the Harvard *Crimson* ran a story under the headline, "War Plaque Lists German Chaplain." At issue was the inclusion of Adolf Sannwald among the names of World War II dead on the wall in the Memorial Church. Sannwald, a visiting fellow at the Harvard Divinity School in the 1920s, became pastor of a Lutheran church in Stuttgart. Drafted into the Wehrmacht in 1942, he was killed on the German–Soviet front in 1943.

According to the account in the *Crimson*, Sannwald was anything but a Nazi. In 1934 he had published a pamphlet that repudiated National Socialist notions of race. Banished to an obscure village, in the late 1930s Sannwald and his family had sheltered fugitive Jews. But contrary to the impression created by the headline, this purported Christian rescuer never became a military chaplain. In fact, as reported, Sannwald had only one opportunity to preach to his fellow soldiers, at an Easter service in 1943. He chose as his topic "the Resurrection and collective guilt."[80] No existing records suggest that any "real" chaplain dared preach on such a provocative theme.

Who Remembers the Wehrmacht Chaplains?

Publications by and about former Wehrmacht chaplains exist in an ongoing conversation, mostly muted but sometimes heated. In 1959, Martin Niemöller, a worldwide celebrity and a convert to pacifism, lambasted the Bundeswehr, on the basis of its officers who had served in the war, as "an Army of mass murderers" and described training for leadership positions in the military as "a school for war crimes."[81] He labeled his fellow clergymen who served as military chaplains in the Bundeswehr as "guides to hell." Given these comments, Protestant leaders distanced themselves from him.[82] Niemöller certainly exaggerated the impact of the chaplains in the 1950s and also during the war. Still, Niemöller called the Bundeswehr chaplains *Höllenlotsen*, which sounds like either "guides to hell" or "guides from hell." But where does one need a guide more than in hell?

A clearer critique appears in a short piece by the theologian Uwe Lütjohann, in the September 1965 issue of *Junge Kirche* (Young Church), a Protestant monthly that presented itself as following the path of the Confessing Church.[83] Lütjohann's two-page essay was a review of a new book edited by Wilhelm Schabel, published in 1963, titled *Herr, in Deine Hände, Seelsorge im Krieg* (Lord, into Your Hands: Pastoral Care in Wartime).[84] The review opened with a recommendation: every pastor should read this book. But it would be a mistake, Lütjohann went on, and a fatal one, "to understand this book as a monument to genuine faith, as a document of true pastoral service, and to think that today, in war or peace, one can simply build on the tradition of the military chaplaincy."[85] Instead he called for heeding the lessons of the past war. The chaplains' reports published in the collection were admirably honest, he observed: "And precisely as a result, it is shockingly clear to what extent they were accessories to injustice, how much they emboldened nationalist and fanatical soldiers, intentionally or unintentionally, in their cruel deeds."[86]

Lütjohann's openness is a stunning contrast to the muted, respectful tones of postwar representations of the Wehrmacht chaplains, and it cracks open a window onto discussions that must have occurred outside public view. Even Lütjohann held back from naming the Wehrmacht's victims, from identifying Jews or Soviet POWs specifically. But they were acknowledged, as was the involvement of the Wehrmacht in their victimization, if vaguely and in general terms. Toward the conclusion, Lütjohann made this statement:

The evil in the church must be pulled out by the roots. The military chaplaincy of the Second World War only helps us now if we learn from its mistakes. Genuine military chaplaincy today leads us back to the law of Christ, that we love our enemies. And only a perverted definition of love can mean killing our enemies.[87]

That old notions of Germanness were discredited as a result of World War II seems obvious. Likewise, Christianity in Germany, despite a flash of popularity in the early period of occupation, seems to have plummeted in credibility because of its alliance with National Socialism. Although the "official story" in German church circles for many years was that the Wehrmacht chaplains were Christian heroes untainted by Nazi politics, the total revamping of the chaplaincy as it emerged in the Bundeswehr also suggests that after 1945, older notions of who chaplains should be and what they were to do were no longer viable. The end of World War II was no zero hour, but, as Hartmut Lehmann has pointed out, it did terminate a relationship between Christianity and the German nation that reached back at least to 1813.[88]

Particularly since unification in 1990, German military chaplains have become agents of internationalism, serving with missions from Afghanistan to Ethiopia, Kosovo, Sudan, and elsewhere. Germans have played a key role in NATO, which offers courses for chaplains at its school in Oberammergau in southern Germany. While there, chaplains stay in barracks built for the 1st Mountain Division, notorious for its massacres of Greek civilians in World War II.[89] In one course, NATO and partner military chaplains are to be educated on "issues affecting their ability to perform cooperative ministry and religious advisory duties in a combined joint theatre of operations. This will include an examination of ethics and reconciliatory techniques to enable chaplains to support the commander and the mission."[90] What a remarkable change.

In June 2021, Mordechai Eliezer (Zsolt) Balla, a forty-two-year-old Orthodox rabbi, was inaugurated as the chief rabbi of the German army (federal military rabbi). Headlines in Israel, Europe, and North America heralded the first Jewish chaplain in Germany since before the Holocaust.[91] Amid surging evidence of right-wing extremism within the Bundeswehr, Rabbi Balla expressed his objectives in modest terms: "It is our goal to make it normal again for Jewish citizens to serve in the German army."[92] An estimated 300 of the Bundeswehr's 180,000 members are Jewish. German officials also announced plans to add a Muslim counterpart soon, to provide pastoral care to the approximately 3,000 to 4,000 Muslims in the Bundeswehr. But so far, no formal steps have been taken.[93]

The appointment of Rabbi Balla was years in the making. In 2019, amid muted fanfare, German and German Jewish authorities signed an agreement to introduce rabbis into the German military. It was sometimes described as return or "reintroduction," but in fact rabbis had never been chaplains in the German military in the sense that Christian clergymen were. During World War I, rabbis indeed served German Jewish soldiers but they were paid by their home congregations, and they were not integrated into the military hierarchy with the status of officers, as were their Christian counterparts.

The agreement signed in 2019 was initiated by the Central Council of Jews with the goal of providing religious counseling to Jewish members of the armed forces. Proponents also expressed the hope that it would help educate non-Jews in the military about Jews and Judaism and in the process help counter the toxins of right-wing extremism and Wehrmacht nostalgia. "This was unthinkable for decades and still can't be taken for granted," Josef Schuster, head of the Central Council said.[94] In his printed statement, Schuster drew a clear line between the German present and the Nazi past: "The Bundeswehr is the army of a democracy and has nothing in common with the Wehrmacht."[95] So is the appointment of a German federal military rabbi a sign that chaplains and their complicity in the Holocaust have been remembered and exorcised – a successful mastering of the past, a true *Vergangenheitsbewältigung* – or an indication of how thoroughly the Wehrmacht chaplains have been forgotten?

Conclusion

"With What Face Should I Remember This?"

People often express surprise to learn that Nazi Germany had Christian chaplains. I too was surprised in the late 1980s when, as a PhD student, I stumbled across records of German military chaplains in World War II. Fifteen years later, by then a professor at the University of Notre Dame, I received a letter asking, "Were there Christian chaplains in the Wehrmacht?" That inquiry had initially been addressed to the military historian Stephen Ambrose,[1] who answered, "No, there were not," but suggested the letter-writer contact the German embassy in Washington, DC. Uncertain, embassy staff referred the question to the German Historical Institute, and they passed it on to me. By this time what seemed surprising to me was that the author of best-selling books about World War II and official representatives of Germany would not know something that had never been concealed and indeed was widely publicized at times. Why had Nazi Germany's military chaplains faded into oblivion?

This book has sought to bring the Wehrmacht chaplains into focus. In the process, it has uncovered some of the motives and mechanisms for forgetting and remembering the approximately 1,000 men who served the Nazi war effort as military chaplains. These men, selected through a procedure meant to weed out troublemakers, met that expectation. Wehrmacht chaplains accompanied German armed forces wherever they went. They also served the SS and Luftwaffe, although they did not have formal appointments with those branches. Chaplains remained on the job until the collapse of Hitler's regime, but they used the upheavals of the final stage of the war to detach themselves from Nazism. The institution of military chaplaincy proved helpful in this regard, as it provided a natural point of contact with the Allies.

Throughout the Nazi years, German military chaplains remained alert to opportunities to prove their worth. When constrained by their superiors or rebuffed by their constituents, they sought new chances to shine, chasing relevance like gamblers trying to win back their losses. Underemployed in the Weimar period, chaplains from the last, lost war found roles in nationalist, militarist, and National Socialist spectacles. Hitler's rise to power sparked hopes for a Christian revival, but once established, Nazi leaders mostly lost interest in the chaplaincy.

Then Germany went to war, and it seemed finally chaplains would be acknowledged. Still, recognition proved fickle. In periods of German military success – Poland in 1939, France in 1940 – chaplains struggled against marginalization. The massive expansion of the war and killing into Soviet territory in 1941 brought a new surge of purpose. Chaplains were needed! Their Christian mission featured prominently in the crusade against the enemy: Communists, Jews, and the imagined Jewish–Bolshevik world conspiracy. Chaplains played a key role in crafting and propagating a narrative of righteousness that transformed German aggressors into Christ figures who suffered but triumphed over their foes. Their narrative had multiple audiences – military leaders, soldiers, the people at home, and chaplains themselves – and it cast all of them in the soft light of God's boundless love.

By the middle years of the war, the Wehrmacht routinely committed atrocities in the everyday reality of long-term genocide. Chaplains turned inward, fixating on the hardships and sacrifices of their men and themselves. When the war effort began to flounder, they found renewed relevance but at a high cost: mass death, now in their own camp, moral decay, and erasure of Germany's victims. As the Nazi system collapsed, institutional self-interest proved useful for pivoting to the new situation. Chaplains found purpose under Allied occupation and during the Cold War, serving as liaisons to the Christian world and advocating for the rights of German POWs. Meanwhile, many of them found time to write and speak, if quietly, and to spin their past for posterity.

Throughout the Nazi years, chaplains had proven to be reliable partners. Starting even before its formal establishment in 1935, the Wehrmacht chaplaincy assembled a record of loyalty to the Nazi German state and its armed forces, and in the six years of war to follow, the chaplains would not deviate from that pattern. With a very few, one-time exceptions, chaplains served the cause effectively and without protest, institutionally or individually. In fact, when it comes to resisting the Third Reich, the chaplaincy, located at the intersection of the military and the churches, has a weaker record than even those compromised institutions. Among the chaplains, there was no Stauffenberg prepared to assassinate the Führer, no Beck, and no Blaskowitz, nor is there evidence that any chaplains participated in their acts of opposition. There was no chaplain counterpart to Monsignor Bernhard Lichtenberg, who prayed publicly for Jews, nor to Edith Stein, who was murdered at Auschwitz; Dietrich Bonhoeffer, Elisabeth Schmitz, who demanded the church show solidarity to all victims; Franz Jägerstätter, or even the flawed heroes Bishop von Galen and Martin Niemoeller.[2]

The reason was not so much ideological fervor, although it existed, as institutional self-interest. Christian leaders felt a need to boost their credibility after the debacle of the Great War, and the military chaplaincy appeared an ideal site for asserting Christianity as strong, manly, national, and relevant. The longstanding rivalry between Catholics and Protestants added another factor: one-upmanship. Meanwhile, the interests of the churches and chaplains dovetailed with the Nazi leadership's own quest for legitimacy at home and abroad, as it prepared for and then waged a war of annihilation.

Looking back on the Wehrmacht chaplains twenty years later, the Protestant theologian Uwe Lütjohann admitted the failure of words. "There are things that cannot be talked about or judged, let alone debated," he wrote: "One takes it in, shaken, silent, ashamed, and at times strengthened in one's faith."[3] Yet he insisted on breaking that silence to expose how chaplains had served destruction:

Their pastoral service is visible in grotesque situations: the chaplain supports and comforts the body lying in the grave with his weapon; the pastor steps silently back from the man who, against all justice, has been condemned to death and abandons him to the firing squad's salvo. Forgiveness is proclaimed as general absolution of people dedicated to death and to killing.[4]

What can be said, what can a person not say? In a postwar trial, Chaplain Tewes could speak of the Jewish children locked in the school at Bila Tserkva and of his and his Protestant colleague's efforts to save them from murder in August 1941. But he did not speak of the weeks that preceded that incident, weeks of German massacres of Jews of all ages in the same city and surrounding countryside. Nor did he talk about the three-and-a-half years that followed, as he continued his ministry, embedded in a brutal system of domination. Did the chaplain's position as a representative of Christianity in the Wehrmacht, the embodiment of a religion of redemption through blood and the agent of an institution created to serve the national war effort, render him unable to see and articulate what he was part of and what he was doing?

Throughout this book, reversing the gaze has cast light on the figure of the Wehrmacht chaplain, the "priest in a Nazi collar," to use the words of Hungarian Holocaust survivor Agnes Mandl Adachi. Born Jewish and baptized into Protestant Christianity in 1944, Adachi lost her family to Nazi killers. Seen from this perspective, the existence of chaplains, their presence and complicity in the German war of annihilation, is not surprising at all but of a piece with the long history of Christianity. In a 1995 interview, survivor Mordechai Singer (born Markus Singer) articulated his view that the Holocaust revealed the lies of Christian history. Singer was born in 1926 to a Hasidic family in Vienna. Before the *Anschluss*, he did not recall experiencing antisemitism, because he lived almost exclusively among Jews. Singer managed to escape to England, where after the war he studied in London:

[At university] you had to do one *goyishe* subject. All the others were about Jewish history, and so on. [. . .] Now the subject I did was church history, and the first chapter was how the church was persecuted by, how the early Christians were persecuted by the Jews. So I wrote back a letter to say, "You're an idiot," to the minister. I said, what are you talking such rubbish for? You complain about persecution? Six million Jews, my parents died just now– you tell me about persecution? For what, it was nothing. So he says stick to the subject. So I said I can't do it, because not – it was about ten years after the Holocaust. I couldn't just do it.[5]

When one works on a topic for a long time, as I have on the Wehrmacht chaplains, one notices connections. Chaplains show up everywhere: in the Imperial Japanese army, among American forces in Vietnam, and in Latin America's Dirty Wars. Their complicity in atrocities is far from unique to the German case. The concept of systemic racism provides insight into the role chaplains play. Glenn Harris, president of Race Forward, defined systemic racism as "the complex interaction of culture, policy and institutions that holds in place the outcomes we see in our lives."[6] In the Nazi empire, Christianity and Christian chaplains were essential components in a system of ideas, structures, and narratives that protected and rewarded the perpetrators of genocide and their communities even as it erased their victims and denied their crimes.

As representatives of Christianity, the dominant religion of their society, the Wehrmacht chaplains practiced complicity that was both active and passive. They prayed for the Führer and blessed the flags and cannons, but at a deeper, unspoken level, they embodied the claim to righteousness and truth and the promise of salvation at the heart of Christian faith. From that position, they were seen by their co-religionists, and saw themselves, as servants of God, part of something intrinsically good. Any egregious failings could be put down to individual sinners, bad apples who, thankfully, could always be forgiven and brought back into the fold through God's boundless mercy. Measured by their own beliefs, their intentions were noble and pure. But the good intentions of privileged individuals often reinforce rather than undermine existing systems, because they hide the damage done.

The military chaplain is an incongruous figure, simultaneously absurd and poignant, because in the modern world, religion is still present but largely unspoken, and the chaplain makes explicit something that usually remains implicit. This idea, from an essay about Heinrich Böll,[7] helps clarify why studying the Wehrmacht chaplains, a small and rather marginal group of men, sheds light on the functioning of the Nazi system as a whole. It also points to the tensions inherent to chaplaincy in other contexts.

Consider the US chaplain for forces in Afghanistan, David Sparks. In August 2021, as American troops were pulling out and the Taliban was sweeping the country, the Associated Press did a feature on Chaplain Sparks at the Dover Air Force Base in Delaware. The focus, as so often with representations of military chaplains, was on death: "Virtually all of America's Afghan war dead arrive back at Dover Air Force Base. Seeing to those remains is such trying work that many do it for just six months. But Sparks was here when the war was launched and the first casualties arrived, through waves of bloodshed, and now, two decades later."[8] The author emphasized the emotional intensity of the chaplain's vocation:

In the belly of C-17s carrying the fallen, his voice quivered in prayer, and in the autopsy suite, he smelled the stench of death. He watched a father reaching for his dead son, repeatedly bellowing the Marine's name, and he heard little boys weep. In anger, families cursed him, and in gratitude they held him tight.[9]

Sparks described the effects of being submerged in death and loss: "'My heart has been torn out so many times,' the 74-year-old says, 'I can hardly count.'" Yet the hundreds of bodies he prayed over and the devastated mourners blurred together, he admitted: "'The movements and the prayer can become routine. And when I discover that I don't really like it,' he says." He comforted himself with the conviction, or at least the hope, that he made a difference. "'They may not remember my name, probably don't,'" he said of the bereaved families he met, "'but I know that I had an impact.'"[10]

Chaplain Sparks's words expose the layers of loyalty and the conflicting affiliations intrinsic to his role. He is emotional about all the dead soldiers and their grieving families yet aware he could do little or nothing for them. The numbness he mentions reflects unease: perhaps he had become part of the machinery that produced and justified their deaths. In the theater in which the chaplain operates, dying and killing are proclaimed acceptable, indeed commendable. The chaplain labors to make death meaningful, even as futility haunts those efforts.[11]

Perhaps holding onto the idea of chaplains as embodying some remnant of Christian morality or basic decency is itself a way to try to salvage faith in the world. Once, in a casual conversation in a playground in Toronto, I told one of the mothers from my son's primary school that I was writing a book about German military chaplains in World War II. She said, "Oh that sounds really important because it will remind people not all Germans were Nazis, that was just about the Nazi Party, and there were Christians there, too." She paused and added tentatively, "The chaplains were doing good, right?" When I responded that it was mixed, she nodded with assurance: "It always is with religion, but they were trying to do what was right."

Indeed, the institution of chaplaincy can create openings for acts of solidarity with marginalized people. These seem most evident in prison chaplaincy, where there is no separate, external enemy. Justin George, a correspondent for the Washington-based Marshall Project, advocates for prison reform. In 2017,

George wrote a story about Rev. Ronald Apollo, a prison chaplain in South Carolina, who was ordered to carry pepper spray. The Federal Bureau of Prisons introduced this policy after a correctional officer was killed in a Pennsylvania prison in 2013. Apollo, a member of the Church of our Lord Jesus Christ of the Apostolic Faith, said it was against his religion to bear arms. A former naval chaplain, Apollo noted he had not even carried a weapon in combat settings, nor would it have been permitted. In addition, he believed it would undermine his mission to the men in prison to do so. He too faced the question at the core of this book: whom or what does a chaplain serve?[12]

Looking from the outside makes it possible to see alternatives beyond God and Hitler. I want to end with a counterpoint to the Wehrmacht chaplains, who remained wrapped in their narratives of righteousness, unable to see the conflicting demands that defined their role. During World War II, Tamara Stephanovna Umnyagina was a junior sergeant in the Soviet Guards and a medical assistant. Half a century later, in an interview with Svetlana Alexievich, she articulated lyrically what it meant to think and feel the human devastation of war and to care for others. Like the Wehrmacht chaplains, Umnyagina was part of a massive and demanding organization; her job, like theirs, was to provide care to the fighting troops. In contrast to the chaplains, however, she was not institutionally a spiritual caregiver and not armed with a sense of rectitude. As a woman in the Red Army, she was an outsider in a way, and the vulnerability and self-consciousness of her narration would be unthinkable for the chaplains.

Umnyagina described how she prepared to meet with the historian: "All night I was remembering, collecting my memories." The process was agonizing, and Umnyagina presented it with a searing awareness of inadequacy:

As soon as I begin telling this story, I get sick again. I'm talking, my insides turn to jelly, everything is shaking. I see it all again, I picture it: how the dead lie – their mouths are open, they were shouting something and never finished shouting, their guts are ripped out. . . . And how frightening! How frightening is hand-to-hand combat, where men go at each other with bayonets . . . Bare bayonets. You start stammering, for several days you can't get the words out correctly. You lose speech. Can those who weren't there understand this? How do you tell about it? With what face? Well, answer me – with what face should I remember this?

The worst part, she confided, was that, "People still hate each other. They go on killing. That's the most incomprehensible thing to me . . . And who is it? Us . . . It's us."

Umnyagina described an experience she had near Stalingrad:

I was carrying two wounded men. I'd carry one for a bit, leave him, go back for the other. And so I carried them in turns. Because they were very badly wounded, I couldn't leave them. How can I explain this simply? They had both been hit high up on the legs; they were losing blood. Minutes were precious here, every minute.

When she got out from under the thick smoke, Umnyagina made a startling discovery:

Suddenly I realized I was carrying one of our tankmen and a German . . . I was horrified: our people are dying there, and I'm saving a German! I panicked . . . There, in the smoke, I hadn't realized . . . I see a man is dying, a man is shouting . . . A-a-a. . . . They were both scorched, black. Identical. But then I made out a foreign medallion, a foreign watch, everything was foreign. That accursed uniform. So what now? I carried our wounded man and thought: 'Should I go back for the German or not?' I knew that if I left him, he would die soon. From loss of blood.

She decided to go back for the man: "It was Stalingrad . . . The most terrible battles. The most, most terrible. My precious one . . . There can't be one heart for hatred and another for love. We have only one, and I always thought about how to save my heart."[13] How did she find those words and that strength, and could any Wehrmacht chaplains have done the same? What does it take to answer the question, "who is it?" – with "us . . . It's us."

Notes

Preface

1 Messerschmidt, "Aspekte der Militärseelsorgepolitik in nationalsozialistischer Zeit," and Messerschmidt, "Zur Militärseelsorgepolitik im Zweiten Weltkrieg."

2 Yelton, *Hitler's Volkssturm*; also Yelton, "Older German Officers."

3 Bergen, "'Germany Is Our Mission'."

4 Weinberg, *Germany, Hitler.*

5 The first pieces of evidence were newspaper clippings in the papers of Franz Dohrmann, Protestant Military Bishop during the war, in BA-MA Freiburg, N282.

6 Klee, Dressen, and Riess, *"The Good Old Days,"* 137–54.

7 Mazower, "Militärische Gewalt"; also Mazower, "Military Violence and National Socialist Values."

8 Brandt, *Priester in Uniform.*

9 Bergen, "Between God and Hitler."

10 Randall Hansen: see Hansen, *Disobeying Hitler.*

11 The phrase "subtle duel" is from Spicer, *Resisting the Third Reich*, 4.

12 Röw, *Militärseelsorge unter dem Hakenkreuz*; Pöpping, *Kriegspfarrer an der Ostfront*; Pöpping, "'Allen alles sein'"; Faulkner Rossi, *Wehrmacht Priests*; Harrisville, *Virtuous Wehrmacht.*

13 Trouillot, *Silencing the Past.* Thanks to Melanie Newton for introducing me to this work and helping me grasp its significance.

14 Important works for me include: Newton, "'The Race Leapt at Sauteurs'"; Fontaine, "Redress for Linguicide"; Nunpa, "Dakota Commemorative March"; Turner, "The Nameless and the Forgotten"; Hartman, *Wayward Lives*; Brown, *Tacky's Revolt.*

15 See, for instance, "Dead Neighbor Archives," in Biddick, *Make and Let Die.*

16 See Shternshis, *When Sonia Met Boris*; also *Yiddish Glory*, with Psoy Korolenko, www.uctv.tv/shows/Yiddish-Glory-The-Lost-Songs-of-World-War-II-with-Anna-Shternshis-and-Psoy-Korolenko-36542

17 Ofer, "Everyday Life of Jews under Nazi Occupation"; Friedländer, *Nazi Germany and the Jews*, 2 vols.: *Years of Persecution* and *Years of Extermination*; Kaplan, *Between Dignity and Despair*; Garbarini, *Numbered Days*; Waxman, "Towards an Integrated History"; and Jockusch, *Collect and Record.*

18 Ringelblum, *Polish–Jewish Relations*; Ofer, "Her View through My Lens"; Auerbach, "In the Fields of Treblinka"; Friedman, *This Was Oswiecim*;

Rubenstein and Altman, *Unknown Black Book*; Boder, *I Did Not Interview the Dead*.
19 Mostly in the USC Shoah Foundation VHA.
20 Works that have influenced my thinking include: Garrard-Burnett, *Terror in the Land of the Holy Spirit*; Long, *Christianity and Genocide in Rwanda*; Mukhopadhyaya, "Buddhism and Ethno-Nationalism of Japan"; Victoria, *Zen at War*; Nunpa, "Sweet-Smelling Sacrifice"; and Tinker, *Missionary Conquest.*

Introduction

1 A vast literature explores the Christian nature of German society in the 1930s and 1940s, notably: Barnett, *For the Soul of the People*; Bergen, *Twisted Cross*; Besier, *Zwischen "nationaler Revolution" und militärischer Aggression*; Conway, *Nazi Persecution*; Ericksen, *Theologians under Hitler*; Gailus, *Protestantismus und Nationalsozialismus*; Griech-Polelle, *Bishop von Galen*; Steigmann-Gall, *Holy Reich*; Heschel, *Aryan Jesus*; Jantzen, *Faith and Fatherland*; Spicer, *Hitler's Priests*; Hastings, *Catholicism and the Roots of Nazism*; and Blaschke and Großbölting, *Was glaubten die Deutschen.*

2 Estimated numbers of Wehrmacht chaplains vary. The estimate of 1,000 is based on a figure of 480 Protestants who served in full-time positions throughout the war and an assumption that about equal numbers of Catholics held full-time positions in the chaplaincy. See "Zusammenstellung der eingesetzten Pfarrer," [1941] BA-MA Freiburg, RH 15/281, p. 35; "Kriegsdienst der evang. Geistlichen Deutschlands, nach den statistischen Angaben der Deutsch-Evangelischen Kirchenkanzlei Berlin, Stand 1.10.1941," in LKA Nuremberg, Kreisdekan Nürnberg/121; and "Aufstellung der Soll- und Iststärke an Evangelischen Kriegspfarrern nach dem Stande vom 25.11.1944," BA-MA Freiburg, N282/8.

3 For discussions, see Bergen, "Between God and Hitler," 124–27; Friedländer, "Wehrmacht, German Society"; Katz, "Murder of Jewish Children." Key documents appear in Klee, Dreßen, and Rieß, *"Schöne Zeiten,"* 135–45; English translations in Heberer, ed., *Children during the Holocaust.*

4 Information about the Jewish history of the city can be found at: https://jewua.org/belaya_tserkov/

5 Lyudmila Sholokhova, biography of Moisei Beregovskii for *YIVO Encyclopedia of Jews in Eastern Europe* (New Haven, CT: Yale University Press, 2008); also see Sholokhova, "Hasidic Music," p. 106 on Beregovsky; Shternshis, liner notes, *Yiddish Glory.*

6 *Oy vey, in 1915 yor, s'iz aroys, oy, a rayer prikaz*; "Oy vey in 1915," in Slobin, *Old Jewish Folk Music*, 267 (song 124); see p. 268 for another version of the song (125). On recruitment of Jewish men into the tsarist army and the myths surrounding it, including the function of the Russian Jewish soldier as "a metonym for the collective suffering of the Jewish people," see Penslar, *Jews and the Military*, 27ff.

7 On Einsatzgruppen killings and the Holocaust in Ukraine, see Earl, *Nuremberg SS-Einsatzgruppen Trial*; Headland, *Messages of Murder*; Dumitru, *State, Antisemitism*; Rubenstein and Altman, *Unknown Black Book*; Brandon and Lower, *Shoah in Ukraine*; Lower, *Nazi Empire-Building*; and Berkhoff, *Harvest of Despair.*

8 See the reminiscences of Ernst Tewes, "Seelsorger bei den Soldaten 1940–1945," 244–87; also Boll and Safrian, "Auf dem Weg nach Stalingrad," 275–77.

9 Tewes, "Seelsorger," 251. Translations from German are my own unless otherwise specified.
10 Ibid.
11 The senior chaplains were divisional chaplains with the 295th Infantry Division, the Catholic Dr. Joseph Maria Reuss and Protestant Wilhelm Kornmann.
12 Invoking the name of Groscurth was significant, because by then he was already well known as a member of the resistance to Hitler within the military, specifically the Abwehr. Groscurth had been shocked by German atrocities in Poland in 1939 and he communicated with Johannes Blaskowitz and tried to gather opposition to Hitler within the Wehrmacht. He participated in the campaign in France as commander of an infantry battalion, then in the invasion of the Soviet Union as General Staff Officer of the 295th Infantry Division. According to his report of events in "Bjelaja Zerkoff," submitted to army officials, soldiers had first approached the SS about the Jewish children before they were rebuffed and turned to the chaplains. See Groscurth, *Tagebücher*, 538 ff. Groscurth was captured at Stalingrad and died in Soviet captivity.
13 Boll and Safrian, "Auf dem Weg," 277.
14 "Meldung des katholischen Kriegspfarrers Tewes und des evangelischen Kriegspfarrers Wilczek an die 295. Infanterie-Division vom 22.8.1941," quoted in Tewes, "Seelsorger," 252.
15 Tewes, "Seelsorger," 252.
16 Girard, *Violence and the Sacred*, 30–33.
17 On viewing violence in the form of atrocity photographs, particularly helpful are Crane, "Choosing Not to Look"; Didi-Huberman, *Images in Spite of All*; Jaskot, "Realism"; and Fehrenbach and Rodogno, *Humanitarian Photography*.
18 YV, Item ID#3666079. Record Group M.40: Documentation from Central Archives in Russia. This document is a copy of a report by the Central Archive of the Ministry of Defense of the USSR, from the regional archives of the Russian Federation in Podolsk. Thank you to Michał Młynarz for research and translation.
19 YV, Item ID#3678209. Record Group M.52.DAKO – State Archives of Kyiv Region, File 2202, Correspondence of the Mayor of Bila Tserkva regarding destruction of the Jewish cemetery, April 17–19, 1943. Thanks to Michał Młynarz for research and translation.
20 United Press story, "Rail City Captured: Belaya Tserkov Falls to Russians – Nazi Peril in Dnieper Bend Grows," Jan. 5, 1944.
21 YV, 3666079. Report by Central Archive of the Ministry of Defense of the USSR.
22 "On the Seventh Square," translated from Yiddish by Eli Jany. Published in *Sovetish Heymland* in the Soviet Union in 1968, but collected in 1941. My thanks to Anna Shternshis for this source.
23 Rabbi Avi Weiss, "The Meaning of Tumah," *Jewish Journal*, April 21, 2015; section of *South Florida Sentinel*. For analysis of the Yiddish vocabulary of the Holocaust, see Schulz, "Gornisht oyser verter," 185–210.
24 On the most recent pogroms, see Veidlinger, *In the Midst of Civilized Europe*.
25 On Soviet evacuations and Jews, see Shternshis, "Between Life and Death."
26 USC Shoah Foundation VHA, Interviewee: Dimitri Kalinski, # 41151, May 11, 1998, Sparks, Nevada. Interviewer: Louise Bobrow. Thanks to Camila Collins Araiza for research.

27 USC Shoah Foundation VHA, Interviewee: Isaac Piasetski, # 39698; March 16, 1998, Miami Beach, Florida. Interviewer: Mahli Lieblich. Thanks to Camila Collins Araiza.

28 Trouillot, *Silencing the Past*, xix.

29 On the myth of the "clean" Wehrmacht, see Smelser and Davies, *Myth of the Eastern Front*. For context see Mailänder, "Making Sense of a Rape Photo"; Beorn, *Marching into Darkness*; Wette, *The Wehrmacht*; Megargee, *War of Annihilation*; Hébert, *Hitler's Generals*; Bartov, *Hitler's Army*; and Hartmann et al., *Der deutsche Krieg im Osten*.

30 Quoted in Noakes and Pridham, *Nazism*, 3: 495.

31 Reichenau was in charge of the area of operations that included Bila Tserkva.

32 Tewes, "Seelsorger," 252.

33 Ibid., 253.

34 Melville, *Billy Budd*, 122. Melville's novella was originally published posthumously, in 1924.

35 Melville's phrase "religion of the meek" is based on Matthew 5:5, "Blessed are the meek for they shall inherit the earth."

36 See Gerlach, "Wannsee Conference," 780.

37 See Gertjejanssen, *Victims, Heroes, Survivors*; Röger, *Kriegsbeziehungen*; and Mailänder, "Making Sense of a Rape Photo."

38 On the connection between German massacres of Black French soldiers in 1940 and Soviet POWs in 1941, see Scheck, *Hitler's African Victims*.

39 This insight is from Weisbrod, "Sozialgeschichte." Weisbrod deals specifically with university professors.

40 See Kunst and Dohrmann, *Gott läßt sich nicht spotten*.

41 The concept of "compensatory compliance" is distinguished from a related phenomenon, "anticipatory obedience," by the element of defensiveness, i.e. the perceived need to prove something, to compensate for some supposed inadequacy by serving the powers that be.

42 On the "unrequited love" the "German Christians" showed for Hitler's movement, see Heschel, *Aryan Jesus*. This concept also applies to chaplains.

43 A similar pattern can be seen in the self-serving accounts of Hitler's generals. See Hébert, "Befehlsempfänger"; Neitzel, *Tapping Hitler's Generals*; Megargee, *Inside Hitler's High Command*; Weinberg, "German Generals."

44 See Voegelin, *Die Politische Religionen*, and Mosse, *Nationalization of the Masses*.

45 On "diffusive religion," see Snape, *God and the British Soldier*.

46 Mühlhäuser, *Eroberungen*, and Mühlhäuser, "Reframing Sexual Violence."

47 Streit, *Keine Kameraden*.

48 See Johnson, "On Agency."

49 Bonhoeffer, *Theological Education Underground: 1937–1940*, in *Dietrich Bonhoeffer* 15: doc. 157, Application for Army and Military Hospital Chaplaincy, to Head Army Chaplain Johannes Radtke, Berlin-Spandau, Sept. 9, 1939, and Enclosure, Curriculum Vitae, with concluding sentence: "Under the present circumstances, I would like to place myself at the service of the military chaplaincy."

50 Arendt, *Eichmann*, 93–97, 148–50.

51 Alexander Wolfram, Pastor, to Propst der Wehrmacht des deutschen Reiches. Luseland, Canada, March 16, 1936, in EZA Berlin 1/A, 2/498, p. 1.

52 On Biberstein see Earl, *Nuremberg SS-Einsatzgruppen Trial*, 116–17, 122–24, and 293; also Harker, *Pearls before Swine*.

53 "His fate demonstrates how annihilationist warfare could turn doing one's duty into becoming an accomplice of crime." Jarausch, *Reluctant Accomplice*, 324–25.

54 The observation that Hitler talked about peace while preparing for war comes from Weinberg, "Propaganda for Peace."

55 See Ryland, *Translating Africa for Germans*, chapters 4–5.

56 Grünzig, *Für Deutschtum und Vaterland*.

57 Lütjohann, "Militärseelsorge," 516.

58 The magnitude of scholarship cannot be captured in a footnote, but a useful distillation of important work in English is available in the Lessons and Legacies series. See Hayes, *Lessons and Legacies*; Cole and Gugliotti, *Lessons and Legacies XIV*, and the twelve volumes between.

59 Messerschmidt, "Aspekte der Militärseelsorgepolitik," and Messerschmidt, "Zur Militärseelsorgepolitik im Zweiten Weltkrieg."

60 Röw, *Militärseelsorge*; Faulkner Rossi, *Wehrmacht Priests*; Pöpping, *Kriegspfarrer an der Ostfront*; Pöpping, "'Allen alles sein'"; Harrisville, *Virtuous Wehrmacht*. Harrisville changes the perspective from chaplains to the Wehrmacht soldiers they served. The same holds true for Schmiedel, *"Du sollst nicht morden"*; another important perspective is provided by Stahel, "Wehrmacht and National Socialist Military Thinking."

61 See Heer and Naumann, *Vernichtungskrieg*; also the catalogue to the revised exhibit: *Verbrechen der Wehrmacht*. In English: Heer and Naumann, *War of Extermination*; and Hamburg Institute for Social Research, *German Army and Genocide*.

62 Missalla, *Für Gott, Führer und Vaterland*; Leugers, *Jesuiten in Hitlers Wehrmacht*; also Güsgen, *Die katholische Militärseelsorge*; Brandt, *Priester in Uniform*; and Brandt, *und auch Soldaten fragten*.

63 Beese, *Seelsorger in Uniform*. Other work on German Protestants, though not focused on military chaplains, includes Ericksen, *Complicity*; and Hockenos, *Then They Came for Me*.

64 See, e.g., Bartov and Mack, *In God's Name*; Jacobs, *Confronting Genocide*; Murphy, *Blackwell Companion to Religion and Violence*; Carlson and Ebel, *Jeremiad to Jihad*; Hassner, *Religion in the Military*; Armstrong, *Fields of Blood*.

65 I am grateful to the late Beate Ruhm von Oppen for encouraging me to use chaplains' military reports. See Ruhm von Oppen, *Religion and Resistance*.

66 Dagmar Pöpping has done invaluable work to locate and present chaplains' view of themselves as recorded in diaries and other writings. See especially Pöpping, "Der schreckliche Gott des Hermann Wolfgang Beyer."

67 A popular image of chaplains as embodiments of Christian patriotism influenced the development of the Wehrmacht chaplaincy and its roles in the war. See the critical study by Zahn, *German Catholics and Hitler's Wars*; and analysis in Ruff, *Battle for the Catholic Past*, 121–52.

68 Valuable works that integrate multiple perspectives into analyses of World War II include Steinert, *Hitler's War*; Fritz, *Frontsoldaten*; Harvey, *Women and the Nazi East*; Merridale, *Ivan's War*; Garbarini, *Numbered Days*; Hoenicke Moore, *Know Your Enemy*; Stargardt, *German War*; and Fritzsche, *An Iron Wind*.

69 For discussion of integrated history, see Friedländer, "Prologue"; also critiques by Goldberg, "The Victim's Voice"; and Waxman, "Towards an Integrated History."

70 Thanks to Steven M. Maddox for drawing my attention to this observation. See also Maddox, *Saving Stalin's Imperial City*; and, for context, Enstad, *Soviet Russians under Nazi Occupation*.

71 See Kühne, *Rise and Fall of Comradeship*.

72 Regina Mühlhäuser has demonstrated how tightly German officers' concept of "decency" was linked to women's bodies: Mühlhäuser, "Historicity of Denial."

73 Herzog, *Sex after Fascism*.

74 *Mit Gott für Volk und Vaterland*.

75 See Shattuck, "Faith, Morale, and the Army Chaplain"; also Zahn, *Military Chaplaincy*.

76 For valuable reflections on the intermingling of past and present in interviews with Wehrmacht veterans, see Weih, *Alltag für Soldaten*, 214–16.

77 See Wieviorka, *Era of the Witness*.

78 Kempowski Archiv #3101, Alphons Satzger. Thanks to Peter Fritzsche for this valuable reference. The cover letter indicates that Dr. Friedrich Knoke sent Satzger's typescript to Walter Kempowski in response to a notice about collecting diaries and letters. It bears the title, "Kriegstagebuch des Divisionspfarrers Alphons SATZGER, 132 Inf. Div., über seine Teilnahme am Russlandfeldzug von 1941/42."

79 Kriegspfarrer Satzger, "Bericht über Kampfhandlungen," Jan. 9, 1942, NARA 242, T-312/419/7995355-6.

80 Kempowski Archiv, 3101, Satzger. The entry mentioning the smell of corpses is dated July 4, 1941.

81 On diaries doctored after the fact, see Turner, "Two Dubious Third Reich Diaries." Turner discusses Bella Fromm, *Blood and Banquets* and Marie Vassiltchikov, *The Berlin Diaries, 1940–1945*. Also relevant is the discussion of Anonymous [Marta Hiller], *A Woman in Berlin*; see Barton, *Writing for Dictatorship*, chapter 5.

82 For me an important perspective came from Hamburg, Sanders, and Tucker, *Russian–Muslim Confrontation*.

83 My work in this area included co-organizing, with the medievalist David Bachrach, a conference at the University of Notre Dame in 2000, titled "Military Chaplains in Their Contexts." See Bachrach, *Religion and the Conduct of War*.

84 For example, see Justin George, "A Chaplain's Conscience vs. the Bureau of Prisons: Stalemate over a can of pepper spray," The Marshall Project (Sept. 25, 2017), online at www.themarshallproject.org/2017/09/25/a-chaplain-s-conscience-vs-the-bureau-of-prisons.

85 See Rowe and Tuck, "Settler Colonialism"; Chalmers, "Settled Memories on Stolen Land"; Daigle, "Spectacle of Reconciliation."

86 See Bergen, *Sword of the Lord*.

87 For details, including an extensive discussion of her recollections of Wallenberg, see the 1990 interview with Agnes Mandl Adachi conducted by Linda Kuzmack in Washington, DC, USHMM RG-50.030.0003.

88 Agnes Adachi, interviewed March 1996 by Marian Weisberg in Queens, NY. USC Shoah Foundation VHA, segment 58, 26:50. Thanks to Sam Meyerson for research.

89 For analysis of a photo of Kun's execution in 1945, see Petö, "Death and the Picture," 51–52.

90 See Shenker, *Reframing Holocaust Testimony*; and Waxman, "Transcending History."
91 Dr. [Eberhard] Müller, "Erfahrungsbericht des evgl. Kriegspfarrers bei der 7. Panzer-Division über die Zeit v. 1. Jan. bis 31. März 1942," p. 2. NARA, T-315/439/307.

Chapter 1

1 Grünzig, *Für Deutschtum*, 101. See also Kitschke, *Die Potsdamer Garnisonskirche*, and Siemens, *Stormtroopers*.
2 Quoted in Grünzig, *Für Deutschtum*, 43.
3 On the "indistinct lines" between conservatism and antisemitism, see Retallack, *German Right*, 272; also discussion on 273–83.
4 Vogel died in February 1933, and there was a big funeral and procession at the Garrison Church, with Nazi uniforms and symbols front and center. See photo in Grünzig, *Für Deutschtum*, 125.
5 See Marks, "Mistakes and Myths."
6 An example is Kulp, *Feldprediger*.
7 On the concept of mythic time, see Sells, "Kosovo Mythology," 180–205.
8 See Hagemann, *Umkämpftes Gedächtnis*, and Planert, *Der Mythos*.
9 See Lehmann, "In the Service of Two Kings," 125–40; Marschke, *Absolutely Pietist*.
10 Especially useful in illustrating this point is Piechowski, *Die Kriegspredigt*.
11 See Trolp, *Die Militärseelsorge*, esp. 11–13.
12 Mommsen, "Die nationalgeschichtliche Umdeutung."
13 See Pressel, *Die Kriegspredigt*; Hammer, *Deutsche Kriegstheologie*; Brakelmann, *Kirche im Krieg*; Hoover, *Gospel of Nationalism*.
14 See Krumeich, "'Gott mit uns.'"
15 P. Otto, "Kriegsbilder aus der Heimat. I. Die Grossstadt," AELKZ 35 (Aug. 28, 1914): 820–21.
16 See Geheran, *Comrades Betrayed*, 6. Geheran estimates that about 80,000 Jewish veterans of the Great War lived in Germany when Hitler became Chancellor.
17 Appelbaum, *Loyalty Betrayed*.
18 "George Salzberger: Compassion and Courage," in Appelbaum, *Loyalty Betrayed*, 25–82. Salzberger materials (diary and interview) translated from German by Peter C. Appelbaum.
19 "Salzberger," in *Loyalty Betrayed*, 77–78.
20 See Smith, *German Nationalism*; Smith, *Butcher's Tale*; also Clark, "Religion and Confessional Conflict," 97–100.
21 Beese, *Seelsorger*.
22 Ernst Max Ferdinand Wölfing, 1847–1928.
23 Beese, *Seelsorger*, 39–40.
24 Weber, *Hitler's First War*, 246–47. For another account of this killing, although with the number of victims given as twelve men, see Westermann, *Drunk on Genocide*, 28.
25 Hastings, *Catholicism*.
26 Ibid., 125.
27 Quoted in ibid., 69.

28 Ibid., 109–10. On the German Christians, see Bergen, *Twisted Cross*.

29 Hosfeld and Pschichholz, *Das Deutsche Reich*.

30 On German atrocities in World War I, see Hull, *Absolute Destruction*; Horne and Kramer, *German Atrocities*; also Audoin-Rouzeau and Becker, *14–18: Understanding the Great War*.

31 See analyses in Hassing, "German Missionaries"; Esherick, *Origins of the Boxer Uprising*, 68–95; Kuss, *German Colonial Wars*; Masters, *"People Who Make Our Heads Spin"*; Bachmann and Kemp, "Was Quashing the Maji-Maji Uprising Genocide?"; and Best, *Heavenly Fatherland*.

32 Ryland, *Translating Africa*, 269.

33 For a lightly fictionalized account of a military chaplain in the Herero/Nama genocide, see Frenssen, *Peter Moor*, 223: "A people savage by nature had rebelled against the authorities God had set over them and besides had stained themselves with revolting murders. Then the authorities had given the sword, which we were to use on the morrow into our hands."

34 For background, see Wiens, *In the Service of Kaiser and King*.

35 In jurisdictions other than Prussia, pastoral care to soldiers had long been organized directly by the churches. See Blankmeister, *Die sächsischen Feldprediger*.

36 Although I have seen this line quoted countless times, I have not been able to find it in Hindenburg's own writings or to determine when, where, and if he said it.

37 Laible, "Bleibt noch eine Hoffnung in dieser schweren Zeit?," AELKZ 43 (Oct. 25, 1918): 941.

38 Conway, "Political Role."

39 Benda, *Great Betrayal*.

40 Hašek, *Good Soldier Svejk*.

41 Houlihan, *Catholicism and the Great War*; also Winter, *Sites of Memory*.

42 Geyer, "There Is a Land."

43 Thimme, *Flucht in den Mythos*.

44 Mosse, *Image of Man*.

45 Todd, *Sexual Treason*.

46 For a look back from the vantage point of the 1930s, see Schlunck and Wibbeling, *Ein Pfarrer im Kriege*; also Lipusch, *Österreich-Ungarns katholische Militärseelsorge*. For a contemporaneous Protestant account, Lehmann, *Der Feldgottesdienst*.

47 "Die evangelischen Geistlichen und die Allgemeine Wehrpflicht," signed Breit, no date but after March 1935, in LKA Bielefeld 4/55/A/61.

48 See his 450-page memoir, published as Hindenburg, *Out of My Life*.

49 Schübel, *Dreihundert Jahre*.

50 Schübel was not the first or only author to use a 300-year time frame. See, e.g., Ihlenfeld, *Preußischer Choral*.

51 See Harry Oelke, "Kein Hurra, aber protestantisches Pflichtgefühl," *Evangelische Sonntags-Zeitung: Christliches Leben in Hessen und Rheinland-Pfalz* (Aug. 24, 2014): 6. Schübel's title had been *Wehrmachtdekan*, the highest rank other than Military Bishop.

52 Kershaw, *Hitler, 1889–1936*; also Hamann, *Hitler's Vienna*.

53 Młynarz, *Socio-Cultural Impact*, 89. Page numbers refer to draft version of the dissertation.

54 Ibid., 90.
55 Ibid., 102–3.
56 Gaydosh, *Bernhard Lichtenberg*.
57 Weber, *Hitler's First War,* 26.
58 Ibid., 48.
59 Ibid., 72–73.
60 Ibid., 97.
61 Ibid., 158.
62 Ibid., 321.
63 Ibid., 342.
64 Memo, Der Chef der Heeresarchive, signed Rabenau, An das Heeresarchiv München, dated Potsdam, Oct. 29, 1941. NARA, T-78/17/689470.
65 In 2019, I found this folder of material in the microfilmed Captured German Documents, held at NARA. Gerhard Weinberg wrote the Guide (GG12) to this particular collection (T-78, OKH/Der Chef der Heeresarchive) in 1957. He provided an extensive description of a set of documents he pronounced "extremely interesting" for someone studying the history of military chaplaincy. Gerhard Weinberg was my PhD supervisor and remains a close mentor and friend.
66 Marschke, *Absolutely Pietist,* 38.
67 Griech-Polelle, *Bishop von Galen.*
68 Friedrich von Rabenau Nachlass, BA-MA Freiburg N62. Rabenau's dissertation is N62/2.
69 On Rabenau, see Ramm, *Mich trägt mein Glaube.* For discussion that reveals Ramm's hagiographic tendencies, see Ringshausen's review of an earlier work, Hans-Joachim Ramm, *"... stets einem Höheren verantwortlich..." Christliche Grundüberzeugungen im militärischen Widerstand gegen Hitler* (Neuhausen-Stuttgart: Hänssler, 1996), in *Kirchliche Zeitgeschichte* 10, no. 2 (1997): 391–94. Ringshausen consulted the materials in BA-MA Freiburg N62, which Ramm evidently did not, and he quotes from Rabenau's letters and sermons but not from the dissertation.
70 Schäfer, *Werner von Blomberg.*
71 BA Berlin-Lichterfelde, R 5101/24294/frame 475: newspaper clipping, "Bischofsweihen in Berlin," *Märkische Volks-Zeitung*: Feb. 18, 1938 [stamped Hanns Kerrl's office, Feb. 19, 1938].
72 Franz Justus Rarkowski, "Hirtenwort an alle Wehrmachtgeistlichen," *Verordnungsblatt* 5 (June 20, 1943): 20. Full title is *Verordnungsblatt des katholischen Feldbischofs der Wehrmacht*; I viewed these bulletins in the Archiv des Katholischen Militärbischofsamts, then located in Bonn.
73 Rarkowski, "Heimatgruß an alle katholischen Wehrmachtangehörigen," *Verordnungsblatt* 3 (Oct. 18, 1939): 11.
74 Hans-Jürgen Brandt, "Franz Justus Rarkowski," in Gatz, *Die Bischöfe,* 594.
75 On Müller (1883–1945), see Schneider, *Reichsbischof.*
76 Shirer, *Rise and Fall*, 235.
77 Wheeler-Bennett, *Nemesis of Power*, 296.
78 See autobiographical material in Dohrmann's notes, dated Munich, July 30, 1965, in BA-MA Freiburg, N282/1, introductory page; for additional perspectives, Kunst and Dohrmann, *Gott läßt sich nicht spotten.*

79 On Werthmann, see BA Berlin Lichterfelde R 5101/24294, microfilm frames 0452-
454, letter (4 pp.) Reichskriegsminister und Oberbefehlshaber der Wehrmacht
(Blomberg), Berlin, June 20, 1936, to Reichsminister des Auswärtigen Berlin, cc
to Reichs- und Preussischen Minister für die kirchlichen Angelegenheiten; also
Gestapo report on Werthmann, BA Berlin Lichterfelde, R 5101/24294/467:
Preussische Geheime Staatspolizei, Geheimes Staatspolizeiamt, Berlin, Aug. 28,
1936, to Church Ministry.
80 *Verordnungsblatt* 8 (May 3, 1944): 13.
81 Ibid.
82 Dodd, *Through Embassy Eyes*, 78.
83 Brief accounts of the Day of Potsdam appear in Conway, *Nazi Persecution*, 19;
Hehl, "Die Kirchen," 165; and Schneider, *Bekennende Kirche*, 102–8. On
Dibelius's address, see Thimme, *Flucht in den Mythos*, 63. For detail, see
Grünzig, *Für Deutschtum*, 141–79.

Chapter 2

1 Keding, *Feldgeistlicher*, 5.
2 Ibid.
3 Keding wrote another book, *Und doch Pfarrer!*, about his experiences in World
War I.
4 Keding, *Feldgeistlicher*, 18–19. Lyrics to "Ich hab mich ergeben" by Hans
Ferdinand Maßmann, 1820. The "Song of the Comrade" refers to "Ich hatt' einen
Kameraden," text by Ludwig Uhland (1809), melody by Friedrich Silcher (died
1860). The Uhland/Silcher song was used during the Spanish Civil War by Germans
of all political persuasions. See Otto and König, *"Ich hatt' einen Kameraden"*; also
Raguer, *Gunpowder and Incense*; and Thomas, "Sacred Destruction?"
5 See typescript of church service: Gottesdienst anlässlich der Einführung der Ev.
Standortpfarrer Keding in der Ev. Garnisonkirche Döberitz. Nov. 17, 1935. EZA
Berlin, 704/19, Subfolder labeled "Döberitz."
6 Fromm, *Blood and Banquets*. Henry Turner points out that parts were certainly
written after the dates on the entries, and after Fromm had arrived in New York.
I accept this observation but consider the diary to be as reliable as Keding's; both
need to be read analytically. Turner, "Two Dubious Third Reich Diaries."
7 Keding, *Feldgeistlicher*, 14.
8 Kershaw, "Working towards the Führer."
9 See photographs in Bergen, *Twisted Cross*, 123 and 131; also description of
ceremony with fifty couples at Berlin's Lazaruskirche, probably in June 1933, in
"Der Sonntag der Kirche," *Täglicher Rundschau*, undated clipping, LKA Bielefeld,
5,1/305,3.
10 For example, Fritz Engelke, "Volk, Staat, Kirche," in *Aus Gottes Garten,
Monatsblätter aus dem Rauhen Haus*, no. 1/2 (1934): 8.
11 In the words of the 1941 guidelines to chaplains: "As in earlier wars, in this war,
too, the military chaplaincy is an important handmaid of the troop leadership:
educating the men to enthusiastic willingness to give their utmost, including their
very lives." Edelmann, "Wesen und Aufgabe der Feldseelsorge," [1941], p. 1, BA-
MA Freiburg, RH 15/282, p. 22.

12 Thomas Breit, "Die evangelischen Geistlichen und die Allgemeine Wehrpflicht," [no date], LKA Bielefeld 4/55, A/ 61, p. 2.
13 Ibid.
14 Ibid., 3.
15 Lipusch, *Österreich-Ungarns katholische Militärseelsorge*, p. III in Vorwort. For context see Houlihan, *Catholicism and the Great War*.
16 "Übersicht über die in den Jahren 1914–1933 gefallenen Theologen, Missionsarbeiter und Pfarrersöhne," 2 pp., no signature, stamped received by Superintendentur Soest, Feb. 1, 1940, in LKA Bielefeld 4/55, A/61.
17 Ibid. Karl Freyburger (1904–1931 in Deutsch-Eylau). See Siemens, *Stormtroopers*.
18 Schieber (Evang. Wehrkreispfarrer V) to Protestant Military Bishop, Ludwigsburg, July 15, 1938, in BA-MA Freiburg, RH 53-5/72, pp. 11–13.
19 There is no evidence Hitler ever met personally with either military bishop or any military chaplains. Even Ludwig Müller, who became Protestant Reich bishop in 1933 and boasted about his ties to Hitler, was already shut out that year. Schneider, *Reichsbischof Ludwig Müller*.
20 Rarkowski, "Heimatgruß an alle katholischen Wehrmachtangehörigen," in *Verordnungsblatt* 3 (Oct. 18, 1939): 11; also "Hirtenwort an alle Wehrmachtgeistlichen," *Verordnungsblatt* 5 (June 20, 1943): 20.
21 Hans-Jürgen Brandt, "Franz Justus Rarkowski," in Gatz, *Die Bischöfe*, 594.
22 Dohrmann's notes, Munich, July 30, 1965, BA-MA Freiburg, N282/1, introductory page.
23 For biographical information on Dohrmann, see Kunst and Dohrmann, *Gott läßt sich nicht spotten*; on Rarkowski, see Brandt, "Franz Justus Rarkowski."
24 Members of the German Christian movement complained repeatedly about Dohrmann. See, e.g., Friedrich Coch, Bishop of Saxony, to Reich Bishop Ludwig Müller, Dresden, March 25, 1935, EZA Berlin 1/A 2/498, p. 36; also Lonicer's reference to tensions with Dohrmann, in Lonicer to Edelmann, Sept. 24, 1943, BA-MA Freiburg, N282/2.
25 See Dohrmann's notes, BA-MA Freiburg, N282/1, p. 62. His account is confirmed by his vicar, Friedrich Münchmeyer; "Erinnerungen an Feldbischof D. Franz Dohrmann," in Kunst and Dohrmann, *Gott läßt sich nicht spotten*, 15. Münchmeyer recalls attempts to oust Dohrmann in 1939 and 1942. He does not name Lonicer but notes that the challenger was a member of the German Christian movement.
26 For discussion of Rarkowski's credentials, see correspondence in AA Bonn R 72265; e.g., Reichswehrminister to Bishop of Berlin Dr. Schreiber, April 29, 1930, "Betr. dem stellvertretenden Katholische Feldpropst."
27 Draft of letter signed Menshausen to Diego von Bergen, Ambassador to the Vatican, Berlin, July 16, 1935, p. 2, AA Bonn, R 72265.
28 File notes, signed Frhr. v. Neurath, Berlin, Sept. 17, 1935, p. 2, AA Bonn, R 72265.
29 Letter from Reichsminister des Auswärtigen, Berlin, Jan. 15, 1936, Streng vertraulich, An den Herrn Reichskriegsminister und Oberbefehlshaber der Wehrmacht. Signed Konstantin von Neurath. BA Lichterfelde R 5101/24294/Microfilm no 260/ Diazoduplikat 87594/vol 0002/p. 1/frame 0437.
30 Ibid., p. 2/0438.
31 Ibid., p. 3/0440.

32 Letter, Oberbefehlshaber des Heeres, Berlin, Feb. 6, 1936, to Reich Church Ministry, saying yes to meet to discuss the kath. Feldbischofsfrage on Feb. 10 at 11 am: BA Berlin Lichterfelde, R 5101/24294/ 0445.

33 "Niederschrift" "vertraulich" on the meeting, which took place on Feb. 10 as planned. Report is dated Feb. 11, 1936. BA Lichterfelde, R 5101/24294/0446.

34 Ibid., p. 2/0447.

35 Bandzählwerk 0002, BA Berlin Lichterfelde, R 5101/24294/frames 0452–54, letter (4 pp.) Der Reichskriegsminister und Oberbefehlshaber der Wehrmacht, Berlin, June 20, 1936, to the Reichsminister des Auswärtigen Berlin, Nachrichtliche an: den Herrn Reichs- und Preussischen Minister für die kirchlichen Angelegenheiten Berlin.

36 BA Berlin Lichterfelde, R 5101/24294, Microfilm no 260, Diazoduplikat 87594. R 5101/24294/0467, Preussische Geheime Staatspolizei, Geheimes Staatspolizeiamt, Berlin, Aug. 28, 1936, to Church Ministry z. H. Herrn Reg. Rat Urlacher oder Vertreter im Amt. Gez. Im Auftrage: Dr. Behrends.

37 BA Berlin-Lichterfelde, R 5101/24294/475: newspaper clipping, "Bischofsweihen in Berlin," *Märkische Volks-Zeitung*: Feb. 18, 1938.

38 Hanns Kerrl letter complaining about being shut out of decision about Rarkowski, (xerox) and von Neurath's response.

39 Cucchiara, "Bonds That Shame"; Hockerts, *Die Sittlichkeitsprozesse*.

40 Quoted in Scholder, *Churches and the Third Reich*, 1:279.

41 See Reichswehrminister to Evang. and Kath. Feldpropst, betr.: Nachweis der arischen Abstammung, Oct. 12, 1933, in BA-MA Freiburg RW 12 I/2, p. 7; and Reichswehrminister to Evang. Feldbischof der Wehrmacht, signed Semler, April 5, 1935, re: "Ernennung von Heerespfarrern," BA-MA Freiburg, RW 12 I/2, p. 17.

42 Memo, Vertraulich! Betr. Heeresdienst der Geistlichen, signed Thuemmel, Evangelisches Konsistorium der Kirchenprovinz Westfalen, dated Münster, March 23, 1936, to Herren Superintendenten, in LKA Bielefeld 4, 55/A/61.

43 OKH, signed Senftleben, Berlin, Feb. 9, 1938, to Dohrmann, BA-MA Freiburg, RW 12 I/2, p. 115.

44 Ronneberger, Wilhelmshaven, to Evang. Feldpropst des Heeres u. der Marine, May 18, 1933, BA-MA Freiburg, RM 26/6, pp. 129–30.

45 Ronneberger, Wilhelmshaven, Dec. 6, 1935, to Dohrmann, in BA-MA Freiburg RM 26/4, p. 15 in file.

46 Ibid.

47 Oberbefehlshaber der Kriegsmarine, signed Schreiber, Berlin, Jan. 6, 1936, to Kommando der Marinestation Ostsee, Kiel; and Nordsee, Wilhelmshaven, BA-MA Freiburg RM 26/4, p. 16 in file.

48 Memo, Luftkreiskommando VI, signed Weigand, Kiel, June 30, 1936. BA-MA Freiburg RM 26/4.

49 Schieber, "Erfahrungsbericht im Anschluss an die Niederschrift von der Standortpfarrerkonferenz Stuttgart am 22. Juni 1936," Ludwigsburg, Aug. 12, 1936, BA-MA Freiburg, RH 53-5/73, p. 4/16.

50 Ronneberger, Naval station chaplain Wilhelmshaven, May 23, 1934, to Admiral Raeder, photocopy from BA-MA Freiburg.

51 "Vorschläge zur Festigung der kirchlichen Verhältnisse in der Marine," attached to Ronneberger, Wilhelmshaven, May 23, 1934, to Admiral Raeder, photocopy from BA-MA, p. 1, stamped 154.

52 Tim Grady says in fact it only happened in exceptional cases that the names were vandalized. Many of the war memorial plaques were burned in November 1938 along with the synagogues in which they were mounted. Grady, *German Jewish Soldiers*, 146.

53 Schieber, "Bericht über die Versammlung der evangelischen Standortpfarrer des Wehrkreises V in Stuttgart am 22. Juni 1936," July 7, 1936, p. 5, BA-MA Freiburg, RH 53-5/73, p. 8. Protestants in the Third Reich commonly employed the phrase, "die Sprache Kanaans" to point to terms associated with Judaism and the Hebrew Bible.

54 See photograph in "Kirchenbücher. Geschichte Garnisonskirche Berlin von F. A. Strauss," in BA-MA Freiburg, N282/15.

55 Klemperer, *I Will Bear Witness*, vol 1, entry dated Nov. 27, 1939, on pp. 275–76.

56 Information on specific Protestant clergy of Jewish background can be found in Lindemann, *"Typisch Jüdisch"*; Hering, section on Sophie Kunert, in *Die Theologinnen*; and Vuletic, *Christen Jüdischer Herkunft*. On Catholics see Leichsenring, *Die katholische Kirche*.

57 See Reichswehrminister to Evang. and Kath. Feldpropst, betr.: Nachweis der arischen Abstammung, Oct. 12, 1933, in BA-MA Freiburg RW 12 I/2, p. 7; and Reichswehrminister to Evang. Feldbischof der Wehrmacht, signed Semler, April 5, 1935, re: "Ernennung von Heerespfarrern," BA-MA Freiburg, RW 12 I/2, p. 17.

58 OKH to Dohrmann, April 29, 1936, BA-MA Freiburg, RW 12 I/2, p. 46.

59 "Verwendung von Ahnenpässen zum Nachweis der Abstammung," *Verordnungsblatt* 4 (May 20, 1937): 13.

60 RH 26-7/298, file folder section B23, page numbered at bottom 12: Generalkommando VII. Armeekorps (Wehrkreiskommando VII), Munich, Jan. 24, 1938, Geheim! Betr.: Nachweis der deutschblütigen Abstammung. Long distribution list, including to Gen.Kdo.VII. A.K.

61 See Leichsenring, *Die katholische Kirche*; Lindemann, "Fate of Christian Pastors"; Gerlach, *And the Witnesses Were Silent*; and Meyer, "Christliche Nichtarier."

62 Rarkowski to Army High Command, Berlin-Tempelhof, Jan. 5, 1937, BA-MA Freiburg, RW 12 II/5, p. 3 of letter/p. 6 of file and p. 5/8.

63 On the German Christian position in 1933, see Scholder, *The Churches*, vol. 1, *Preliminary History*. For discussion of German Christian influence in the military chaplaincy, see Bergen, "Germany Is Our Mission."

64 Clipping *Berliner Tageblatt* 195 (April 26, 1934), "Für die grosse Volkskirche," in ZSA Potsdam DC I 1933–35, 00200. After German unification in 1990, this archive became the BA Potsdam, which has since been closed. The record of the Church Ministry are now in the BA Berlin-Lichterfelde.

65 Grimm to Dohrmann, via Wehrkreispfarrer VI, Heeresoberpfarrer Koblanck, Düsseldorf-Gerresheim, July 12, 1936, 3 pp. in BA-MA Freiburg RW 12 I/5, pp. 16–17 in file.

66 Ibid., p. 2/p. 17 in file.

67 Curt Koblanck transferred from Potsdam 1934 as Heeresoberpfarrer to Münster. See Hermle, *Handbuch*.

68 Evang. Wehrkreispfarrer VI Koblanck to Dohrmann, Münster, July 13, 1936, BA-MA Freiburg, RW 12 I/5, pp. 18–19 in file.

69 Correspondence from Generalkommando VI. Armeekorps, Münster, July 29, 1936, BA-MA Freiburg, RW 12 I/5.

70 Dohrmann's note to Grimm, July 22, 1936, BA-MA Freiburg, RW 12 I/5 in file on p. 21.

71 Wehrkreiskommando VIII, Abt. I c., Breslau, April 11, 1935, signed Der Chef des Stabes, to Chef der Heeresleitung und Reichswehrministerium – Wehrmachtsamt, BA-MA Freiburg RH 15/262, p. 19.

72 On Gottfried Adolf Krummacher's appointment in Posen, see Dohrmann to Chaplain XXI (draft), Nov. 15, 1939, RW 12 1/9, p. 10, BA-MA Freiburg; Superintendent Clarenbach, Soest, identified Chaplain Dietwald Wilms of Dinker near Hamm, as a German Christian; Clarenbach to recruiting station, Oct. 7, 1942, and list dated May 21, 1940, 4,55/A/61, LKA Bielefeld. See RH 15/282, BA-MA Freiburg, and Dohrmann's report mentioning Professor Hermann Wolfgang Beyer, Oct. 14, 1943, RH 15/280, p. 113, BA-MA Freiburg. Reference to Pastor Gerhard May of Cilli/Unterst. in report of meeting of base chaplains in Salzburg, 1944, RH 15/280, pp. 143–44, BA-MA Freiburg.

73 BA Berlin Lichterfelde, R 5101/24302/1433 ff, Reichsminister f d kirchl. Angelegenheiten, Berlin, Dec. 18, 1942, to OKH (Chef der Heeresrüstung . . .), re: vetting Kriegspfarreranwärtern (ev.), frame 1434, p. 2.

74 The Catholic military bishop decried assaults from neo-pagan publicists on the "religious tradition of the German army." The problem, he said, was not that the publications attacked "Christianity as such," but that they mocked "the Christian, heroic death of German soldiers." Rarkowski to Army High Command, Berlin-Tempelhof, Jan. 5, 1937, p. 3, BA-MA Freiburg, RW 12 II/5, p. 6.

75 Otto Jäger to Reich Bishop Ludwig Müller, Pilkallen, May 6, 1935, EZA Berlin, 1/A 2/498, file pp. 22–24.

76 Ibid.

77 Ibid., pp. 2–3 of letter/23–24 in file.

78 J. Bendrat to Kreisleiter Pg. Uschdraweit, Pilkallen, Aug. 11, 1935, EZA Berlin, 1/A 2/498, p. 26. See Strübind, *Die unfreie Freikirche*.

79 Kreisleiter to Landrat Pg. Gunia, Osterode, Pilkallen, Aug. 13, 1935, EZA Berlin, 1/A 2/498, p. 27.

80 Wolfram to Generalsuperintendent Zoenner, Luseland, Canada, March 16, 1936; and Wolfram to Dohrmann, Luseland, March 16, 1936, EZA Berlin, 1/A 2/498, pp. 79–80.

81 See Evangelischer Wehrkreispfarrer VI to Evang. Feldbischof, Münster, Nov. 28, 1936; also Evangelischer Wehrkreispfarrer VI to Evang. Feldbischof, Münster, Oct. 24, 1936; both in BA-MA Freiburg, RW 12 I/5, pp. 75 and 77.

82 Koblanck, Evangelischer Wehrkreispfarrer VI to Evang. Feldbischof, Münster, Jan. 18, 1937, BA-MA Freiburg, RW 12 I/5, p. 73.

83 Koblanck, Evang. Wehrkreispfarrer to Evang. Feldbischof, Münster, June 3, 1937, BA-MA Freiburg, RW 12 I/5, p. 133; a copy of Thurmann's contract dated Sept. 23, 1937 is in BA-MA Freiburg, RW 12 I/5, p. 152.

84 *Vater, ich rufe dich!*, subtitled *Gebet während der Schlacht* (Prayer during the Battle), was composed by Schubert in 1815, using a poem by Theodor Körner, who was killed in battle in 1813. The words, not standard Christian fare, call on the deity to "lead me to triumph or lead me to perish."

85 Młynarz, *Socio-Cultural Impact*, 109.
86 Spicer, *Resisting the Third Reich*, 4; on the related concept of "antagonistic cooperation," see Hockerts and Graf, *Distanz und Nähe*.
87 Rarkowski to Army High Command, Berlin-Tempelhof, Jan. 5, 1937, BA-MA Freiburg, RW 12 II/5, p. 3 of letter/p. 6 of file.
88 Ibid.
89 Griech-Polelle, "Impact of the Spanish Civil War"; also Hanebrink, *Specter Haunting Europe*.
90 Rarkowski to Army High Command, Berlin-Tempelhof, Jan. 5, 1937, BA-MA Freiburg, RW 12 II/5, p. 3 of letter/p. 6 of file.
91 Ibid., p. 4/7.
92 Ibid., p. 5/8.
93 See draft of complaint from Dohrmann to Kommandierender General des VI. Armeekorps, Münster, Dec. 16, 1936, BA-MA Freiburg, RW 12 I/5, p. 126; the final version was worded even more strongly: Dohrmann to Oberst Mummentey, Dec. 17, 1936, BA-MA Freiburg, RW 12 I/5, p. 127.
94 Army High Command to Protestant and Catholic military bishops, Sept. 29, 1938, BA-MA Freiburg, RW 12 I/2, p. 145.
95 See circular from Oberkommando der Wehrmacht, Berlin, Jan. 5, 1939, BA-MA Freiburg, RW 12 I/2, p. 176.
96 Order from Reichskreigsminister und Oberbefehlshaber der Wehrmacht v. Blomberg, May 25, 1937, in BA-MA Freiburg, N282/6.
97 Blomberg to Army High Command, May 25, 1937, BA-MA Freiburg, N 282/6.
98 Senftleben, *Deutsches Wehrrecht*.
99 "Dienstplan der Gruppe Seelsorge ab 1.11.1939," 4 pp., Oct. 31, 1939, in BA-MA Freiburg N 282/17.
100 This photograph is on the cover of Steigmann-Gall, *Holy Reich*.
101 Weikart, "Doctored Photo"; also Weikart, *Hitler's Religion*.
102 Ibid.
103 Protestant Navy Chaplain Ronneberger to Pastor Lüneburg, Aug. 7, 1937, Wilhelmshaven, BA-MA Freiburg RM 26/4, p. 56.
104 Complaint from Protestant Bishop of Mecklenburg Schultz, Schwerin, Jan. 15, 1938, to Hitler, in BA Koblenz R 43II/150, fiche 2, pp. 94–95.
105 Letter to the editor, from Oberingenieur Urbanczyk, Nov. 30, 1938, sent by *Das Schwarze Korps* to OKH, Berlin, Dec. 16, 1938, BA-MA Freiburg, RW 12 I/6, p. 29.
106 Keding mentioned celebrating Christmas 1937 in Burgos with other chaplains but he did not provide names nor have I found evidence that other German chaplains were present. Perhaps he was referring to other German Protestant theologians associated with the Condor Legion or to Italian or Spanish chaplains. Keding, *Feldgeistlicher*, 37.
107 Hehl and Kösters, *Priester unter Hitlers Terror*.
108 Heschel, *Aryan Jesus*.
109 Theodor Fliedner to Konsistorialkasse Berlin, Buchhalterei 2, Madrid, Oct. 7, 1936, EZA Berlin 7/4128. The saga of Pastor Fliedner, his mission in Spain, enthusiasm for the Spanish Republic in the early 1930s, and discontent with Germany's support for Franco is detailed in a folder labeled "Akten betr die

Foerderung des Evangeliums in Spanien," Oct. 1927–March 1939, EZA Berlin 7/4128.

110 See Preston, *Spanish Holocaust*; Cazorla-Sanchez, "Beyond They Shall Not Pass"; Schüler-Springorum, *"Krieg und Fliegen."*

111 E. W. Bohle, *Spanien, wie es keiner kennt,* 4. Copy in EZA Berlin 51/NId1, Spanien und Kommunismus 1935.

112 Keding, *Feldgeistlicher,* 9.

113 Ibid., 20–21.

114 Ibid., 26–27.

115 Ibid., 36.

116 Kunst and Dohrmann, *Gott lässt sich nicht spotten.*

117 For a related example of self-serving narratives, see Weinberg, "German Generals."

118 Schäfer, *Werner von Blomberg.*

119 On the Protestant side, relations were especially complex, because Reich Bishop Müller was a close friend of Blomberg's. By some accounts, Müller was one of the first people outside police circles to see the dossier on Gruhn and attempt to warn Blomberg about it. See Deutsch, *Hitler and his Generals,* 9, 91–95.

120 Brauchitsch had his own marriage and divorce issues. See Löffler, *Walther von Brauchitsch (1881–1948).*

121 Klemperer, *I Will Bear Witness,* entry for March 20, 1938, on pp. 251–52.

122 Baedeker, *Das Volk,* 19.

123 Ibid., 20.

124 Quoted in Wall, "Confessing Church," 427.

125 Quoted in ibid., 429.

126 See the extensive correspondence, involving Senftleben in Group S, Dohrmann, Lonicer, Münchmeyer, Bauerle, and many others, on the "Denkschrift evangelischer Heerespfarrer über die Auswirkung des Kirchenkampfes." Senftleben's file notation, April 27, 1939, followed by a huge list of chaplains queried about the text, with "nein" written after their names; copies of their written responses are appended. BA-MA Freiburg RH 15/262, pp. 139–45, 152–241.

127 Reichsminister für die kirchlichen Angelegenheiten to Oberkommando des Heeres, der Chef der Heeresrüstung und Befehlshaber des Ersatzheeres, Nov. 7, 1942, BA Potsdam 51.01/23847, pp. 10–11. The Bundesarchiv Potsdam has been closed since I used these files, which are now at the BA Berlin Lichterfelde. The numbering system has been altered slightly but these materials can be found using the BA Potsdam numbers.

128 Chef der Sicherheitspolizei und des SD to Reichsminister für die kirchlichen Angelegenheiten, Sept. 12, 1944, BA Potsdam 51.01/21842, p. 40.

129 Quoted in Fest, *Hitler,* 539 and 572. Fest gives the source as Zoller, *Hitler privat,* 84.

130 Memo signed Kauffmann, May 20, 1939, Oberkommando des Heeres to Evang. Feldbishop, BA-MA Freiburg RH 53-5/72, p. 30 in file.

131 Oberkommando des Heeres, "Merkblatt über Feldseelsorge," Berlin, Aug. 21, 1939, in BA-MA Freiburg RW 12/I/2, pp. 177–78 in file.

132 "Vertraulich! Einschreiben! An alle Standortpfarrer i.N. und Lazarettpfarrer!," signed Kormann, kommissarischer Wehrmachtspfarrer, stellv. ev. Wehrkreispfarrer XII, nd [Aug. 1939]; BA-MA Freiburg N 127/13, pp. 1–2.

133 Personnel file Keding. EZA Berlin 5/4278, Pfarrstellen, 1928–43.

Chapter 3

1 Böll, *Briefe*.
2 Ibid., Dec. 21, 1939, Osnabrück, p. 30.
3 Ibid. April 18, 1940, p. 54.
4 Protestant Kriegspfarrer, 1st Infantry Division, twelve-page activity report for period May 5, 1939–Sept. 11, 1940, NARA, T-315/2/75, signed illegible [Kaurad?], Heerespfarrer, p. 3.
5 Ibid., p. 4/frame 76.
6 Ibid., p. 5/77.
7 Friedlander, *Origins of Nazi Genocide*; Heberer, "Exitus heute in Hadamar"; Knittel, "Autobiography, Moral Witnessing."
8 Griech-Polelle, *Bishop von Galen*.
9 See Scheck, *Hitler's African Victims*.
10 "Bin ich nicht durch den Krieg zum Mörder geworden?" Activity report May 1939–Sept. 1940, NARA, T-315/2/78, p. 6.
11 Ibid., p. 7/fr. 79.
12 Ibid., p. 8/fr. 80.
13 Ibid., p. 9/81. The biblical passage itself poses a translation challenge, because that line is a common expression in German, but not in English. It is included in the Luther Bible but not in many widely used Bibles, and some editions, based on evidence that this line was not part of the original text, simply say Jesus rebuked them. Others include an additional, significant clause at the end of the sentence: "for the Son of Man came not to destroy men's lives but to save them."
14 Ibid., p. 11/83.
15 "Bestimmungen für die Führung von Kriegstagebüchern und Tätigkeitsberichten," OKH, Berlin, April 23, 1940. NARA, T-78/17/689329ff.
16 "Kriegstagebücher und Tätigkeitsberichte," NARA, T-78/17/689329, p. 1.
17 "Kriegstagebücher und Tätigkeitsberichte," NARA, T-78/17/unnumbered page of doc, from frame 689335.
18 Kruk, *Last Days*, 4.
19 Ibid. See also description of German attacks on people fleeing Jedrzejow in Kukielka, *Escape*, 1–2.
20 On horses in the Wehrmacht, see Chaney, "Behind the Lines."
21 Aly, *"Final Solution."*
22 Böhler, *Auftakt zum Vernichtungskrieg*; Böhler, *"Grösste Härte"*; Rossino, *Hitler Strikes Poland*; Matthäus, Böhler, and Mallmann, *War, Pacification*; Clark, "Johannes Blaskowitz," 28–50.
23 See Bergen, "Instrumentalization of *Volksdeutschen*."
24 Koschorke, *Polizeireiter in Polen*, 41–48. Thanks to Edward Westermann for alerting me to this source.
25 3 pp. letter from A. Kretschmer, Berlin Dahlem, to Bauerle, Feb. 18, 1940, p. 1. LKM Ludwigsburg NL Bernhard Bauerle. Thanks to Eberhard Gutekunst and Andrea Kittel for permitting me to see these materials
26 Böll, *Briefe*, Sept. 27, 1939, Osnabrück, p. 18.
27 The song referred to may be "Arthur McBride and the Sergeant," a well-known antiwar song dating back to the nineteenth century. The lyrics originated not in

France but in Ireland, but the sergeant, who was trying to recruit men to fight for England in France, ends up hit over the head, his weapons tossed into the sea. Bob Dylan recorded a version of this song in 1992.

28 Krakowski, "Fate of Jewish Prisoners."
29 YV Item ID: 3556095, Record Group: O.3, File: 2138, Testimony of Tuchman, born in Przemyśl (Peremyshl, Ukr), regarding his experiences in the Przemyśl Ghetto, Janowska, Lwów, Stalowa Wola and Kraków. Thanks to Michał Młynarz for research and translation from Polish.
30 Ibid.
31 YV 3555567, 0.3, 1653. Testimony of Józef (Yosef) Kneppel, born in Przemyśl, Poland, 1905. Thanks to Michał Młynarz for research and translation.
32 Protestant Wehrmachtpfarrer Schmidt, 75. Inf. Div, report dated Zamosc, June 6, 1941 for period July 13, 1940 to May 13, 1941. BA-MA Freiburg, RH 26-75/157.
33 Mayer-Ullmann, Wehrmachtoberpfarrer, "Tätigkeitsbericht für die Zeit v. 1.3. bis 15.4.41," April 17, 1941, AOK Abt IV d. NARA, T-312/661/8294846-7.
34 The 1st Army was activated on September 3, 1939, and remained located in the western theater throughout the war. It took part in the invasion of France in May 1940, then was stationed in southwestern France with its headquarters in Bordeaux. Its most famous generals included von Witzleben and Blaskowitz.
35 NARA, T-312/5, Records of German Field Commands, Armies, 1st Army (AOK 1). The whole roll is photo albums.
36 Torrie, *German Soldiers*, 148; for in-depth analysis, see 128–64.
37 Page of three photos with handwritten captions, no further labeling. NARA, T-312/5/7505196.
38 NARA, T-312/5/7505197. The date given was Oct. 20, 1939.
39 NARA, T-312/5/7505197–99.
40 NARA, T-312/5/7505208. A caption specified the location as "the withdrawal of the French behind the border in the sector Hornbach-Brenschalbach, Oct. 18, 1939."
41 NARA, T-312/5/7505209.
42 NARA, T-312/5/7505211.
43 NARA, T-312/5/7505251.
44 NARA, T-312/5/7505433.
45 NARA, T-312/5/7505311.
46 E.g., Meyer-Erlach, *"Das deutsche Leid."*
47 NARA, T-312/5/7505323.
48 NARA, T-312/5/7505333. Battle of Spicheren, aka Battle of Forbach, Aug. 6, 1870.
49 IVd, Ev. Kriegspfarrer, Tätigkeitsbericht, 1st Infantry Division, dated O.U. Sept. 23, 1940, covering the period Nov. 5, 1939–Sept. 11, 1940, "während des Einsatzes im Westen," NARA, T-315/2/73 (p. 1). Signed Heerespfarrer [K–].
50 Ibid., p. 2.
51 Bauerle, Tätigkeitsbericht des Evang. Kriegspfarrers beim Armeeoberkommando 16 für die Zeit des Einsatzes gegen Frankreich Mai–Juni 1940. NARA, T-312/522/8123111 (p. 1).
52 Wehrmachtpfarrer G. May, July 2, 1940, IVd (ev) Tätigkeitsbericht über den Einsatz in Narvik, May 1–July 2, 1940, 3 Geb Div W2620H. starts on NARA, T-315/174/219.
53 Ibid.

54 May, IVd (ev) Tätigkeitsbericht über den Einsatz in Narvik, May 1–July 2, 1940, 3 Geb Div W2620H. NARA, T-315/174/222, p. 2.

55 Ibid., 224, p. 4.

56 Tätigkeitsbericht, AOK 20, Tätigkeitsbericht für Jan. 1941, O.Qu./Qu.2. starts on NARA T-312/992/9185287; p. 4/9185290 = *Kriegsgräber. Unterhaltung der Kriegsgräber.*

57 Wehrmachtoberpfarrer, Winkler, A.O.K. Norwegen, Abt. IV d, O.U., Feb. 5, 1941, An A.O.K. Norwegen – Abt. O.Qu. NARA, T-312/992/9185309.

58 Ibid., 9185310/p. 2.

59 Protestant Wehrmachtoberpfarrer Winkler, Evang. u. Kath. Kriegspfarrer beim Armee-Oberkommando Norwegen, O.U., June 2, 1941. Tätigkeitsbericht für Mai 1941, An das Armee-Oberkommando Norwegen – Abt. O. Qu. NARA, T-312/992/9185541.

60 Abschrift, Protestant Wehrmachtoberpfarrer Winkler, Evang. u. Kath. Kriegspfarrer beim Armee-Oberkommando Norwegen, O.U., June 2, 1941. Tätigkeitsbericht fuer Mai 1941, An das Armee-Oberkommando Norwegen – Aug. 11, 1941. Kuffner, Wehrmachtoberpfarrer. NARA, T-312/992/9185542 (p. 2).

61 Geheim, Tätigkeitsbericht für Monat Juni 41, O.U., June 30, 1941, Signed on p. 5, illeg; p. 4/9187001 labeled Kriegsgefangene. T-312/994 is Gebirgs-Armeeoberkommando 20 (20th Mountain Army). Starting on T-312/994/9186984, period June 1–June 30, 1941 AOK 20, 12843/1. Anlagen zum Tätigkeitsbericht, AOK 20, O,Qu. NARA, T-312/994/9186998. Hansson was arrested in 1941; after the war he served briefly as acting Chief of Defense in Norway in 1946. He divorced his wife, Øyvor Hansson (née Styren), whom he had married in 1915. She was a Quisling devotee and founder of the nationalist women's organization. Hansson was himself a longtime friend of Quisling. See Dahl, *Quisling.*

62 Wehrmachtpfarrer Pohlmann, ev. Divisionspfarrer bei der 710. Inf. Div., Jan. 9, 1942, report for Oct. 1–Dec. 31, 1941, reports on pp. 1–2/20–21, [included with Alfred Goßmann, kath. div. Pfar. bei der 710. Inf. Div., 1944; Wolf Künzel (sp?), evgl. near Heröya and Skien … [Norway], BA-MA Freiburg RH 26-710/15, pp. 20–21.

63 Stevens, *Trial of Nikolaus von Falkenhorst.* Falkenhorst was sentenced to death by a British military court in 1946.

64 Protestant Hermann, report, AOK 18, Aug. 27, 1940, NARA, T-312/756/84002301 (p. 2).

65 Report from Roussig, April 4, 1941, bei der 12. Inf. Div., for Jan. 1–March 31, 1941, in Bauerle file labeled by him "Seelsorgeberichte" (not his own reports). LKM Ludwigsburg NL Bauerle.

66 Bauerle, Tätigkeitsbericht des Evang. Kriegspfarrers beim Armeeoberkommando 16 für die Zeit des Einsatzes gegen Frankreich Mai–Juni 1940. NARA, T-312/522/8123112, p. 2.

67 Ibid.

68 Ibid., 8123113, p. 3; ellipses in original.

69 Ibid., 8123114, p. 4.

70 Némirovsky, *Suite Française*, 325.

71 Ibid., 326.

72 Torrie, *German Soldiers*, 66–67, 92–93.

73 Protestant Kriegspfarrer, 1st Infantry Division, activity report for May 5, 1939–Sept. 11, 1940, NARA, T-315/2/82, p. 10.

74 IVd, Ev. Kriegspfarrer, Tätigkeitsbericht, 1st Infantry Division, dated O.U. Sept. 23, 1940, covering Nov. 5, 1939–Sept. 11, 1940, "während des Einsatzes im Westen," NARA, T-315/2/82, p. 10.

75 2 pp. report April 10, 1941, from kath. Kriegspfarrer bei der 12. Inf. Div., for July 1, 1940 to March 31, 1941, signed Schmidt, p. 1. BA-MA Freiburg RH 26-12/112.

76 Evang. Kriegspfarrer der 12. Inf. Div., 9.4.1941, gez. Roussig, Tätigkeitsbericht for June 23, 1940–March 31, 1941, in Vendée. BA-MA Freiburg RH 26-12/112, p. 1.

77 See Moscovitz, "Aumônerie générale."

78 Tätigkeitsbericht. AOK 16, IVd., Handwritten, Cover page, 8123106, June 24, 1940, signed Robert Franke, kath. Wehrmachtdekan. Z.Zt. Kriegspfarrer b AOK 16, Sept. 22, 1939–June 24, 1940. AOK 16, W 4091/4. NARA, T-312/522/8123107.

79 Ibid., 8123108, p. 2.

80 Ibid., 8123109, p. 3. The parenthetical comment is confusing, because chaplains should have been recognizable by the absence of epaulets on their uniforms.

81 Protestant Wehrmachtoberpfarrer Hermann, report, AOK 18, Aug. 27, 1940, NARA, T-312/756/84002300, p. 1. The phrase "to arm them with emboldening and comforting faith" is quoted from the *Merkblatt über Feldseelsorge*, Aug. 21, 1939, section 1.

82 Protestant Hermann, report, AOK 18, Aug. 27, 1940, NARA, T-312/756/84002301, p. 2.

83 Cover letter Aug. 22, 1940, signed Heeresoberpfarrer [Klum?], NARA, T-312/756/8400306; Aug. 22, 1940 AOK 18, W.5966y; Tätigkeitsbericht, AOK 18, IVd (Katholisch); NARA, T-312/756/8400305, Tätigkeitsbericht laut Verordnung "Allgem.H.M.1940" Ausschr. 538.

84 IVd, Ev. Kriegspfarrer, Tätigkeitsbericht, 1st Infantry Division, dated O.U. Sept. 23, 1940, covering the period Nov. 5, 1939–Sept. 11, 1940, "während des Einsatzes im Westen," NARA, T-315/2/81, p. 9.

85 On the flip side, see Scheck, *Love between Enemies*.

86 2 pp. report from Kriegspfarrer [Krause or Krauss?], April 1, 1941, Ev. Kriegspfarrer bei der 95. I.D., Tätigkeitsbericht for Jan. 1–March 31, 1941, p. 2 in LKM Ludwigsburg NL Bauerle.

87 Kath. Kriegspfarrer bei der 5. Pz. Div. Oppeln, July 16, 1940, Tätigkeitsbericht über die Zeit des Einsatzes während des Feldzuges in Belgien und Frankreich. Signed Kitzmann [or Kretschmann?], Kriegspfarrer. NARA, T-315/259/247.

88 For context, see Meinen, *Wehrmacht und Prostitution*.

89 Report April 10, 1941, kath. Kriegspfarrer bei der 12. Inf. Div., for July 1, 1940–March 31, 1941, signed Schmidt, p. 1. BA-MA Freiburg RH 26-12/112.

90 Dr. theol. Krummacher, Ev. Kriegspfarrer b.d. 208 I.D., 2 pp. Tätigkeitsbericht (duplicated) by April 6, 1941, for Jan.–March 1941, p. 1, in LKM Ludwigsburg NL Bauerle.

91 See Hushion, *Intimate Encounters*.

92 Evang. Kriegspfarrer der 12. Inf. Div., April 9, 1941, signed Roussig, Tätigkeitsbericht for June 23, 1940–March 31, 1941, in Vendée. BA-MA Freiburg RH 26-12/112, p. 2.
93 Protestant Hermann, report, AOK 18, Aug. 27, 1940, NARA, T-312/756/84002301, p. 2.
94 *Verordnungsblatt* 5 (May 25, 1941): 25, death of Robert Franke. Franke was born in 1895, served as a divisional chaplain in World War I, entered the Wehrmacht chaplaincy in 1936, and was promoted in 1940 to Wehrmachtdekan.
95 Tätigkeitsbericht des Wehrmachtpfarrers Gleditsch, evgl. Kriegspfarrer bei der 5. Panzer-division über die Einsatzzeit im Westen vom 10. Mai bis 12. Juli 1940. May 10–July 12, 1940, IVd, Tätigkeitsbericht, p. 1/239. Materials start at NARA, T-315/259/236.
96 Ibid., p. 2/240.
97 Ibid.
98 Kath. Kriegspfarrer bei der 5. Pz. Div. Oppeln, den 16. Juli 1940, Taetigkeitsbericht über die Zeit des Einsatzes während des Feldzuges in Belgien und Frankreich. Signed Kitzmannn [or Kretschmann?], Kriegspfarrer. NARA, T-315/259/247.
99 Ibid., 248, p. 2.
100 Photo Album no. 67, including photos showing 1st Army activities on the Front during the period covered. Nov. 1939–Jan. 1940, begins NARA, T-312/5/7505304. Photo of two men on bikes is at 7505309.
101 NARA, T-312/5/7505310. It is not clear what the flags are, with black and white lines, but they are neither a swastika nor a Union Jack.
102 NARA, T-312/5/7505385.
103 Ibid., 7505386.
104 Ibid., 7505387.
105 Ibid., 7505433.
106 See, e.g., pamphlet, "Ein kleiner Spaziergang durch Saloniki," Andenken vom Einmarsch der Deutschen Truppen in Saloniki – April 9, 1941. Italienische Buchdruckerei A. Akuaroni, Ermu – Strasse 19 – Saloniki [1942]. NL Hans Radtke, EZA Berlin 704/36.
107 Wehrmachtoberpfarrer [Schloss], Kath. Kriegspfarrer beim Wehrmachtbefehlshaber Südost, July 14, 1941, Report for April 1–June 30, 1941, p. 3. T-312/464/8052331.
108 Ibid.
109 Ibid., 8052332, p. 4.
110 Ibid., 8052333, p. 5.
111 See Dordanas, "Jewish Community of Thessaloniki."
112 *Verordnungsblatt* 4 (April 21, 1941): 21.
113 Wehrmachtoberpfarrer [Schloss], Kath. Kriegspfarrer beim Wehrmachtbefehlshaber Südost, July 14, 1941, Report for April 1–June 30, 1941, p. 6. NARA, T-312/464/8052334.
114 Ibid., 8052335, p. 7.
115 Radtke, 1941. Tätigkeitsbericht über Einsatz im Südosten. AOK 12, Ev. Armeepfarrer, Sept. 10, 1941, p. 2. NARA, T-312/464/8052321.

116 Wehrmachtoberpfarrer [Schloss], Dec. 40–June 41, AOK 12, 19535, Tätigkeitsbericht. AOK 12, IVd kath., p. 2. NARA, T-312/464/8052328.
117 Ibid., 8052330.
118 Quoted in Mazower, "Military Violence and National Socialist Value," 131.
119 Ev. Kriegspfarrer der 73. Inf. Div. Dr. theol. U. Bergfried, as of Aug. 20, 1941, in Florina, Skopje, p. 3 of report for period May 11, 1941–July 12, 1941. BA-MA Freiburg, RH 26-73/89.
120 Zakić, *Ethnic Germans*, 138–39.
121 Mayer-Ullmann, AOK 17 Abt IV d/E u. K, April 3, 1941, Tätigkeitsbericht, March 16–March 31, 1941. NARA, T-312/661/8294848.
122 Mayer-Ullmann, AOK 17 Abt. IV d/E u. K, April 18, 1941, Tätigkeitsbericht for the period April 1–April 15, 1941. NARA, T-312/661/8294850.
123 Chef der Sicherheitspolizei und des SD to Reichsminister für die kirchlichen Angelegenheiten, March 11, 1941, re. Pfarrer Kurt Richter, BA Potsdam 51.01/23846, p. 9.
124 On the Catholic accused of striking the young boys, see Reichsminister für die kirchlichen Angelegenheiten to Chef der Heeresrüstung und Befehlshaber des Ersatzheeres, May 19, 1941, BA Potsdam 51.01/21839, p. 69.
125 Reichsminister für die kirchlichen Angelegenheiten to Chef der Heeresrüstung und Befehlshaber des Ersatzheeres, March 10, 1941, BA Potsdam 51.01/21839, p. 48.
126 One communication rejected both proposed names because of their activity in youth work. Reichsminister für die kirchlichen Angelegenheiten to Chef der Heeresrüstung und Befehlshaber des Ersatzheeres, BA Potsdam 51.01/21839, p. 69.
127 Edelmann, "Wesen und Aufgabe der Feldseelsorge," [1941], p. 1, BA-MA Freiburg, RH 15/282, p. 22.
128 "Bestimmungen für besondere Dienstverhältnisse der Kriegspfarrer beim Feldheer," June 18, 1941, BA-MA Freiburg, N282/3.
129 Correspondence from Dr. Albert M. Koeniger, o.ö. Professor des Kirchenrechts an der Rhein. Friedrich-Wilhelms-Universität Bonn, to the office of the Catholic Military Bishop, with copy to the Church Ministry, no date (reply dated June 14, 1941), pp. 294–96 in file, BA Potsdam 51.01/23158; also copy of Maximilian Schedlbauer, Kriegspfarrer, 337. Inf. Div., to Catholic Military Bishop, June 3, 1941, p. 298 in same file. See also a later, related case: Chef der Sicherheitspolizei und des SD to Reich Minister for Church Affairs, Berlin, July 30, 1941, BA Potsdam 51.01/23158, pp. 299–300.
130 Böll, *Briefe* (May 3, 1941), 184–85.
131 Ibid. (May 25, 1941), 190.

Chapter 4

1 YV Visual Centre, Item 7934915 – Testimony of Nina (Vera) Bela Gelman, born in Zhytomyr, Ukraine, 1932. Interview conducted in Russian, in Israel. Thanks to Michał Młynarz for research and translation. On analyzing interviews, see Shternshis, *When Sonia Met Boris*.
2 Kopstein and Wittenberg, *Intimate Violence*.

3 Streit, *Keine Kameraden*; see also Hartmann, *Unternehmen Barbarossa.*
4 For accounts of mass killings of Jews in song, see Shternshis, "Yiddish Glory."
5 See Jantzen and Thiesen, *European Mennonites.*
6 For discussion, see Uziel, "Wehrmacht Propaganda Troops."
7 See Knopp, *Weltenbrand.*
8 Lower, *Nazi Empire-Building*, 73–78. About Jeckeln, Lower notes that "the evident Nazi leap to genocide that occurred in Ukraine was mainly his doing and occurred while he was in the Zhytomyr region between late July and mid-September 1941" (p. 76).
9 Berkhoff, *Harvest of Despair*, chapter 4, "Prisoners of War." Berkhoff is particularly interested in the "myriad attempts by civilian bystanders to save the lives of the prisoners" (p. 89). On the POW camp at Zhytomyr, see 99–101.
10 quoted in Poliakov, *Harvest of Hate*, 134. Here Poliakov is translating and abridging a document read into the record of the Nuremberg trials on Feb. 18, 1946 as Exhibit #USSR-293. Roesler was describing a mass shooting operation he observed in late July 1941.
11 On soldiers photographing scenes of killing, see Struk, *Photographing the Holocaust*, 70–73.
12 YV, Item 3560179. Record Group: O.3 – Testimonies Department, File: 6916. Aleksander Ivanovich Iakimenko (Yakimenko), born in a village near Malin, Zhytomyr Oblast, Ukrainian SSR, USSR, 1930. Audio testimony and transcript. His emphasis.
13 The term "violent display" is Lee Ann Fujii's. See Fujii, "Talk of the Town"; also Fujii, *Show Time.*
14 Thanks to Ryan Masters for drawing this image to my attention. USHMM has a number of photos of this event: e.g., USHMM 17541, 17546, 18458, and 18451. See also Hellbeck, "A 'Great Antibolshevik Show.'"
15 Uziel, "Wehrmacht Propaganda Troops," 19–20.
16 Yad Vashem, Item 3656886. Record Group: TR.3 – Eichmann Trial. File: 780. Report issued by the Reich Security Head Office (RSHA) regarding activities of the Einsatzgruppen in various locations in the east, the establishment of the Kaunas Ghetto and the murder of Jews. This report was prepared on Aug. 15, 1941.
17 Timothy Snyder's definition, which encompasses the territories ravaged both by Stalin and Hitler, fits here as well. Snyder, *Bloodlands.*
18 "Fateful Months" is from Browning, *Fateful Months.* See also Browning, with Matthäus, *Origins of the Final Solution.*
19 The term is from Shepherd, *War in the Wild East.*
20 Regimental commissar Janis Mistris, Acting Head of the Political Department of the 201st Latvian Rifle Division, To the Head of the Political Administration of the Western Front; To the Head of the Political Department of the 33rd Army, Political Report #131/s, Jan. 12, 1942, from the village of Riabushki. Latvijas Nacionālā arhīva Latvijas Valsts arhīvs. PA-301. Fonds "Lielā Tēvijas kara vēstures komisija" LNA LVA, PA-301. F.,3. Apr.,81.1., 32.-34. 1p. I am grateful to Konstantin Fuks for finding and translating this document.
21 See Enstad, "Prayers and Patriotism"; and Berkhoff, "Was There a Religious Revival."
22 "Die religiöse Lage bei den Russlanddeutschen," subsection of "Aktenvermerk, Betr. Transnistrienschleusung," signed Dr. Foe [?], Litzmannstadt, Feb. 3, 1943, in

AP Łódź, L-3578/10 (Berichte der Kommandos der Einsatzgruppe D über das Schwarzmeerdeutschtums . . . 1941–44), p. 8/file p. 50.

23 Klee and Dreßen, *"Gott mit uns,"* 122: quote from SS-Sturmbannführer Karl Hennicke.

24 On perpetrators confiding in Christian clergy see Krondorfer, *Male Confessions.*

25 Kranz, *Eine katholische Jugend*; on Kranz, see Phayer, *Catholic Church and the Holocaust*, 79–81.

26 Tewes, "Seelsorger," 244–87; also Boll and Safrian, "Auf dem Weg nach Stalingrad," 275–77.

27 Order signed Keitel, "Betr.: Richtlinien für die Durchführung der Feldseelsorge," Berlin, May 24, 1942, p. 1, BA Potsdam, 51.01/21839, p. 147.

28 Rarkowski, "Hirtenwort des katholischen Feldbischofs an die katholischen Wehrmachtangehörigen zu dem großen Entscheidungskampf im Osten," Berlin, July 29, 1941, 4 pp.; bound with *Verordnungsblatt*; quotations from pp. 1–3.

29 Wehrmachtdekan Gmeiner, 4-page report, July 12, 1941, "Tätigkeitsbericht des Kath. Armeepfarrers beim A.O.K. 11 früher (Oberkommando der Truppen des deutschen Heeres in Rumänien) über die Zeit vom 20.5. bis 30.6.1941." NARA, T-312/354/7927741–44.

30 Ofer, "Holocaust in Transnistria," 136.

31 Albrecht, Protestant divisional chaplain, 2nd Mountain Division, "Tätigkeitsbericht bis 3.11.1941," Nov. 10, 1941, NARA, T-315/101/747. Zapadnaya Litsa was a German naval base on the Kola Peninsula, 45 km from the border with Norway. The Soviets allowed the Germans to use this territory in a deal worked out during the Molotov–Ribbentrop period.

32 Wehrmachtpfarrer Pohlmann, Protestant divisional chaplain with the 710th Infantry Division, report dated Jan. 9, 1942, for period Oct. 1–Dec. 31, 1941, reports on p. 1/20: "Reise vom 26.11.-2.12. in den nahen Nordbezirk, insbesondere zu Luftwaffeneinheiten. . ."; Dec. 3–4, "Seelsorge bei Erschiessung von 3 Norwegern"; Dec. 28/29, "Seelsorge b. Erschiessung von 11 Norwegern," p. 2/21. BA-MA Freiburg, RH 26-710/15, pp. 20–21b. The proclivity of Wehrmacht and SS men to highlight their involvement against other targets of Nazism in areas with few or no Jews, or after they had killed the Jews, as a way to assert their importance has been observed for northern Russia, where Wehrmacht units massacred many Roma. Holler, "Like Jews?"

33 Beorn, *Marching into Darkness*; see also Gerlach, *Kalkulierte Morde*; and Walke, *Pioneers and Partisans.*

34 26 pp. report, signed Wehrmachtoberpfarrer illeg., for July 1, 1941–Jan. 31, 1942, dated March 6, 1942, p. 3. This whole folder is reports from the Protestant divisional chaplain with the 15th Division in Belarus (Weißrußland). Once Mogilev was taken by the Germans, he reverted back to the divisional staff. BA-MA Freiburg, RH 26-15/62.

35 Ibid.

36 For discussion in another context, see Kucich, *Imperial Masochism.*

37 Catholic divisional priest, 7th Tank Division, entry for May 3–8, 1942, in "Tätigkeitsbericht, 1.1.42–12.5.42," p. 7, NARA, T-315/439/329.

38 Dr. [Eberhard] Müller, Protestant divisional chaplain, 7th Tank Division, Tätigkeitsbericht, June 22–Sept. 30, 1941, p. 4, NARA, T-315/439/301.

39 Ibid., 299.
40 Ibid.
41 See Dieckmann, *Deutsche Besatzungspolitik in Litauen.*
42 NL Bernhard Bauerle, in LKM Ludwigsburg.
43 Landwehr, "So sah ich sie sterben."
44 Pöpping, "'Der schreckliche Gott."
45 On the influence of the "German Christian" Movement in the chaplaincy, see Bergen, "'Germany Is Our Mission."
46 Perau, *Priester*, 29 and 33. There's an extensive Yizkor book for Tomaszow-Lubelski, in Yiddish (Brooklyn: Tomashover Relief Committee, 1965), available in the New York Public Library digital collection. https://digitalcollections.nypl .org/items/6cc2c990–324c-0133-929c-58d385a7b928.
47 See "Tomaszow Lubelski," translated chapter from *Pinkas Hakehillot Polin/ Encyclopedia of Jewish Communities in Poland* (Jerusalem: Yad Vashem, 1999), vol. 7: 237–41. online: www.jewishgen.org/yizkor/pinkas_poland/pol7_00237b .html
48 Paulovicova, *Rescue of Jews*, 296–97. She footnotes Ivan Kamenec et al., *Vatikán a Slovenská Republika 1939–1945: Dokumenty* (Bratislava: Slovak Academic Press, 1992), 71.
49 Madigan, "Two Popes," 27–32.
50 Biliuță, "To Murder or Save"; see also Harward, *Romania's Holy War.*
51 Adrian Cioflâncă, comments in response to paper by D. Bergen on Wehrmacht chaplains, at conference on Memories of World War II, Chisinau, Moldova, 2011; on the role of the Romanian Orthodox Church in massacres of Jews, see also Popa, "7th Roşiori (Cavalry) Regiment," 52–53.
52 Tilli, "'Deus Vult!'"
53 On the related concept of the "settler colonial mesh," see Woolford, *This Benevolent Experiment*, 3.
54 On how this process worked in Poland in 1939, see Böhler, *Auftakt zum Vernichtungskrieg*; for the case of Spain in 1936, see Preston, *Spanish Holocaust.* Also relevant is Hull, *Absolute Destruction.*
55 For a later chapter of efforts to sort the population, see Penter, "Local Collaborators," and Exeler, "What Did You Do during the War."
56 Sudermann, *Lebenserinnerungen*, quoted in Gerhard Rempel, "Dove and Swastika: Russian Mennonites under Nazi Occupation," unpublished manuscript; see also Rempel, "Mennonites and the Holocaust."
57 Genesis 24:1–26 tells the story of Rebekah and how Abraham's servant identified her at the well, and Genesis 29:1–12 depicts Jacob, who drew water for the shepherdess Rachel.
58 Tingler, "Religion, Ethno-Nationalism."
59 Accounts of Jesus "cleansing the temple" appear in Matthew 21:12–17, Mark 11:15–19, Luke 19:45–47, and John 2:13–22.
60 Bergen, *Twisted Cross*, 161–62.
61 Sermon on Jesus and the temple, cited in Harrisville, "Unholy Crusaders," 621.
62 For example, a Catholic chaplain maintained that the church in Juchnow, east of Smolensk, had already been used as a granary for twenty years. Diary entry for Nov. 20, 1941, Perau, *Priester*, 42.

63 See Hanebrink, *Specter Haunting Europe.*

64 War reporter Franz Tautphocus, "Erster Gottesdienst nach 24 Jahren," press clipping stamped Reich Minister Kerrl, Berlin [source not named], Aug. 18, 1941, BA Berlin Lichterfelde R 5101/22183/1070 (microfilm).

65 Rarkowski, "Hirtenwort des katholischen Feldbischofs an die katholischen Wehrmachtangehörigen zu dem großen Entscheidungskampf im Osten," Berlin, July 29, 1941, quotations from pp. 1–3.

66 Ibid.

67 To appreciate the significance of Luther in this context, see Probst, *Demonizing the Jews.*

68 See, for example, description of German destruction of synagogues in Przemyśl, in YVa, Item 3555567. Record Group: 0.3 – Testimonies Department. File: 1653. Testimony of Józef (Yosef) Kneppel, born in Przemysl, Poland, 1905.

69 See Montague, *Chełmno.*

70 Quoted in Lower, "Anti-Jewish Violence," 145.

71 YV, Item 3556728. Testimony of Karolina (Pfeffer) Berger, born in Przemyślany (Peremyshliany – Ukr), Poland, 1917, regarding her experiences in the Przemyślany Ghetto, Chrzanów forests, with the partisans and in hiding.

72 YV, Item 3541092. Record Group: M.1 – Central Historical Commission (CHC) of the Central Committee of Liberated Jews in the US Zone, Munich. Sub-Record Group: M.1.E – Testimonies Collection. File: 1080. Altman, Pepa: Testimony on her fate in Przemyślany.

73 For example, see Hildebrand, *Odyssee*, 249. Hildebrand, a Mennonite from Ukraine who worked for the Germans, describes learning of the murder of the Jews in Vitebsk in the winter of 1941–42. "The ghetto had disappeared. I asked a soldier where the Jews had gone. He informed me that there was a new district commander, and he had said the ghetto was a security threat for the Wehrmacht. After that the Jews were shot. From that point on my faith in victory vanished. People who commit crimes like that will not succeed in the long run."

74 Quoted by Langer, "Introduction," xii. Langer's note: cited in Rhodes, *Masters of Death*, 146.

75 For discussion, see Braun, "Symbol of the Cross," 5–33.

76 On Stangl, see Sereny, *Into That Darkness.*

77 See Nevermann, "Warum zog ich nicht die Notbremse?," 282–84.

78 Faulkner Rossi provides some examples of SS men confessing to Catholic chaplains: *Wehrmacht Priests*, 126–28.

79 Heinz Keller, "Ob das der Herrgott von uns will?," in Brandt, *Priester in Uniform*, 130–31. Heinz Keller was with the 2nd Medical Corps, 46th Infantry Division, in the Crimea and the Caucasus.

80 Relevant scholarship includes: Koonz, *Mothers in the Fatherland*; Schulz, "Weibliche Häftlinge"; Paul, *Zwangsprostitution*; Schwarz, *Eine Frau an seiner Seite*; Steinbacher, *"Musterstadt" Auschwitz*; Flaschka, "Race, Rape and Gender"; Bos, "Her Flesh Is Branded," 59–85; Röger, *Kriegsbeziehungen*; Mailänder, "Making Sense of a Rape Photo."

81 Berkhoff, "Was There a Religious Revival," 548–49.

82 Harrisville, "Unholy Crusaders."

83 Werner, *Constructed Mennonite*, 147.

84 Neufeld, *Family Torn Apart*, 103.

85 Gertjejanssen, *Victims, Heroes, Survivors*; Mühlhäuser, *Erorberungen.*

86 Tönsmeyer, "Besatzung," 281–98; Dallin, *German Rule in Russia.*

87 See accounts in Desbois, *Holocaust by Bullets.*

88 For a literary representation of the humiliations experienced by Soviet women with Germans in their homes, see Grossman, "The Old Teacher."

89 Benedikt Heinrich Wundshammer was a prolific and well-known photojournalist attached to a propaganda company in the Luftwaffe. See David F. Crew, "Benno Wundshammer: Photo-Journalism and German History, 1933–1987," research project: www.visual-history.de/en/project/benno-wundshammer-photo-journalism-and-german-history-1933-1987/

90 See Kay, *Making of an SS Killer*, 43–56.

91 YV, Item 3560918. Record Group: O.3, Testimonies Department. File: 4722. Six pages, original document in Russian. The informant's full name is Giorgi Valerianovich Shantir. The interview took place in Moscow in 1987. Thanks to Michał Młynarz for research and translation.

92 See interviews (in Russian) in Pavel Chukhraj, dir., *Children from the Abyss,* from the USC Shoah Foundation "Broken Silence" Series, 2002.

93 Wehrmachtdekan Gmeiner, July 12, 1941, "Tätigkeitsbericht des Kath. Armeepfarrers beim AOK 11 (früher Oberkommando der Truppen des deutschen Heeres in Rumänien) über die Zeit vom 20.5. bis 30.6.1941." NARA, T-312/354/7927741-7927744.

94 Andrea Löw, "Stanisławów (now Ivano-Frankivsk)," *United States Holocaust Memorial Museum Encyclopedia of Camps and Ghettos, 1933–1945*, vol 2, *Ghettos in German-Occupied Eastern Europe* (Washington, DC: USHMM, 2012); see also Pohl, *Nationalsozialistische Judenverfolgung in Ostgalizien*; and Sandkühler, *"Endlösung" in Galizien.*

95 Certeau, *Practice of Everyday Life*, 36–38.

96 Mühlhäuser, "Reframing Sexual Violence."

97 Dr. [Eberhard] Müller, "Erfahrungsbericht des evgl. Kriegspfarrers bei der 7. Panzer-Division über die Zeit v. 1. Jan. bis 31. März 1942," p. 1. NARA, T-315/439/306.

98 Ibid., 307, p. 2.

99 Werner, *Constructed Mennonite*, 147. The reference is to Stern, *Remembering Pinochet's Chile.*

100 Hildebrand, *Odyssee*, 268.

101 Sudermann quoted in Rempel, "Mennonites and the Holocaust."

102 Dr. Müller, "Vierteljahres (Seelsorge) – Bericht des ev. Divisions-Pfarrers der 7. Pz. Division für die Zeit vom 1.10 bis 31.12.41," not dated. NARA, T-315/439/303–305.

103 Two years later, the Catholic Military Vicar Georg Werthmann was still lamenting the prohibition on using church buildings in the east for church services for the soldiers. See list of complaints signed Werthmann, Catholic military bishop to Army High Command, July 9, 1943, p. 5, BA-MA Freiburg, RH 15/280, p. 123.

104 See, for example, a Protestant chaplain's account of using a dilapidated church on the road to Stalingrad for services of worship in June 1942: Baedeker, *Das Volk*, 53–54.

105 Silecky, "Fathers in Uniform"; also Budz and Kloes, "Ethnonationalism."
106 Biondich, "Controversies Surrounding the Catholic Church," 31–59.
107 Biliuță, "To Murder or Save."
108 Jarausch, *Reluctant Accomplice.*
109 Jews in Minsk were already ghettoized by the time Jarausch arrived in the city. See Epstein, *Minsk Ghetto.*
110 Jarausch, *Reluctant Accomplice*, 250–51.
111 Ibid., 291.
112 See H. Wilhelmy, "Aus Meinem Leben," 1977 (manuscript), quoted in Scholder, *Über den Umgang*, 21.
113 See Bergen, "Between God and Hitler"; also Mazower, "Military Violence."

Chapter 5

1 Heinrich Pachowiak, "Auf den Hinterhöfen," in Brandt, *Priester in Uniform*, 27–28.
2 Eismann, "Le Militärbefehlshaber in Frankreich"; Neumaier, "Escalation of German Reprisal Policies."
3 Hilberg, "Development of Holocaust Research," 34. Hilberg cites Herbert, "German Military Command in Paris"; also Hilberg, *Sources*, 192–93.
4 See Hanley, *Last Human Face,* 116.
5 See reference to "genocidal attempts, whether cerebral, endemic, systematic, or otherwise," in Moore, *Genocide of the Mind*, xv–xvi. Thanks to Martina Cucchiara for bringing this concept to my attention.
6 The term "universe of moral obligation" is from Fein, *Genocide.*
7 Angrick, *Besatzungspolitik*; Oldenburg, *Ideologie und militärisches Kalkül*; Penter and Titarenko, "Local Memory"; Beorn, *Marching into Darkness.*
8 See Tönsmeyer, "Besatzung," 281–98; Gertjejanssen, *Victims, Heroes, Survivors*; Westermann, *Drunk on Genocide*, 175–96.
9 Streit, *Keine Kameraden.*
10 Manoschek, *"Serbien ist Judenfrei."*
11 Hürter, "Die Wehrmacht vor Leningrad"; see also Kirschenbaum, *Legacy of the Siege*; Peri, *War Within.*
12 Important works include: Röw, *Militärseelsorge*; Pöpping, *Kriegspfarrer an der Ostfront*; Faulkner Rossi, *Wehrmacht Priests*; Harrisville, "We No Longer Pay Heed"; and Harrisville, *Virtuous Wehrmacht.*
13 On Krymchaks and Mountain Jews, see Feferman, *Holocaust in the Crimea.*
14 USC Shoah Foundation VHA. Interview #41658: Nama Bakshi (Maiden name – Sholom). Date of birth: July 31, 1928. Interviewed March 11, 1998 in Simferopol (Crimea), Ukraine. Thanks to Sharon Minos for research and translation from Russian.
15 Rubenstein and Altman, *Unknown Black Book*; Berkhoff, "Was There a Religious Revival," 548 (on Ukrainians crossing themselves at sight of white cross painted on German tanks).
16 Particularly important here are: Tönsmeyer, "Besatzung"; Dallin, *German Rule in Russia*; Rowe-McCulloch, *Holocaust and Mass Violence*; Röger, *Kriegsbeziehungen*; Hushion, *Intimate Encounters*; Mühlhäuser, *Eroberungen*; and for switching perspective: Penter, "Local Collaborators on Trial"; and Exeler, "What Did You Do during the War?"

17 Interview with Giorgi Valerianovich Shantir, Moscow, 1987. YV, Item ID: 3560918. Record Group: O.3. File 4722. Shantir, whose father was ethnic Russian and his mother Jewish, was recognized as having "dual nationality" in the Soviet system. His mother, Ida (née Soloveichik) Isaakovna, died in the Vitebsk ghetto.

18 USC Shoah Foundation VHA, Interview #49666. Lidiia Andrushchenko (birth name Lidia Kogan), born in Zvenigorodka (Kyi, Ukraine), USSR, Oct. 7, 1925. Interviewed June 3, 1998 in Buky (Celo) (Cherkasy Oblast), Ukraine, in Russian. Thanks to Sharon Minos for locating this account and translating from Russian.

19 For a literary representation, including discussion of Wehrmacht soldiers' toilet practices, see Grossman, "The Old Teacher"; for analysis, Mühlhäuser, "Reframing Sexual Violence"; for details as recounted by German POWs, Neitzel and Welzer, *Soldaten*.

20 The term is from Rowe-McCulloch, *Holocaust and Mass Violence*, which differentiates the "violence of occupation" from the "violence of invasion" and "violence of retreat."

21 YV, Item 3560179. Record Group: O.3 – Testimonies Department. File: 6916. Aleksander Ivanovich Iakimenko (Yakimenko), born in a village near Malyn, Zhytomyr Oblast, Ukrainian SSR, USSR, 1930. Audio testimony and transcript. Thanks to Michał Młynarz.

22 For details see Alphons Satzger, typescript diary, Kempowski Archiv #3101, entry for Feb. 1, 1942, p. 39. Akademie der Künste, Berlin.

23 See report by Gmeiner, "Tätigkeitsbericht des Kath. Armeepfarrers bei der 11. Armee, 1.10–31.12.1942," dated Jan. 20, 1942. NARA T-312/419/7995346–52: p. 5/7995350 is a list of chaplains to receive decorations with details on Chaplain Satzger; see also Satzger, "Bericht über Kampfhandlungen," Jan. 9, 1942, p. 1, NARA, T-312/419/7995355.

24 *"Ein kleiner Spaziergang durch Saloniki,"* Andenken vom Einmarsch der Deutschen Truppen in Saloniki – 9 April 1941. Italienische Buchdruckerei A. Akuaroni, Ermu – Strasse 19 – Saloniki [1942]. NL Hans Radtke, EZA Berlin 704/36.

25 Envelope in NL Hans Radtke, EZA Berlin 704/36.

26 Edelmann, "Wesen und Aufgabe der Feldseelsorge," [1941], p. 1, BA-MA Freiburg, RH 15/282, p. 22.

27 Heinrich Lonicer to Colonel Radtke, OKH, [April 1942], BA-MA Freiburg, N282/2; program for Lonicer's service: "Feldgottesdienst," April 19, 1942, Poltawa, included.

28 Evangelischer Armeepfarrer bei der Panzerarmee Afrika, dated Oct. 20, 1942, covering the period July 1–Sept. 30, 1942. Signed Ziskus (sp?), p. 3/. NARA, T-313/436/8729346.

29 Ibid.

30 Thiel, 58th Infantry Division, "Seelsorgebericht, 1.10–31.12.1942," Jan. 30, 1943, pp. 1–2, LKM Ludwigsburg NL Bauerle.

31 Four-page (double-sided) duplicate of "I 20 687/42 für Reg. II," dated Berlin, May 24, 1942, Oberkommando der Wehrmacht, signed Keitel, "Betr.: Richtlinien für die Durchführung der Feldseelsorge," p. 1. BA Potsdam 51.01/21839, p. 147.

32 Ibid., reverse of p. 1/file p. 147.

33 Ibid., p. 3/148.
34 See remarks in appendix to report by Stellv. Ev. Wehrkreispfarrer IX, Karig, "Möglichkeiten und Schwierigkeiten der Truppenseelsorge," for meeting of base chaplains in Kassel, Feb. 17, 1943, p. 4, in BA-MA Freiburg, RH 15/273, p. 15.
35 "Schreiben von Kriegspfarrern an Angehörige Gefallener oder Verstorbener," OKH order of July 14, 1942, printed in *Verordnungsblatt* 8 (Aug. 15, 1942): 45.
36 Oberkommando der Wehrmacht, Dec. 8, 1942, reprinted as "Schreiben von Soldaten, die im Zivilberuf Geistliche sind, an Angehörige Gefallener oder Verstorbener," in *Verordnungsblatt* 3 (April 1, 1943): 13.
37 Stellv. Ev. Wehrkreispfarrer IX, Kassel, March 13, 1943, signed Karig, to OKW through Evang. Feldbischof, re: Standortpfarrerversammlungen. BA-MA Freiburg, RH 15/273, pp. 9–11 in file, p. 1/9.
38 Ibid., p. 2/reverse.
39 Ibid., p. 7/18.
40 Karig, Protestant chaplain for Military District 9, Kassel, "Möglichkeiten und Schwierigkeiten der Truppenseelsorge," copy of speech, attached to Karig to Armed Forces High Command, report on gatherings of base chaplains in Kassel, Eisenach, and Frankfurt/M., March 13, 1943, p. 5, BA-MA Freiburg, RH 15/273, p. 16.
41 Abschrift zu den Vorgängen bei I 12 115/42, letter from Deutsche Evangelische Kirche Kirchenkanzlei, Berlin, Nov. 13, 1942, to Oberkommando der Wehrmacht durch den Reichsmin. f.d. kirchl. Ang. BA Potsdam 51.01/23847; p. unnumbered, at end of file.
42 Erzbischof von Breslau, Nov. 26, 1942, An den Herrn Reichsmin f.d. kirchl. Angel. BA Potsdam 51.01/23159.
43 Franz Dohrmann, *Ansprache des Evangelischen Feldbischofs der Wehrmacht an die evangelischen Wehrmachtangehörigen*, [1943], p. 1. BA-MA Freiburg, RW 15/278, pp. 206–7 in file.
44 Ibid., p. 2.
45 Ibid., p. 3.
46 Ibid., p. 4.
47 "Bericht über die Standortpfarrerversammlungen der evgl. Standort- und Lazarettpfarrer im Wehrkreis XII," 4 pp., no name at end; meeting took place Feb. 23–25, 1943 for 26 Standort- and 54 Lazarettpfarrer from Mannheim, Koblenz, and Trier. Akten über Standortpfarrer, Versammlungen, 1943–1944, BA-MA Freiburg, RH 15/273, file p. 2/p. 1 of report.
48 "If instruction on the oath falls away, we are concerned that a not insignificant proportion of the recruits will swear the oath of allegiance without understanding what the oath really means. Instruction by a military superior, which sometimes occurs, does not always go into the religious meaning of the oath and therefore only half fulfills its goal." Ibid., p. 4/15.
49 The SS received complaints about clergy in the Wehrmacht holding church services in the Warthegau attended only by Poles. Archive of the Main Commission for the Investigation of Crimes against the Polish Nation (now Institute of National Remembrance), Warsaw, Reichsstatthalter im Warthegau/210, p. 24 in file is Ausschnitt aus dem Lagebericht des Höheren SS- und Polizeiführers beim Reichsstatthalter in Posen im Wehrkreis XXI. – Inspekteur der Sicherheitspolizei

und des SD.-Posen, from May 17–23, 1941. These clippings are from the office of the Reichsstatthalter.

50 A chaplain's report from Belgium describes German chaplains burying fallen enemy soldiers, of unspecified nationality. 1. Infanterie-Division, Abt. IVd/e (Ev. Kriegspfarrer), Feldpostnummer 04089, dated O.U. Sept. 23, 1940; covering the period Nov. 5, 1939–Sept. 11, 1940, p. 5. NARA, T-315/2/77. The following year, another chaplain, a Catholic, reported from Greece that he buried wounded Greek and English soldiers and seemed to think it obvious that German chaplains and physicians would treat the enemy wounded: "Regelung der Seelsorge der engl. Verwundeten bei der San.Komp.3/572 mit St.A.Dr. Schiersner in Ekali, wo sich ein sterbender engl. Offz. befand." Kath. Kriegspfarrrer beim Wehrmachtbefehlshaber Südost, Report for April 1–June 30, 1941, dated July 14, 1941, p. 6. NARA, T-312/464/8052334.

51 See photographs by Heinz Mittelstädt from the opening of the cathedral in Zhytomyr in summer 1941, with the same sentence at the beginning of five captions supplied by the Wehrmacht photo service: "On the Soviet front: (Ukraine). German soldiers restore to the oppressed Ukrainian people the gift of their faith in God." BArch Bild 183-B09383, B09404, B09408, B09438, B09573, and L26913.

52 Erzbischofliches Ordinariat, der Generalvikar, Freiburg i.Br., Dec. 1, 1941, To Excellenz Wienken [Fulda Bishops conference], Re: Verbot der Seelsorge an gefangenen Polen. BA Berlin Lichterfelde, R 5101/22297/frame 334. The order, signed by Dr. Freisler, allowed for one pernicious exception: "Nur die von einem zum Tode verurteilten Polen vor der Hinrichtung erbetene Seelsorge ist gestattet. Sie übt ein deutscher Geistlicher aus."

53 Letters requesting permission to provide pastoral care to imprisoned Dutch Catholics, priests incarcerated in Strafanstalt Stuhm (the Bishop of Ermland lists them by name), March 1942, in BA Berlin Lichterfelde, R 5101/22297/340 ff.

54 A request to provide pastoral care to a group of French Catholic women prisoners is in BA Berlin Lichterfelde, R 5101/22297/344 ff.

55 Bishop of Berlin Konrad von Preysing, June 19, 1944, to Reich Church Ministry, Betr: Seelsorge in dem Konzentrationslager Ravensbrueck, BA Berlin Lichterfelde R 5101/22297/346.

56 Copy, Stellv. Generalkommando V.A.K., Wehrkreiskommando V, Stuttgart, May 19, 1942, An das OKH, Berlin, labeled Akten über Standortpfarrer i.N. BA-MA Freiburg, RH 15/272; p. 3 in file is Abschrift dated May 19, 1942, from stellv. Generalkommando V.A.K. to Gauleiter der NSDAP, Gau Baden, Reichsstatthalter Robert Wagner, Karlsruhe.

57 Ibid., p. 2 in file.

58 Ibid., p. 3 in file is Abschrift dated May 19, 1942, from stellv. Generalkommando V.A.K. to Gauleiter der NSDAP, Gau Baden, Reichsstatthalter Robert Wagner, Karlsruhe.

59 Ibid., p. 4 in file is Abschrift von Abschrift of response from Wagner, Der Gauleiter, Karlsruhe, May 16, 1942, to stellv. Kommandierenden General im V.A.K. Befehlshaber im Wehrkreis V und im Elsaß, Herrn General der Infanterie Oßwald.

60 Graf, Catholic chaplain, 8. Jäger-Div, "Tätigkeitsbericht" for Aug. 7–31, 1942, dated Sept. 3, 1942. NARA, T-315/465/286–87.

61 For example: Report of Catholic chaplain (Peterck?), Kriegspfarrer a.K., "Anlage zum Kriegstagebuch Stab 18.I.D. (mot) Abt. Ib," p. 1: dated Jan. 5, 1943. BA-MA Freiburg, RH 26-18/108. He held 105 religious services with 6,662 participants, 1,523 of whom took mass. Of the total number of services, 20 were devotions in the barracks (*Bunkerandachten*) and 7 Christmas services in the area of Staraja Russa.

62 "Tätigkeitsbericht über den Einsatz im Westen vom 10. Mai bis 9. Juli 1940," Stettin, Aug. 1, 1940, NARA, T-315/87/637–38. Faulkner Rossi discusses the sacrament of penance as it appeared in Catholic chaplains' reports and letters but does not touch on general absolution. Faulkner Rossi, *Wehrmacht Priests*, 123–28.

63 NARA, T-315/101/beginning at frame 671; 2nd Mountain Division; frames 743–50 chaplains' reports, NARA, T-315/101/744–46, Kath. Div. Pfarrer, 2. Geb. Div., dated im Felde, Oct. 1, 1941, Tomaschek, to Kath. Feldbischof der Wehrmacht. Norway.

64 Graf, Catholic chaplain, 8. Jäger-Div, "Tätigkeitsbericht" for Dec. 1, 1942–Jan. 1, 1943, dated Jan. 9, 1943, p. 2. NARA, T-315/465/693.

65 Excoriations of soldiers for immoral behavior and accounts of his efforts to warn and improve them appear in many reports from Catholic Chaplain Graf, 8th Light Infantry Division, for example: "Tätigkeitsbericht" dated Jan. 6, 1942, in France. NARA, T-315/465/1028.

66 Herzog makes a related point in *Sex after Fascism*; see also Herzog, "Pleasure and Evil," 154–56.

67 Catholic Chaplain Graf, 8th Light Infantry Division, France, "Tätigkeitsbericht" for Feb. 1–15, 1942. NARA, T-315/465/1031.

68 In the Lutheran and Roman Catholic system of counting, "Thou shalt not commit adultery" is the 6th commandment; for most Protestants, Eastern Orthodox Christians, and Jews it is the 7th. Coogan, *Ten Commandments*, 27–28.

69 Protestant Chaplain Busse, 122nd Infantry Division, "Seelsorgebericht," for Jan. 1–March 31, 1943, dated March 31, 1943, p. 1. LKM Ludwigsburg NL Bauerle. On long-distance marriage ceremonies, see Heineman, *What Difference*, 46–48.

70 Würthwein, Prot. Kriegspfarrer a.K., 218 I.D., 5-pp *Seelsorgebericht*, for Oct. 1–Dec. 31, 1942, dated Jan. 3, 1943, p. 2. LKM Ludwigsburg NL Bauerle.

71 Bauerle, "Gruß zum 12. Sonntag nach Trinitatis," Aug. 23, 1942, p. 1, in LKM Ludwigsburg NL Bauerle, materials labeled "Sonntagsgruß."

72 A shocking illustration is Westermann, *Drunk on Genocide*, 190.

73 On unsympathetic nurses who obstructed the work of the chaplains, see report by Pastor Engelbrecht, Fulda, "Die Seelsorge im Res.-Lazarett," summarized in Karig, deputy Protestant military chaplain, District 9, to Supreme Command and Protestant military bishop, Kassel, March 13, 1943, p. 1, BA-MA Freiburg, RH 15/273, p. 9.

74 Wehrmachtoberpfarrer Hunzinger, report for July 1, 1941–Jan. 31, 1942, dated March 6, 1942, p. 23. BA-MA Freiburg, RH 26-15/62. This whole folder contains reports from "ev. Divisionspfarrer der 15. Div, Weißrußland."

75 D. Dr. Doerne, "Lazarettseelsorge," report from conference of base and military hospital chaplains in Military District 4, Dresden, July 7, 1943, in *Mitteilungblatt des Ev. Feldbischofs* 3 (Oct. 15, 1943): 5, BA-MA Freiburg, RW 12 I/13, p. 5.

76 See list of complaints signed Werthmann, Catholic military bishop to Army High Command, July 9, 1943, p. 5, BA-MA Freiburg, RH 15/280, p. 123. For more on Werthmann, see Faulkner, "Against Bolshevism."

77 Wehrmachtpfr Krüger, Ev. Div.Pfr b.d. 18 I.D. (mot.), "Seelsorgebericht für 1.7.–30.9.1942," dated Oct. 20, 1942, p. 5. LKM Ludwigsburg NL Bauerle.

78 Aufsatz Nr. 19 "Die Soldatenpredigt im Kriege," Leitgedanken aus einem Vortrag bei einem Frontlehrgang im Osten von Wehrmachtdekan Schackla. Abschrift aus dem *Mittelungsblatt des Ev. Feldbischofs* 4 (Oct. 10, 1942): 1–8 in file. BA-MA Freiburg, RW 12 I/12, p. 1.

79 "Die Soldatenpredigt im Kriege," Schackla, p. 2/reverse.

80 Ibid., p. 3/2 in file.

81 Ibid., p. 4/reverse.

82 Aufsatz Nr. 19 "Die Soldatenpredigt im Kriege," Leitgedanken aus einem Vortrag bei einem Frontlehrgang im Osten von Wehrmachtdekan Schackla. Abschrift aus dem *Mittelungsblatt des Ev. Feldbischofs* 4 (Oct. 10, 1942): 1–8 in file. BA-MA Freiburg, RW 12 I/12, p. 5/3.

83 Lipp, divisional Catholic priest, 1st Mountain Division, "Tätigkeitsbericht 16.12.1941–31.5.1942," June 22, 1942, p. 5, NARA, T-315/48/1315.

84 Herzog, "Pleasure and Evil," 154.

85 E.g., having the Abitur was often a bond between members of the Wehrmacht and was recognized as such. Giles, "Ich hab' Dich gern," 2.

86 Buchbender and Sterz, *Das andere Gesicht des Krieges*, 46.

87 Catholic Chaplain Graf, 8. Jäger-Division, "Tätigkeitsbericht" for Nov. 1–Dec. 1, 1942, dated Dec. 1, 1942, p. 2. NARA, T-315/465/695.

88 By one estimate, more than 20,000 German soldiers were executed by order of German military courts during World War II. See Thomas, "'Nur das ist für die Truppe Recht," 48.

89 Kriegspfarrer Busse, 122nd Light Infantry Division, "Seelsorgebericht, 1.10–31.12.1942," Dec. 31, 1942, p. 2, LKM Ludwigsburg NL Bauerle.

90 Some 258 Jehovah's Witnesses were executed on order of the Reich Military Court. I have not found evidence as to whether military chaplains ministered to any of them. Kehoe, "Reich Military Court."

91 Schmiedel, *"Du sollst nicht morden."*

92 E.g., "Mystici Corporis Christi," Encyclical of Pope Pius XII on the Mystical Body of Christ, 1943. Item 2 states: "the greatest joy and exaltation are born only of suffering," www.vatican.va/content/pius-xii/en/encyclicals/documents/hf_p-xii_enc_29061943_mystici-corporis-christi.html

93 "Gruss zum Sonntag Misericordias Domini (April 19, 1942)," signed Eure Amtsbrüder in der Heimat, to Liebe Amtsbrüder! In LKM Ludwigsburg NL Bauerle

94 Rarkowski, "Hirtenwort an alle Wehrmachtgeistlichen," *Verordnungsblatt* 5 (June 20, 1943): 20.

95 Chaplain Hunzinger, "Verhandlungsbericht über die Arbeitstagung der ev. Standort- und Lazarettpfarrer des Wehrkreises X in Hamburg am Montag, dem 8. März 1943." BA-MA Freiburg, RH 15/273, p. 2/file p. 42. For context, see Hagemann and Schüler-Springorum, *Home/Front.*

96 "Meßweinversorgung," *Verordnungsblatt* 7, no. 4 (May 20, 1943): 16.

97 "Meßweinversorgung," *Verordnungsblatt* 7, no. 7 (Oct. 1, 1943): 31.

98 Westermann, *Drunk on Genocide*, 4–7.

99 Ev. Armeepfarrer beim Oberkommando der Panzerarmee Afrika, O.U., "Tätigkeitsbericht für 1.1.–31.3.1942," April 1, 1942. NARA, T-313/436/8729339.

100 Wehrmachtpfarrer Krüger, "Tätigkeitsbericht für 1.5.–31.12.1942, Anlage zum Kriegstagebuch Stab 18.I.D.(mot) Abt. Ib," p.1: dated Jan. 11, 1943. BA-MA Freiburg, RH 26-18/108.

101 Wehrmachtoberpfarrer Bauerle to the ev. Kriegspfarrer of the 16th Army, "Rundschreiben Armeepfarrer '16'" [unlabeled page of one of his circulars], LKM Ludwigsburg NL Bauerle.

102 Roussig, Evang. Divi. Pfarrer, 12. Inf. Div., April 26, 1943, "Tätigkeitsbericht für 16.12.1941–28.2.1943," BA-MA Freiburg, RH 26-12/144.

103 Letter, signed [illeg.], Neustadt/Orla, Aug. 1, 1941, An Herrn Marinepfarrer Ronneburger! [sic] NL Friedrich Ronneberger, EZA Berlin 621/29.

104 Quoted in Würthwein, Protestant military chaplain, 218th Infantry Division, "Seelsorgebericht, 1.10–31.12.1942," Jan. 3, 1943, p. 4, LKM Ludwigsburg NL Bauerle.

105 Oberkommando des Heeres to Reichsminister für die kirchlichen Angelegenheiten, Berlin, May 4, 1943, BA Potsdam 51.01/21839, p. 211.

106 Reichsminister für die kirchlichen Angelegenheiten to Oberkommando des Heeres, May 13, 1943, BA Potsdam 51.01/21839, p. 212.

107 BA-MA Freiburg RH 15/272, p. 100: file entry dated Oct. 25, 1943, OKW, initialed among others by Senftleben.

108 Spicer and Cucchiara, trans., Becker-Kohen, *Evil that Surrounds Us*; also see Schrafstetter, *Flucht und Versteck*.

109 Spicer and Cucchiara, trans., Becker-Kohen, *Evil that Surrounds Us*, 70–75.

110 Ibid., 109–11. The only military chaplain that features in Becker-Kohen's account is an American chaplain she encounters at the time of liberation.

111 USC Shoah Foundation VHA, Xenia Stephens, segments 23–25. Thanks to Jessica Bush for finding this account.

112 For context see Hellbeck, *Stalingrad*.

113 *Verordnungsblatt* 6, no. 11 (Nov. 15, 1942): 59.

114 *Verordnungsblatt* 7, no. 4 (May 20, 1943): 15.

115 *Verordnungsblatt* 7, no. 8 (Dec. 1, 1943): 33.

116 *Verordnungsblatt* 7, no. 7 (Oct. 1, 1943): 29.

117 *Verordnungsblatt* 7, no. 3 (April 1, 1943): 11.

118 See Shepherd, "Continuum of Brutality"; and Westermann, *Hitler's Police Battalions*, 177, 221.

119 *Verordnungsblatt* 7, no. 2 (March 1, 1943): 7.

120 Ibid.

121 *Verordnungsblatt* 7, no. 1 (Jan. 15, 1943): 1–2.

122 Catholic chaplain (Hermann Raible) with the 15th Infantry Division, "Tätigkeitsbericht," Feb. 1–May 31, 1942. BA-MA Freiburg, RH 26-15/63, pp. 1–2.

123 Ibid. The name of the man to be executed appears in the original.

124 Most chaplains' activity reports from this period are terse. Typical is the following excerpt: "Zusammenfassung: Im Laufe der Berichtszeit hielt ich 32 Gottesdienste mit 358 Kommunionen. Die Zahl der Beerdigungen in dieser Zeit beträgt 10," Lake, Catholic divisional chaplain, 12th Infantry Division, "Tätigkeitsbericht für die Zeit vom 1.3.–30.6.43," Sept. 22, 1943. BA-MA Freiburg, RH 26-12/156.

125 Raible, "Tätigkeitsbericht," Feb. 1–May 31, 1942, BA-MA Freiburg, RH 26-15/63, pp. 4–5.

126 On the Wehrmacht and atrocities around Minsk and Mogilev, see Beorn, *Marching into Darkness*.

127 Raible, "Tätigkeitsbericht," Feb. 1–May 31, 1942, BA-MA Freiburg, RH 26-15/63, p. 5.
128 Tewes, "Seelsorger bei den Soldaten," 253.

Chapter 6

1 See Weinberg, *A World at Arms*; also Weinberg, "Germany's War for World Conquest."
2 See Majstorović, "Red Army Troops Encounter the Holocaust."
3 For context, see Prusin, "'Fascist Criminals to the Gallows!'"
4 See Bade, Skowronski, and Viebig, *NS-Militärjustiz*.
5 On the last year of the war, see Fritz, *Endkampf*; Grier, *Hitler, Dönitz*; and Bessel, *Germany 1945*.
6 See, for instance, Enstad, "Prayers and Patriotism"; Berkhoff, "Was There a Religious Revival"; and for a personal account, Sofiia Zabramnaia, Interview 33735, USC Shoah Foundation VHA, 1997. Thanks to Anna Heffernan for research and translation from Russian.
7 "How I Was Saved from Hitler: The Recollections of the Teacher Emilia Borisovna Kotlova, from Letters to Ilya Ehrenburg 1945, Kiev, Jan. 13, 1945," in Rubenstein and Altman, *Unknown Black Book*, 81–87.
8 Hoenicke Moore, *Know Your Enemy*, 345.
9 Quinnett, "The German Army Confronts the NSFO."
10 Laasch, stellv. Ev. Wehrkreispfarrer XI, an alle Standort- und Res. Laz. Pfarrer im Wehrkreis XI, Hanover, Jan. 22, 1944. BA-MA Freiburg, RH 15-11/71.
11 See Messerschmidt and Wüllner, *Die Wehrmachtjustiz*; Kittermann, "Those Who Said, 'No!'"; Messerschmidt, "Kriegsdienstverweigerer."
12 Laasch, Jan. 22, 1944.
13 Ibid.
14 See Messerschmidt and Wüllner, *Die Wehrmachtjustiz*, 199–218; Kirschner, "Wehrkraftzersetzung," 405–25; and Welch, "Securing the German Domestic Front."
15 Gerlach, *Extremely Violent Societies*.
16 See Fritz, "Inside the Ghetto"; and Frojimovics and Kovács, "Jews in a 'Judenrein' City."
17 Blatman, *Death Marches*.
18 USC Shoah Foundation VHA, Michael Jackson, Interview #26142 (tapes 1–19); conducted Feb. 21, 1997, in Allentown, PA, by Jeannie Miller. Relevant portions on tapes 1, 14, 16, and 18. Thanks to Camila Collins Araiza for research assistance.
19 This interpretation, that Christians saw the Holocaust as proof of Christian triumph over Judaism, was articulated by Rubenstein, *After Auschwitz*.
20 USC Shoah Foundation VHA, Tomas Stern, Interview # 11109 (tapes 1–6); conducted Jan. 21, 1996, in Caracas, Venezuela, by Debora Avram. Quote from Tape 1, 28:30. Thanks to Susana Benhaki for research and translation from Spanish.
21 Hockenos, "German Protestant Church and Its *Judenmission*."
22 USC Shoah Foundation VHA, Iuliia Penziur (born Fleishman), Interview #33811; conducted July 6, 1997, in Bershad (Vinnytsia Oblast), Ukraine. Thanks to Sharon Minos for research and translation from Russian.

23 USC Shoah Foundation VHA, Ernest Light, Interview #19576, interviewed by Isabel Alcoff, Pittsburgh, 1996. Thanks to Marilyn Campeau for research.
24 Ibid.
25 Report from Heeresgruppenpfarrer E, April 28, 1944, to Ev. Feldbischof, re: meeting in Athens, April 19–20, 1944. BA-MA Freiburg, RH 15/273, p. 215.
26 See Benbassa and Rodrigue, *Sephardi Jewry*; Fleming, *Greece*; Mazower, *Inside Hitler's Greece*; Bowman, *Agony of Greek Jews*; Dalven, *Jews of Ioannina*.
27 Tagesordnung des Frontlehrganges der kath. Kriegspfarrer im Bereich der 1. Armee, includes talk on June 2, 1944 by Wehrmachtpfarrer Kurschatke, "Der Divisionspfarrer im Kampfeinsatz – Erfahrungen an der Ostfront." BA-MA Freiburg, RH 15/273, p. 220.
28 Ev. Heeresgruppenpfarrer Mitte, OU., May 22, 1944, signed Dr. Schuster, to Ev. Feldbischof, re: Frontlehrgang für ev. Kriegspfarrer, im Gebiet des Wehrmachtbefehlshabers Weissruthenien und im Bereich der 9. Armee ... May 31–June 2, 1944 ... in Schirowize bei Slonim, BA-MA Freiburg, RH 15/273, p. 224. On the NSFO see Echternkamp, "Der politische Offizier," in Shahar, *Deutsche Offiziere*.
29 See, on an earlier period, Shepherd, "Continuum of Brutality."
30 See Angrick and Klein, *Endlösung in Riga*; also Schneider, *Reise in den Tod*.
31 "Tagesordnung für den Frontlehrgang der evangelischen Kriegspfarrer der 18. Armee und der Armeegruppe Narwa," June 1–5, 1944 in Riga; includes "experience reports" on "Seelsorge bei Absetzbewegungen," by Wehrmachtoberpfarrer Koehn and Wehrmachtpfarrer Beckherrn; and Wehrmachtoberpfarrer Bauerle on "Einheitliche Ausrichtung der Feldseelsorge." BA-MA Freiburg, RH 15/273, p. 227.
32 Perau, *Priester*, 159–61.
33 Leonhard, *Wieviel Leid*, 89.
34 Werthmann, "Bericht über die Dienstreise nach Krakau in der Zeit vom 15.-17.3.1944," p. 6/file p. 173. BA-MA Freiburg, RH 15/280.
35 Ibid., p. 10/file p. 177.
36 Schuster, Ev. Heeresgruppenpfarrer Mitte, to Evang. Feldbischof, "Bericht über den Frontlehrgang der ev. Kriegspfarrer in Gebiet des Wehrmachtbefehlshabers Weissruthenien und der 9. Armee, May 31–June 2, 1944 in Schirowize bei Slonim," June 6, 1944. BA-MA Freiburg, RH 15/273, p. 233.
37 Werthmann, "Bericht über die Dienstreise vom 13.–20. Juni 1944 zur Teilnahme an den Frontlehrgängen der Katholischen Kriegspfarrer der 2. und 4. Armee," pp. 11–12. BA-MA Freiburg, RH 15/280, pp. 206–20. On German military atrocities in Belarus, see Beorn, *Marching into Darkness*; Gerlach, *Kalkulierte Morde*; and Walke, *Pioneers and Partisans*.
38 Werthmann, "Dienstreise vom 13.–20. Juni 1944."
39 Kurt Bunkert, to Landeskirchenrat der Pfalz, Speyer, July 13, 1944, ZASP 150.15/1 (A–F), collection #4872: Ludwig Diehl.
40 Perau, *Priester*, 176. Allusions from Psalm 16:6, "Das Los ist mir gefallen aufs Liebliche"; Ps 22:1, "Mein Gott, mein Gott, warum hast Du mich verlassen?" Ps 116:13, "Ich will den Kelch des Heils nehmen und des Herrn Namen predigen"; Ps 23:5, "Du ... schenkest mir voll ein." All appear in the New Testament too, quoted by Jesus.

41 Pfarrer Alexander Jehnke, Riedheim, two-page report for Kirchengemeinde Sobieski (dt. Mühlenrode), Kreis Kalisch (u. Schieratz), no date, but specified he was responding to a letter of Feb. 7, 1952. BA Koblenz Ost-Dok. 1/118, p. 43 in file. The Ost-Dok collection has since been relocated to BA Bayreuth.

42 "The military district is seriously overfilled with military hospitals etc. The existing Protestant pastoral forces are inadequate and help is urgently needed." Der Wehrmachtbevollmächtigte beim Reichsprotektor und Befehlhaber im Wehrkreis Böhmen und Mähren, Prague, June 3, 1944, to OKW via Evang. Feldbischof, BA MA Freiburg, RW 12 I/10, p. 69.

43 Wehrmachtoberpfarrer Hofer to Catholic Military Bishop, Seelsorgebezirk XVIII/3, Innsbruck, Oct. 19, 1944. BA-MA Freiburg, RH 15/272, p. 253 and back of 252: (out of order).

44 Perau, *Priester*, 241.

45 On the better known SS counterpart, see Ingrao, *SS Dirlewanger Brigade*.

46 Perau, *Priester*, 241. "Work, for the Night Is Coming" is a popular Christian hymn; those words come from John 9:4.

47 In March 1944, Wehrmachtoberpfarrer Schall received "serious war injuries" and had to be sent back to his civilian base: he took over pastoral care in District V/10. Chaplain Satzger was wounded in September 1942, moved to a military hospital in Augsburg, then to Bad Tölz in February 1944. BA-MA Freiburg, RW 12 I/4, Entwurf, p. 104 in file, dated March 17, 1944, [from Evang. Wehrkreispfarrer V] to Stadtpfarrer Geißler – Tübingen, et al.

48 Reports from Dohrmann's office: "Aufstellung der Soll- und Iststärke an Evangelischen Kriegspfarrern nach dem Stande vom 25.11.1944." BA MA Freiburg, N282/8.

49 Ibid.

50 On British Army chaplains and D-Day, see Reynolds, *To War without Arms*.

51 Ev. Armeepfarrer bei der 10. Armee, to Evang. Feldbischof, Feb. 28, 1944, re: Dienstbesprechung der evangelischen Kriegspfarrer bei der 10. Armee, BA-MA Freiburg, RH 15/273, pp. 211–13.

52 For context see Janz, "From Battlegrounds to Burial Grounds," 147–62.

53 Evang. Divisionspfarrer Rosenthal, 14. Infanterie-Division, Tätigkeitsbericht, Jan. 4, 1944, p. 1. BA-MA Freiburg, RH 26-14/84.

54 For analysis, see Walke, "Split Memory."

55 Interview with Giorgi Valerianovich Shantir, YV 3560918/4722.

56 *Verordnungsblatt* 4 (May 3, 1944): 13

57 *Verordnungsblatt* 5 (July 1, 1944): 21, two death announcements. Gehrmann, chaplain with an armored division, was born in 1909 in Deutsch-Eylau. He had a Kriegsverdienstkreuz II. Klasse "mit Schwertern und Ostmedaille" and had been a military chaplain since November 1939, serving four years with a Panzerdivision.

58 Werthmann, "Dienstreise vom 13.–20. Juni 1944," p. 2/207.

59 Wehrmachtdekan and Heeresgruppenpfarrer Kauder was born in 1890 in Schubin; decorated in World War I; and served as Wehrkreispfarrer 1935 to 1939 in Kassel. He became Armeepfarrer in 1939 and was promoted to Heeresgruppenpfarrer in 1942. *Verordnungsblatt* 8, no. 5 (July 1, 1944): 21.

60 For context, see Rudling, "The Invisible Genocide," 57–81; Marples, "History, Memory"; Laputska, "World War II Crimes."

61 July 20, 1944, OKW an den Reichsmin. f.d. kirchl. Angelegenheiten, signed Wulff.
    BA Potsdam 51.01/21948, p. 13.

62 From January 1941, Zimmermann held the position of Wehrmachtoberpfarrer; he
    became Divisionspfarrer des Feldheeres in 1939. *Verordnungsblatt* 7 (Oct. 15,
    1944): 1.

63 Rochus Schneider, Navy Chaplain and Catholic Chaplain to Admiral Skagerrak: born
    June 24, 1912 in Bremen and called up Dec. 13, 1939 as navy chaplain. On Jan. 14,
    1942 he was named active navy chaplain. *Verordnungsblatt* 4 (Jan. 1, 1945).

64 Ibid.

65 To see the approval procedure at work, e.g., Ministry of Church Affairs to Armed
    Forces High Command, May 22, 1944, BA-MA Freiburg, RH 15/272, pp. 216–17;
    Church Affairs to OKW, BA-MA Freiburg, RH 15/272, p. 116; same file, OKW
    (Gruppe S) memo to military bishops, March 21, 1944, p. 113; report of Gestapo
    Hanover on Pastor Friedrich Voges, in Deputy Chief Command, District 11, to
    OKH, Nov. 17, 1944, BA-MA Freiburg, RH 15/270, p. 25.

66 Wohl was born in 1906 in Austria. SD report, Jan. 7, 1944, in Acta betr. kath.
    Glaubensgenossen beim Militär ... in der Provinz Schlesien, vom Nov. 1911. BA
    Potsdam, 51.01/22306, p. 221. The term "Volksgemeinschaft" is notoriously diffi-
    cult to translate: "racial community," "ethnic community," and "people's commu-
    nity" all capture some elements.

67 Ministry for Church Affairs, signed Haugg, to OKH, April 21, 1944, re: kath.
    Standortpfarrer i.N. für den Standort Moers, BA-MA Freiburg, RH 15/272, p. 136.

68 Ibid., notation at bottom of page, OKH to kath. Feldbischof, May 8, 1944.

69 For the case of the Catholic Priest Schosser, see Chef der Sicherheitspolizei und des
    SD, an den Reichsmin. f.d. kirchl. Angelegenheiten, Aug. 30, 1944, BA Potsdam
    51.01/21842, p. 40.

70 Re: complaint about Emil Engelhardt, BA-MA Freiburg, RW 12 I/4.

71 SD report on prospective Catholic chaplain, dated May 3, 1944. Dyllus was born in
    1895 in Gleiwitz. BA Potsdam 51.01/22306, p. 236.

72 BA Potsdam 51.01/22306, [p. 236], May 17, 1944 – "Keine Bedenken" from
    Church Ministry.

73 BA Potsdam 51.01/21842, p. 43, Der Chef der Sicherheitspolizei und des SD,
    Sept. 22, 1944 report to Reichsmin. f.d. kirchl. Angelegenheiten on Blahut.

74 BA Potsdam 51.01/21842, p. 44, Der Chef der Sicherheitspolizei und des SD,
    Sept. 22, 1944 report to Reichsmin. f.d. kirchl. Angelegenheiten on Sperlik.

75 Werthmann, Berlin, May 5, 1944, "Bericht über die Dienstreise nach Prag und
    Holoubkau vom 19.–23.4.1944," p. 2/181. BA-MA Freiburg, RH 15/280.

76 Ibid., p. 3/182. The term used, which I translated as "battle between peoples," was
    Volkstumskampf.

77 Ibid.

78 On Schinzinger: Werthmann, kath. Feldgeneralvikar, Berlin, Dec. 22, 1944,
    "Dienstreisebericht," to Prague Dec. 1944, (p. 5/237). BA-MA Freiburg, RH 15/
    280, pp. 232–37.

79 See Bergen, "Death Throes."

80 BA Potsdam 51.01/22306, [Volksdeutsche], p. 242, SD report, Dec. 19, 1944, to
    Reichsmin. f.d. kirchl. Angel. signed Hahnenbruch (sp?). Chmiel was born in
    1911 in Lubitzka.

81 Church Ministry to OKH, Jan. 9, 1945. BA Potsdam 51.01/22306, p. 243.

82 Born in 1910, Peter Weiland had been in Engerau since 1939, with previous posts in Pressburg, Karlsbad, and St. Joachimsthal. Reich Ministry for Church Affairs, "Personalien," signed Haugg, Berlin, Jan. 29, 1945, p. 7. BA-MA Freiburg, RH 15/270, p. 2.

83 Reich Ministry for Church Affairs, signed Muhs, to Oberkommando der Wehrmacht, Berlin, May 22, 1944,' 3 pp. BA MA Freiburg, RH 15/272, p. 216, reverse, and 217 in file.

84 Ibid.

85 Ibid.

86 Ibid.

87 Ibid. For Dohrmann's original letter, see the Evangelische Feldbischof der Wehrmacht to Reich Minister for Church Affairs, Attn Landgerichtsrat Dr. Haugg, Potsdam, April 14, 1944. BA Potsdam 51.01/23847, p. 171.

88 Ministry for Church Affairs to OKW, Berlin, May 22, 1944. BA MA Freiburg, RH 15/272, p. 216, reverse, and 217 in file.

89 Werthmann, e.g., proposed turning contested cases over to the relevant military intelligence post for a binding decision. Re: Beauftragung von Standortpfarrern i.N. Kath. Feldbischof, signed Feldgeneralvikar Werthmann, to OKW AHA/Ag/S (III), July 7, 1944, BA-MA Freiburg RH 15/272, p. 210.

90 Ministry for Church Affairs to OKW, "Betrifft: Beauftragung von Standortpfarrern im Nebenamt," May 22, 1944, BA Potsdam 51.01/23847, pp. 173–75: discussion of the four Catholics begins on back of p. 174. Related correspondence on Neumann in BA Potsdam 51.01/21840, p. 8 (Abschrift zu den Akten); a copy of the same notice regarding Neumann, with a red border, labeled Schnellbrief, dated Oct. 19, 1943, appears in BA Potsdam 51.01/21842, p. 7; also Abschrift Geheime Staatspolizei, Staatspolizeileitstelle Reichenberg, to Wehrkreiskommando VIII, "Betr.: Ernennung des Kaplans Franz Neumann geb. am 8.7.1913 in Gross-Borowitz, ... zum Heeresstandortpfarrer," Reichenberg, Aug. 7, 1943. BA Potsdam 51.01/21842, p. 11.

91 BA Potsdam 51.01/23847, pp. 173–75: letter from Reichsmin. f. d. kirchl. Angel., to OKW, May 22, 1944, "Betrifft: Beauftragung von Standortpfarrern im Nebenamt."

92 BA Potsdam 51.01/21840, p. 11 in the file, June 12, 1944, kath. Feldbischof der Wehrmacht, signed Werthmann I.V., to Reichsmin. f. d. kirchl. Angel.

93 BA Potsdam 51.01/21840, p. 12, Reichsmin. f.d. kirchl. Angel, June 26, 1944, An das Oberkommando der Wehrmacht, "Betrifft: Beauftragung von Standortpfarrern im Nebenamt." Many of these communications contain excerpts and entire copies of earlier correspondence.

94 See the exhibit, "Haft unterm Hakenkreuz. Bautzen I und Bautzen II 1933–1945," Gedenkstätte Bautzen, Stiftung Sächsische Gedenkstätte, www.stsg.de/cms/baut zen/ausstellungen/nationalsozialismus_1933-1945.

95 BA Potsdam 51.01/21842 – on Hornig: p. 26, from OKH to Reichsmin. f.d.kirchl. Angel, Feb. 11, 1944; p. 28 in 51.01/21842 – as of May 13, 1944 the Church Ministry still objected.

96 OKW, Aug. 2, 1944, to Chef H Rüst u BdE/Gr S. BA-MA Freiburg, RH 15/272, p. 221.

97 For list of all eight contested names, see Abschrift, OKH, Chef H. Rüst u BdE, Berlin, Aug. 12, 1944, an Evgl. Feldbischof der Wehrmacht; Kath. Feldbischof der Wehrmacht, signed Geißler. BA Potsdam 51.01/23847, p. 148 in file.

98 Memo Reichsmin. f. d. kirchl. Angel. Aug. 31, 1944, Vermerk: with Haugg's name on it. BA Potsdam 51.01/23847, p. 146.

99 A list of names of prospective Catholic chaplains included university professor Dr. Josef Jatzke, born 1901 in Groß-Hermsdorf, proposed as part-time base chaplain for Olmütz. Army High Command to Church Ministry, Aug. 11, 1944, BA Potsdam 51.01/21842, p. 42.

100 BA Potsdam 51.01/23820. No internal label on file.

101 On the question of whether base chaplains and chaplains in military hospitals could be decorated, see Army High Command to Military Bishops, March 21, 1944, BA-MA Freiburg, RH 15/272, p. 104. For a case where several War Merit Crosses were withdrawn from base and military hospital chaplains, see Army High Command, Jan. 30, 1945, in BA-MA Freiburg, RH 15/270, p. 13; the same file contains a great deal of related correspondence.

102 Stellv. Ev. Wehrkreispfarrer XIII, Nürnberg O., Feb. 7, 1944, to Evang. Feldbischof, signed Wehrmachtoberpfarrer Schach. BA-MA Freiburg, RH 15/272, p. 80.

103 OKH, March 21, 1944, to Feldbischöfe. BA-MA Freiburg, RH 15/272, p. 104.

104 Bunke, Stellvertretender Ev. Wehrkreispfarrer III, "Vorschlagsliste 1 für die Verleihung des K.V.K. II. Kl. o. Schw.," Berlin-Spandau, April 18, 1944. BA-MA Freiburg, RH 15/272, p. 123.

105 On Bunke and Dannenbaum, see Sandvoß, *"Es wird gebeten."*

106 "Only recently we had the behavior of military pastor Bunke, which had to be addressed in an ongoing instruction of all military district chaplains." Reich Ministry for Church Affairs I 1022/44 to OKW, Berlin, May 22, 1944, (copy), 3 pp. BA MA Freiburg, RH 15/272, pp. 216–17.

107 Army High Command to AHA/Tr. Abteilung, Jan. 30, 1945, in BA-MA Freiburg, RH 15/270, p. 13.

108 OKH, Berlin, March 21, 1945, Entwurf, in response to "Vorgang" described. BA-MA Freiburg, RH 15/270, p. 29 in file.

109 Ibid.

110 See Faulkner Rossi, "Against Bolshevism." Faulkner Rossi accepts Werthmann's version of events, including Rarkowski's dementia, but Pöpping is skeptical. I tend toward Pöpping here.

111 Gatz, *Bischöfe*, 594.

112 See, e.g., Faulkner Rossi, "Against Bolshevism."

113 See Faulkner Rossi, *Wehrmacht Priests*, 86–89 and 318 (note 78).

114 Gatz, *Bischöfe*, 808: Georg Werthmann (1898–1980) served the Bundeswehr from 1955 to 1962 under Bishops Joseph Wendel and Franz Hengsbach.

115 For analysis of some forms of opportunism, see Goda, "Black Marks."

116 Grier, "Hitler's Favorite General," 8.

117 Ibid.; also Grier, *Hitler, Dönitz*, 613. In contrast, Grier shows, Dönitz was prepared to sacrifice many German lives to please Hitler. Between April 24 and 27, 1945, Dönitz readied approximately 12,000 naval troops to be flown into Berlin to fight as infantry. Due to lack of fuel and airfields, only 150–300 were actually sent there.

118 National Socialist staff in Army High Command reprimanded a chaplain for saying a German soldier condemned to death had died "brave as a soldier." Circular from Laasch, stellv. Ev. Wehrkreispfarrer XI, "An alle Ev. Standort- und Reservelazarettpfarrer im Wehrkreis XI," Hanover, June 28, 1944, p. 2, in BA-MA Freiburg, RH 53-11/71. For analysis, see Fritsche, "Proving One's Manliness."

119 See circular from Laasch, stellv. Ev. Wehrkreispfarrer XI, "An alle Ev. Standort- und Reservelazarettpfarrer im Wehrkreis XI," Hanover, June 28, 1944, p. 2, in BA-MA Freiburg, RH 53-11/71. Thanks to David Yelton for this citation.

120 Pfarrer Börner, ev. Standortpfarrer i.N., Chemnitz, Feb. 25, 1944. BA-MA Freiburg, RH 15/272, p. 154.

121 Result in response to case precipitated by Pfarrer Börner: Entwurf, OKH (Ch H Rüst und BdE), April 28, 1944, to Evang. Feldbischof. BA-MA Freiburg, RH 15/272, p. 155.

122 Entwurf, OKH (Ch H Rüst und B d E), May 16, 1944, to Evang. Feldbischof. BA-MA Freiburg, RH 15/272, p. 139.

123 Excerpt from *Verordungsblatt des Katholischen Feldbischofs der Wehrmacht* 5 (July 1, 1944): 26. BA Potsdam 51.01/23847, p. 127.

124 *Verordnungsblatt* 8, no. 7 (Oct. 15, 1944): 34.

125 *Verordnungsblatt* 9, no. 4 (Jan. 1, 1945): 2.

126 On absence of chaplains in the Luftwaffe, see guidelines prepared by Group S of Army High Command, signed Edelmann, "Wesen und Aufgabe der Feldseelsorge," [1941], p. 7, BA-MA Freiburg, RH 15/282, p. 28.

127 SS Main Personnel Office – Amt II W to OKW, Berlin-Charlottenburg, Sept. 14, 1944, BA-MA Freiburg, RH 15/272, p. 263. It is unclear what happened, but the back of the page has a note dated Sept. 26, 1944, initialed by Senftleben, that says he spoke on the telephone with SS Personalhauptamt-Hauptsturmführer Holzbach and informed him that Pastor Langer was not a member of the military but a part-time military hospital chaplain so did not need to be released.

128 See discussion in Motadel, *Islam and Nazi Germany's War*.

129 Most Greek Catholics came from Western Ukraine in the province of Galicia. On Jan. 14, 1942, Metropolitan Sheptyts'kyi signed as National Council chairman, (together with OUN leader Anij Mel'nyk and other national leaders from Galicia) a letter "to His Excellency, the Führer Adolf Hitler," which contained protests about "Ukrainians being prohibited from taking part in the armed struggle against their traditional enemy." The letter assured that "leading circles in Ukraine" were willing to cooperate with Germany. Quoted in Magocsi, *A History of Ukraine*, 677. See also Himka, "Christianity and Radical Nationalism."

130 Silecky, "Fathers in Uniform"; also Khromeychuk, "*'Undetermined' Ukrainians.*" On comparable Belarusian case, see Pomiecko, "It's never too late."

131 Rudling, "They Defended," 343; see also Shkandrij, *In the Maelstrom*.

132 See Hoare, *Bosnian Muslims*; also Greble, *Sarajevo*.

133 Geheim, Kath. Wehrkreispfarrer I, Königsberg Pr., July 18, 1944, to Kath. Feldbischof, re: arrest of Standortpfarrer i.N. Kunke./Königsberg. signed Hunzinger. BA-MA Freiburg, RH 15/272, p. 240.
134 Schröder, *Waches Gewissen*.
135 Boehm, "The 'Free Germans.'"
136 Ibid., 291.
137 Schröder, *Waches Gewissen*, 201–3.
138 "Predigt zum 20. August 1944." Ibid., 207.
139 "An die Bildungsträger und Geistlichen," Aug. 31, 1944. Ibid., 210.
140 Perau, *Priester*, entry dated Klerinowo, July 22, 1944, p. 177. Presumably he meant Kalinowo, in what was then East Prussia.
141 Rarkowski, *Verordnungsblatt* 6 (Aug. 12, 1944): 30–31.
142 On the Wednesday Circle, see Dörner, "'Der Krieg ist verloren!,'" 105–22.
143 Martin Röw discusses the importance of *Predigtskizzen*, outlines of sermons, of which several hundred were provided to Catholic military chaplains. Röw, *Militärseelsorge*, 207–10; see also Missalla, *Für Gott*, 119–68.
144 Laasch, circular stellv. ev. Wehrkreispfarrer XI, Hanover, Advent 1943, An die Herren Ev. Standort- und Lazarettpfarrer des Wehrkreises XI, p. 1. BA-MA Freiburg, RH 53-11/71.
145 Laasch, Advent 1943, BA-MA Freiburg, RH 53-11/71.
146 Laasch wrote that he included a lecture titled "Abseits der Kirche," which was not preserved in the file. Laasch, June 28, 1944, p. 1. BA-MA Freiburg, RH 53-11/71.
147 Ibid.
148 Ibid.
149 Ibid.
150 Laasch circular, Hanover, Nov. 16, 1944, BA-MA Freiburg, RH 53-11/71.
151 Ibid.
152 Ibid.
153 Ibid.
154 Laasch, Dec. 2, 1944, BA-MA Freiburg RH 53-11/71.
155 Sermon Wehrmachtspfarrer Dr. Hugo Gotthard Bloth, Prague, Feb. 25, 1945, in Krause and Marzahn, *Er führte sie*.
156 Wehrmacht soldier to wife and child, Easter Sunday 1945, in ibid.

Chapter 7

1 Elfriede Braun to Bishop Ludwig Diehl, Sept. 5, 1944, re: husband Erich, POW in Washington, DC. She quotes from his letter of Aug. 12, 1944, in the papers of Pastor Ludwig Diehl in ZASP Speyer, 150.15/1 (A–F).
2 LKM Ludwigsburg NL Bauerle.
3 It is difficult to confirm whether any chaplains indeed were given this choice or if it was a commonly told tale, inspired perhaps by Maximilian Kolbe.
4 *Mit Gott für Volk und Vaterland*; see also Ericksen, *Complicity*.
5 Schrör, in Gatz, *Erinnerungen rheinischer Seelsorger*, 309.
6 Quoted in Schwinge, *Bundeswehr und Wehrmacht*, 75.

7 It is no coincidence that the biography of the wartime Protestant military bishop was put together by a clergyman who played a central role in reestablishing the military chaplaincy in West Germany. See Kunst and Dohrmann, *Gott läßt sich nicht spotten*.

8 In Alexievich, *Unwomanly Face of War*, 311–12.

9 USHMM, RG 06.005.05M, Reel 8, no page numbers. Doc. is 3 pp. but pages numbered 2, 3, and 4. Thanks to David Yelton for bringing this document to my attention.

10 USHMM, RG 06.005.05M, Reel 8. On Rabbi Wall, see Wall, "We Will Be." Also see Townsend, *Mission at Nuremberg*, on the Lutheran Henry Gerecke; and Brennan, *Priest*.

11 Menkis, "But You Can't See the Fear"; on Canadian and British chaplains at Buchenwald, Celinscak, *Distance*, 102 and 177–90.

12 Eichhorn to Zelda, Jonny, Mike, Jerry, Judy and all, Dec. 14, 1944, "Somewhere in France," in Palmer and Zaid, *GI's Rabbi*, 137–40.

13 USC Shoah Foundation VHA, Frank Yturbide, #41172, interviewed May 10, 1998, in Reno, Nevada, by Louise Bobrow. Tape 2, 26:37–27:38. Thanks to Paloma Alaminos for research.

14 Wall, "We Will Be," 205–9.

15 Judah Nadich, USC Shoah Foundation VHA, #50887, interviewed March 23, 2000 and May 18, 2000 in New York City by Nancy Fisher. Thanks to Paloma Alaminos for research.

16 Ibid., Tape 1, 16:55.

17 Ibid., Tape 1, 29:15–29:21 and Tape 2, 0:30–1:39.

18 Ibid., Tape 2, 10:25, 4, 23:53, and 5, 2:30.

19 Ibid., Tape 6, 18:53–23:18.

20 See Bergen, "I Am (Not) to Blame."

21 See US Army Signal Corps photographs from May 6, 1945, near Regen, Germany, showing Lt. Col. Crane, chaplain from the 4th Armored Division, 3rd US Army, with three uniformed Germans, conflated in the caption as "the Chief of Chaplains of the German Army." One of the men shown (on the left) is Catholic Military Vicar Georg Werthmann, https://thechaplainkit.com/chaplains/foreign-chaplains/germany/

22 Faulkner, "Against Bolshevism."

23 On Rarkowski, see Missalla, *Wie der Krieg*.

24 Document no. 227, Statement of Friedrich August Ronneberger, Wilhelmshaven, April 12, 1946, in *Trial of the Major War Criminals*, vol. 41: 80.

25 Ibid., 81.

26 Ibid., 82.

27 Ibid., 82–83.

28 Ibid., 83.

29 For the Admiral's postwar praise for the Navy Chaplaincy, see Raeder, *Mein Leben*, 350–56.

30 Schröder, *Waches Gewissen*. The Soviets also recruited other chaplains into the Free Germany Committee: the Catholic Joseph Kaiser and the Protestant Matthäus Klein. See Boehm, "Free Germans."

31 French efforts were particularly important in this regard, led by chief military chaplains in the French occupation zones of Germany and Austria, the Catholic

Robert Picard de la Vacquerie and the Protestant Marcel Sturm. See Schröber, "Franco-German Rapprochement," 143–65. Also see Snape, *Royal Army Chaplains*.

32 See Théofilakis, "Rodolph," 163–74. Also of interest in the same volume are Overmans, "German Treatment of Jewish Prisoners of War," 45–53; and Debons, "All Things Are Possible," 54–64.

33 Hanley, *Last Human Face*.

34 Brennan, *Priest*, 98.

35 In his Preface, Morgenschweis emphasizes that Pohl "has written the conversion story himself" (*Credo*, 9) and that he, on his own accord and without undue external influence, longed to convert to Catholicism: "Pohl came to his conversion solely under the influence of God's grace" (10). The chaplain needs to insist on Pohl's independent decision-making and authorship in order to uphold the integrity of the conversion experience. Pohl, *Credo*.

36 A counter-example: Karl Brandt, who was sentenced to death for his role in the program to kill people with disabilities, proudly maintained his anti-Christian, pagan worldview until the end. He accused Christians of hypocrisy and said that "only the pagan dies joyfully" (letter of April 6, 1947, reprinted in *Deutsche Hochschullehrer Zeitung* 10/1, 1962). Brandt was hanged in 1948.

37 For George Mosse, "respectability" is a crucial aspect in the construction of modern masculinity, while masculinity, in turn, is closely linked to "modern national consciousness." "Respectability ... provides society with essential cohesion." Mosse, *Image of Man*, 192f.

38 Krondorfer, "Perpetrator's Confession"; see also Kellenbach, *Mark of Cain*. For more on Heinrich Vogel (1902–1989) and his role in the Confessing Church and after Nazi years, see Barnett, *For the Soul of the People*, 235, 282–83.

39 Smelser and Davies, *Myth of the Eastern Front*; also Bendersky, *"Jewish Threat."*

40 See *Bundeswehr: Armee für den Krieg. Aufbau und Rolle der Bundeswehr als Aggressionsinstrument des westdeutschen Imperialismus* (Berlin: Deutscher Militärverlag, 1968). The author is given as "Autorenkollektiv des Deutschen Instituts für Militärgeschichte."

41 Werkner, *Soldatenseelsorge versus Militärseelsorge*; Hierold, "Die rechtlichen Strukturen," 39–53; also Uzulis, *Die Bundeswehr*, 52–53. For an apologetic view of the Wehrmacht and continuities after 1945, see Schwinge, *Bundeswehr und Wehrmacht*. The first villain named as a "Gegner der Traditionswürdigkeit der Wehrmacht" is Manfred Messerschmidt (17).

42 Blaschke and Oberhem, *Bundeswehr und Kirchen*, vol. 11, *Die Bundeswehr*.

43 Werthmann, "In Memoriam" Friedrich Wolf. *Militärseelsorge* 4 (Dec. 1970): 334.

44 Corum, "Adenauer," 29–52; also see Lüdtke, "Coming to Terms."

45 Lubbers, "Die Neuordnung der Militärseelsorge," 13.

46 Ibid., 20.

47 "Die Verhandlungen über die Errichtung einer Katholischen Militärseelsorge in der Bundesrepublik im Spiegel der Presse," in Katholisches Militärbischofsamt, ed., *Katholische Militärseelsorge*, 44, 55, 165, and 166.

48 Elert, "Zur Frage des Soldateneides," 385–455.

49 Ibid., 419. See also Hébert, *Hitler's Generals*.

50 Elert, "Zur Frage des Soldateneides," 420.

51 Ibid., 454.
52 See Federal Government of Germany, "Commemorating Resistance Fighters," July 20, 2017, www.bundesregierung.de/breg-en/news/commemorating-german-resist ance-fighters-402858.
53 Of interest in this context is Bloch, *Faith for This World*. Chaplain Eberhard Müller, whose 1941 sermon is quoted in the epilogue to this book, features extensively in Bloch's study.
54 Article ms, author unknown (Rüb?), "The Changing Role of Military Chaplaincy: From Raising Military Morale to Praying Peace," 9 pp. Translated from German. Here p. 8.
55 Marx, *Eighteenth Brumaire*, 15.
56 See the essays in Lepp and Nowak, *Evangelische Kirche*.
57 Herman, *Rebirth of the German Church*.
58 Littell, *German Phoenix*.
59 Examples: Schabel, *Herr, in Deine Hände*; Schübel, *Dreihundert Jahre*; Baedeker *Das Volk das im Finstern*.
60 Perau, *Priester*, entry from April 8, 1945.
61 Ibid., 240.
62 Ibid. General Otto Lasch (1893–1971).
63 Loeffel, *Family Punishment*. For a case where "Sippenhaft" was invoked for the family of a military chaplain, see Schröder, *Waches Gewissen*.
64 Perau, *Priester*, 241.
65 Diary of Alphons Satzger, typescript, p. 19, Kempowski Archiv, #3101.
66 Ibid.
67 Ibid., 20.
68 On the ratline, see Steinacher, *Nazis auf der Flucht*.
69 Isaiah 9:2, Matthew 4:16.
70 Leonhard, *Wieviel Leid*, 41–42.
71 Rosenberg, *Mythus des 20. Jahrhunderts*, 614.
72 Leonhard, *Wieviel Leid*, 42.
73 Published diaries and memoirs of chaplains include: Alberti, *Als Kriegspfarrer*; Perau, *Priester*; Baedeker, *Das Volk*; and Leonhard, *Wieviel Leid*. Also see Brandt, *Priester*. The most extensive collections of personal papers of a German World War II chaplain that I found are the NL Bernhard Bauerle, LKM Ludwigsburg, and the NL Hans Radtke, EZA Berlin. There are relevant materials in the papers of Pastors Hans Stempel and Ludwig Diehl in ZASP Speyer.
74 *Militärseelsorge. Zeitschrift des Katholischen Militärbischofsamtes Bonn* – no. 4, Dec. 1970: Georg Werthmann, "Unsere 'Ehemaligen'," pp. 329–32: Diözese Essen, pp. 329–30.
75 Judt, *Postwar*.
76 Goes, *Unruhige Nacht*, 29.
77 Bondanella, "L'uomo della croce," 32–44.
78 Ibid., 39.
79 See the movie, *Father of Mercy*, directed by Cinzia Th. Torrini, 2004. It has thousands of enthusiastic reviews on Netflix, e.g., "one of the best religious movies I have ever seen."

80 Joyce Palmer Ralph, "Vita: Adolf Sannwald," in *Harvard Magazine*, July–Aug. 1995: 44–45.

81 Hockenos, *Then They Came for Me*.

82 Pauli, *Wehrmachtsoffiziere*, 184.

83 Lütjohann, "Militärseelsorge."

84 Schabel, *Herr in Deine Hände*.

85 Lütjohann, "Militärseelsorge," 515.

86 Ibid.

87 Ibid., 516.

88 Lehmann, "God Our Old Ally," 107.

89 See Mazower, "Military Violence," for mention of a chaplain's role.

90 M4–37, NATO & Partner Chaplain Operations Course, www.natoschool.nato.int/ Academics/Resident-Courses/Course-Catalogue/Course-Description?ID=38

91 Christoph Strack, "Germany's Military Appoints First Rabbi since Before Holocaust," *Deutsche Welle*, June 21, 2021; "German Army Taps Chief Rabbi for First Time in a Century and 76 Years after Holocaust," *Israel Times*, June 4, 2021; *Chicago Sun Times*. The *Israel Times* story mentions that another ten rabbis would play roles in the military and also notes that the Bundeswehr does not document the religious affiliations of its members, so there could in fact be fewer than 300 Jewish soldiers. Also it gives a figure of 1,600 for Muslim Bundeswehr members.

92 Strack, "Germany's Military," *Deutsche Welle*, June 21, 2021.

93 Christoph Strack, "Being Muslim in Germany's Bundeswehr Means no Pastoral Care," *Deutsche Welle*, July 25, 2020. See also "German Army to Recruit First Imam," Anadolu Agency, May 23, 2015, www.aa.com.tr/en/world/german-army-to-recruit-first-imam/44276#.

94 "In Previously 'Unthinkable' Move, German Military Has Its 1st Rabbi in over a Century," *Los Angeles Times*, June 22, 2021. Associated Press story.

95 Address by the President of the Central Council of Jews in Germany, Dr. Josef Schuster, on the Inauguration of the Federal Military Rabbi, June 21, 2021, Leipzig. Zentralrat der Juden in Deutschland, p. 1, www.zentralratderjuden.de/fileadmin/ user_upload/pdfs/MR_Pressemappe/Adress_Dr._Schuster.pdf

Conclusion

1 See among many other books, Stephen E. Ambrose, *The Supreme Commander: The War Years of General Dwight D. Eisenhower* (Garden City, NY: Doubleday, 1970); *D-Day, June 6, 1944: The Climactic Battle of World War II* (New York: Simon & Schuster, 1994); *The Victors: Eisenhower and His Boys: The Men of World War II* (New York: Simon & Schuster, 1998); *Band of Brothers: E. Company, 506th Regiment, 101st Airborne from Normandy to Hitler's Eagle's Nest* (New York: Simon & Schuster, 1992 and 2001).

2 Griech-Polelle, *Bishop von Galen*; Clark, "Johannes Blaskowitz," 28–50; Hoffmann, *Stauffenberg*; Gaydosh, *Bernhard Lichtenberg*; Spicer, *Resisting the Third Reich*; Hockenos, *Then They Came for Me*; Gailus, *Mir aber zerriss es das Herz*; Barnett, *After Ten Years*; Spector, "Edith Stein's Passing Gestures."

3 Lütjohann, "Militärseelsorge," 514.

4 Ibid., 515.

5 USC Shoah Foundation VHA, Interview with Mordechai Singer (b. Markus Singer), Interview # 9773 (tapes 1–5), interviewed Dec. 7, 1995 in Brooklyn, NY by Lorrie Fein. (27:30) [Tape 4]. Thanks to Masha Koyama for research.

6 Quoted in N'dea Yancey-Bragg, "What Is Systemic Racism? Here's What It Means and How You Can Help Dismantle It," *USA Today* (Jan. 29, 2021).

7 Rymar, "Die Gnade," 164.

8 Matt Sedensky, "Last Rites for Afghan War's 'Holy Ground'," *Toronto Star* (Aug. 15, 2021), IN3.

9 Ibid.

10 Ibid.

11 See the collection of short stories, Klay, *redeployment*, including a remarkable story about a chaplain, "Prayer in the Furnace," 129–67.

12 Justin George, "A Chaplain's Conscience vs. the Bureau of Prisons," *ABA Journal* (Oct. 2, 2017), www.abajournal.com/news/article/a_chaplains_conscience_vs._the_bureau_of_prisons/. The chaplain prevailed: Justin George, "The Bureau of Prisons Yields to a Chaplain's Conscience," *The Marshall Project*, Jan. 26, 2018, www.themarshallproject.org/2018/01/26/the-bureau-of-prisons-yields-to-a-chaplain-s-conscience

13 Quoted in Alexievich, *Unwomanly Face of War*, 323, 330–31.

Bibliography

Archives

*Note that some of the archives I used have changed names, moved location, or no longer exist.

Akademie der Künste, Kempowski Archiv, Berlin, Germany

Archiv des Katholischen Militärbischofsamts (AKM), Bonn, Germany (now in Berlin)

Archive of the Main Commission for the Investigation of Crimes against the Polish Nation (now Institute of National Remembrance), Warsaw, Poland

Archiwum Pansytwowe w Łódźi (AP Łódź), Poland

Bundesarchiv Bayreuth (BA Bayreuth)

Bundesarchiv Berlin-Lichterfelde (BA Berlin-Lichterfelde), Germany

Bundesarchiv Koblenz (BA Koblenz)

Bundesarchiv Potsdam (BA Potsdam), Germany (no longer exists; collections have been moved to other Bundesarchiv locations)

Bundesarchiv-Militärarchiv, Freiburg/Br. (BA-MA Freiburg), Germany

Evangelisches Zentralarchiv, Berlin (EZA Berlin), Germany

Landeskirchenarchiv, Bielefeld (LKA Bielefeld), Germany

Landeskirchenarchiv, Nuremberg (LKA Nuremberg), Germany

Landeskirchliches Museum, Ludwigsburg (LKM Ludwigsburg), Germany

National Archives Research Administration (NARA), Washington, DC

Politisches Archiv des Auswärtigen Amts (AA), Bonn, Germany (now in Berlin)

USC Shoah Foundation Visual History Archive (VHA), Los Angeles, United States (online)

United States Holocaust Memorial Museum Archives (USHMM), Washington, DC, United States

Yad Vashem Archives (YV), Jerusalem, Israel

Zentralarchiv der Evangelischen Kirche der Pfalz (ZASP), Speyer, Germany

Published Primary Sources

Alberti, Rüdiger. *Als Kriegspfarrer in Polen: Erlebnisse und Begegnungen in Kriegslazaretten.* Dresden: Ungelenk, 1940.

Anonymous [Marta Hiller]. *A Woman in Berlin: Diary 20 April 1945 to 22 June 1945.* London: Virago, 2005.

Baedeker, Dietrich. *Das Volk, das im Finstern wandelt: Stationen eines Militärpfarrers 1938–1946*. Hanover: Lutherisches Verlagshaus, 1987.

Benda, Julien. *The Great Betrayal (La trahison des clercs)*. Translated by Richard Aldington. London: George Routledge & Sons, 1928.

Blankmeister, Franz. *Die sächsischen Feldprediger: Zur Geschichte der Militärseelsorge in Krieg und Frieden*. Leipzig: Fr. Richter, 1893.

Boder, David P. *I Did Not Interview the Dead*. Urbana: University of Illinois Press, 1949.

Böll, Heinrich. *Briefe aus dem Krieg 1939–1945*. Vol. 1. Cologne: Kiepenheuer & Witsch, 2001.

Bonhoeffer, Dietrich. *Dietrich Bonhoeffer Works*. Edited by Victoria J. Barnett. Translated by Claudia D. Bergmann et al. Minneapolis: Fortress, 2011.

Brandt, Hans Jürgen, ed. *Priester in Uniform: Seelsorger, Ordensleute und Theologen als Soldaten im Zweiten Weltkrieg*. Augsburg: Pattloch, 1994.

Buchbender, Ortwin and Reinhold Sterz. *Das andere Gesicht des Krieges: Deutsche Feldpostbriefe 1939–1945*. Munich: Beck, 1982.

Dodd, Martha. *Through Embassy Eyes*. New York: Harcourt Brace, 1939.

Elert, Werner. "Zur Frage des Soldateneides." *Deutsches Pfarrerblatt: Bundesblatt der Deutchen Evangelischen Pfarrervereine* 52, no. 13 (1952): 385–455.

Frenssen, Gustav. *Peter Moor: A Narrative of the German Campaign in South-West Africa*. Translated by Margaret May Ward. London: Constable, 1908.

Fromm, Bella. *Blood and Banquets: A Berlin Social Diary*. New York: Garden City Publishing, 1943.

Gatz, Erwin, ed. *Erinnerungen rheinischer Seelsorger aus den Diözesen Aachen, Köln und Lüttich (1933–1986)*. Aachen: Einhard, 1988.

Goes, Albrecht. *Unruhige Nacht*. Hamburg: Wittig, 1950.

Groscurth, Helmuth. *Tagebücher eines Abwehroffiziers, 1938–1940: Mit weiteren Dokumenten zur Militäropposition gegen Hitler*. Edited by Helmut Krausnick, Harold C. Deutsch, and Hildegard von Kotze. Stuttgart: Deutsche Verlags-Anstalt, 1970.

Grossman, Vasily. "The Old Teacher." In Robert Chandler, ed. *The Road: Stories, Journalism, Essays*. Translated by Elizabeth Chandler. New York: NYRB Classics, 2010; 84–115.

Hamburg Institute for Social Research, ed. *The German Army and Genocide: Crimes against War Prisoners, Jews, and Other Civilians, 1939–1944*. New York: New Press, 1999.

Harnack, Falk, director. *Unruhige Nacht*. Federal Republic of Germany: co-produced by Carlton Film, Filmaufbau, and Real-Film, 1958; 95 mins.

Hašek, Jaroslav. *The Good Soldier Svejk and His Fortunes in the World War*. Translated by Cecil Parrott. New York: Crowell, 1974.

Herman, Stewart W. *The Rebirth of the German Church*. New York: Harper, 1946.

Hildebrand, Peter. *Odyssee wider Willen: Das Schicksal eines Auslandsdeutschen*. Oldenburg: Heinz Holzberg, 1984.

Hindenburg, Paul von. *Out of My Life*. Translated by F. A. Holt. London: Cassell, 1920.

Ihlenfeld, Kurt, ed. *Preußischer Choral: Deutscher Soldatenglaube in drei Jahrhunderten*. Berlin-Steglitz: Echart, 1935.

Jarausch, Konrad. *Reluctant Accomplice: A Wehrmacht Soldier's Letters from the Eastern Front*. Princeton, NJ: Princeton University Press, 2011.

Katholisches Militärbischofsamt, ed. *Katholische Militärseelsorge in der Bundeswehr: Ein Neubeginn (1951–1957)*. Cologne: J. P. Bachem, 1986.

Keding, Karl. *Feldgeistlicher bei Legion Condor: Spanisches Kriegstagebuch eines evangelischen Legionspfarrers*. Berlin: Ostwerk, [1938].

Und doch Pfarrer! Ein Mann findet zu Christus. Potsdam: Stiftungsverlag, 1940.

Klay, Phil. *Redeployment*. New York: Penguin, 2014.

Klee, Ernst and Willi Dreßen. *"Gott mit uns": Der deutsche Vernichtungskrieg im Osten, 1939–1945.* Frankfurt am Main: Fischer, 1989.

Klee, Ernst, Willi Dreßen, and Volker Rieß. *"Schöne Zeiten": Judenmord aus der Sicht der Täter und Gaffer.* Frankfurt am Main: Fischer, 1988.

Klemperer, Victor. *I Will Bear Witness: A Diary of the Nazi Years*, Vol. 1: *1933–1941*; Vol. 2: *1941–1945*. Translated by Martin Chalmers. New York: Random House, 1998 and 1999.

Koschorke, Helmuth. *Polizeireiter in Polen.* Berlin: Franz Schneider, 1940.

Kranz, Gisbert. *Eine katholische Jugend im Dritten Reich: Erinnerungen, 1921–1947.* Freiburg: Herder, 1990.

Krause, Werner and Wolfgang Marzahn, eds. *Er führte sie aus Dunkel und Angst: Predigten und Andachten Pommerscher Pastoren aus Kriegs- und Nachkriegsjahren.* Leer: Gerhard Rautenberg, 1986.

Kruk, Herman. *The Last Days of the Jerusalem of Lithuania: Chronicle from the Vilna Ghetto and the Camps, 1939–1944.* Edited by Benjamin Harshav. Translated by Barbara Harshav. New Haven, CT: Yale University Press, 2002.

Kukielka, Renya. *Escape from the Pit.* New York: Sharon, 1947.

Kulp, Johannes. *Feldprediger und Kriegsleute als Kirchenliederdichter.* Leipzig: Schloeßmann, 1941.

Kunst, Hermann and Franz Dohrmann. *Gott läßt sich nicht spotten: Franz Dohrmann Feldbischof unter Hitler.* Hanover: Lutherisches Verlagshaus, 1983.

Kunze, Gerhard. *Evangelisches Kirchenbuch für Kriegszeiten.* Göttingen: Vandenhoeck & Ruprecht, 1939.

Landwehr, Gordian. "So sah ich sie sterben." In Hans Jürgen Brandt, ed. *Priester in Uniform: Seelsorger, Ordensleute und Theologen als Soldaten im Zweiten Weltkrieg.* Augsburg: Pattloch, 1994; 349–50.

Lipusch, Viktor. *Österreich-Ungarns katholische Militärseelsorge im Weltkriege.* Graz: Berger, 1938.

Lehmann, Paul Gerhard. *Der Feldgottesdienst: Betrachtungen eines Frontoffiziers.* Göttingen: Vandenhoeck & Ruprecht, 1917.

Leonhard, Hans. *Wieviel Leid erträgt ein Mensch? Aufzeichnungen eines Kriegspfarrers über die Jahre 1939 bis 1945.* Amberg: Buch & Kunstverlag Oberpfalz, 1994.

Lütjohann, Uwe. "Militärseelsorge im 2. Weltkrieg und heute." *Junge Kirche. Protestantische Monatshefte* 26 (Sept. 10, 1965): 514–17.

Melville, Herman. *Billy Budd, Sailor.* New and definitive text edited by Harrison Hayford and Merton M. Sealts, Jr. Chicago, IL: University of Chicago Press, 1962.

Meyer-Erlach, Wolf. *"Das deutsche Leid" – Ein Schauspiel in vier Akten.* Munich: Deutsche Bühnenbücherei, 1923.

Mit Gott für Volk und Vaterland: Die Württembergische Landeskirche zwischen Krieg und Frieden 1903–1957. Stuttgart: Haus der Geschichte Baden-Württemberg and Landeskirchlichen Museum Ludwigsburg, 1995.

Neitzel, Sönke, ed. *Tapping Hitler's Generals: Transcripts of Secret Conversations, 1942–1945*. Translated by Geoffrey Brooks. Barnsley: Frontline Books, 2007.

Neitzel, Sönke and Harald Welzer, eds. *Soldaten: The Secret World War II Transcripts of German POWs*. Translated by Jefferson Chase. New York: Alfred A. Knopf, 2012.

Némirovsky, Irène. *Suite Française*. Translated by Sandra Smith. New York: Knopf, 2006.

Neufeld, Justina D. *A Family Torn Apart*. Kitchener, ON: Pandora, 2003.

Nevermann, Hans Richard. "Warum zog ich nicht die Notbremse? Erinnerungen 40 Jahre nach dem Überfall auf die Sowjetunion." *Junge Kirche*, no. 6 (1981): 282–84.

Noakes, Jeremy and Geoffrey Pridham, eds. *Nazism, 1919–1945*. 3rd ed. Exeter: University of Exeter Press, 2001.

Palmer, Greg and Mark Zaid, eds. *The GI's Rabbi: World War II Letters of David Max Eichhorn*. Lawrence: University Press of Kansas, 2004.

Perau, Josef. *Priester im Heere Hitlers: Erinnerungen 1940–1945*. Essen: Ludgerus, 1963.

Piechowski, Paul. *Die Kriegspredigt von 1870/71*. Leipzig: Scholl, 1917.

Pohl, Oswald. *Credo: Mein Weg zu Gott*. Landshut: Girnth, 1950.

Raeder, Erich. *Mein Leben*. Beltheim-Schnellbach: Bublies, 2009; original publication 1956.

Reynolds, Alexander. *To War without Arms: The Journal of Reverend Alexander Reynolds, May–November 1944: The D-Day Diary of an Army Chaplain*. Edited by Simon Trew. Devizes: Sabrestorm Publishing, 2019.

Rosenberg, Alfred. *Der Mythus des 20. Jahrhunderts: Eine Wertung der seelisch-geistigen Gestaltenkämpfe unserer Zeit*. Munich: Hoheneichen, 1935.

Rubenstein, Joshua and Ilya Altman, eds. *The Unknown Black Book: The Holocaust in the German-Occupied Territories*. Translated by Christopher Morris and Joshua Rubenstein. Bloomington: Indiana University Press, 2010.

Schabel, Wilhelm. *Herr in Deine Hände: Seelsorge im Krieg*. Bern: Scherz, 1963.

Schlunck, Rudolf and Wilhelm Wibbeling, eds. *Ein Pfarrer im Kriege, Kriegserlebnisse des renitenten Pfarrers Rudolf Schlunck*. Kassel: Neuwerk, 1931.

Schröder, Johannes. *Waches Gewissen – Aufruf zum Widerstand: Reden und Predigten eines Wehrmachtpfarrers aus sowjetischer Gefangenschaft 1943–1945*. Edited by Christiane Godt, Peter Godt, Hartmut Lehmann, Silke Lehmann, and Jens-Holger Schjörring. Göttingen: Wallstein, 2021.

Senftleben, Otto. *Deutsches Wehrrecht, ein Grundriß*. Berlin: Junker & Dünnhaupt, 1935.

Shirer, William L. *The Rise and Fall of the Third Reich: A History of Nazi Germany*. New York: Simon & Schuster, 1960; 50th anniversary edition, 2010.

Spicer, Kevin P. and Martina Cucchiara, eds. and trans. *The Evil that Surrounds Us: The WWII Memoir of Erna Becker-Kohen*. Bloomington: Indiana University Press, 2017.

Stevens, E. H., ed. *Trial of Nikolaus von Falkenhorst, formerly Generaloberst in the German Army*. London: William Hodge, 1949.

Tewes, Ernst. "Seelsorger bei den Soldaten 1940–1945: Aufzeichnungen und Erinnerungen." In Georg Schwaiger, ed. *Das Erzbistum München und Freising in der Zeit der nationalsozialistischen Herrschaft.* Vol. 2. Munich: Schnell & Steiner, 1984; 244–87.

Trial of the Major War Criminals before the International Military Tribunal at Nuremberg, 14 November 1945–1 October 1946. Vol. 41. English edition. Nuremberg: International Military Tribunal, 1949.

Vassiltchikov, Marie. *The Berlin Diaries, 1940–1945.* London: Chatto and Windus, 1985.

Voegelin, Eric. *Die Politischen Religionen.* Reprint. Munich: Peter J. Opitz, 1996.

Wall, Max B. "'We Will Be': Experiences of an American Jewish Chaplain in the Second World War." In Doris L. Bergen, ed. *The Sword of the Lord: Military Chaplains from the First to the Twenty-First Centuries.* Notre Dame, IN: University of Notre Dame Press, 2004; 187–214.

Zoller, Albert. *Hitler privat: Erlebnisbericht seiner Geheimsekretärin.* Düsseldorf: Droste, 1949.

Secondary Sources

Abzug, Robert. *Inside the Vicious Heart: Americans and the Liberation of Nazi Concentration Camps.* New York: Oxford University Press, 1985.

Alexievich, Svetlana. *The Unwomanly Face of War: An Oral History of Women in World War II.* Translated by Richard Pevear and Larissa Volokhonsky. New York: Random House, 2017.

Aly, Götz. *"Final Solution": Nazi Population Policy and the Murder of the European Jews.* Translated by Belinda Cooper and Allison Brown. New York: Arnold, 1999.

Ambrose, Stephen E. *The Victors: Eisenhower and His Boys: The Men of World War II.* New York: Simon & Schuster, 1998.

Angrick, Andrej. *Besatzungspolitik und Massenmord. Die Einsatzgruppe D in der südlichen Sowjetunion 1941–1943.* Hamburg: Hamburger Edition, 2003.

Angrick, Andrej and Peter Klein. *Endlösung in Riga: Ausbeutung und Vernichtung 1941–1944.* Darmstadt: Wissenschaftliche Buchgesellschaft, 2006.

Apold, Hans. "Feldbischof Franz Justus Rarkowski im Spiegel seiner Hirtenbriefe." *Zeitschrift für die Geschichte und Altertumskunde Ermlands* 39, no. 100 (1978): 86–128.

Appelbaum, Peter C. *Loyalty Betrayed: Jewish Chaplains in the German Army during the First World War.* London: Vallentine Mitchell, 2014.

Apsel, Joyce and Ernesto Verdeja, eds. *Genocide Matters: Ongoing Issues and Emerging Perspectives.* London: Routledge, 2013.

Arendt, Hannah. *Eichmann in Jerusalem: A Report on the Banality of Evil.* New York: Viking, 1963.

Armstrong, Karen. *Fields of Blood: Religion and the History of Violence.* New York: Knopf, 2014.

Audoin-Rouzeau, Stéphane and Annette Becker. *14–18: Understanding the Great War.* Translated by Catherine Temerson. New York: Hill and Wang, 2002.

Auerbach, Rachel. "In the Fields of Treblinka." In Alexander Donat, ed. *The Death Camp Treblinka.* New York: Holocaust Library, 1979; 17–76. Published 1947 in Yiddish.

Bachmann, Klaus and Gerhard Kemp. "Was Quashing the Maji-Maji Uprising Genocide? An Evaluation of Germany's Conduct through the Lens of International Criminal Law." *Holocaust and Genocide Studies* 35, no. 2 (2021): 235–49.

Bachrach, David S. *Religion and the Conduct of War, c. 300–1215.* Woodbridge: Boydell, 2003.

Bade, Claudia, Lars Skowronski, and Michael Viebig, eds. *NS-Militärjustiz im Zweiten Weltkrieg: Disziplinierungs- und Repressionsinstrument in europäischer Dimension.* Göttingen: Vandenhoeck & Ruprecht, 2015.

Bamberg, Hans-Dieter. *Militärseelsorge in der Bundeswehr – Schule der Anpassung und des Unfriedens.* Cologne: Paul Rugenstein, 1970.

Barish, Louis. *Rabbis in Uniform: The Story of the American Jewish Military Chaplains.* New York: Jonathan David, 1962.

Barnett, Victoria J. *Bystanders: Conscience and Complicity during the Holocaust.* Westport, CT: Praeger, 1999.

   For the Soul of the People: Protestant Protest against Hitler. New York: Oxford University Press, 1992.

   ed. *"After Ten Years": Dietrich Bonhoeffer and Our Times.* Minneapolis, MN: Fortress, 2017.

Barton, Deborah. *Writing for Dictatorship, Refashioning for Democracy: German Women Journalists in the Nazi and Post-war Press.* PhD diss., University of Toronto, 2014.

Bartov, Omer. *The Eastern Front, 1941–1945: German Troops and the Barbarisation of Warfare.* London: Palgrave Macmillan, 1985.

   Hitler's Army: Soldiers, Nazis, and War in the Third Reich. New York: Oxford University Press, 1991.

Bartov, Omer and Phyllis Mack, eds. *In God's Name: Religion and Genocide in the Twentieth Century.* New York: Berghahn, 2000.

Beese, Dieter. *Seelsorger in Uniform. Evangelische Militärseelsorge im Zweiten Weltkrieg. Aufgabe – Leitung – Predigt.* Hanover: Lutherisches Verlagshaus, 1995.

Benbassa, Esther and Aron Rodrigue. *Sephardi Jewry: A History of the Judeo-Spanish Community, 14th–20th Centuries.* Berkeley: University of California Press, 2000.

Bendersky, Joseph W. *The "Jewish Threat": Anti-Semitic Politics in the U.S. Army.* New York: Basic Books, 2000.

Beorn, Waitman Wade. *Marching into Darkness: The Wehrmacht and the Holocaust in Belarus.* Cambridge, MA: Harvard University Press, 2014.

Bergen, Doris L. "Between God and Hitler: German Military Chaplains and the Crimes of the Third Reich." In Omer Bartov and Phyllis Mack, eds. *In God's Name: Genocide and Religion in the Twentieth Century.* New York: Berghahn, 2001; 123–38.

   "Death Throes and Killing Frenzies: A Response to Hans Mommsen." *Bulletin of the German Historical Institute*, Washington, DC 27 (2000): 25–38.

   "'Germany Is Our Mission – Christ Is Our Strength': The *Wehrmacht* Chaplaincy and the 'German Christian' Movement." *Church History* 66, no. 3 (1997): 522–36.

   "'I Am (Not) to Blame': Guilt and Shame in Eyewitness Accounts of the Holocaust." In Wendy Lower and Lauren Faulkner Rossi, eds. *Lessons and Legacies XII.* Evanston, IL: Northwestern University Press, 2017; 87–107.

"Instrumentalization of *Volksdeutschen* in German Propaganda in 1939: Replacing/ Erasing Poles, Jews, and Other Victims." *German Studies Review* 31, no. 3 (2008): 447–70.

Twisted Cross: The German Christian Movement in the Third Reich. Chapel Hill: University of North Carolina Press, 1996.

Bergen, Doris L., ed. *The Sword of the Lord: Military Chaplains from the First to the Twenty-First Centuries.* Notre Dame, IN: University of Notre Dame Press, 2004.

Berkhoff, Karel. *Harvest of Despair: Life and Death in Ukraine under Nazi Rule.* Cambridge, MA: Belknap, 2004.

"Was There a Religious Revival in Soviet Ukraine under the Nazi Regime?" *Slavonic and East European Review* 78, no. 3 (2000): 536–67.

Besier, Gerhard, ed. *Zwischen "nationaler Revolution" und militärischer Aggression: Transformationen in Kirche und Gesellschaft während der konsolidierten NS-Gewaltherrschaft (1934–1939).* Munich: Oldenbourg, 2001.

Bessel, Richard. *Germany 1945: From War to Peace.* New York: Harper Perennial, 2009.

Best, Jeremy. *Heavenly Fatherland: German Missionary Culture and Globalization in the Age of Empire.* Toronto, ON: University of Toronto Press, 2021.

Biddick, Kathleen. "Dead Neighbor Archives: Jews, Muslims, and the Enemy's Two Bodies." In *Make and Let Die: Untimely Sovereignties.* Brooklyn, NY: Punctum, 2016.

Biliuţă, Ionuţ. "To Murder or Save Thy Neighbour? Romanian Orthodox Clergymen and Jews during the Holocaust (1941–1945)." In Kevin P. Spicer and Rebecca Carter-Chand, eds. *Religion, Ethnonationalism, and Antisemitism in the Era of the Two World Wars.* Montreal: McGill-Queen's University Press, 2022; 305–30.

Biondich, Mark. "Controversies Surrounding the Catholic Church in Wartime Croatia in 1941–45." In Sabrina P. Ramet, ed. *The Independent State of Croatia, 1941–45.* London: Routledge, 2007; 31–59.

Black, Johann. *Militärseelsorge in Polen.* Stuttgart: Seewald, 1981.

Blaschke, Olaf and Thomas Großbölting, eds. *Was glaubten die Deutschen zwischen 1933 und 1945? Religion und Politik im Nationalsozialismus.* Frankfurt am Main: Campus, 2020.

Blaschke, Peter H. and Harald Oberhem. *Bundeswehr und Kirchen.* Vol. 11. In Hubert Reinfried and Hubert F. Walitschek, eds. *Die Bundeswehr. Eine Gesamtdarstellung.* Regensburg: Walhalla and Praetoria, 1985.

Blatman, Daniel. *The Death Marches: The Final Phase of Nazi Genocide.* Translated by Chaya Galai. Cambridge, MA: Belknap Press of Harvard University Press, 2011.

Bloch, Brandon. *Faith for This World: Protestantism and the Reconstruction of Constitutional Democracy in Germany, 1933–1968.* PhD diss., Harvard University, 2018.

Boehm, Eric H. "The 'Free Germans' in Soviet Psychological Warfare." *Public Opinion Quarterly* 14, no. 2 (1950): 285–95.

Böhler, Jochen. *Auftakt zum Vernichtungskrieg: Die Wehrmacht in Polen 1939.* Frankfurt am Main: Fischer Taschenbuch, 2006.

ed. *"Grösste Härte ..." Verbrechen der Wehrmacht in Polen September/Oktober 1939.* Warsaw: Deutsches Historisches Institut, 2005.

Boll, Bernd and Hans Safrian. "Auf dem Weg nach Stalingrad: Die 6. Armee 1941/42."
    In Hannes Heer and Klaus Naumann, eds. *Vernichtungskrieg: Verbrechen der
    Wehrmacht 1941–1944*. Hamburg: Hamburger Edition, 1998; 260–96.
Bondanella, Peter. "L'uomo della croce: Rossellini and Fascist Cinema." In Peter
    Bondanella, ed. *The Films of Roberto Rossellini*. Cambridge: Cambridge
    University Press, 1993; 32–44.
Bos, Pascale. "'Her Flesh Is Branded: "For Officers Only".' Imagining and Imagined
    Sexual Violence against Jewish Women during the Holocaust." In Hilary Earl and
    Karl A. Schleunes, eds. *Lessons and Legacies XI: Expanding Perspectives on the
    Holocaust in a Changing World*. Evanston, IL: Northwestern University Press,
    2014; 59–85.
Bowman, Steven B. *The Agony of Greek Jews, 1940–1945*. Palo Alto, CA: Stanford
    University Press, 2009.
Brakelmann, Günter, ed. *Kirche im Krieg: Der deutsche Protestantismus am Beginn
    des II. Weltkriegs*. Munich: Christian Kaiser, 1988.
Brandon, Ray and Wendy Lower, eds. *The Shoah in Ukraine: History, Testimony,
    Memorialization*. Bloomington: Indiana University Press, 2008.
Brandt, Hans Jürgen, ed., *... und auch Soldaten fragten: Zur Aufgabe und Problematik
    der Militärseelsorge in drei Generationen*. Paderborn: Bonifatius, 1992.
Braun, Christina von. "The Symbol of the Cross: Secularization of a Metaphor from the
    Early Church to National Socialism." In Doris L. Bergen, ed. *Lessons and
    Legacies VIII: From Generation to Generation*. Evanston, IL: Northwestern
    University Press, 2008; 5–33.
Brennan, Sean. *The Priest Who Put Europe Back Together: The Life of Rev. Fabian
    Flynn, CP*. Washington, DC: Catholic University of America Press, 2018.
Brown, Vincent. *Tacky's Revolt: The Story of an Atlantic Slave War*. Cambridge, MA:
    Belknap Press, 2020.
Browning, Christopher R. *Fateful Months: Essays on the Emergence of the Final
    Solution*. New York: Holmes & Meier, 1985; Rev. ed., 1991.
Browning, Christopher, with contributions by Jürgen Matthäus. *The Origins of the
    Final Solution: The Evolution of Nazi Jewish Policy, September 1939–March
    1942*. Lincoln: University of Nebraska Press, 2004.
Budz, Kateryna and Andrew Kloes. "Ethnonationalism as a Theological Crisis:
    Metropolitan Andrey Sheptytsky and the Greek Catholic Church in Western
    Ukraine, 1923–1944." In Kevin P. Spicer and Rebecca Carter-Chand, eds.
    Religion, Ethnonationalism, and Antisemitism in the Era of the World Wars.
    Montreal: McGill-Queen's University Press, 2022; 274–304.
Carlson, John D. and Jonathan H. Ebel, eds. *From Jeremiad to Jihad: Religion,
    Violence and America*. Oakland: University of California Press, 2012.
Carter-Chand, Rebecca. "A Relationship of Pragmatism and Conviction: The
    International Salvation Army and the German Heilsarmee in the Nazi Era."
    Kirchliche Zeitgeschichte 33, no. 2 (2020): 323–35.
Cazorla-Sanchez, Antonio. "Beyond They Shall Not Pass: How the Experience of
    Violence Re-Shaped Political Values in Early Franco Spain." *Journal of
    Contemporary History* 40, no. 3 (2005): 503–20.
Celinscak, Mark. *Distance from the Belsen Heap: Allied Forces and the Liberation of a
    Nazi Concentration Camps*. Toronto, ON: University of Toronto Press, 2015.

Certeau, Michel de. *The Practice of Everyday Life*. Translated by Steven F. Rendall. Berkeley: University of California Press, 1984.

Chalmers, Jason. "Settled Memories on Stolen Land: Settler Mythology at Canada's National Holocaust Monument." *American Indian Quarterly* 43, no. 4 (2019): 379–407.

Chaney, Sandra. "Behind the Lines in the Ukraine and Caucasus, 1942–1943: The Wartime Diaries and Photos of Senior Staff Veterinarian, Dr. Eugen Kohler." Paper presented at the German Studies Association conference. Portland, OR, 2019.

Clark, Christopher. "Johannes Blaskowitz – Der Christliche General." In Ronald Smelser and Enrico Syring, eds, *Die Militärelite des Dritten Reichs*. Berlin: Ullstein, 1997; 28–50.

"Religion and Confessional Conflict." In James Retallack, ed. *Imperial Germany, 1871–1918*. Oxford: Oxford University Press, 2008; 83–105.

Cole, Tim and Simone Gigliotti. *Lessons and Legacies XIV: The Holocaust in the Twenty-First Century*. Evanston, IL: Northwestern University Press, 2020.

Conway, John S. *The Nazi Persecution of the Churches, 1933–1945*. New York: Basic, 1968.

"The Political Role of German Protestantism, 1870–1990." *Journal of Church and State* 34, no. 4 (1992): 819–42.

Coogan, Michael. *The Ten Commandments: A Short History of an Ancient Text*. New Haven, CT: Yale University Press, 2015.

Corum, James S. "Adenauer, Amt Blank, and the Founding of the Bundeswehr 1950–1956." In James S. Corum, ed. *Rearming Germany*. Leiden: Brill, 2011; 29–52.

Crane, Susan. "Choosing Not to Look: Representation, Repatriation, and Holocaust Atrocity Photography." *History and Theory* 47, no. 3 (2008): 309–30.

Crew, David F. "Benno Wundshammer: Photo-Journalism and German History, 1933–1987." Research project. www.visual-history.de/en/project/benno-wundshammer-photo-journalism-and-german-history-1933-1987/

Cucchiara, Martina. "The Bonds That Shame: Reconsidering the Foreign Exchange Trials against the Catholic Church in Nazi Germany, 1935/36." *European History Quarterly* 45, no. 4 (2015): 689–712.

Dahl, Hans Fredrik. *Quisling: A Study in Treachery*. Cambridge: Cambridge University Press, 1999.

Daigle, Michelle. "The Spectacle of Reconciliation: On (the) Unsettling Responsibilities to Indigenous Peoples in the Academy." *Environment and Planning, D: Society and Space* 37, no. 4 (2019): 703–21.

Dallin, Alexander. *German Rule in Russia: A Study of Occupation Policies*. Boulder, CO: Westview, 1981.

Dalven, Rae. *The Jews of Ioannina*. Philadelphia, PA: Cadmus, 1990.

Damman, Martin. *Soldier Studies: Cross-Dressing in der Wehrmacht*. Berlin: Hantje Cantz, 2018.

Davis, Belinda. "Europe Is a Peaceful Woman, America Is a War-Mongering Man? The 1980s Peace Movement in NATO-Allied Europe." In Maria Bühner and Maren Möhring, eds. *Europäische Geschlechtergeschichte in Quellen und Essays*. Wiesbaden: Franz Steiner, 2018; 97–110.

Debons, Delphine. "'All Things Are Possible for Him Who Believes' (Mark 9:23): The Regulation of Religious Life in Prisoner of War Camps in the Second World War." In Anne-Marie Pathé and Fabien Théofilakis, eds. *Wartime Captivity in the Twentieth Century: Archives, Stories, Memories*. Translated by Helen McPhail. New York: Berghahn, 2016; 54–64.

Desbois, Patrick. *The Holocaust by Bullets: A Priest's Journey to Uncover the Truth behind the Murder of 1.5 Million Jews*. New York: Palgrave Macmillan, 2008.

Deutsch, Harold C. *Hitler and His Generals: The Hidden Crisis, January–June 1938*. Minneapolis: University of Minnesota Press, 1974.

Didi-Huberman, Georges. *Images in Spite of All: Four Photographs from Auschwitz*. Translated by Shane B. Lillis. Chicago, IL: University of Chicago Press, 2008.

Dieckmann, Christoph. *Deutsche Besatzungspolitik in Litauen 1941–1944*. 2 vols. Göttingen: Wallstein, 2011.

Dordanas, Stratos N. "The Jewish Community of Thessaloniki and the Christian Collaborators: 'Those That Are Leaving and What They Are Leaving Behind'." In Giorgos Antoniou and A. Dirk Moses, eds. *The Holocaust in Greece*. Cambridge: Cambridge University Press, 2018; 208–27.

Dörfler-Dierken, Angelika. "The Changing Role of Protestant Military Chaplains in Germany: From Raising Military Morale to Praying for Peace." *Religion, State and Society* 39, no. 1 (2011): 79–91.

Dörner, Bernward. "'Der Krieg ist verloren!' 'Wehrkraftzersetzung' und Denunziation in der Truppe." In Norbert Haase and Gerhard Paul, eds. *Die anderen Soldaten: Wehrkraftzersetzung, Gehorsamsverweigerung und Fahnenflucht im Zweiten Weltkrieg*. Frankfurt am Main: Fischer, 1995; 105–22.

Dumitru, Diana. *The State, Antisemitism, and the Holocaust: Romania and the Soviet Union*. New York: Cambridge University Press, 2015.

Earl, Hilary. *The Nuremberg SS-Einsatzgruppen Trial, 1945–1958*. New York: Cambridge University Press, 2009.

Echternkamp, Jörg. "Der politische Offizier als normativer Typus." In Galili Shahar, ed. *Deutsche Offiziere: Militarismus und die Akteure der Gewalt*. Göttingen: Wallstein, 2016; 221–50.

Eismann, Gaël. "Le Militärbefehlshaber in Frankreich et la genèse de la 'solution finale' en France (1941–1942)." *Vingtième Siècle: Revue d'histoire* 132 (2016): 43–59.

Enstad, Johannes Due. "Prayers and Patriotism in Nazi-Occupied Russia: The Pskov Orthodox Mission and Religious Revival, 1941–1944." *Slavonic and East European Review* 94, no. 3 (2016): 468–96.

Soviet Russians under Nazi Occupation. Cambridge: Cambridge University Press, 2018.

Epstein, Barbara. *The Minsk Ghetto, 1941–1943: Jewish Resistance and Soviet Internationalism*. Berkeley: University of California Press, 2008.

Ericksen, Robert P. *Complicity in the Holocaust: Churches and Universities in Nazi Germany*. New York: Cambridge University Press, 2012.

Theologians under Hitler: Gerhard Kittel, Paul Althaus, and Emanuel Hirsch. New Haven, CT: Yale University Press, 1985.

Esherick, Joseph. *The Origins of the Boxer Uprising*. Los Angeles: University of California Press, 1987.

Exeler, Franziska. "What Did You Do during the War? Personal Responses to the Aftermath of Nazi Occupation." *Kritika: Explorations in Russian and Eurasian History* 17, no. 4 (2016): 805–35.

Faulkner, Lauren N. "Against Bolshevism: Georg Werthmann and the Role of Ideology in the Catholic Military Chaplaincy, 1939–1945." *Contemporary European History* 19, no. 1 (2010): 1–16.

Faulkner Rossi, Lauren. *Wehrmacht Priests: Catholicism and the Nazi War of Annihilation.* Cambridge, MA: Harvard University Press, 2015.

Feferman, Kiril. *The Holocaust in the Crimea and the Northern Caucasus.* Jerusalem: Yad Vashem Publications, 2016.

Fehrenbach, Heide and Davide Rodogno, eds. *Humanitarian Photography: A History.* New York: Cambridge University Press, 2015.

Fein, Helen. *Accounting for Genocide: Victims and Survivors of the Holocaust.* New York: Free Press, 1979.

Genocide: A Sociological Perspective. New York: Sage, 1993.

Fest, Joachim C. *Hitler.* Translated by Richard and Clara Winston. New York: Harcourt Brace Jovanovich, 1974.

Flaschka, Monika. *Race, Rape and Gender in Nazi-Occupied Territories.* PhD diss., Kent State University, 2009.

Fleming, Katherine. *Greece: A Jewish History.* Princeton, NJ: Princeton University Press, 2008.

Fontaine, Lorena Sekwan. "Redress for Linguicide: Residential Schools and Assimilation in Canada." *British Journal of Canadian Studies* 30, no. 2 (2017): 183–204.

Förster, Jürgen. "The Wehrmacht and the War of Extermination against the Soviet Union." *Yad Vashem Studies* 14 (1981): 7–34.

Friedlander, Henry. *The Origins of Nazi Genocide.* Chapel Hill: University of North Carolina Press, 1995.

Friedländer, Saul. *Nazi Germany and the Jews.* Vol. 1, *The Years of Persecution.* Vol. 2, *The Years of Extermination.* New York: HarperCollins, 1997 and 2007.

"Prologue." In Jonathan Petropoulos, Lynn Rapaport, and John K. Roth, eds. *Lessons and Legacies IX: Memory, History, and Responsibility: Reassessments of the Holocaust, Implications for the Future.* Evanston, IL: Northwestern University Press, 2010; 3–15.

"The Wehrmacht, German Society, and the Knowledge of the Mass Extermination of the Jews." In Omer Bartov, Atina Grossmann, and Mary Nolan, eds. *Crimes of War: Guilt and Denial in the Twentieth Century.* New York: New Press, 2002; 17–30.

Friedman, Philip. *This Was Oswiecim: The Story of a Murder Camp.* Translated by Joseph Leftwich. London: United Jewish Relief Appeal, 1946.

Fritsche, Maria. "Proving One's Manliness: Masculine Self-Perceptions of Austrian Deserters in the Second World War." *Gender and History* 24, no. 1 (2012): 35–55.

Fritz, Regina. "Inside the Ghetto: Everyday Life in Hungarian Ghettos." In Ferenc Laczó, ed. *The Holocaust in Hungary in Contexts: New Perspectives and Research Results.* Special issue. *Hungarian Historical Review* 4, no. 3 (2015): 606–40.

Fritz, Stephen G. *Endkampf: Soldiers, Civilians, and the Death of the Third Reich.* Lexington: University Press of Kentucky, 2004.

Frontsoldaten: The German Soldier in World War II. Lexington: University of Kentucky Press, 1995.

Fritzsche, Peter. *An Iron Wind: Europe under Hitler.* New York: Basic, 2016.

Frojimovics, Kinga and Éva Kovács. "Jews in a 'Judenrein' City: Hungarian Jewish Slave Laborers in Vienna (1944–1945)." In Ferenc Laczó, ed. *The Holocaust in Hungary in Contexts: New Perspectives and Research Results.* Special issue. *Hungarian Historical Review* 4, no. 3 (2015): 705–36.

Fujii, Lee Ann. *Show Time: The Power of Violent Display.* Ithaca, NY: Cornell University Press, 2021.

"'Talk of the Town': Explaining Pathways to Participation in Violent Display." *Journal of Peace Research* 54, no. 5 (Sept. 2017): 661–73.

Fulbrook, Mary. *A Small Town near Auschwitz: Ordinary Nazis and the Holocaust.* Oxford: Oxford University Press, 2012.

Gailus, Manfred. *Mir aber zerriss es das Herz: Der stille Widerstand der Elisabeth Schmitz.* Göttingen: Vandenhoeck & Ruprecht, 2010.

Protestantismus und Nationalsozialismus: Studien zur nationalsozialistischen Durchdringung des protestantischen Sozialmilieus in Berlin. Cologne: Böhlau, 2001.

Gailus, Manfred and Hartmut Lehmann, eds. *Protestantische Mentalitäten 1870–1970.* Göttingen: Vandenhoeck & Ruprecht, 2004.

Garbarini, Alexandra. *Numbered Days: Diaries and the Holocaust.* New Haven, CT: Yale University Press, 2006.

Garrard-Burnett, Virginia. *Terror in the Land of the Holy Spirit: Guatemala under General Efrain Rios Montt, 1982–1983.* Oxford: Oxford University Press, 2010.

Gatz, Erwin, ed. *Die Bischöfe der deutschsprachigen Länder 1875/1803 bis 1945: Ein biographisches Lexikon.* Berlin: Duncker & Humblot, 1983.

Gaydosh, Brenda L. *Bernhard Lichtenberg: Roman Catholic Priest and Martyr of the Nazi Regime.* Lanham, MD: Lexington Books, 2017.

Geheran, Michael. *Comrades Betrayed: Jewish World War I Veterans under Hitler.* Ithaca, NY: Cornell University Press, 2020.

Gerlach, Christian. *Extremely Violent Societies: Mass Violence in the Twentieth-Century World.* Cambridge: Cambridge University Press, 2010.

Kalkulierte Morde: Die deutsche Wirtschafts- und Vernichtungspolitik in Weißrussland 1941 bis 1944. Hamburg: Hamburger Edition, 1999.

"The Wannsee Conference, the Fate of German Jews, and Hitler's Decision in Principle to Exterminate All European Jews." *Journal of Modern History* 70, no. 4 (1998): 759–812.

Gerlach, Wolfgang. *And the Witnesses Were Silent: The Confessing Church and the Persecution of the Jews.* Translated by Victoria J. Barnett. Lincoln: University of Nebraska Press, 2000.

Gertjejanssen, Wendy Jo. *Victims, Heroes, Survivors: Sexual Violence on the Eastern Front during World War II.* PhD diss., University of Minnesota, 2004.

Geyer, Michael. "'There Is a Land Where Everything Is Pure: Its Name Is Land of Death': Some Observations on Catastrophic Nationalism." In Greg Eghigian and Matthew Paul Berg, eds. *Sacrifice and National Belonging in Twentieth-Century Germany.* College Station: Texas A&M University Press, 2002; 118–47.

Giles, Geoffrey J. "'Ich hab' Dich gern wie ein Mädchen': Homosexuality in Hitler's Wehrmacht." Paper presented at the German Studies Association meeting, Portland, OR, 2019.

Girard, René. *Violence and the Sacred*. Translated by Patrick Gregory. London: Athlone, 1988.

Goda, Norman J. W. "Black Marks: Hitler's Bribery of His Senior Officers during World War II." *Journal of Modern History* 79, no. 2 (2000): 413–52.

Goldberg, Amos. "The Victim's Voice and the Melodramatic Aesthetics in History." *History and Theory* 48, no. 3 (2009): 220–37.

Goltermann, Svenja. *The War in Their Minds: German Soldiers and Their Violent Pasts in West Germany*. Translated by Philip Schmitz. Ann Arbor: University of Michigan Press, 2020.

Grady, Tim. *The German Jewish Soldiers of the First World War in History and Memory*. Liverpool: Liverpool University Press, 2011.

Greble, Emily. *Sarajevo, 1941–1945: Muslims, Christians and Jews in Hitler's Europe*. Ithaca, NY: Cornell University Press, 2014.

Griech-Polelle, Beth A. *Bishop von Galen: German Catholicism and National Socialism*. New Haven, CT: Yale University Press, 2002.

"The Impact of the Spanish Civil War upon the Roman Catholic Clergy in Nazi Germany." Paper presented at the American Historical Association, Seattle, WA, 2005.

Grier, Howard D. *Hitler, Dönitz, and the Baltic Sea: The Third Reich's Last Hope, 1944–1945*. Annapolis, MD: Naval Institute Press, 2007.

"Hitler's Favorite General: Ferdinand Schörner." Unpublished Stukes Lecture, Erskine College, SC, March 22, 2021.

Grünzig, Matthias. *Für Deutschtum und Vaterland: Die Potsdamer Garnisonkirche im 20. Jahrhundert*. Berlin: Metropol, 2017.

Güsgen, Johannes. *Die katholische Militärseelsorge in Deutschland zwischen 1920 und 1945*. Cologne: Böhlau Verlag, 1989.

Haase, Norbert and Gerhard Paul, eds. *Die anderen Soldaten: Wehrkraftzersetzung, Gehorsamsverweigerung und Fahnenflucht im Zweiten Weltkrieg*. Frankfurt am Main: Fischer, 1995.

Hagemann, Karen. *Umkämpftes Gedächtnis: Die Antinapoleonischen Kriege in der deutschen Erinnerung*. Paderborn: Schöningh, 2019.

Hagemann, Karen and Stefanie Schüler-Springorum, eds. *Home/Front: The Military, War and Gender in Twentieth Century Germany*. Oxford: Berg, 2002.

Hájková, Anna, ed. *Sexuality, Holocaust, Stigma*. Special issue *German History* 39, no. 1 (2021).

Hamann, Brigitte. *Hitler's Vienna: A Dictator's Apprenticeship*. Translated by Thomas Thornton. New York: Oxford University Press, 1999.

Hamburg, Gary, Thomas Sanders, and Ernest Tucker, eds. *Russian–Muslim Confrontation in the Caucasus: Alternative Visions of the Conflict Between Imam Shamil and the Russians, 1830–1859*. London: Routledge Curzon, 2004.

Hammer, Karl. *Deutsche Kriegstheologie 1870–1918*. Munich: Kösel, 1971.

Hanebrink, Paul. *A Specter Haunting Europe: The Myth of Judeo-Bolshevism*. Cambridge, MA: Belknap, 2018.

Hanley, Boniface F. *The Last Human Face: Franz Stock: A Priest in Hitler's Army*. Self-published, 2010.

Hansen, Randall. *Disobeying Hitler: German Resistance after Operation Valkyrie.* Toronto, ON: Random House, 2014.

Harker, Ian. *Pearls before Swine: The Extraordinary Story of the Rev. Ernst Biberstein, Lutheran Pastor and Murder Squad Commander.* Canterbury: Holocaust Studies Centre, 2017.

Harrisville, David. "Unholy Crusaders: The Wehrmacht and the Re-Establishment of Soviet Churches during Operation Barbarossa." *Central European History* 52, no. 4 (2019): 620–49.

The Virtuous Wehrmacht: Crafting the Myth of the German Soldier on the Eastern Front, 1941–1944. Ithaca, NY: Cornell University Press, 2021.

"'We no Longer Pay Heed to Humanitarian Considerations': Narratives of Perpetration in the Wehrmacht, 1941–44." In Timothy Williams and Susanne Buckley-Zistel, eds. *Perpetrators and Perpetration of Mass Violence: Actions, Motivations and Dynamics.* New York: Routledge, 2018; 117–32.

Hartman, Saidiya. *Wayward Lives, Beautiful Experiments: Intimate Histories of Riotous Black Girls, Troublesome Women, and Queer Radicals.* New York: Norton, 2019.

Hartmann, Christian. *Unternehmen Barbarossa: Der deutsche Krieg im Osten 1941–1945.* Munich: Beck, 2011.

Hartmann, Christian, Johannes Hürter, Peter Lieb, and Dieter Pohl, eds. *Der deutsche Krieg im Osten 1941–1944: Facetten einer Grenzüberschreitung.* Berlin: De Gruyter, 2012.

Harvey, Elizabeth. *Women and the Nazi East: Agents and Witnesses of Germanization.* New Haven, CT: Yale University Press, 2003.

Harward, Grant T. *Romania's Holy War: Soldiers, Motivation, and the Holocaust.* Ithaca, NY: Cornell University Press, 2021.

Hassing, Per. "German Missionaries and the Maji Maji Rising." *African Historical Studies* 3, no. 2 (1970): 373–89.

Hassner, Ron E., ed. *Religion in the Military Worldwide.* Cambridge: Cambridge University Press, 2014.

Hastings, Derek. *Catholicism and the Roots of Nazism: Religious Identity and National Socialism.* Oxford: Oxford University Press, 2010.

Hayes, Peter, ed. *Lessons and Legacies: The Meaning of the Holocaust in a Changing World.* Evanston, IL: Northwestern University Press, 1991.

Headland, Ronald. *Messages of Murder: A Study of the Reports of the Einsatzgruppen of the Security Police and the Security Service, 1941–1943.* Cranbury, NJ: Fairleigh Dickinson University Press, 1992.

Heberer, Patricia L. *"Exitus heute in Hadamar": The Hadamar Facility and "Euthanasia" in Nazi Germany.* PhD diss., University of Maryland, 2001.

ed., *Children during the Holocaust.* Plymouth: Alta Mira, 2011.

Hébert, Valerie. "Befehlsempfänger und Helden oder Verschwörer und Verbrecher? Konzeptionen, Argumente und Probleme im OKW-Prozeß." In Kim Priemel and Alexa Stiller, eds. *NMT: Die Nürnberger Militärtribunale zwischen Geschichte, Gerechtigkeit und Rechtschöpfung.* Hamburg: Hamburger Edition, 2013; 255–87.

Hitler's Generals on Trial: The Last War Crimes Tribunal at Nuremberg. Lawrence: University Press of Kansas, 2010.

Heer, Hannes and Klaus Naumann, eds. *Verbrechen der Wehrmacht. Dimensionen des Vernichtungskrieges 1941–1944*. Hamburg: Institut für Sozialforschung der Hamburger Edition, 2002.
  Vernichtungskrieg: Verbrechen der Wehrmacht 1941–1944. Hamburg: Hamburger Edition, 1998.
  War of Extermination: The German Military in World War II. Translated by Roy Shelton. New York: Berghahn, 2000.
Hehl, Ulrich von. "Die Kirchen in der NS-Diktatur: Zwischen Anpassung, Selbstbehauptung und Widerstand." In Karl Dietrich Bracher et al., eds. *Deutschland, 1933–1945: Neue Studien zur nationalsozialistischen Herrschaft*. Düsseldorf: Droste, 1992.
Hehl, Ulrich von and Christoph Kösters. *Priester unter Hitlers Terror. Eine biographische und statistische Erhebung*. 4th ed. Paderborn: Kommission für Zeitgeschichte, 1998.
Heineman, Elizabeth D. *What Difference Does a Husband Make? Women and Marital Status in Nazi and Postwar Germany*. Berkeley: University of California Press, 2003.
Hellbeck, Jochen. "A 'Great Antibolshevik Show': Zhytomyr, August 7, 1941." Paper presented at Rutgers University, New Brunswick, NJ, Nov. 18, 2021.
  Stalingrad: The City That Defeated the Third Reich. Translated by Christopher Tauchen and Dominic Bonifiglio. New York: Public Affairs, 2015.
Henisch, Peter. *Negatives of My Father*. Translated by Anne Close Ulmer. Riverside, CA: Ariadne, 1990.
Herbert, Ulrich. "The German Military Command in Paris." In Ulrich Herbert, ed. *National Socialist Extermination Policies: Contemporary German Perspectives and Controversies*. New York: Berghahn, 2000; 128–62.
Hering, Rainer. *Die Theologinnen: Sophie Kunert, Margarete Braun, Margarete Schuster*. Hamburg: Verein für Hamburgische Geschichte, 1997.
Hermle, Siegfried. *Handbuch der deutschen evangelischen Kirchen 1918 bis 1949*. Göttingen: Vandenhoeck & Ruprecht, 2017.
Herzog, Dagmar. "Pleasure and Evil: Christianity and the Sexualization of Holocaust Memory." In Jonathan Petropoulos and John K. Roth, eds. *The Gray Zone*. New York: Berghahn, 2005; 147–64.
  Sex after Fascism: Memory and Morality in Twentieth-Century Germany. Princeton, NJ: Princeton University Press, 2005.
Heschel, Susannah. *The Aryan Jesus: Christian Theologians and the Bible in Nazi Germany*. Princeton, NJ: Princeton University Press, 2008.
Hierold, Alfred. "Die rechtlichen Strukturen der Militärseelsorge im Deutschen Reich und in der Bundesrepublik Deutschland: Aufgaben, Chancen und Gefahren." In Hans Jürgen Brandt, ed. *und auch Soldaten fragten: Zur Aufgabe und Problematik der Militärseelsorge in drei Generationen*. Paderborn: Bonifatius, 1992; 39–53.
Hilberg, Raul. "The Development of Holocaust Research – A Personal Overview." In David Bankier and Dan Michman, eds. *Holocaust Historiography in Context*. New York: Berghahn and Yad Vashem, 2008; 25–36.
  Sources of Holocaust Research: An Analysis. Chicago, IL: Ivan R. Dee, 2001.
Himka, John-Paul. "Christianity and Radical Nationalism: Metropolitan Andrei Sheptytsky and the Bandera Movement." In Catherine Wanner, ed. *State*

Secularism and Lived Religion in Soviet Russia and Ukraine. Washington, DC: Woodrow Wilson Center Press, 2012; 93–116.

"The Lviv Pogrom of 1941: The Germans, Ukrainian Nationalists, and the Carnival Crowd." *Canadian Slavonic Papers* 53, no. 2–4 (2011): 209–43.

"Metropolitan Andrei Sheptytsky and the Holocaust." *Polin: Studies in Polish Jewry* 26 (2013): 337–60.

Hoare, Marko Attila. *The Bosnian Muslims in the Second World War.* Oxford: Oxford University Press, 2014.

Hockenos, Matthew D. *Church Divided: German Protestants Confront the Nazi Past.* Bloomington: Indiana University Press, 2004.

"The German Protestant Church and Its *Judenmission*, 1945–1950." In Kevin P. Spicer, ed. *Antisemitism, Christian Ambivalence, and the Holocaust.* Bloomington: Indiana University Press, 2007; 173–200.

Then They Came for Me: Martin Niemöller, the Pastor Who Defied the Nazis. New York: Basic Books, 2018.

Hockerts, Hans Günter. *Die Sittlichkeitsprozesse gegen katholische Ordensangehörige und Priester 1936/1937.* Mainz: Matthias Grünewald, 1971.

Hockerts, Hans Günter and Friedrich Wilhelm Graf, eds. *Distanz und Nähe zugleich? Die christlichen Kirchen im "Dritten Reich."* Munich: NS-Dokumentationszentrum München, 2017.

Hoenicke Moore, Michaela. *Know Your Enemy: The American Debate on Nazism, 1933–1945.* Cambridge: Cambridge University Press, 2010.

Hoffmann, Peter. *Stauffenberg: A Family History, 1905–1944.* Montreal: McGill-Queen's University Press, 2003.

Holler, Martin. "'Like Jews?' The Nazi Persecution and Extermination of Soviet Roma under the German Military Administration: A New Interpretation Based on Soviet Sources." *Dapim: Studies on the Holocaust* 24, no. 1 (2010): 137–76.

Hoover, Arlie J. *The Gospel of Nationalism: German Patriotic Preaching from Napoleon to Versailles.* Wiesbaden: F. Steiner, 1986.

Horne, John and Alan Kramer, *German Atrocities, 1914: A History of Denial.* New Haven, CT: Yale University Press, 2001.

Horowitz, Sara R. "Gender, Genocide, and Jewish Memory." *Prooftexts* 20, nos. 1 and 2 (2000): 158–90.

Hosfeld, Rolf and Christin Pschichholz. *Das Deutsche Reich und der Völkermord an den Armeniern.* Göttingen: Wallstein, 2017.

Houlihan, Patrick. *Catholicism and the Great War: Religion and Everyday Life in Germany and Austria-Hungary, 1914–1922.* Cambridge: Cambridge University Press, 2015.

"Imperial Frameworks of Religion: Catholic Military Chaplains of Germany and Austria-Hungary in the 1st World War." *First World War Studies* 3, no. 2 (2012): 165–82.

Hull, Isabel V. *Absolute Destruction: Military Culture and the Practices of War in Imperial Germany.* Ithaca, NY: Cornell University Press, 2005.

Hürter, Johannes. "Die Wehrmacht vor Leningrad: Krieg und Besatzungspolitik der 18. Armee im Herbst und Winter 1941/42." *Vierteljahrshefte für Zeitgeschichte* 49, no. 3 (2001): 377–440.

Hushion, Stacy. *Intimate Encounters and the Politics of German Occupation in Belgium, 1940–1945*. PhD diss., University of Toronto, 2014.

Ingrao, Christian. *The SS Dirlewanger Brigade: The History of the Black Hunters*. Translated by Phoebe Green. Oak Park, IL: Skyhorse, 2013.

Jacobs, Stephen L., ed. *Confronting Genocide: Judaism, Christianity, Islam*. Lanham, MD: Lexington Books, 2009.

Jantzen, Kyle. *Faith and Fatherland: Parish Politics in Hitler's Germany*. Minneapolis, MN: Fortress, 2008.

Jantzen, Mark and John D. Thiesen, eds. *European Mennonites and the Holocaust*. Toronto, ON: University of Toronto Press, 2021.

Janz, Nina. "From Battlegrounds to Burial Grounds: The Cemetery Landscapes of the German Army during the Second World War." In Sarah K. Danielsson and Frank Jacob, eds. *War and Geography: The Spatiality of Organized Mass Violence*. Paderborn: Schöningh, 2017; 147–62.

Jaskot, Paul B. "'Realism'? The Place of Images in Holocaust Studies." In Sara R. Horowitz, ed. *Lessons and Legacies X: Back to the Sources*. Evanston, IL: Northwestern University Press, 2012; 68–88.

Jockusch, Laura. *Collect and Record! Jewish Holocaust Documentation in Early Postwar Europe*. New York: Oxford University Press, 2012.

Johnson, Walter. "On Agency." *Journal of Social History* 37, no. 1 (special issue, 2003): 113–24.

Judt, Tony. *Postwar: A History of Europe since 1945*. New York: Penguin, 2005.

Kaplan, Marion. *Between Dignity and Despair: Jewish Life in Nazi Germany*. New York: Oxford University Press, 1998.

Katz, Steven T. "Murder of Jewish Children." In *Holocaust Studies: Critical Reflections*. New York: Routledge, 2019.

Kay, Alex J. *The Making of an SS Killer: The Life of Colonel Alfred Filbert, 1905–1990*. New York: Cambridge University Press, 2016.

Kehoe, Thomas J. "The Reich Military Court and Its Values: Wehrmacht Treatment of Jehovah's Witness Conscientious Objectors." *Holocaust and Genocide Studies* 33, no. 3 (2019): 351–71.

Kellenbach, Katharina von. *The Mark of Cain: Guilt and Denial in the Post-War Lives of Nazi Perpetrators*. Oxford: Oxford University Press, 2013.

Keren, Michael and Shlomit Keren. "Chaplain with a Star of David: Reverend Leib Isaac Falk and the Jewish Legions." *Israel Affairs* 14, no. 2 (2008): 184–201.

Kershaw, Ian. *Hitler, 1889–1936: Hubris*. London: Penguin, 1998.

"'Working towards the Führer': Reflections on the Nature of the Hitler Dictatorship." *Contemporary European History* 2, no. 2 (1993): 103–18.

Khromeychuk, Olesya. *"Undetermined" Ukrainians' Post-War Narratives of the Waffen SS "Galicia" Division*. Oxford: Peter Lang, 2013.

Kirschenbaum, Lisa A. *The Legacy of the Siege of Leningrad 1941–1945: Myths, Memories, and Monuments*. Cambridge: Cambridge University Press, 2006.

Kirschner, Albrecht. "Wehrkraftzersetzung." In Wolfgang Form, Wolfgang Neugebauer, and Theo Schiller, eds. *NS-Justiz und politische Verfolgung in Österreich 1938–1945: Analysen zu den Verfahren vor dem Volksgerichtshof und dem Oberlandesgericht Wien*. Munich: DeGruyter, 2006; 405–748.

Kissi, Edward. *Africans and the Holocaust: Perceptions and Responses of Colonized and Sovereign Peoples*. London: Routledge, 2020.

Kitschke, Andreas. *Die Potsdamer Garnisonskirche: "nec soli cedit."* Potsdam: Potsdamer Verlag, 1991.

Kittermann, David. "Those Who Said, 'No!': Germans Who Refused to Execute Civilians during World War II." *German Studies Review* 11, no. 2 (1988): 241–54.

Klee, Ernst, Willi Dressen, and Volker Riess, eds. *"The Good Old Days": The Holocaust as Seen by Its Perpetrators and Bystanders*. Translated by Deborah Burnstone. Old Saybrook, CT: Konecky & Konecky, 1991.

Knittel, Susanne C. "Autobiography, Moral Witnessing, and the Disturbing Memory of Nazi Euthanasia." In Stephanie Bird, Mary Fulbrook, Julia Wagner, and Christiane Wienand, eds. *Reverberations of Nazi Violence in Germany and Beyond: Disturbing Pasts*. London: Bloomsbury Academic, 2016; 65–81.

Knopp, Guido. *Weltenbrand: Die Kriege der Deutschen im 20. Jahrhundert*. Zurich: Pendo, 2012.

Koonz, Claudia. *Mothers in the Fatherland: Women, the Family, and Nazi Politics*. New York: St. Martin's, 1987.

The Nazi Conscience. Cambridge, MA: Harvard University Press, 2005.

Kopstein, Jeffrey S. and Jason Wittenberg. *Intimate Violence: Anti-Jewish Pogroms on the Eve of the Holocaust*. Ithaca, NY: Cornell University Press, 2018.

Krakowski, Shmuel. "The Fate of Jewish Prisoners of War in the September 1939 Campaign." *Yad Vashem Studies* 12 (1977): 297–333.

Krausnick, Helmut and Hans-Heinrich Wilhelm. *Die Truppe des Weltanschauungskrieges: Die Einsatzgruppen der Sicherheitspolizei und des SD 1938–42*. Stuttgart: DVA, 1981.

Krech, Volkhard. "Secularisation, Re-Enchantment, or Something In-Between? Methodical Considerations and Empirical Observations Concerning a Controversial Historical Idea." In Marion Eggert and Lucian Hoelscher, eds. *Religion and Secularity*. Vol. 4. Leiden: Brill, 2013; 77–108.

Krimmer, Elisabeth. *German Women's Life Writing and the Holocaust: Complicity and Gender in the Second World War*. New York: Cambridge University Press, 2018.

Krondorfer, Bjorn. *Male Confessions: Intimate Revelations and the Religious Imagination*. Stanford, CA: Stanford University Press, 2010.

"A Perpetrator's Confession: Gender and Religion in Oswald Pohl's Conversion Narrative." *Journal of Men, Masculinities and Spirituality* 2, no. 2 (2008): 62–81.

Krumeich, Gerd. "'Gott mit uns'? Der Erste Weltkrieg als Religionskrieg." In Gerd Krumeich and Hartmut Lehmann, eds. *"Gott mit Uns": Nation, Religion und Gewalt im 19. und frühen 20. Jahrhundert*. Göttingen: Vandenhoeck & Ruprecht, 2000; 273–84.

Kucich, John. *Imperial Masochism: British Fiction, Fantasy, and Social Class*. Princeton, NJ: Princeton University Press, 2006.

Kühne, Thomas. *The Rise and Fall of Comradeship: Hitler's Soldiers, Male Bonding, and Mass Violence in the Twentieth Century*. Cambridge: Cambridge University Press, 2017.

ed. "Masculinity and the Third Reich." *Central European History* 51, no. 3 (2018). With contributions by Thomas Kühne, Jason Crouthamel, Patrick Farges,

Michael J. Geheran, Edward B. Westermann, Elissa Mailänder, and Christopher Dillon.

Kuss, Susanne. *German Colonial Wars and the Context of Military Violence.* Translated by Andrew Smith. Cambridge, MA: Harvard University Press, 2017.

Laczó, Ferenc, ed. *The Holocaust in Hungary in Contexts: New Perspectives and Research Results.* Special issue. *Hungarian Historical Review* 4, no. 3 (2015).

Langer, Lawrence. "Introduction." In Piotr Rawicz, *Blood from the Sky.* Translated by Peter Wiles. New Haven, CT: Yale University Press, 2003; v–xvii.

Laputska, Veranika. "World War II Crimes in Belarusian Internet Mass-Media: The Cases of Anthony Sawoniuk and Vladimir Katriuk." *Journal of Belarusian Studies* 8, no. 1 (2016): 50–77.

Lehmann, Hartmut. "'God Our Old Ally': The Chosen People Theme in Late Nineteenth- and Early Twentieth-Century German Nationalism." In William R. Hutchison and Hartmut Lehmann, eds. *Many Are Chosen: Divine Election and Western Nationalism.* Minneapolis, MN: Fortress, 1994; 85–114.

"In the Service of Two Kings: Protestant Prussian Military Chaplains, 1713–1918." In Doris L. Bergen, ed. *The Sword of the Lord: Military Chaplains from the First to the Twenty-First Century.* Notre Dame, IN: University of Notre Dame Press, 2004; 125–40.

Lehmhöfer, Lutz. "Gegen den gottlosen Bolschewismus: Zur Stellung der Kirchen zum Krieg gegen die Sowjetunion." In Gerd R. Ueberschär and Wolfram Wette, eds. *Der deutsche Überfall auf die Sowjetunon.* Frankfurt am Main: Fischer, 1991; 131–39.

Leichsenring, Jana. *Die katholische Kirche und "ihre Juden": Das "Hilfswerk beim Bischöflichen Ordinariat Berlin" 1938–1945.* Berlin: Metropol, 2007.

Lepp, Claudia and Kurt Nowak, eds. *Evangelische Kirche im geteilten Deutschland (1945–1989/90).* Göttingen: Vandenhoeck & Ruprecht, 2001.

Leugers, Antonia. *Jesuiten in Hitlers Wehrmacht. Kriegslegitimation und Kriegserfahrung.* Paderborn: Schöningh, 2009.

Lindemann, Gerhard. "The Fate of Christian Pastors of Jewish Descent in Hanover, 1925–1947." *Kirchliche Zeitgeschichte* 10, no. 2 (1997): 359–63.

"Typisch Jüdisch": Die Stellung der Ev.-luth. Landeskirche Hannovers zu Antijudaismus, Judenfeindschaft und Antisemitismus 1919–1949. Berlin: Duncker & Humblot, 1998.

Littell, Franklin Hamlin. *The German Phoenix: Men and Movements in the Church in Germany.* New York: Doubleday, 1960.

Locke, Hubert. *Learning from History: A Black Christian's Perspective on the Holocaust.* Westport, CT: Greenwood, 2000.

Loeffel, Robert. *Family Punishment in Nazi Germany: Sippenhaft, Terror and Myth.* New York: Palgrave Macmillan, 2012.

Löffler, Jürgen. *Walther von Brauchitsch (1881–1948): Eine politische Biographie.* Frankfurt am Main: Peter Lang, 2001.

Long, Timothy. *Christianity and Genocide in Rwanda.* New York: Cambridge University Press, 2010.

Loveland, Ann. *American Evangelicals and the U.S. Military, 1942–1993.* Baton Rouge: Louisiana State University Press, 1997.

Lower, Wendy. "Anti-Jewish Violence in Western Ukraine, Summer 1941." In *The Holocaust in Ukraine: New Sources and Perspectives. Conference Presentations.* Washington, DC: Center for Advanced Holocaust Studies, 2013.
  Nazi Empire-Building and the Holocaust in Ukraine. Chapel Hill: University of North Carolina Press, 2005.

Lubbers, Franz. "Die Neuordnung der Militärseelsorge: Ein Rückblick aus staatlicher Sicht." In Katholisches Militärbischofsamt, ed. *Katholische Militärseelsorge in der Bundewehr: Ein Neubeginn (1951–1957).* Cologne: J. P. Bachem, 1986; 13–21.

Lüdtke, Alf. "'Coming to Terms with the Past': Illusions of Remembering, Ways of Forgetting the Nazi Past in West Germany." *Journal of Modern History* 65, no. 3 (1993): 542–72.

Maddox, Steven. *Saving Stalin's Imperial City: Historic Preservation in Leningrad, 1930–1950.* Bloomington: Indiana University Press, 2014.

Madigan, Kevin. "Two Popes, One Holocaust." *Commentary* 130, no. 5 (2010): 27–32.

Magocsi, Paul Robert. *A History of Ukraine: The Land and Its Peoples.* 2nd ed. Toronto: University of Toronto Press, 2010.

Mailänder, Elissa. "Making Sense of a Rape Photo: Sexual Violence as Social Performance on the Eastern Front, 1939–1944." *Journal of the History of Sexuality* 26, no. 3 (2017): 489–520.

Majstorović, Vojin. "Red Army Troops Encounter the Holocaust: Transnistria, Moldavia, Romania, Bulgaria, Yugoslavia, Hungary, and Austria, 1944–1945." *Holocaust and Genocide Studies* 32, no. 2 (2018): 249–71.

Manoschek, Walter. *"Serbien ist Judenfrei!" Militärische Besatzungspolitik und Judenvernichtung in Serbien 1941/42.* Munich: Oldenbourg, 1993.

Marhoefer, Laurie. "Lesbianism, Transvestitism, and the Nazi State: A Microhistory of a Gestapo Investigation, 1939–1943." *American Historical Review* 121, no. 4 (2016): 1167–95.

Marks, Sally. "Mistakes and Myths: The Allies, Germany, and the Versailles Treaty, 1918–1921." *Journal of Modern History* 85, no. 3 (2013): 632–59.

Marples, David R. "History, Memory, and the Second World War in Belarus." *Australian Journal of Politics and History* 58, no. 3 (2012): 513–23.

Marschke, Benjamin. *Absolutely Pietist: Patronage, Factionalism, and State-Building in the Early Eighteenth-Century Prussian Army Chaplaincy.* Halle: Verlag der Franckeschen Stiftungen, 2005.

Marx, Karl. *The Eighteenth Brumaire of Louis Bonaparte.* New York: International Publishers, 1963.

Masters, Ryan. *"The People Who Make Our Heads Spin": White Violence in German East Africa.* PhD diss., University of Toronto, 2019.

Matthäus, Jürgen, Jochen Böhler, and Klaus-Michael Mallmann. *War, Pacification, and Mass Murder, 1939: The Einsatzgruppen in Poland.* Lanham, MD: Rowman and Littlefield, 2014.

May, Georg. *Interkonfessionalismus in der deutschen Militärseelsorge von 1933–1945.* Amsterdam: Grüner, 1978.

Mazower, Mark. *Inside Hitler's Greece: The Story of Greek Jews during the Second World War.* New Haven, CT: Yale University Press, 1993.
  "Militärische Gewalt und nationalsozialistische Werte: Die Wehrmacht in Griechenland 1941 bis 1944." In Hannes Heer and Klaus Naumann, eds.,

Vernichtungskrieg: Verbrechen der Wehrmacht, 1941–1944. Hamburg: Hamburger Edition HIS, 1995; 157–90.

"Military Violence and National Socialist Values: The *Wehrmacht* in Greece 1941–1944." *Past & Present* 134 (Feb. 1992): 129–58.

Megargee, Geoffrey P. *Inside Hitler's High Command.* Lawrence: University Press of Kansas, 2000.

War of Annihilation: Combat and Genocide on the Eastern Front, 1941. Lanham, MD: Rowman and Littlefield, 2006.

Meinen, Insa. *Wehrmacht und Prostitution im besetzten Frankreich.* Bremen: Edition Temmen, 2002.

Menkis, Richard. "'But You Can't See the Fear that People Lived Through': Canadian Jewish Chaplains and the Canadian Encounter with Dutch Survivors, 1944–45." *American Jewish Archives Journal* 60, no. 1–2 (2008): 24–50.

Merridale, Catherine. *Ivan's War: Life and Death in the Red Army, 1939–1945.* London: Faber and Faber, 2005.

Messerschmidt, Manfred. "Aspekte der Militärseelsorgepolitik in nationalsozialistischer Zeit." *Militärgeschichtliche Mitteilungen* 1 (1968): 63–106.

"Kriegsdienstverweigerer und Deserteure des Zweiten Weltkriegs: Die Osnabrücker Friedensgespräche, 1996." *Osnabrücker Jahrbuch Frieden und Wissenschaft* 4 (1997): 167–71.

Die Wehrmachtjustiz 1933–1945. Paderborn: Ferdinand Schöningh, 2005.

"Zur Militärseelsorgepolitik im Zweiten Weltkrieg." *Militärgeschichtliche Mitteilungen* 1 (1969): 37–85.

Messerschmidt, Manfred and Fritz Wüllner. *Die Wehrmachtjustiz im Dienste des Nationalsozialismus. Zerstörung einer Legende.* Baden-Baden: Nomos, 1987.

Meyer, Beate. "'Christliche Nichtarier'. Getaufte 'Juden' im Nationalsozialismus zwischen der Hoffnung auf Schutz und dem Stigma des Opportunismus." In Regina Laudage-Kleeberg and Hannes Sulzenbacher, eds. *Treten Sie ein! Treten Sie aus! Warum Menschen ihre Religion wechseln.* Berlin: Parthas, 2012; 218–28.

Missalla, Heinrich. *Für Gott, Führer und Vaterland: Die Verstrickung der katholischen Seelsorge in Hitlers Krieg.* Munich: Kösel, 1999.

Wie der Krieg zur Schule Gottes wurde: Hitlers Feldbischof Rarkowski. Eine notwendige Erinnerung. Oberursel: Publik-Forum, 1997.

Młynarz, Michał. *The Socio-Cultural Impact of the Post-World War II Mass Population Movements on Urban Space and Identity in the Polish Borderlands: A Comparative Analysis of Jelenia Góra and Drohobych.* PhD diss., University of Toronto, in preparation.

Mommsen, Wolfgang J. "Die nationalgeschichtliche Umdeutung der christlichen Botschaft im Ersten Weltkrieg." In Gerd Krumeich and Hartmut Lehmann, eds. *"Gott mit Uns": Nation, Religion und Gewalt im 19. und frühen 20. Jahrhundert.* Göttingen: Vandenhoeck & Ruprecht, 2000; 249–62.

Montague, Patrick. *Chełmno: The History of Hitler's First Death Camp.* London: Bloomsbury, 2020.

Moore, Mari Jo., ed. *Genocide of the Mind: New Native American Writing.* New York: Bold Type Books, 2003.

Moscovitz, Emmanuelle. "The Aumônerie générale des israélites de France and the preservation of funeral traditions in internment camps, 1940–1944." *Revue d'histoire de la Shoah* 215, no. 1 (2022): 131–49.

Mosse, George. *The Image of Man: The Creation of Modern Masculinity*. New York: Oxford University Press, 1996.

The Nationalization of the Masses: Political Symbolism and Mass Movements in Germany from the Napoleonic Wars through the Third Reich. New York: H. Fertig, 1975.

Motadel, David. *Islam and Nazi Germany's War*. Cambridge, MA: Harvard University Press, 2014.

Mühlhäuser, Regina. *Eroberungen: Sexuelle Gewalttaten und intime Beziehungen deutscher Soldaten in der Sowjetunion 1941–1945*. Hamburg: Hamburger Edition, 2010.

"The Historicity of Denial: Sexual Violence against Jewish Women during the War of Annihilation, 1941–1945." In Hilary Earl and Karl Schleunes, eds. *Lessons and Legacies XI*. Evanston, IL: Northwestern University Press, 2014; 31–58.

"Reframing Sexual Violence as a Weapon and Strategy of War: The Case of the German Wehrmacht during the War and Genocide in the Soviet Union, 1941–1944." *Journal of the History of Sexuality* 26, no. 3 (2017): 366–401.

Mukhopadhyaya, Ranjana. "Buddhism and Ethno-Nationalism of Japan during the Second World War." Paper presented at symposium on Religion and Ethno-Nationalism in the Era of the Two World Wars, University of Toronto, May 2017.

Murphy, Andrew R., ed. *The Blackwell Companion to Religion and Violence*. Malden, MA: Wiley-Blackwell, 2011.

Neumaier, Christoph. "The Escalation of German Reprisal Policies in Occupied France." *Journal of Contemporary History* 41, no. 1 (2006): 113–31.

Newton, Melanie J. "'The Race Leapt at Sauteurs': Genocide, Narrative, and Indigenous Exile in the Caribbean Archipelago." *Caribbean Quarterly* 60, no. 2 (2014): 5–28.

Nunpa, Chris Mato. "Dakota Commemorative March: Thoughts and Reactions." *American Indian Quarterly* 28, no. 1–2 (2004): 216–37.

"A Sweet-Smelling Sacrifice: Genocide, the Bible, and the Indigenous Peoples of the United States, Selected Examples." In Steven Leonard Jacobs, ed., *Confronting Genocide: Judaism, Christianity, Islam*. Lanham, MD: Lexington, 2009; 47–63.

Ofer, Dalia. "Everyday Life of Jews under Nazi Occupation: Methodological Issues." *Holocaust and Genocide Studies* 9, no. 1 (1995): 42–69.

"Her View through My Lens: Cecilia Slepak Studies Women in the Warsaw Ghetto." In Judith Tydor Baumel-Schwartz and Tova Cohen, eds. *Gender, Place, and Memory in the Modern Jewish Experience: Re-placing Ourselves*. London: Valentine Mitchell, 2003; 29–50.

"The Holocaust in Transnistria: A Special Case of Genocide." In Lucjan Dobroszycki and Jeffrey S. Gurock, eds. *The Holocaust in the Soviet Union: Studies and Sources on the Destruction of the Jews in the Nazi-Occupied Territories of the USSR, 1941–1945*. Armonk, NY: M. E. Sharpe, 1993; 133–54.

Oldenburg, Manfred. *Ideologie und militärisches Kalkül: Die Besatzungspolitik der Wehrmacht in der Sowjetunion 1942*. Cologne: Böhlau, 2004.

Otto, Uli and Eginhard König. *"Ich hatt' einen Kameraden": Militär und Kriege in historisch-politischen Liedern in der Jahren von 1740 bis 1914.* Mainz: Conbrio, 1999.

Overmans, Rüdiger. "German Treatment of Jewish Prisoners of War in the Second World War." In Anne-Marie Pathé and Fabien Théofilakis, eds. *Wartime Captivity in the Twentieth Century: Archives, Stories, Memories.* Translated by Helen McPhail. New York: Berghahn, 2016; 45–53.

Paul, Christa. *Zwangsprostitution: Staatlich errichtete Bordelle im Nationalsozialismus.* Berlin: Hentrich, 1994.

Pauli, Frank. *Wehrmachtsoffiziere in der Bundeswehr. Das kriegsgediente Offizierkorps der Bundeswehr und die Innerer Führung 1955 bis 1970.* Paderborn: Ferdinand Schöningh, 2010.

Paulovicova, Nina. *Rescue of Jews in the Slovak State (1939–1945).* PhD diss. University of Alberta, 2012.

Penslar, Derek J. *Jews and the Military: A History.* Princeton, NJ: Princeton University Press, 2013.

Penter, Tanja. "Local Collaborators on Trial: Soviet War Crimes Trials under Stalin." *Cahiers du monde russe* 49, no. 2–3 (2008): 341–64.

Penter, Tanja and Dmitrii Titarenko. "Local Memory on War, German Occupation and Postwar Years." *Cahiers du monde russe* 52 (2011): 441–74.

Peri, Alexis. *The War Within: Diaries from the Siege of Leningrad.* Cambridge, MA: Harvard University Press, 2020.

Petö, Andrea. "Death and the Picture: Representations of War Criminals and Construction of a Divided Memory about World War II in Hungary." In Andrea Petö and Klaartje Schrijvers, eds. *Faces of Death: Visualizing History.* Pisa: Plus-Pisa University Press, 2009; 39–56.

Phayer, Michael. *The Catholic Church and the Holocaust, 1930–1965.* Bloomington: Indiana University Press, 2000.

Planert, Ute. *Der Mythos vom Befreiungskrieg: Frankreichs Kriege und der deutsche Süden: Alltag – Wahrnehmung – Deutung 1792–1842.* Paderborn: Schöningh, 2007.

Pohl, Dieter. *Nationalsozialistische Judenverfolgung in Ostgalizien 1941–1944.* Munich: Oldenbourg, 1996.

Poliakov, Léon. *Harvest of Hate: The Nazi Program for the Destruction of the Jews of Europe.* Rev. ed. New York: Holocaust Library, 1979.

Popa, Ion. "The 7th Roşiori (Cavalry) Regiment and the Holocaust in Romania and the Soviet Union." *Dapim: Studies on the Holocaust* 32, no. 1 (2018): 38–56.

——— "Sanctuary from the Holocaust? Roman Catholic Conversion of Jews in Bucharest, Romania, 1942." *Holocaust and Genocide Studies* 29, no. 1 (2015): 39–56.

Pöpping, Dagmar. "'Allen alles sein': Deutsche Kriegspfarrer an der Ostfront 1941–1945." In Konstantin Lindner, Ulrich Riegel, and Andreas Hoffmann, eds. *Alltagsgeschichte in Religionsunterricht: Kirchengeschichtliche Studien und religionsdidaktische Perspektiven.* Stuttgart: Kohlhammer, 2013; 173–86.

——— *Kriegspfarrer an der Ostfront: Evangelische und katholische Wehrmachtseelsorge im Vernichtungskrieg 1941–1945.* Göttingen: Vandenhoeck & Ruprecht, 2017.

——— "Der schreckliche Gott des Hermann Wolfgang Beyer: Sinnstiftungsversuche eines Kirchenhistorikers zwischen Katheder und Massengrab." In Manfred Gailus and

Clemens Vollnhals, eds. *Für ein artgemäßes Christentum der Tat. Völkische Theologen im Dritten Reich*. Göttingen: Vandenhoeck & Ruprecht, 2016; 261–78.

Pomiecko, Aleksandra. "'It's never too late to fight for one's family and nation': Attempts at 'Belarusifying' Soldiers in German-sponsored Armed Formations 1941–1944." *Journal of Slavic Military Studies* 33, no. 2 (2020): 259–76.

Pressel, Wilhelm. *Die Kriegspredigt 1914–18 in der Evangelischen Kirche Deutschlands*. Göttingen: Vandenhoeck & Ruprecht, 1967.

Preston, Paul. *The Spanish Holocaust: Inquisition and Extermination in Twentieth-Century Spain*. London: HarperCollins, 2012.

Probst, Christopher J. *Demonizing the Jews: Luther and the Protestant Church in Nazi Germany*. Bloomington: Indiana University Press, 2012.

Prusin, Alexander Victor. "'Fascist Criminals to the Gallows!' The Holocaust and Soviet War Crimes Trials, December 1945–February 1946." *Holocaust and Genocide Studies* 17, no. 1 (2003): 1–30.

Quinnett, Robert L. "The German Army Confronts the NSFO." *Journal of Contemporary History* 13, no. 1 (1978): 53–64.

Raguer, Hilary. *Gunpowder and Incense: The Catholic Church and the Spanish Civil War*. Translated by Gerald Howson. London: Routledge, 2007.

Ramm, Hans-Joachim. *Mich trägt mein Glaube. Friedrich von Rabenau. General und Christ im Widerstand. Tagebuch einer Gestapohaft*. Saarbrücken: Fromm, 2011.

Reese, Günter. "Seelsorgerliche Bedenken gegen eine bedenkliche Seelsorge." *Junge Kirche* 7/8 (1982): 351–58.

Rempel, Gerhard. "Mennonites and the Holocaust: From Collaboration to Perpetration." *Mennonite Quarterly Review* 84, no. 4 (2010): 507–49.

Retallack, James. *The German Right, 1860–1920: Political Limits of the Authoritarian Imagination*. Toronto: University of Toronto Press, 2006.

Rhodes, Richard. *Masters of Death: The SS-Einsatzgruppen and the Invention of the Holocaust*. New York: Knopf, 2002.

Rigg, Bryan Mark. *Hitler's Jewish Soldiers: The Untold Story of Nazi Racial Laws and Men of Jewish Descent in the German Military*. Lawrence: University Press of Kansas, 2002.

Ringelblum, Emanuel. *Polish–Jewish Relations during the Second World War*. Translated by Dafna Allon et al. Evanston, IL: Northwestern University Press, 1992.

Rock, Stella, ed. *The Changing Nature of Military Chaplaincy*. Special issue. *Religion, State and Society* 39, no. 1 (2011).

Röger, Maren. *Kriegsbeziehungen. Intimität, Gewalt und Prostitution im besetzten Polen 1939 bis 1945*. Frankfurt am Main: Fischer, 2015.

Rossino, Alexander B. *Hitler Strikes Poland: Blitzkrieg, Ideology, and Atrocity*. Lawrence: University Press of Kansas, 2003.

Röw, Martin. *Militärseelsorge unter dem Hakenkreuz: Die katholische Feldpastoral 1939–1945*. Paderborn: Ferdinand Schöningh, 2014.

Rowe, Aimee Carrillo and Eve Tuck. "Settler Colonialism and Cultural Studies: Ongoing Settlement, Cultural Production, and Resistance." *Cultural Studies Critical Methodologies* 17, no. 1 (2017): 3–13.

Rowe-McCulloch, Maris. *The Holocaust and Mass Violence in the German-Occupied City of Rostov-on-Don, 1941–1943*. PhD diss., University of Toronto, 2019.

Rubenstein, Richard. *After Auschwitz: History, Theology, and Contemporary Judaism*, originally published in 1966. 2nd ed. Baltimore, MD: Johns Hopkins University Press, 1992.

Rudling, Per Anders. "The Invisible Genocide: The Holocaust in Belarus." In John-Paul Himka and Joanna Michlic, eds. *Bringing the Dark Past to Light: The Reception of the Holocaust in Post-Communist Europe*. Lincoln: University of Nebraska Press, 2013; 57–81.

'"They Defended Ukraine': The 14. Waffen-Grenadier-Division der SS (Galizische Nr. 1) Revisited." *Journal of Slavic Military Studies* 25, no. 3 (2012): 329–68.

Ruff, Mark Edward. *The Battle for the Catholic Past in Germany, 1945–1980*. Cambridge: Cambridge University Press, 2017; 121–52.

Ruhm von Oppen, Beate. *Religion and Resistance to Nazism*. Princeton, NJ: Center of International Studies, 1971.

Ryland, Glen P. *Translating Africa for Germans: The Rhenish Mission in Southwest Africa*. PhD diss., University of Notre Dame, IN, 2013.

Rymar, Nikolaj. "Die Gnade, 'leiden zu dürfen'. Anfänge der lyrischen Prosa in Heinrich Bölls Roman *Kreuz ohne Liebe*." In Natalia Bakshi, Dirk Kemper, and Iris Bäcker, eds. *Religiöse Thematiken in den Deutschsprachigen Literaturen der Nachkriegszeit (1945–1955)*. Munich: Wilhelm Fink, 2013; 151–66.

Sandkühler, Thomas. *'Endlösung' in Galizien: Der Judenmord in Ostpolen und die Rettungsinitiative von Berthold Beitz 1941–1944*. Bonn: Dietz, 1996.

Sandvoß, Hans-Rainer. *"Es wird gebeten, die Gottesdienst zu überwachen." Religionsgemeinschaften in Berlin zwischen Anpassung, Selbstbehauptung und Widerstand von 1933 bis 1945*. Berlin: Lukas, 2014.

Schäfer, Kirstin A. *Werner von Blomberg – Hitlers erster Feldmarschall*. Paderborn: Schöningh, 2006.

Scheck, Raffael. *Hitler's African Victims: The German Army Massacre of Black French Soldiers in 1940*. New York: Cambridge University Press, 2006.

Love between Enemies: Western Prisoners of War and German Women in World War II. Cambridge: Cambridge University Press, 2021.

Schmiedel, David. *"Du sollst nicht morden": Selbstzeugnisse christlicher Wehrmachtssoldaten aus den Vernichtungskrieg gegen die Sowjetunion*. Frankfurt: Campus, 2017.

Schneider, Gertrud. *Reise in den Tod: Deutsche Juden in Riga 1941–1944*. Berlin: Hentrich, 2006.

Schneider, Thomas Martin. *Reichsbischof Ludwig Müller: Eine Untersuchung zu Leben, Werk und Persönlichkeit*. Göttingen: Vandenhoeck & Ruprecht, 1993.

Schneider, Ulrich. *Bekennende Kirche zwischen "freudigem Ja" und antifaschistischem Widerstand*. Kassel: Brüder Grimm, 1986.

Scholder, Klaus. *The Churches and the Third Reich*. 2 vols. Translated by John Bowden. Philadelphia, PA: Fortress, 1988. Vol. 1, *Preliminary History and the Time of Illusions, 1918–1934*.

Über den Umgang mit unserer jüngsten Geschichte. Munich: Bayerische Landeszentral für politische Bildungsarbeit, 1979.

Schrafstetter, Susanne. *Flucht und Versteck. Untergetauchte Juden in München: Verfolgungserfahrung und Nachkriegsalltag*. Göttingen: Wallstein, 2015.

Schröber, Ulrike. "Franco-German Rapprochement and Reconciliation in the Ecclesial Domain: The Meeting of Bishops in Bühl (1949) and the Congress of Speyer (1950)." In Birgit Schwelling, ed. *Reconciliation, Civil Society, and the Politics of Memory: Transnational Initiatives in the 20th and 21st Century*. Bielefeld: Transcript, 2012; 143–65.

Schübel, Albrecht. *Dreihundert Jahre evangelische Soldatenseelsorge*. Munich: Evangelischer Presseverband für Bayern, 1964.

Schüler-Springorum, Stefanie. *"Krieg und Fliegen": Die Legion Condor im Spanischen Bürgerkrieg*. Paderborn: Brill/Schöningh, 2010.

Schulz, Christa. "Weibliche Häftlinge aus Ravensbrück in Bordellen der Männerkonzentrationslager." In Claus Füllberg-Stolberg et al., eds. *Frauen in Konzentrationslagern Bergen-Belsen, Ravensbrück*. Bremen: Edition Temmen, 1994; 135–46.

Schulz, Miriam. "'Gornisht oyser verter'?! *Khurbn-shprakh* as a Mirror of the Dynamics of Violence in German-Occupied Eastern Europe." In Gaëlle Fisher and Caroline Mezger, eds. *The Holocaust in the Borderlands: Interethnic Relations and the Dynamics of Violence in Occupied Eastern Europe*. Göttingen: Wallstein, 2019; 185–210.

Schwarz, Gudrun. *Eine Frau an seiner Seite. Die Ehefrauen in der "SS-Sippengemeinschaft."* Berlin: Aufbau, 2000.

Schwinge, Erich. *Bundeswehr und Wehrmacht: Zum Problem der Traditionswürdigkeit*. Bonn: Ring Deutsches Soldatenverbünde, 1992.

Seidman, Naomi. *Faithful Renderings: Jewish–Christian Difference and the Politics of Translation*. Chicago, IL: University of Chicago Press, 2006.

Sells, Michael. "Crosses of Blood: Sacred Space, Religion and Violence in Bosnia Herzegovina." *Sociology of Religion* 64, no. 3 (2003): 309–31.

"Kosovo Mythology and the Bosnian Genocide." In Omer Bartov and Phyllis Mack, eds. *In God's Name: Genocide and Religion in the Twentieth Century*. New York: Berghahn, 2001; 180–205.

Sereny, Gitta. *Into That Darkness: An Examination of Conscience*. New York: Vintage Books, 1983.

Shattuck, Jr., Gardiner H. "Faith, Morale, and the Army Chaplain in the American Civil War." In Doris L. Bergen, ed. *The Sword of the Lord: Military Chaplains from the First to the Twenty-First Centuries*. Notre Dame, IN: University of Notre Dame Press, 2004; 105–23.

Shenker, Noah. *Reframing Holocaust Testimony*. Bloomington: Indiana University Press, 2015.

Shepherd, Ben H. "The Continuum of Brutality: Wehrmacht Security Divisions in Central Russia, 1942." *German History* 21, no. 1 (2003): 49–81.

War in the Wild East: The German Army and Soviet Partisans. Cambridge, MA: Harvard University Press, 2004.

Shkandrij, Myroslav. *In the Maelstrom: The Waffen-SS "Galicia" Division*. Montreal: McGill-Queen's University Press, 2023.

Sholokhova, Lyudmila. *Biography of Moisei Beregovskii for YIVO Encyclopedia of Jews in Eastern Europe*. New Haven, CT: Yale University Press, 2008.

"Hasidic Music for the An-Ski Collection: a History of Collecting and Classification." *Musica Judaica* 19 (5770/2009–2010): 103–30.

Shternshis, Anna. "Between Life and Death: Why Some Soviet Jews Decided to Leave and Others to Stay in 1941." *Kritika: Explorations in Russian and Eurasian History* 15, no. 3 (2014): 477–504.

Liner Notes. Yiddish Glory: The Lost Songs of World War II. Six Degrees Records, 2018.

When Sonia Met Boris: An Oral History of Jewish Life under Stalin. New York: Oxford University Press, 2017.

Siemens, Daniel. *Stormtroopers: A New History of Hitler's Brownshirts.* New Haven, CT: Yale University Press, 2017.

Silecky, Ariana. *Fathers in Uniform: The Greek Catholic Chaplains of the 14th SS Galicia Division, 1943–1947.* MA thesis, University of Alberta, 2006.

Slobin, Mark, ed. and trans. *Old Jewish Folk Music: The Collections and Writings of Moshe Beregovski.* Syracuse, NY: Syracuse University Press, 2000.

Slomovitz, Albert Isaac. *The Fighting Rabbis: Jewish Military Chaplains and American History.* New York: New York University Press, 1999.

Smelser, Ronald M. and Edward J. Davies II. *The Myth of the Eastern Front: The Nazi–Soviet War in American Popular Culture.* Cambridge: Cambridge University Press, 2008.

Smith, Helmut Walser. *The Butcher's Tale: Murder and Anti-Semitism in a German Town.* New York: W. W. Norton, 2002.

German Nationalism and Religious Conflict: Culture, Ideology, Politics 1870–1914. Princeton, NJ: Princeton University Press, 1995.

Snape, Michael. *God and the British Soldier: Religion and the British Army in the Era of the Two World Wars.* London: Routledge, 2005.

The Royal Army Chaplains' Department, 1796–1953: Clergy under Fire. Woodbridge: Boydell and Brewer, 2008.

Snyder, Timothy. *Bloodlands: Europe between Hitler and Stalin.* New York: Basic, 2010.

Spector, Scott. "Edith Stein's Passing Gestures: Intimate Histories, Empathic Portraits." *New German Critique* 75 (Autumn 1998): 28–56.

Spicer, Kevin P. *Hitler's Priests: Catholic Clergy and National Socialism.* DeKalb: Northern Illinois University Press, 2008.

Resisting the Third Reich: The Catholic Church in Hitler's Berlin. DeKalb: Northern Illinois University Press, 2004.

Stahel, David. "The Wehrmacht and National Socialist Military Thinking." *War in History* 24, no. 3 (2017): 336–61.

Stargardt, Nicholas. *The German War: A Nation Under Arms, 1939–1945.* New York: Basic, 2015.

Steigmann-Gall, Richard. *The Holy Reich: Nazi Conceptions of Christianity, 1919–1945.* New York: Cambridge University Press, 2003.

Steinacher, Gerald. *Nazis auf der Flucht: Wie Kriegsverbrecher über Italie nach Übersee entkamen.* Innsbrück: Studien Verlag, 2008.

Steinbacher, Sybille. *"Musterstadt" Auschwitz: Germanisierungspolitik und Judenmord in Ostoberschlesien.* Munich: K. G. Saur, 2000.

Steinert, Marlis G. *Hitler's War and the Germans: Public Mood and Attitude during the Second World War.* Translated and edited by Thomas E. J. de Witt. Athens: University of Ohio Press, 1977.

Steinweis, Alan. *Studying the Jew: Scholarly Antisemitism in the Third Reich.* Cambridge, MA: Harvard University Press, 2006.

Stern, Steve J. *Remembering Pinochet's Chile: On the Eve of London.* Durham, NC: Duke University Press, 2004.

Streit, Christian. *Keine Kameraden: Die Wehrmacht und die sowjetischen Kriegsgefangenen 1941–1945.* Stuttgart: Deutsche Verlags-Anstalt, 1978.

Strübind, Andrea. *Die unfreie Freikirche: Das Bund der Baptistengemeinden im "Dritten Reich."* Neukirchen-Vluyn: Neukirchener Verlag, 1991.

Struk, Janina. *Photographing the Holocaust: Interpretations of the Evidence.* London: I. B. Tauris, 2004.

Théofilakis. Fabien. "'Rodolph – How Nice He Is!' Contact between German Prisoners of War and French Civilians, 1944–1948." In Anne-Marie Pathé and Fabien Théofilakis, eds. *Wartime Captivity in the Twentieth Century: Archives, Stories, Memories.* Translated by Helen McPhail. New York: Berghahn, 2016; 163–74.

Thimme, Anneliese. *Flucht in den Mythos: Die Deutschnationale Volkspartei und die Niederlage von 1918.* Göttingen: Vandenhoeck & Ruprecht, 1969.

Thomas, Jürgen. "'Nur das ist für die Truppe Recht, was ihr nützt . . .' Die Wehrmachtjustiz im Zweiten Weltkrieg." In Norbert Haase and Gerhard Paul, eds. *Die anderen Soldaten. Wehrkraftzersetzung, Gehorsamsverweigerung und Fahnenflucht im Zweiten Weltkrieg.* Frankfurt am Main: Fischer, 1995; 37–49.

Thomas, Maria. "Sacred Destruction? Anticlericalism, Iconoclasm and the Sacralization of Politics in Twentieth-Century Spain." *European History Quarterly* 47, no. 3 (2017): 490–508.

Tilli, Jouni. "'Deus Vult!' The Idea of Crusading in Finnish Clerical War Rhetoric, 1941–1944." *War in History* 24, no. 3 (2017): 363–85.

Timm, Annette. "The Challenges of Including Sexual Violence and Transgressive Love in Historical Writing on World War II and the Holocaust." *Journal of the History of Sexuality* 26, no. 3 (2017): 351–65.

Tingler, Jason. "Religion, Ethno-Nationalism, and Genocidal Violence in Chełm, 1939–1944." Paper presented at the conference on Religion and Ethno-Nationalism in the Era of the World Wars, University of Toronto, May 2017.

Tinker, George E. *Missionary Conquest: The Gospel and Native American Cultural Genocide.* Minneapolis, MN: Fortress, 1993.

Todd, Lisa M. *Sexual Treason in Germany during the First World War.* New York: Palgrave Macmillan, 2017.

Tönsmeyer, Tatjana. "Besatzung als europäische Erfahrungs- und Gesellschaftsgeschichte. Der Holocaust im Kontext des Zweiten Weltkrieges." In Frank Bajohr and Andrea Löw, eds. *Der Holocaust. Ergebnisse und neue Fragen der Forschung.* Frankfurt am Main: Fischer, 2015; 281–98.

Torrie, Julia S. *German Soldiers and the Occupation of France, 1940–1944.* Cambridge: Cambridge University Press, 2018.

Townsend, Tim. *Mission at Nuremberg: An American Army Chaplain and the Trial of the Nazis.* New York: HarperCollins, 2014.

Trolp, Werner. *Die Militärseelsorge in der hannoverschen Armee.* Göttingen: Vandenhoeck & Ruprecht, 2012.

Trouillot, Michel-Rolph. *Silencing the Past: Power and the Production of History.* Boston, MA: Beacon Press, 1995.

Turner, Henry Ashby. "Two Dubious Third Reich Diaries." *Central European History* 33, no. 3 (2000): 415–22.

Turner, Sasha. "The Nameless and the Forgotten: Maternal Grief, Sacred Protection, and the Archive of Slavery." *Slavery and Abolition* 28, no. 2 (2017): 232–50.

Uziel, Daniel. "Wehrmacht Propaganda Troops and the Jews." Translated by William Templer. *Yad Vashem Studies* 29 (2001): 27–65.

Uzulis, André. *Die Bundeswehr: Eine politische Geschichte von 1955 bis heute.* Hamburg: Mittler, 2005.

Veidlinger, Jeffrey. *In the Midst of Civilized Europe: The Pogroms of 1918–1921 and the Onset of the Holocaust.* New York: Metropolitan Books, 2021.

Victoria, Brian Daizen. *Zen at War*, 2nd ed. Lanham, MD: Rowman & Littlefield, 2006.

Vuletić, Aleksandar-Saša. *Christen Jüdischer Herkunft im Dritten Reich: Verfolgung und organisierte Selbsthilfe, 1933–1939.* Mainz: Philipp von Zabern, 1999.

Walke, Anika. *Pioneers and Partisans: An Oral History of Nazi Genocide in Belorussia.* New York: Oxford University Press, 2015.

"Split Memory: The Geography of Holocaust Memory and Amnesia." *Slavic Review* 88, no. 1 (2018): 174–97.

Wall, Donald D. "The Confessing Church and Hitler's Foreign Policy: The Czechoslovakian Crisis of 1938." *Journal of the American Academy of Religion* 44, no. 3 (1976): 423–38.

Waxman, Zoë. "Towards an Integrated History of the Holocaust: Masculinity, Femininity, and Genocide." In Christian Wiese and Paul Betts, eds. *Years of Persecution, Years of Extermination: Saul Friedländer and the Future of Holocaust Studies.* London: Continuum, 2010; 311–21.

"Transcending History? Methodological Problems in Holocaust Testimony." In Dan Stone, ed. *The Holocaust and Historical Methodology.* New York: Berghahn, 2012; 143–57.

Weber, Thomas. *Hitler's First War.* Oxford: Oxford University Press, 2010.

Webster, Ronald. "Opposing Victors' Justice: German Protestant Churchmen and Convicted War Criminals in Western Europe after 1945." *Holocaust and Genocide Studies* 15 (2001): 47–70.

Weih, Ruth. *Alltag für Soldaten? Kriegserinnerungen und soldatischer Alltag in der Varangerregion 1940–1944.* PhD diss., Christian Albrecht University, Kiel, 2005.

Weikart, Richard. "A Doctored Photo of Hitler Discovered: Unraveling Hitler's Religious Deception," *The Stream* (Dec. 4, 2016). https://stream.org/a-doctored-photo-of-hitler-discovered-unraveling-hitlers-religious-deception/

Hitler's Religion: The Twisted Beliefs That Drove the Third Reich. Washington, DC: Regnery History, 2016.

Weinberg, Gerhard L. "The German Generals and the Outbreak of War, 1938–1939." In *Germany, Hitler, and World War II: Essays in Modern German and World History.* New York: Cambridge University Press, 1995; 129–45.

Germany, Hitler, and World War II: Essays in Modern German and World History. New York: Cambridge University Press, 1995.

"Germany's War for World Conquest and the Extermination of Jews." Meyerhoff Lecture. Washington, DC: US Holocaust Memorial Museum, 1995.

"Propaganda for Peace and Preparation for War." In *Germany, Hitler and World War II.* New York: Cambridge University Press, 1995; 68–83.

A World at Arms: A Global History of World War II. Rev. ed. New York: Cambridge University Press, 2005.

Weisbrod, Bernd. "Sozialgeschichte und Gewalterfahrung im 20. Jahrhundert." In Paul Nolte, Manfred Hettling, Frank-Michael Kuhlemann, and Hans-Walter Schmuhl, eds. *Perspektiven der Gesellschaftsgeschichte*. Munich: Beck, 2000; 112–23.

Welch, S. R. "Securing the German Domestic Front in the Second World War: Prosecution of Subversion before the People's Court." *Australian Journal of Politics and History* 53, no. 1 (2007): 44–56.

Werkner, Ines-Jacqueline. *Soldatenseelsorge versus Militärseelsorge. Evangelische Pfarrer in der Bundeswehr*. Baden-Baden: Nomos, 2001.

Werner, Hans. *The Constructed Mennonite: History, Memory, and the Second World War*. Winnipeg: University of Manitoba Press, 2013.

Westermann, Edward B. *Drunk on Genocide: Alcohol and Mass Murder in Nazi Germany*. Ithaca, NY: Cornell University Press, 2021.

Hitler's Police Battalions: Enforcing Racial War in the East. Lawrence: University Press of Kansas, 2005.

Wette, Wolfram. *The Wehrmacht: History, Myth, Reality*. Translated by Deborah Lucas Schneider. Cambridge, MA: Harvard University Press, 2006.

Wheeler-Bennett, J. W. *The Nemesis of Power: The German Army in Politics 1918–1945*. 2nd ed. London: Macmillan, 1967.

Whitt, Jacqueline E. *Bringing God to Men: American Military Chaplains and the Vietnam War*. Chapel Hill: University of North Carolina Press, 2014.

Wiens, Gavin. *The Imperial German Army between Kaiser and King: Monarchy, Nation-Building, and War, 1866–1918*. London: Palgrave Macmillan, 2023.

Wieviorka, Annette. *The Era of the Witness*. Translated by Jared Stark. Ithaca, NY: Cornell University Press, 2006.

Winter, Jay. *Sites of Memory, Sites of Mourning: The Great War in European Cultural History*. Cambridge: Cambridge University Press, 1995.

Wölfel, Ute. "At the Front: Common Traitors in West German War Films in the 1950s." *Modern Language Review* 110, no. 3 (2015): 739–58.

Wollaston, Isabel. "The Absent, the Partial and the Iconic in Archival Photographs of the Holocaust." *Jewish History and Culture* 12, no. 3 (2010): 439–62.

Woolford, Andrew. *This Benevolent Experiment: Indigenous Boarding Schools, Genocide, and Redress in Canada and the United States*. Lincoln: University of Nebraska Press, 2015.

Yelton, David K. *Hitler's Volkssturm: The Nazi Militia and the Fall of Germany, 1944–1945*. Lawrence: University Press of Kansas, 2002.

"Older German Officers and National Socialist Activism: Evidence from the German Volkssturm." *Journal of Military History* 83, no. 2 (2019): 455–85.

Zahn, Gordon C. *German Catholics and Hitler's Wars: A Study in Social Control*. New York: Sheed and Ward, 1962.

The Military Chaplaincy: A Study of Role Tension in the Royal Air Force. Toronto, ON: University of Toronto Press, 1969.

Zakić, Mirna. *Ethnic Germans and National Socialism in Yugoslavia in World War II*. Cambridge: Cambridge University Press, 2017.

Zemel, Carol. *Looking Jewish: Visual Culture and Modern Diaspora*. Bloomington: Indiana University Press, 2015.

Index

absolution, 101
  general, 160, 198, 231
Adachi, Agnes, 20–21, 231
Adenauer, Konrad, 215
Advent, 200
Afghanistan, 19, 227, 232
Ailly-le-Haut-Clocher, 101
Albania, 226
Albert, Franz, 41, 183
Alberts, chaplain, 191
Alexievich, Svetlana, 206, 234
Allenstein. *See* Olsztyn
Allgemeine Evangelisch-Lutherische
  Kirchenzeitung, 25, 31
Alsace, 41, 159
Altman, Pepa, 133
Ambrose, Stephen, 229
ancestry passes, 58
Andersch, Alfred, 197
Andriivka, 220
Andrushchenko, Lidiia, 152
Anschluss. See Austria, annexation of
antisemitism, 18, 26, 50, 57, 231. *See also*
  massacres of Jews
  accusation of deicide, 151
  blamed on Jews, 57
  in Bundeswehr, 228
  as factor in support for Nazi movement, 28
  used to deride Christianity, 161
Apollo, Ronald, 234
Arctic Circle, 180
Arendt, Hannah, 14
Armed Forces High Command, 112
  instructions to chaplains, 200
Armenian genocide, 28
Armenians, 149
Army Group Center, 178, 184
Army High Command, 64, 82, 99, 112
  made responsible for chaplaincy, 66
  restrictions on chaplains, 155, 186, 190–91,
  193
Army Personnel Office, 58

Arrow Cross, 20
Arrow to the Heart, 222
Aryan clause, 58
Aryan papers
  chaplain with Jewish ancestry, 166
  required of chaplains, 58
Aryan Paragraph, 58
Associated Press, 232
Athens, 154, 178
atrocities, 69, 207
  chaplains as witnesses of, 178–79, 223
Augustine, 212
Auschwitz, 6, 175, 178–79, 184, *209*, 230
Austria, 45, 175
  annexation of, 47, 72–73
Austro-Hungarian Army
  chaplains in, 48

Babyn Yar, 6, 121, 134, 172
Baedeker, Dietrich, 72, 220
Bakshi, Nama, 149, 151
Balkans, 178
Balla, Mordechai Eliezer (Zsolt), 36–38, 228
Baltimore, 209
Banat
  South, 109
baptism, 63, *151*, 167, 176, 200
Baptists, 63
Barth, Karl, 217
Bartsch, Albert, 170
Bastert, Hermann, 188
Bathsheba, 122
Battle of Moscow, 120
Baudissin, Wolf Graf von, 217
Bauerle, Bernhard, 17, 57, 83, 90, 95, 161,
  164–65, 178
  ambivalent witness to murder of Jews, 124
  in France 1940, 96
Bautzen, 189
Bavaria, 27–28, 36–37, 167, *195*
Bavarian Soviet Republic, 27
beatitudes, 30

Oßwald, Herbert, 159
Osterkirche, *213*

Pacelli, Eugenio, 125
Pachowiak, Heinrich, 147
Pahl, Georg, *42*
Pančevo, 109
Panzerarmee Afrika, 154
Paris, 210
partisans, 9–10, 18, 109, 124, 172, 180, 183, 185
  massacres of, 178
Passover, 128, 177
Pastors Emergency League, 58
Pechmann, Wilhelm von, 54
penal battalion, 181
Pentecost, 219
Perau, Josef, 125, 178–79, 182, 198
  memoir of, 218–19
Peremyshlyany, 133
Perlach, 27
Peus, Ferdinand, 186
Philippians 4 verse 7, 38
phoney war, 97
photographs, 17, *42*, 63, 67, 71, 78, 88, 126, 134, 196, 211, 216
  of church openings, 113–15, *116*, 131, *135*, 136, 140
  of German atrocities, 18, 117, 119, 125, 154, 223, *224*
  Wehrmacht albums, 86–87, *88*, 102, *104–5*
physicians
  chaplains' relations with, 158, 161
Piatsetski, Isaac, 6–7
Pioneers, German, 107, 133
Pius XII, 125
plunder, 84, 99, 107, 133, 145, 179, 220
pogrom, 6, 72, 114, 223
  November, 47, 67, 74, 133, 186
Pohl, Oswald, 212
Pohlmann, chaplain, 122
Poland, 10, 128, 158, 207
  German atrocities in, 13, 81, 83, *85*, 91, 125, 133
  German war on, 7, 13, 34, 77, 81–82, 133
  massacres of Jews in, 3, 84
  Wehrmacht chaplains in, 78–79, 83, 86, 91–92, 109, 125, 181
Polish Catholic priests, 83
  killed by Germans, 199
political religion, 12, 203
Pomeranian reserves, 199
Pöpping, Dagmar, 125
Pöschl, Josef, 169
Positive Christianity, 27

Potsdam, 22, 41, 51
Potsdam, Day of, *42*
Prague, 186, 202
prayer, 73, 79, 89, 92, 98, 124, *138*, 142, 203, 221, 233
  in battle, 25, 157
  of blessing, 34
  Catholic prayer book, 83, 180, 185
  for Hitler, 12, 74, 232
  Jewish, 177, 208
  for peace, 73
  as postwar defense, 211
  of repentance, 25
  for victory, 25
prisoners of war
  chaplains in Soviet hands, 220
  chaplains' role aiding German, 212
  French, 97
  German, 198, 205, 230
  German in French hands, 212
  German in Soviet hands, 204, 206, 212, 214
  German in US hands, 203, 207
  Jewish, 84
  Norwegian, 91
  Soviet, 10, 15, 18, 37, 114, 116, *127*, *129*, 133, 153, 171
  Ukrainians after World War II, 196
Protectorate of Bohemia and Moravia, 187
Protestant Church's Foreign Office, 69
Protestant military bishop, 155, 192, *See also* Dohrmann, Franz
Prussia, 25, 30, 37, 39, 53
Przemyśl, 84–85
Psalm 31 verse 16, 147, 154
Psalm 90 verses 5–7, 35

Rabenau, Friedrich von, 36–38
Radom, *209*
Radtke, Hans, 153
Raeder, Erich, 56–57, 211
Raible, Hermann, 170
Ramcke Parachute Brigade, 154
rape, 10, 100, 139, 159
Rarkowski, Franz Justus, 11, 41, 59, 70–71, 183
  1937 memo, 64–66
  biography, 39
  consecration, 53
  messages, 122, 131, 164
  sidelined, 192, 211, 214
  struggle for credibility, 51–52, 54
  and World War I, 50, 59
ratline, 220
Raubvogel, Lucy Gross, 133
Ravensbrück, 158

For EU product safety concerns, contact us at Calle de José Abascal, 56–1°,
28003 Madrid, Spain or eugpsr@cambridge.org.